D1769596

3036000000435521

```
HD
8066     Bimba
.B513    The history of the
1968     American working class
(1)
```

Date Due			
MAR 4 1976			
MAY 11 1985			
OCT 31 1991			

VOID

LIBRARY-ALLEGHENY CAMPUS
808 RIDGE AVENUE
PITTSBURGH, PA. 15212

PRINTED IN U.S.A.

The HISTORY of THE AMERICAN WORKING CLASS

By ANTHONY BIMBA

GREENWOOD PRESS, PUBLISHERS
NEW YORK   1968

Copyright, 1927, by
INTERNATIONAL PUBLISHERS CO., INC.

Reprinted with the permission of
International Publishers Co., Inc.

HD
8066
.B513
1968
(1)

First Greenwood reprinting, 1968

Library of Congress catalogue card number: 68-30818

Printed in the United States of America

PREFACE

THE aim of this book is to give a popular presentation of the main phases of the development and struggles of the working class in the United States, together with their economic and social background, and to draw the inevitable lessons therefrom.

Particular attention was paid to those phases of the subject which have been neglected by the historians of our labor movement, which, however, are of great importance. For instance, the rôle of the state in the class struggle is hardly mentioned by them. The historians also fail to expose the real mission of the conservative leadership of the labor movement. They record mostly events and deal only with the organizational aspects of the labor movement without pointing out or emphasizing their causes and their effects.

An attempt was made in this book to interpret movements and events from the standpoint of the materialist conception of history, which holds that the social and political structure of society is not the result of the free choice and the free will of the people; it is not the work of a few individuals, or a product of someone's high ideals and humanitarian dreams. It is rather a product of historical development, and the foundation of this development and of this political and social structure are the material conditions. Therefore, the labor organizations, labor movements and labor struggles also have an economic basis. The class struggle is not an invention of a few agitators. It is the result of economic, social and political conditions or relationships. As long as these conditions prevail, the class struggle will continue.

This survey of American labor history is not and does not claim to be "impartial," as other labor histories pretend to be. It openly takes side with the working class against the bourgeoisie.

The reader who desires to study the subject further will find references to the necessary material. One of the aims in this work was to stimulate such a desire amongst the readers.

I take this opportunity to thank Solon De Leon and Alexander Trachtenberg for reading the manuscript and for their coöperation in its preparation for publication. Their advice on many questions was of great help to me.

A. B.

1927

PREFACE TO THIRD EDITION

IN the present edition of the book, I have added a short chapter summarizing the important events in the labor movement during the period 1933-36. Errors which crept into the previous text have been noted in an errata page at the end of the book. Further revisions, including an elaboration of the points treated in the book, as well as new material, are now in progress and will be included in a later edition.

A. B.

January, 1936.

CONTENTS

		PAGE
PREFACE		v

CHAPTER
I.	EUROPEAN BACKGROUND OF AMERICAN SOCIETY	9
II.	THE WHITE SLAVES AND THEIR MASTERS	12
III.	NEGRO SLAVERY IN AMERICA	20
IV.	"FREE" WORKERS IN THE COLONIAL PERIOD	30
V.	WORKERS AND THE AMERICAN REVOLUTION	39
VI.	LIFE OF THE WORKING MASSES AFTER THE REVOLUTION	49
VII.	THE BOURGEOISIE CAPTURES THE STATE POWER	54
VIII.	INDUSTRIAL DEVELOPMENT, 1783–1860	61
IX.	DEVELOPMENT OF THE WORKING CLASS, 1783–1860	66
X.	LABOR ORGANIZATIONS AND LABOR STRUGGLES, 1783–1819	71
XI.	LABOR ORGANIZATIONS AND THEIR STRUGGLES, 1819–1837	81
XII.	THE LABOR MOVEMENT FROM 1837–1860	101
XIII.	ERA OF UTOPIAN SOCIALISM	108
XIV.	THE WORKERS IN THE CIVIL WAR	115
XV.	ECONOMIC DEVELOPMENT AFTER THE CIVIL WAR	136
XVI.	LABOR ORGANIZATION AND STRUGGLES, 1860–1873	143
XVII.	PERIOD OF MILITANT LABOR STRUGGLES, 1873–1880	152
XVIII.	AWAKENING OF THE LABOR MOVEMENT, 1880–1886	166
XIX.	STRIKES, KNIGHTS OF LABOR, TRADE UNIONS, AND ANARCHISTS, 1880–1886	176
XX.	THE STRUGGLE BETWEEN THE KNIGHTS AND THE FEDERATION, 1886–1900	189
XXI.	THE SOCIALISTS, TRADE UNIONS, AND POLITICAL ACTION, 1886–1900	199
XXII.	STRIKES AND STRUGGLES FOR THE EIGHT-HOUR DAY, 1886–1900	209

CONTENTS

CHAPTER		PAGE
XXIII.	The Industrial "Miracles" of the Twentieth Century	221
XXIV.	The Labor Organizations, 1900–1914	226
XXV.	Strikes and Labor Cases, 1900–1914	239
XXVI.	The Trade Unions and the World War	247
XXVII.	American Socialists and the World War	256
XXVIII.	After the World War, 1918–1920	265
XXIX.	The Beginning of the Communist Movement	280
XXX.	Period of Militant Labor Struggles, 1921–1927	293
XXXI.	The Political Movement of the Working Class Since 1929	315
XXXII.	The Revolutionary Trade Union Movement	334
XXXIII.	The Crisis, 1929–1933	350
XXXIV.	Recent Tendencies, 1933–1936	373
Index		382
Errata		386

THE HISTORY OF THE AMERICAN WORKING CLASS

CHAPTER I

European Background of American Society

The discovery of America at the end of the fifteenth century was mainly a result of commercial and business necessity. The thirst of the European ruling classes to acquire new wealth and the glory which goes with it inspired and made possible the famous voyage of Christopher Columbus across the Atlantic.

The discovery of America was an accidental result of the search for shorter and safer trade routes from Europe to Asia. Once America was found, the sole aim of the first white explorers was to plunder the American Indians, resorting, when necessary, to the most murderous means. That is why they were more interested in the southern part of the continent than in the northern, for in the former there lived numerous tribes of Indians, some of them highly civilized in their own way, and rich. The northern part of America, where Canada and the United States now lie, did not attract the first Europeans, because here the climate was cold and there were no ready riches to be seized. Therefore, a whole century passed before England and other European countries became interested in colonizing North America. Only toward the end of April, 1607, did a group of Englishmen, numbering 120, reach North America and settle on the spot where Jamestown, Va., stands to-day. This was the first permanent English colony in America. Then followed Germans, French, Dutch, and others. The Spanish had settled a few years earlier, at St. Augustine, Fla. A bitter struggle was waged between the ruling classes of the European countries, in which thousands of workers and farmers died, to determine to which nation the American continent should belong. England defeated its rivals and became the supreme ruler of the North American continent as far west as the Mississippi River.

Colonization of America on a large scale would not have started even by the beginning of the seventeenth century had not a great change occurred in conditions in Europe. Hundreds of thousands of men and women were forced to desert their old homes and search for new abodes.

At that time Europe was passing through a tremendous transformation. With the growth of commerce and industry there had appeared a new class—the capitalist class. This capitalist class or bourgeoisie was gaining strength and destroying the old feudal system root and branch. Through revolutions and wars it was shattering the political power and privileges of the landed lords and monarchs. The old economic system based on serfdom was rapidly disintegrating and giving way to a new economic system based on wage-slavery. A change in the methods of producing the necessaries of life brought with it a change in all social and political institutions.

"The bourgeoisie," say Marx and Engels in the *Communist Manifesto*, "wherever it has got the upper hand, has put an end to all feudal, patriarchal, idyllic relations. It has pitilessly torn asunder the motley feudal ties that bound man to his 'natural superiors,' and has left remaining no other nexus between man and man than naked self-interest, than callous 'cash payment.' It has drowned the most heavenly ecstasies of religious fervor, of chivalrous enthusiasm, of philistine sentimentalism, in the icy water of egotistical calculation. It has resolved personal worth into exchange value, and in place of the numberless indefeasible chartered freedoms, has set up that single, unconscionable freedom—*Free Trade*. In one word, for exploitation, veiled by religious and political illusions, it has substituted naked, shameless, direct, brutal exploitation."

It was a period of great changes and revolutions in Europe.

"The forces of feudalism," according to A. M. Simons, "were not yet completely conquered and the new class was compelled constantly to fight to hold its position and gain greater power. It was a time when nations and religions were being born, and when in all fields of social life mighty forces were struggling for the mastery.

"As fast as the merchant or the manufacturing class attained power, its members set about divorcing the former serfs and peasants from the soil, and dissolving all old feudal relations, in order that the workers might be 'free' to hunt for employers. So it was that in nearly all the leading European nations the people were being driven out of their ancient homes" (Simons: *Social Forces in American History*, p. 13).

These peasants and workers, driven from the land, sought shelter in the rising cities. But industry could not absorb these millions of human beings as rapidly as their numbers increased. Their conditions became so wretched that the poorest of our times are almost fortunate by comparison. Even those who were lucky enough to obtain employment were steeped in misery. They were forced to work inhumanly long hours. Their pay was inhumanly meager. Of the slums of London and other English cities, for example, Friedrich Engels could say as late as the middle of the nineteenth century:

"Here live the poorest of the poor, the worst paid workers with thieves and the victims of prostitution indiscriminately huddled together . . . and those who have not yet sunk in the whirlpool of moral ruin which surrounds them, are sinking daily deeper, losing daily more and more of their power to resist the demoralizing influence of want, filth and evil surroundings" (F. Engels: *Conditions of the Working Class in England in 1844*, p. 27).

England was no exception. In all the other countries of Western Europe hundreds of thousands of "free" men and women were on the point of starvation, roaming from place to place, seeking shelter and food. The "religious" wars in Germany, lasting for decades, devastated that country and left multitudes of workers destitute. The savage war between France and Holland laid waste the province of the Palatinate, and thousands of human beings were bereft of their belongings. In Ireland hordes of peasants were driven from the land by the English ruling class; and finding no occupation in the cities—for the same English masters had closed the cotton mills of Ireland in order to avoid competition with their own textile enterprises—sank into desperation till the great famine of 1740 forced them to flee from Ireland and seek food in other lands. In France conditions were no better; it is estimated that during the year 1715 about one-third of the people of France, 6,000,000 in all, perished of hunger.

Such was the state of the masses of the poor in Europe during the seventeenth and the beginning of the eighteenth centuries. Ready to risk any danger in order to save themselves from starvation, they besieged the ports and begged to be taken to America by the colonizers.

The colonizers were the same commercial adventurers, capitalists, exploiters, wealth-seekers, privileged masters of Europe. The governments gave them great tracts of land in America and said in effect: "Take these wretches of the cities and villages, transport them to America, and exploit them to your hearts' content." It was these helpless creatures who by their unceasing toil laid the foundation for the wealth and power now possessed by the ruling class of this country.

Thus was American society born in the era of the rise of capitalism. It did not have to pass through a long, gradual process of development covering hundreds of years as was the case with other nations. The European settlers in America created a bourgeois order in spite of the fact that in the beginning it retained some characteristics of feudalism.

"They (the European settlers) were now to build up a society in a new world. As materials to this end they brought with them a vast store of things that mankind has been countless ages in acquiring: the knowledge of reading, and printing and gunpowder, of making tools of iron and steel, of spinning and weaving and making of clothing, social and governmental institutions, churches, laws, creeds, beliefs, prejudices, superstitions. All these things, developed in the complex civilization of Europe, were now transported to a world where they had hitherto been unknown (Simons: *Loc. cit.*, p. 21).

CHAPTER II

THE WHITE SLAVES AND THEIR MASTERS

As soon as we mention slavery in America, there arises before us the terrible picture of Negro slavery. Very few realize that there was a time in this country when white people were bought and sold. Few know that our forefathers, working-men and women, were once purchased for dollars or tobacco.

The colonies were nearly all settled by chartered companies whose purposes were purely commercial and whose success depended on their securing immigrants.

"The London Company," says Gustavus Myers, "thrice chartered to take over to itself the land and resources of Virginia and populate its zone of rule, was endowed with sweeping rights and privileges which made it an absolute monopoly. . . . In its intense aim to settle New Netherlands and make use of its resources, Holland, through the States General, offered extraordinary inducements to promoters of colonization. . . . Any man who should succeed in planting a colony of 50 'souls,' each of whom was to be more than 15 years old, was to become at once a patroon with all the rights of lordship. He was permitted to own 16 miles along shore or on one side of a navigable river" (Gustavus Myers: *History of the Great American Fortunes*, Vol. I, pp. 11-14).

The settlement of New York was carried on by the Dutch West India Company, made up of many of the biggest land owners.

"Like so many petty monarchs each had his distinct flag and insignia; each fortified his domain with fortresses, armed with cannon and manned by his paid soldiery. The colonists were but humble dependents; they were his immediate subjects and were forced to take oath of fealty and allegiance to him" (*Ibid.*, p. 21).

By the middle of the eighteenth century a number of land speculating companies had grown up. To these companies belonged many governors and almost all of our "forefathers," such as George Washington. Washington was one of the leaders of the Ohio Company, organized in 1749. King George gave these speculators 500,000 acres of land. In 1787, after the revolution, while Washington was in Philadelphia presiding over the secret constitutional convention, agents of this company were in New York buying up Congressmen and won 5,000,000 acres of land, paying not more than 8 or 9 cents an acre. In 1792 this same company obtained another concession of nearly 1,000,000 acres almost free. Thus was formed the American aristocracy, and thus did it begin to amass its great wealth (James Oneal: *The Workers in American History*, pp. 34-35).

THE WHITE SLAVES AND THEIR MASTERS 13

The "fathers" of our country lived as well as, if not better than, the feudal lords of Europe. Indeed, many European men of wealth and power envied the American aristocracy their opulent establishments. Not alone in the southern colonies, as in Virginia, were the landowners masters over everything. In the North, where manufacturing and commerce were in full bloom, as in New York, aristocracy of the same type were in firm control.

"The soil was owned by a few. The masses were mere retainers or tenants as in the monarchies of Europe. The feudal lord was also the dominant manufacturer and trader. He forced his tenants to sign covenants that they should trade in nothing else than the produce of the manor; that they should trade nowhere else but at his store; that they should grind their flour at his mill, and buy bread at his bakery, lumber at his sawmills, and liquor at his brewery. Thus he was not only able to squeeze the last penny from them by exorbitant prices, but it was in his power to keep them everlastingly in debt to him. He claimed, and held, a monopoly in his domain of whatever trade he could seize. These feudal tenures were established in law; woe to the tenant who presumed to infract them. He became a criminal and was punished as a felon" (Myers: *Loc. cit.,* Vol. I, p. 46).

As to the hard-working habits of a southern landlord, McMaster says:

"The daily life of such men was a strange mixture of activity and sloth. When they were not scouring the country in search of a fox, when they were not riding 20 miles to a cockfight or a barbecue, they seem to have indulged in all the idleness of an Eastern pasha. Travelers from a colder climate were amazed to see a man in the best of health rise at 9, breakfast at 10, and then lie down on the coolest pallet in the house to drink toddy, bombo, or sangaree, while a couple of slaves fanned him and kept off the flies. At 2 he ate his dinner; supper he rarely touched. At 10 he went to bed" (McMaster: *History of the People of the United States,* Vol. II, pp. 12-13).

Such was the governing class of the colonies. Under the iron rule of this society, masses of white slaves, poor white workers, and black slaves had to live.

How did these over-lords get their white slaves?

The slogan "Bread and Freedom" brought the European workers to America. They were told in effect: "In America there are tracts of fertile soil awaiting you. Woods so thick that you cannot pass through them, great fields of natural wealth, rivers full of fish. And all free! Only step in and everything is yours. Also, in America there is freedom. In Europe we have bloodshed, wars. Wars between nations, wars between religions. Prisons full of people, misery and death everywhere. The whole atmosphere smells of tyranny. In America there is no such thing. There is no exploitation. There are no wars. Every one can worship his own god without any fear!"

That is how America was painted by the land speculators and shipping companies. The poor Europeans had heard of such places only in myths and had lived there only in their dreams. But now they were really going to see and own such a place. All they had to do was to cross the Atlantic.

The shipping companies and speculators agreed to take them across, but only on condition that they were to be bound out to service until they had paid back the expenses connected with their voyage. The starving workers agreed to these terms with pleasure. Thousands of them were brought to America, often in ships that were not fit to carry human beings. Many were drowned, many more died at sea. Those who reached America were sold to the land speculators.

"The 'adventurers' who 'founded Virginia' never saw the American coast. They remained in England and invested their money in the venture, while others known as 'planters' went as colonists. The history of the corporation is one of swindle and plunder.... After 1610, one governor established a military system by which workmen were driven in squads to their daily tasks, and severely punished for disobedience. A persistent neglect of labor was to be punished by galley service from one to three years. Penal servitude was also instituted; for 'petty offenses' they worked 'as slaves in irons for a term of years.' The victims claimed that there were whippings, hangings, shootings, and breaking on the wheel" (Oneal: *Loc. cit.,* p. 25).

In 1629 Charles I granted to Lord Baltimore the present state of Maryland and a large part of Delaware. Colonization was carried on under a system of which the following is a description: "The first adventurers were allowed 2,000 acres for a yearly rent of 400 pounds of wheat for every five servants imported, 100 acres for less than five servants at a yearly rent of 20 pounds of wheat, and 50 acres for those importing children less than 16 years of age . . ." (*Ibid.,* pp. 30-31).

"One step above the slaves were the convict bond-servants, or men and women in a state of temporary involuntary servitude. These people were either political offenders or felon convicts. . . .

"The felons formed the great source of supply, and had been sent over in very considerable numbers from the earliest days of colonization. . . .

"But the indentured servant and redemptioner did not cease to come when the colonies became the United States. Speaking generally, the indentured servants were men, women, and even children who, unable to pay their passage, signed a contract called an indenture before leaving the old world. This indenture bound the owner or master of the ship to transport them to America, and bound the emigrant after arrival in America to serve the owner, master, or other assign, for a certain number of years. On reaching port the owner or master whose servants they then became sold them for their passage to the highest bidder or for what he could get.

"The redemptioner, on the other hand, was an immigrant who signed no indenture before embarking, but agreed with the shipping merchant that after reaching America he should be given a certain time (generally a month) in which to find somebody to redeem him by paying the passage money, or freight, as it was called. Should he fail to find a redeemer within a specified time, the ship captain was at liberty to sell him to the highest bidder, in which case the redemptioner became an indentured servant and was subject to the laws governing such cases.

THE WHITE SLAVES AND THEIR MASTERS

"The contract signed, the newcomer became in the eyes of the law a slave, and in both the civil and criminal code was classed with Negro slaves and Indians. None could marry without the consent of the master or mistress under penalty of an addition of one year's service to the time set forth in the indenture. They were worked hard, were dressed in the cast-off clothes of their owners, and might be flogged as often as the master or mistress thought necessary. If they ran away, at least two days might be added to their time of service for each day they were absent. Father, mother and children could be sold to different buyers. Such remnants of cargoes as could not find purchasers within the time specified were bought in lots of 50 or more by a class of speculators known as 'soul drivers,' who drove them through the country like so many cattle and sold them for what they would bring.

"In the middle and southern states almost all labor, skilled and unskilled, was done by slaves, redemptioners, and indentured servants. The advertisements of redemptioners mention weavers, gardeners, spinners, carpenters, smiths, wheelwrights, shoemakers, and school teachers, stonecutters, bricklayers, tailors, hatters, harness makers—men and women skilled in every sort of labor then needed in the country" (McMaster: *The Acquisition of Political, Social, and Industrial Rights of Man in America,* pp. 31-35).

The average price of a white slave, with five years of service due, was about £10 in 1672, according to Bancroft, while a Negro was worth £20 or £25. The system existed throughout the colonies. White slaves were publicly advertised and sold in the market places of Philadelphia, Boston, and New York, as well as in Jamestown and St. Augustine (Bancroft: *History of the United States,* Vol I, p. 125).

When the prisons of Europe were empty, elaborate plans for enticing the people to go to America were invented. The shipping companies and governments who were interested in the colonization of the new continent cleverly hid from the Europeans the terrible conditions of the slaves on this side. They printed and widely distributed all sorts of information about the "earthly paradise" in America. They bribed American workers to write letters to their relatives and friends in Europe, telling of the wonderful conditions in the new world (*Documentary History of American Industrial Society,* Vol. I, p. 342).

"These alluring pictures of land where work was plenty, where wages were high, where food was cheap and good, and tithes unknown," says McMaster, even as late as 1830, "awakened such interest that even the terrors of the ocean and the horrors of emigrant ship were overcome" (McMaster: *History,* etc., Vol. VI, pp. 80-81).

The advertising campaign was successful. Throngs of immigrants poured in, most of whom could not pay their passage money and so became slaves.

"From 1682 to 1804 the proportion of white slaves to the whole number of immigrants to Pennsylvania steadily increased, till they constituted two-thirds during the last 19 years. This enormous exodus from Germany and Holland is suggestive of the work of the emigrant hunters in these countries" (Oneal: *Loc. cit.,* p. 61).

The hardships the slaves had to undergo during their voyage to America were terrific. Often more than half of them suffocated on board ship and were thrown overboard.

"One ship sailing in 1730 with 150 emigrants, had only 13 survivors. Another sailed in 1745 with 400 Germans, of whom only 50 lived to see America. Still another bearing 1,500 lost 1,100 from deaths on the voyage. Children seldom survived the journey, 'many a time parents were compelled to see their children die of hunger, thirst, or sickness, and then see them cast into the water; many a mother was cast into the water with her child'" (Oneal: *Loc. cit.*, p. 64).

Geiser in his book *Redemptioners* speaks extensively about deaths from hunger and disease. On one ship sailing from Holland

"the hunger was so great on board that all the bones about the ship . . . were pounded with a hammer and eaten; and what is more lamentable, some of the deceased persons, not many hours before their death, crawled on their hands and feet to the captain, and begged him for God's sake to give them a mouthful of bread or a drop of water to keep them from perishing, but their supplications were in vain; he most obstinately refused, and thus did they perish. . . . Sometimes whole families die in quick succession; so that often many dead persons lie in the berths beside the living ones, when contagious diseases have broken out" (*Ibid.*, p. 65).

At first only men came to the new world. Until 1621 women did not dare to make the trip. In the early days men did not come to America to live. Their only aim was to get wealth and go back to the land where they were born. But as soon as colonies began to be formed, women were needed to insure their success. And this problem was easily solved: if slavery of men was possible, why not slavery of women?

Hunting and enticing of women began in Europe. The streets and alleys of England, Germany, and Holland were at the time full of women fighting hunger and starvation. Prostitution was rampant. If it was possible to empty the prisons by taking the criminals to America and selling them into slavery, why was it not possible to do the same with prostitutes or with girls who had been deceived and whom the church and state regarded as great criminals?

The traffic in women was not, however, confined to these unfortunates. Also "maids of virtuous education, young, handsome, and well recommended," were induced by the promise of prosperity to cross the ocean. They were married to men who could pay the price of their passage and who could support them. The price gradually "rose from 120 to 150 pounds of tobacco, or even more . . ." (Bancroft: *Loc. cit.*, Vol. I, p. 116).

From that time on a large and profitable trade in white women slaves began. They were brought in droves to America and sold for tobacco or for gold and silver.

But the shipping companies, speculators, and agents of the colony

THE WHITE SLAVES AND THEIR MASTERS 17

owners were not satisfied with adult Europeans alone. They also bought or stole children, brought them to America, and sold them into slavery.

"The London Company of adventurers who settled Virginia was eager to employ child labor in developing the resources of the colony. In 1619 its records acknowledge the arrival of 100 children, 'save such as dyed on the waie,' and another 100, 12 years old or over, is asked for. In 1627 many ships arrived, bringing 1,400 and 1,500 children kidnapped by 'spirits' in European ports, and a few years later they sent a request to London for another supply of 'friendless boyes and girles'" (Oneal: *Loc. cit.*, pp. 59-60; *see* Solomon: *Domestic Service,* p. 22).

Only part of these children reached America and were sold into slavery. The majority of them died on shipboard and were cast into the water.

Words fail to describe the hardships of these white men, women, and child slaves. Their existence was so wretched as almost to defy belief. Especially the women slaves had to suffer from the lords and masters.

"One of the common offenses in the seventeenth century was bastardy, due in part to the degraded character of many servants, men and women, who came or were shipped to the colony, and the fact that many of the women were at the mercy of their masters and forced to enter into illicit relations with them. Masters also opposed marriage among the women servants as this often meant an interruption of their work through confinement and the birth and care of children, while the death of a mother meant the loss of the sum invested in her" (Oneal: *Loc. cit.,* pp. 45-46).

Numerous laws were passed to punish bastardy. The punishment for women offenders was generally much more severe than for men, the latter usually escaping by paying a fine. Sometimes the man offender was only required to appear before the parish church and confess his sin, while the woman was brutally whipped. But in spite of the severe punishments imposed upon the unfortunate women, the number of the offenses became more frequent and the list of illegitimate children grew larger every year.

When a female servant gave birth to a child, the father of which was her master, the church was authorized to sell her into slavery for a period of two years, the price being paid in tobacco to the parish. Occasionally, when masters were fined for this offense the violated mothers were required to repay their masters by an extension of their terms of servitude. Since the birth of a bastard child to a servant entitled the master to lengthen her period of slavery, it is easy to understand that the masters would take advantage of this situation.

Near the close of the century, church wardens were empowered to bind out illegitimate boys until they were 30 years old. Their power to do the same with orphan children until the age of 20 was also frequently exercised. Poor children, whose parents were unable to provide for them properly, were also bound out by the church for a long term of years (Bruce: *Institutional History of Virginia,* Vol. I, Chapters V and IX).

The conditions of the white slaves were harder than those of the black slaves.

"Negroes being a property for life, the death of slaves, in the prime of youth or strength, is a material loss to the proprietor; they are, therefore, almost in every instance, under more comfortable circumstances than the miserable Europeans, over whom the rigid planter exercises an inflexible severity. They are strained to their utmost to perform their allotted labor. ... They groan beneath a worse than Egyptian bondage. By attempting to lighten the intolerable burden, they often render it more insupportable" (*Documentary History,* etc., Vol. I, pp. 343-344).

Woe to the slave who attempted to escape from his servitude and was caught. The masters had organized an effective system of finding runaways. The papers regularly carried advertisements describing escaped slaves and offering a reward for their return. When they were recaptured, their punishment was cruel. The lash was not spared.

Revolt was a second road to freedom sometimes tried by the white slaves. Not many of them had the courage to try this method, but still several revolts broke out. The slaves had no organization which would help them win their fight, and, of course, they lacked class consciousness. Their masters even sought to prevent their talking with slaves of another owner. But the common oppression, the same unbearable burden of toil and suffering developed among them a spirit of unity and solidarity. Their hard life taught them that their common enemy was the master class.

The Boston *Chronicle* of September 26, 1768, describes one of the revolts of the colonial white slaves as follows:

"News came that on August 17th, about 200 of the Spaniards and Italians introduced by Dr. Turnbull, and which he was settling at Musquito's, rose and seized a schooner which was employed in carrying provisions of the settlement. They tried to capture other vessels also and get away to Havana; but the wind was against them. An express was sent to St. Augustine. Two sloops full of troops were sent to prevent them getting away from Musquito's. The Spaniards, upon the troops arriving, took to the bushes. It is apprehended that Dr. Turnbull will have much trouble with the settlers he has introduced" (*Documentary History,* etc., Vol. I, pp. 343-344).

The master class was stricken with fear lest the slaves rebel and make an end of their rule. Therefore, they did everything to prevent their slaves from acquiring weapons. As early as 1672 only those slaves were accepted into military training and allowed to carry weapons whose period of servitude was about to end. A slave whose term of service was almost up would not turn his gun against his tyrant and thereby run the risk of having his slavery prolonged. In 1699 the governor of Virginia, Nicholson, proposed to the house of representatives of the colony that the agricultural workers—the white slaves—be trained in the use of arms. The house immediately answered the governor that the workers had no time to indulge in military training because it was necessary for them to till the soil and to harvest the crops. On the other hand, such a policy would be dangerous because it would be very difficult to control armed slaves or those skilled in the use of weapons. How were they to be sure that some fine day the slaves would not revolt and massacre all of their masters or try to win their freedom?

The colonial masters took these questions seriously and used every means at their disposal to protect themselves from the wrath of their discontented slaves. This was also one of the main reasons why the propertied class of the colonies were so much afraid of invasion by foreign armies. They were in mortal fear lest the slaves assist an invader in their desire for liberty and vengeance.

Finally, it must not be supposed that white slaves in America consisted only of European prisoners or those who sold themselves to the shipping companies for their passage. During the colonial period slavery was a common punishment for crime. In view of the fact that the government and courts were in the hands of the slave-owners, it is only natural that such a law was often used against the poor and exploited white workers and farmers.

CHAPTER III

NEGRO SLAVERY IN AMERICA

No matter how industriously the European rulers emptied their prisons and lured the poor to America to sell them as slaves, still the colonial masters were not satisfied. They wanted more slaves on the fruits of whose toil they could live even more luxuriously and splendidly. And with what joy did the landowners of Virginia hail the Dutch ship *Treasurer* which landed at Jamestown in August, 1619, and set on shore 20 strong Negroes for sale.

This was the beginning of Negro slavery in America. These 20 inhabitants of "wild" Africa were the pioneers who opened the road of suffering for their race in America. Now the question of labor power was solved for the ruling class in America by putting to work the Negro slaves in addition to the white slaves; now the owners were able to amass further stores of wealth and to send the roots of their rule still deeper into the life of the new continent.

In 1630 another ship, the *Fortune,* arrived with a larger cargo of Negroes, who were sold for "85 barrels of rum and 5 barrels of tobacco."

The first American ship to bring Negroes from Africa was called the *Desire,* and was built in 1636. The trade at the beginning grew very slowly. In 1635 in all of Virginia there were only 26 Negro slaves (Spears: *The American Slave-Trade,* p. 9). At first no companies or ships would limit their activities to the hunting of Negroes in Africa. The slave-trade was only an addition to their trade in other commodities.

Eventually slavery was established not only in the southern colonies, but in the North also. We find it in New York and in New England. The center of activity of the famous Incorporated West Indies Company of Dutch plunderers was located on Manhattan Island, where the city of New York now stands. This company stated in its charter that "it will attempt to supply the colonists with as many slaves as it can." If slavery was not able to establish itself in the northern colonies as firmly as in the South, the reasons are to be found in the economic conditions existing there. It was found that slavery was useful only in that part of the country where there were large tracts of fertile soil good for raising cotton and tobacco. Slavery did not pay on such small farms as were found in New England. Even in the colonial period it was clear that slave labor-power was not adaptable for industry and commerce, which were growing fast in the northern part of the country. Industry required "free" workers, proletarians, who did not cost the employers anything, for whom the latter were not responsible, and who could be hired and fired at any time. It was economics, not morals, which caused the slight spread of Negro slavery in the North.

"While the colonies were under the British crown slavery and the slave-trade existed in each one of them. But in those where no great staple such as rice and tobacco was grown, where for climatic and economic reasons slavery was not a profitable form of labor, and where the demand for skilled and unskilled laborers was fully supplied by 'redemptioners' and 'bond-servants,' the moral aspects of slave-holding aroused strong feelings; and repeated attempts were made to cut off the slave-trade and stop the source of supply . . ." (McMaster: *Cambridge Modern History*, Vol. VII, p. 361).

After 1650, however, slavery spread like wildfire. Hundreds of thousands of Africans were captured and brought to America. Even after the War of Independence which overthrew English rule and gave birth to the United States of America, the slave-trade was not discontinued. Instead, it was carried on more extensively. In 1860, just before the Civil War, the number of Negro slaves in this country was 4,442,000 (Commons: *Races and Immigrants in America*, p. 53).

The constitution of the United States not only did not prohibit the importation of slaves, but it contains a paragraph which says that Congress has no right or power to prohibit "importation of such persons as any of the states now existing shall think proper to admit . . . prior to 1808." At the end of that period Congress did enact a law which prohibited the importation of Negroes into the United States. But the law had many loopholes, and little attention was paid to it. The slave-trade was illegal; but it continued. The faster the raising of cotton spread in the southern states, the more slaves were needed, and the more they were imported from Africa.

Of course the planters and slave-owners did not explain their adherence to slavery on purely economic grounds. Far from it. They did everything to conceal their material aims in slavery and the slave-trade, and loudly declared to the world that they were performing a holy mission by bringing "wild" Negroes to America and thus converting them to Christianity and saving their "unfortunate souls" from eternal hell! They claimed that their aim was

"To preach and baptize into the Christian religion, and, by propagation of the Gospel, to recover out of the arms of the devil, a number of poor and miserable souls wrapt up unto death in almost invincible ignorance; to endeavor the fulfilling and accomplishment of the number of the elect which shall be fathered out of all corners of the earth and to add our myte to the treasury of Heaven" (Spears: *Loc. cit.*, p. 10).

At the beginning of the nineteenth century, when the movement for abolition of slavery had begun to spread, and when the question came up in Congress, there were some legislators who talked of the immorality of the slave-trade. Then Henry Clay took the floor and shouted into the faces of these "moralists": "This trade has nothing to do with morality. It should be clear to every one that this question must be considered from the commercial standpoint." Clay fully expressed the real interests of the masters.

The legislature of South Carolina had passed a law prohibiting the importation of slaves into the colony. This law was enacted for the simple reason that at that time the labor of the "free" workers was more profitable. But conditions changed when Whitney invented the cotton gin and for the first time the raising of cotton became a profitable occupation in South Carolina. White workers were not as adaptable for that heavy toil as the Negro workers. The conviction on the part of the colonial fathers in South Carolina that slavery was immoral soon disappeared, and the legislature annulled the anti-slavery law. The results were more than substantial. During the period 1804-1807 as many as 39,075 Negro slaves were imported into the state. Little was said about the immoral aspects of slavery from then on in South Carolina!

"Did the introduction of slavery pay?" asks Spears in his book, *The American Slave-Trade*:

"Let the facts answer. The planters in the tobacco, rice, cotton, and sugar regions not only increased in number from year to year, but they built finer houses, bought finer clothes and books, and lived in more expensive fashion from generation to generation.

"In Georgia, the one colony where no slaves were allowed in early days, the planters became so eager for them that their regular toast when drinking together was 'Here's for the one thing needful'!

"In short, to sum up the facts, slaves were introduced into United States territory in answer to a demand for labor. They were purchased by men who were accustomed to the purchase and sale of laborers, and no one's conscience was in any way hurt by the transaction. It was a good business proposition for that day, and for two centuries, at least, thereafter" (Spears: *Loc. cit.*, p. 13).

Virginia was another great slave-holding colony. Cultivation of tobacco required hard labor and the Negroes were able to supply it.

"Tobacco," says Henry Cabot Lodge, "founded this colony and gave it wealth. . . . The clergy were paid and the taxes levied in tobacco. The whole prosperity of the colony rested upon it for more than a century. . . .

"Tobacco planting made slaves necessary and profitable, and fastened slavery upon the provinces. The method of cultivation, requiring intense labor and watching for a short period, and permitting complete idleness for the rest of the year, fostered habits which alternated feverish exertion and languid indolence" (Simons: *Loc. cit.*, p. 42).

In the seaports of London, Bristol and Liverpool, the slave-trade increased enormously, and the traders became rich. Whoever was able to get a ship plunged into the traffic.

"In those days the ship-chandlers of Liverpool made special displays in their windows of such things as handcuffs, legshackles, iron collars, short and long chains, and furnaces and copper kettles designed for slavers' use. The newspapers were full of advertisements of slaves and slaver goods. The young bloods of the town deemed it fine amusement to circulate hand bills in which Negro girls were offered for sale" (Spears: *Loc. cit.*, p. 18).

The American trader-capitalists began to envy this highly profitable English enterprise. When Pennsylvania in 1800 proposed in Congress to start gradual emancipation of the Negro slaves, a representative from Rhode Island arose and angrily declared:

"We want money; we want a navy; therefore we must use means in order to attain these things. . . . Why should we stand and look how England has acquired all the slave-trade? Why can't our country have this very profitable trade for itself?"

It did not take long for the colonial business men of New England to decide what to do. They also embarked on the slave-trade. The seaports were opened wide for vessels carrying Negroes from Africa.

"If the infamy of holding of slaves belongs to the South, the greater infamy of supplying slaves must be shared by England and the North. While the states were yet colonies, to buy Negroes and to sell them into slavery had become a source of profit to the inhabitants of many New England towns. Scarce a year passed by but numbers of slavers went out from Boston, from Medford, from Salem, from Providence, from Newport, from Bristol, in Rhode Island, to Africa, where they bought or forcibly took Negroes, brought them to America, and sold them into slavery to the planters of the South" (McMaster: *History,* etc., Vol. I, p. 15).

The Puritans of New England were great religious fanatics. A smile on the Sabbath was to them an act of the devil. But these same Puritan fathers were among the boldest and most merciless slave-hunters. They made rum in their breweries, carried it to Africa, and there exchanged it for slaves: the slaves were then brought to the American colonies or the West Indies and sold to the planters for molasses; the molasses was brought to New England and turned into rum; and again that rum went to Africa and was exchanged for slaves, who were brought to the colonies and sold for molasses. The slave-trade continually grew, new breweries were built, the Puritan fathers got richer and richer, the number of churches constantly increased, and the prayers of the "righteous" ascended to heaven!

The Puritan fathers did not divorce themselves from this very profitable trade even after it was outlawed. Rather, they became the greatest smugglers the world has ever known.

When the governments of England and America began to suppress illegal dealers in human flesh, the crimes of the slave-trade became unspeakable. The smugglers of New England, as well as of Spain and

England, began to arm their vessels and to resist seizure. When they saw that it was impossible to escape, they drowned their human cargo. Thus, the English slaver *Brillante* crossed the ocean 10 times and brought to Cuba 5,000 Negroes. But once four battleships surrounded the smugglers when they were carrying 600 Negroes, and there was no hope of escape. Captain Homans instructed his crew to chain the slaves together by their necks, and at the middle of the chain an anchor was attached. When the government ships were about to capture the *Brillante*, the anchor was thrown into the water and with it went all of the 600 slaves. When the smugglers were captured their vessel was searched and not a single Negro was found. Captain Homans laughed and poked fun at his captors.

Smuggling was so successful that in 1828 46,160 Negroes were brought to Rio de Janeiro alone, from which port as well as from Cuba the slaves were easily transported to the United States. This bloody trade was profitable indeed. At that time it was possible to get a Negro in Africa for about $20, but after he was brought to America his value rose to $500 (Spears: *Loc. cit.*, pp. 143-144).

Horrible indeed were the methods employed by captains and agents of the slave-vessels in obtaining Negroes in Africa. In those days traveling on the seas was dangerous, and those who hired themselves out to go to Africa for slaves were the lowest elements of society—criminals and drunkards. In the beginning, when the slave-trade was not very extensive, Negroes could be gotten in Africa almost free of charge. A captain could buy several dozen of them for a barrel of rum. But as the trade expanded and it became difficult to secure fresh victims, the price rose. Then the slavers began to employ most cruel means to accomplish their mission. They armed their agents and gave them plenty of drink before sending them ashore. Under cover of darkness, while the Negroes were peacefully sleeping, these drunken criminals would attack the native villages, kill those who could not be subdued, and capture the rest, chain them together, and cram them into the ship's hold.

"When every available inch of space in the hold had been filled, the slaver turned westward and made for some southern port. The coastline had scarcely disappeared from view when the hatches were taken off and the terrors of the voyage began. Every fine day at sunrise the slaves were driven on deck. Such as were noisy had the thumbscrews put on. Such as were hard to manage were chained in pairs by the arms, or the ankles, or the necks. At the first signs of insurrection the leaders were shot down and cast into the sea. Their food was salt pork and beans. Their sole exercise was dancing and capering about the deck. This they were made to do. If any refused, the cat-o'-nine tails or the rope's end was vigorously applied. When the sun set, the whole band went below. There the space assigned each to lie down in was 6 feet by 16 inches. The bare boards were their beds. To make them lie close the lash was used. For one to turn from his right side to his left was impossible, unless the long line of cramped and stiffened sufferers turned with him. But the misery of a night was as nothing to the misery of a stormy day. Then the hatches were fastened down, tarpaulins were drawn over the gratings, and ventilation ceased; the air grew thick and stifling; the floor became wet with perspiration; the groaning and panting of the pent-up Negroes could be heard on deck; their mouths became parched, their tongues swollen. When the storm was over, the hatches opened and the tarpaulins drawn away, the air that would come from the hold was like that from an oven. The hardiest in the crew could not inhale it without growing faint. The stench was terrible. It was not uncommon for as many as five dead bodies to be brought up and flung over the ship's side. On a slaver making the middle passage a mortality of 30 per cent was not rare" (McMaster: *History*, etc., Vol. II, p. 15).

When the ship arrived at one of the American ports, the Negroes were put on sale and widely advertised in the press. Here are two examples taken from the *Virginia Gazette:*

"Virginia, August 9, 1736. The ship *Withers* is just arrived from the coast of Africa, with nearly 300 choice slaves, which are to be put up to sale at York this day, and to continue there until Saturday next; and at West Point on Monday, the 16th instant, and there to continue till they are sold."

"April 22, 1837. The ship *Johnston* of Liverpool is lately arrived at York from Angola, with 490 choice young slaves. The sale of them began on Tuesday . . ." (*Documentary History*, etc., Vol. II, p. 52).

But not only those who were freshly brought from Africa were put up for sale. If the slave-holder went bankrupt, or decided to go out of business, he sold his slaves to somebody else. There were plenty of speculators whose only source of subsistence was to buy slaves from one master and sell them to another.

The slave-owner looked upon his slave as upon any other commodity, which had a certain value. The slave had no political or social rights. No law would protect him. The owner could treat him any way he wished; nobody listened to his sufferings, nobody was interested in his troubles.

But, on the other hand, the owner was interested in the slave's physical condition because he had invested a certain amount of capital in him. Death or sickness of his slaves meant financial loss to him. Or, if the slaves were physically run down, they could not perform their duties as well as strong and healthy slaves. In this case the same rule applied to slaves as to beasts of burden.

Care of the physical condition of the slaves was placed on the same level as the care of horses and other animals. A certain Richard Carbin gave the following instructions to his agent in 1759:

"The care of Negroes is the first thing to be recommended that you give me timely notices of their wants that may be provided with all necessities. . . .

"Next to the care of Negroes is the care of stock. . . .

"Take an exact account of all the Negroes and stock at each plantation and send to me . . ." (*Documentary History*, etc., Vol. I, pp. 109-110).

Instructions by Alexander Telfair, of Savannah, Ga., to overseers of his plantation near Augusta, dated June 11, 1832, were as follows:

"The allowance for every grown Negro however old and good for nothing and every young one that works in the field is a peck of corn each week, and a pint of salt, and a piece of meat, not exceeding 14 pounds per month.

"No Negro to have more than 50 lashes inflicted for any offense, no matter how great the crime.

"You will give tickets to any of the Negroes who apply for them, to go anywhere about the neighborhood, but do not allow them to go off without it, nor suffer any strange Negroes to come on it without pass.

"No night meeting and preaching to be allowed on the place, except on Saturday night and Sunday morning . . ." (*Ibid.*, pp. 126-127).

The Christian church recognized slavery, and together with the slave-owners defended and supported it. The southern church and its clergy, with very few exceptions, were ready to give their all for the continuation of slavery when the struggle for its abolition had been started.

H. B. Bonner has the following to say about the Christian church and its relations to slavery:

"Negro slavery was recognized by all the Christian governments of Europe and America; it was supported by the great bulk of the clergy and justified by Christian writers of nearly every denomination except the Quakers. Clergymen and missionaries were among the slave-holders, and churches were supported from slave property.

"George III, hereditary defender of the faith, always upheld slavery and regarded its abolition with abhorrence. He even issued an injunction under his own hand commanding the Governor of Virginia, under pain of the highest displeasure, to assent to no law by which the importation of slaves could be in any respect prohibited or obstructed. . . .

"It was not Christianity which freed the slave; Christianity accepted slavery; Christian ministers defended it; Christian merchants trafficked in human flesh and blood, and drew their profits from this unspeakable horror of the middle passage. Christian slaveholders treated their slaves as they did the cattle in their fields: they worked them, scourged them, mated them, parted them, and sold them at will . . ." (Bonner: *Christianity and Conduct,* pp. 28-32).

A slave could not think for himself. He was not allowed to show any independence. He was good and useful only when he performed the duties of an ordinary beast of burden and was entirely and in all circumstances devoted to and dependent upon his master. What discipline was imposed upon the slaves and how strongly they were enslaved spiritually, we can judge from the following rules laid down in 1803 for the slaves of one of the sugar plantations. Among other things, the rules provide:

"You cannot resign him to the guidance of his own discretion, but, like a soldier in the ranks, he must be a *mere machine,* without either will or motion, other than you impress upon him. The basis of this discipline consists in accustoming your Negroes to absolute submission to order; for if you suffer them to disobey in one instance they will do so in another; and by this an

NEGRO SLAVERY IN AMERICA

independence of spirit will be acquired, that will demand repeated punishment to suppress it and to reëstablish your relaxed authority. . . ."

A struggle of the black slaves against their masters was almost impossible. First of all, they had no opportunity for any kind of education. Indeed, they did not know what education meant. Their masters were careful not to allow them to learn to write, and in many instances they were not even allowed to read.

Furthermore, the Negroes had no organization and the masters were very vigilant in preventing them from forming any. The slaves of one owner were carefully segregated from the slaves of another owner.

In vain would one search for a conscious and organized struggle on the part of the slaves under such conditions. Nevertheless they felt the burden of their oppression and struggled against it as best they could. What was in their hearts against their servitude and sufferings would sometimes burst forth and take physical forms.

As with the white slaves, one form of this struggle was the attempt to run away. To escape from their masters, to hide from them, to feel that they were free, to become human beings in the true sense of the word, used to be the hope, the desire and inextinguishable thirst in the bosom of many slaves. Numbers of them even tried in practice to achieve that great goal of their life. In spite of the fact that the roads to freedom were everywhere blocked and strewn with the greatest dangers, in spite of the fact that blood-thirsty hounds were set upon their trails, here and there the slaves used to gather their courage together, brave the hazards, face death itself, and flee from the will and the law of their oppressors. The newspapers of those days are dotted with advertisements for escaped slaves. Here is one from the *Virginia Gazette*, April 23, 1767:

"Run away from the subscriber in Norfolk, about the 20th of October last, two young Negro fellows, viz.: Will, about 5 feet 8 inches high, middling black, well made, is an outlandish fellow, and when he is surprised the white of his eyes turns red. . . . Peter, about 5 feet 9 inches high, a very black, slim fellow, has a wife at Little Town, and a father at Mr. Philip Burt's quarters. . . . They are both outlawed, and £10 apiece offered to any person that will kill the said Negroes, and bring their heads, or 30 shillings for each if brought home alive.—John Brown" (*Documentary History*, etc., Vol. II, pp. 92-93).

An attempt to escape was not the only means employed by the slaves to free themselves from the hands of their oppressors.

"The intolerable conditions of the blacks provoked at least 25 rebellions of these slaves in the United States before the American Revolution. . . .

"During Governor Hunter's administration of New York in 1712, a party of Negroes, armed with guns, knives, and hatchets, fired a building and shot and slashed those who ran to the spot. Soldiers captured the slaves and 21 were executed. 'One was broken on the wheel, and several were burned at the stake, while the rest were hanged.' In 1774 a revolt in Georgia was suppressed and a few leaders burned at the stake after having murdered four and injured as many more. About 1,000 blacks revolted in Virginia in 1800 and marched on the city of Richmond. A swollen stream interfered with their march; the leaders were captured and executed" (Oneal: *Loc. cit.*, pp. 75-76).

McMaster says:

"In 1829 a Negro named David Walker wrote, printed and scattered over the South a pamphlet entitled *Walker's Appeal*. It was addressed to the free blacks, who were urged to make the cause of the slave their own; it censured the meekness and nonresistance of the blacks . . . advised an insurrection when the time was ripe. The effect was immediate. Copies found in the hands of Negroes in Richmond (Va.), in New Orleans, in Savannah, in Tarborough (N. C.), were seized and formally transmitted by the governors of Virginia, Louisiana, Georgia, and North Carolina to their respective legislatures; and sharp laws against the free blacks were enacted by Georgia and Louisiana.

"The excitement produced by *Walker's Appeal* had not subsided when the danger of writings of this sort was brought home to the slave owners by a rising of slaves in Virginia—an outbreak known as 'Nat Turner's Insurrection.' It was quickly put down; and every Negro concerned in it, together with many who were not, was hanged, shot, mutilated, or beheaded. The insurrection was at once attributed to Negro preachers and 'incendiary publications' such as Walker's pamphlet and the *Liberator*, a newspaper recently started at Boston by William Lloyd Garrison. To attack the *Liberator* now became habitual in all slave-holding states. The corporation of one city forbade any free Negro to take a copy of it from the post office. A vigilance committee in another offered $1,500 for the detection and conviction of any white person found circulating copies. The governors of Georgia and Virginia called on the mayor of Boston to suppress it, and the legislature of Georgia offered $5,000 to any person who should secure the arrest and conviction of Garrison under the laws of the state" (McMaster: "History of the Slavery Question," in *Cambridge Modern History*, Vol. VII, pp. 386-387).

These and other attempts of the slaves put fear into the hearts of the masters. They commenced persecutions and with the greatest vigilance began to watch the movements of their slaves. For instance, the "most respectable citizens" of Charleston were so greatly alarmed that they got together and presented a demand to the government of South Carolina that the slaves be further restricted. They called the attention of the government and the "community" especially to the question of free Negroes who were coming in contact with the slaves and agitating the latter to revolt against their owners. They also pointed out that here and there were whites who were spreading rebellion. These "citizens" demanded that the government take immediate steps against the danger.

The masters looked upon the free Negroes with the greatest contempt and antagonism. Nevertheless, the number of free Negroes continuously increased, for here and there an owner would die and in his will he would free his slaves. Some of the owners, also, were so afraid of losing their lives at the hands of their rebellious chattels that they voluntarily let them go free. Then the northern states one after another, seeing that slavery did not pay, passed laws freeing the slaves within their borders. Naturally, these Negroes who were free and class-conscious would get in touch with their brothers in bondage and stir them to action against their owners. This state of affairs appeared highly menacing to the planters of the South; menacing to their earthly paradise and to their very lives.

How the slave owners hated the free Negroes can be judged from the following words of Henry Clay: "Of all the descriptions of our population the free persons of color are by far, as a class, the most corrupt, depraved, and abandoned."

So afraid were the slave-holders of slave revolts that in 1816 they organized "The American Society for Colonizing the Free People of Color of the United States," which had as its aim to purchase or obtain in some part of the earth a tract of land to which they could transport the freed American Negroes. Still earlier "good hearted" citizens of England had gotten the idea of transporting free Negroes back to Africa and establishing for them a new "fatherland." They purchased a piece of land in Africa and founded a Negro colony named Sierra Leone. The Americans greeted this step of the English masters enthusiastically as the best way of getting rid of "undesirable" and "depraved" free "people of color." On December 30, 1800, the Virginia House of Delegates requested the Governor to correspond with the President "on the subject of purchasing lands without this state whither persons obnoxious to the laws or dangerous to the peace of society may be removed (Spears: *Loc. cit.*, p. 163). Therefore, this American Society was formed primarily for the purpose of deporting from the United States the "undesirable" Negro citizens. The organization also bought a piece of land in Africa near Sierra Leone and removed there those elements which were "dangerous" to the "happiness" and "welfare" of society. The climate of the American colony in Africa was so bad that the deported Negroes died like flies from various diseases.

CHAPTER IV

"Free" Workers in the Colonial Period

During the colonial period the main occupation of this country was agriculture and the large landowners were the ruling class. Nevertheless, commerce and industry always played an important rôle. As the colonization of the continent went on, cities and towns arose and grew in size and importance. Boston, New York, Philadelphia, Jamestown, Baltimore and other centers were founded very early in our history.

In the beginning the cities were mainly centers of commerce, especially with Europe. But soon various industries began to appear and thus began industrial capitalism, which to-day rules supreme. If agriculture was based almost entirely on slave labor-power, industry grew and prospered on the basis of "free" labor-power.

In the early days of our country the industries were carried on under the roofs of handicraftsmen. The handicraftsman had his own tools and he himself was the worker. Take, for example, the shoemaker. He made the complete shoe himself. There was no division of labor. He owned all of the tools which were necessary in the making of a shoe. He either went from house to house, from farm to farm, and made the shoes for the people, or took orders and made them in his own home. Later he took into his home another worker and taught him the trade. At this time the shoemaker was "three in one"; the worker, the owner of the means of production, and the "boss" or employer. Here we already find a small division of labor between the shoemaker-employer and the shoemaker-apprentice. A little later the shoemaker-employer might get another apprentice and thereby the division of labor would be increased. Then production expanded, labor became more productive, and the shoemaker-boss became a still greater "boss."

Step by step industry developed. It became increasingly inconvenient for the shoemaker-boss to move from house to house with his tools and his employees. Increasingly he found it more convenient and profitable to settle in his own shop in the town. As his enterprise grew, he had not only two or three apprentices, but also two or three mechanics in his employ.

"But with the growth of towns into cities and an increase in rural population of the immediate neighborhood, two parallel developments occurred. The master workman continued to take custom orders as before, but began to employ journeymen in addition to his own work. He also began to stock up with finished products made by the same journeymen for sale to sojourners and visitors.

"From the standpoint of ownership and production the retail-shop stage introduced a change in the position of the journeyman. He retained his hand tools but lost ownership of the shop and the raw material. Likewise he lost control of the market and the price-bargain. Thus we have industrial classes: the journeyman, who owned no capital and depended upon his wages for a living; and the retail merchant-employer, who owned the capital, and, since he no longer performed manual labor, looked for his remuneration to his investment and his managerial ability" (Commons and Associates: *History of Labor in the United States*, Vol. I, pp. 56-57).

Here we see the beginnings of the division between labor and capital, between worker and employer. One more step in the development of the industry and our journeyman or mechanic-worker loses even his hand tools of production. The development of the bourgeois system of production is a continuous process of separation of the worker from the means of production. When this development is complete and the bourgeois system of production is established, the factory, the machinery, and the raw materials are entirely in the hands of the employer. Now the worker has nothing to do with the means of production. He becomes a proletarian in the true sense of the word.

Though the journeyman lost ownership of the shop and raw material, though he had to depend entirely on his wages for his living, he still had his skill, which in this stage of the development of industry had not yet been taken from him. He was still interested in the protection of this skill. He thought that the fewer journeymen there were in his particular line of work, the higher wages he would get. Therefore, he tried to prevent outsiders from coming into his trade. Of course, he could not entirely close the doors of his craft because he had not enough power. On the other hand the demand for his product was constantly increasing and he could not satisfy this demand by himself. He was, therefore, compelled to take the unskilled worker and train him in the trade. He saw to it, however, that the period of apprenticeship was as long as possible, often from five to seven years.

Industry continued developing. In spite of all limitations and restrictions, the army of journeymen constantly increased. Immigration from Europe was reaching larger proportions. Half-skilled and unskilled workers began to enter industry and take the place of the skilled. The development of machinery and the ever greater division of labor in the shops made it possible for the unskilled workers to take away from the skilled workers or journeymen position after position. Naturally the skilled workers began to think that all of their troubles were the result of the influx of half-skilled and unskilled workers into their industry. They started to organize into societies or "labor unions" and declared war against their own brothers—the half-skilled and unskilled.

This division between skilled and unskilled exists even to-day to a certain degree and is very harmful to the unity of the working class. The struggle between skilled and unskilled workers is beneficial only to the employing class.

As an industry develops, it also creates competition between employers, a competition as to which of them will be able to produce and sell goods more cheaply. The one who can produce the goods at lowest cost to himself can undersell his competitors, acquire more and better markets for his products, and therefore make higher profits. The skilled mechanics of those days imagined that their interests were identical with the interests of their employers. For example, they believed, as they were told by their employers, that if the prices of the goods were higher, the workers would gain proportionately in the way of higher wages. Therefore we find in many instances the employers and the workers of this period going hand in hand against those employers who did not maintain standard prices for their goods. Various appeals are on record in which these mechanics asked the public not to buy the goods advertised in the newspapers, which were offered for sale at lower prices (*Ibid.*, pp. 57-60).

The life of these "free" wage workers in the colonial period was nothing to be envied. The government, controlled by the master class and faithfully defending the interests of the employers, saw to it that the workers did not get decent living wages. In some colonies the government even regulated the occupations of the workers.

"For instance, in Virginia agriculture afforded more profitable opportunities than most industrial pursuits, and there even the paternalistic inducements of financial aid and other protection failed to attract capital and mechanics to some of the most important trades. Not succeeding by these measures and finding their services indispensable, Virginia, totally disregarding their own wishes, forced such mechanics as 'brickmakers, carpenters, joiners, sawyers, and turners' to practice their trades by forbidding them 'to take part in any tillage of the soil.' Similarly, Massachusetts, when troubled in 1646 by a scarcity of farm labour impressed all manner of workmen into that service. The reason for the action was stated as follows: 'Because ye harvest of hay, corne, flax and hemp comes usually so neare together yt much losse can hardly be avoyded, it is ordered & decreed . . . that artificers or handicrafts men' be required to aid the harvest when crops may be injured by delay" (*Ibid.*, p. 43).

In almost all colonies the government controlled the earnings of the workers. Massachusetts colony passed a law in 1630 which forbade carpenters, joiners, bricklayers, and others to take more than 2 shillings a day (*Ibid.*, p. 51).

"One year after the passage of this act there was an increase in the demand for labor and the clause penalizing the employers for paying wages higher than the legal rates was repealed. The towns were then authorized to appoint a board of three men to fix wages when the employers and workmen failed to agree. As the workers had no political power it is evident that the town boards always represented the masters and any interference was seldom to their disadvantage. While the employers were exempt from penalties for violating the act the workmen continued to be fined. The law was later repealed, but another took its place in 1636, giving towns jurisdiction in fixing wages. But in 1640 prices collapsed and there was danger of the workers reaping some benefits from the lower prices. The colonial legislature then went over the heads of the towns and commanded the workmen to reduce wages to correspond with reduced prices and those who failed to respond were fined as usual" (Oneal: *Loc. cit.,* p. 42).

We also must not forget that there were always enough slaves whom the masters used very effectively against the "free" laborers.

"Competition of this sort made the lot of the free laborer hard indeed, but it was made harder still by the usages of the time. He worked from sunrise to sunset, earned less wages in winter than in summer, was paid at irregular intervals, and if not paid at all had no lien on the product of his labor. If he were so unfortunate as to fall into debt, though it were for but a sixpence or penny, he might at the will of his creditor be torn from his family and cast into jail, there to remain until the debt and the prison charges were paid or he died of hunger or disease" (McMaster: *The Acquisition,* etc., pp. 32-35).

"Intrenched in their possessions the landed class looked down with haughty disdain upon the farming and laboring classes. On the other hand, the farm laborer with his 16 hours work a day for a 40-cent wage, the carpenter straining for his 52 cents a day, the shoemaker drudging for 73 cents a day and the blacksmith for his 70 cents, thought over this injustice as they bent over their tasks. They could sweat through their lifetime at honest labor, producing something of value and yet be a constant prey to poverty while a few men, by means of bribes, had possessed themselves of estates worth tens of thousands of pounds and had preëmpted great stretches of the available lands" (Myers: *Loc. cit.,* Vol. I, pp. 35-36).

Small wages, long hours of labor, the impossibility of supplying their families with decent food and clothes, drove many to extremities. In desperation a man would lose his patience and in order to save himself from starvation, would become a thief or highwayman, would make an attempt on the property of the rich. Then the government would outlaw him and the church would consign him to eternal damnation. He was an outcast, and was looked upon by every one as a criminal who must carry the mark of his crime till the end of his days, even after he had gone to jail and paid dearly for his mistake. Others were sent out of this world forever, with a noose around their neck, for thievery or robbery.

"In Massachusetts, Connecticut and Rhode Island, in 1789, 10 crimes were punishable by death. In Pennsylvania, in 1718, 12 crimes on first conviction and several others on second conviction were capital offenses. In 1776 this list contained 20 crimes, and the second conviction for any crime save larceny entailed death. In Virginia and afterwards in Kentucky, to swear falsely, to destroy or conceal a will, to obtain money on false pretenses, to steal a horse, or a record of writ of court, or commit robbery in the highway, were but a few of 27 offenses for which a man or woman might suffer death.

"For such misdeeds as did not merit death on the first conviction, the common punishments were branding, whipping, cropping the ears, standing on the pillory, sitting in the stocks, or ducking. In Maryland each county was required to have an assortment of branding irons and use them unsparingly. S L on either cheek meant seditious libeller. T on the left hand meant thief. The man with an R on the shoulder was a vagabond or rogue, an F on the cheek a coiner twice convicted. New Hampshire branded her burglars with the letter B on the right hand for the first offense, on the forehead if the crime was done on the Lord's day. Connecticut put an F on the forehead of the forger of a deed, and an I on the villain who sold arms to the Indians, and cut off the ears of counterfeiters.

"Publicity in the opinion of the fathers was a great corrective and deterrent of crime. In Pennsylvania therefore the robber and the thief, whether man or woman, after receiving at the whipping post 31 lashes well laid on, was condemned to wear in plain view on the left sleeve of the outer garment, between the shoulder and the elbow, a Roman T; the letter must be four inches each way and one inch wide, must be of red, blue, or yellow cloth, as the magistrate pleased, must be worn from sunrise to sunset and for a period of six months. If found without the letter the penalty for the first offense was 21 lashes, and for the second, 39 lashes and a T branded on the forehead.

"Every pauper who received any aid from any county, city or place, as also his wife and children must wear on the sleeve of the outer garment in plain view a large P of red or blue cloth, and the first letter of the place to which he belonged (McMaster: *The Acquisition,* etc., pp. 35-38).

Of course the laws provided that these rigorous punishments be imposed upon everybody—rich and poor alike. But in practice they were inflicted only upon the "offenders" from the working class. For a very small and insignificant offense the worker was flogged, compelled to stand in the pillory, and carry brands on his body till the end of his days. On the other hand, the rich criminals—the grafters, the robbers, murderers, the exploiters of labor, instead of being persecuted were held in high esteem and looked upon as paragons of morality.

"In the churches the colonists prayed to God as the Father of all men and showed great humility. But in actual practice the propertied men recognized no such thing as equality and dispensed with humility. The merchants imitated in a small way the seignorial pretensions of the land nabobs. Few merchants were there who did not have a bonded laborer or two, whose labor they monopolized and whose career was their property for a long term of years. Limited bondage, called apprenticeship, was general. Penniless boys, girls and adults were impressed by sheer necessity into service" (Myers: *Loc. cit.,* Vol. I, pp. 51-52).

Before the advance of the modern age of machinery, skill was absolutely necessary to the worker in making a living. Therefore the question of acquiring that skill or training was important for every youth of the working class. We find instance after instance where these youths, in order to learn a trade, used practically to sell themselves into slavery, though there was a definite limit to the period of this slavery. We see, then, that even the so-called free worker was hardly able to escape slavery in those days, at least till he learned his trade.

"FREE" WORKERS IN THE COLONIAL PERIOD

We find that equally bad conditions prevailed during the colonial period with regard to the social and political life of these poorer classes, the free workers and poor farmers. They had practically no political rights. Ownership of property was not only the key to higher society, but also a prerequisite to the right to vote. The aristocratic master class looked upon labor with the greatest contempt. Those who earned their livelihood with their own hands were considered by the masters and parasites as unfit for anything but to toil and bear the heavy burden of life till the end of their days. The rich not only thought, but openly and brazenly said that only those who were well off should enjoy the luxury and wealth created by the hands of others. "Only those who have no brains work." Therefore the government must be in the hands of those who "have brains," that is, those who own property and live upon the sweat and labor of others.

Government is necessary to protect property. Property is everything. Property is the foundation of society. Therefore, only those who own property are interested in the "maintenance" and "welfare" of society. Society does not mean anything to poor John Doe, who only toils day in and day out and who owns nothing but his ten fingers and scissors and a needle in them. What do all of these institutions, this great wealth of our society, which is accumulated in the hands of the few, mean to him? Nothing!

That is how the master class of those days reasoned and argued. And they could come to only one conclusion: a great wall of ownership of property must be erected between the poor and the government.

The crown of England appointed governors to various colonies. On the other hand the colonists had a right to elect their own "parliament," and the parliaments of the colonies under the direct supervision of the governors took care of public affairs. Therefore, around this parliament or assembly of the colony the masters built a Chinese wall of the ownership of property in order that the workers and poor farmers might not intrude and try to use it for their class interests.

In Massachusetts only those who owned a tract of land or other property worth 40 shillings had a right to vote. In Maryland only those could vote who had 50 acres of land or other property valued at £40. In New Jersey it was necessary to own 200 acres of land or £50. In New York only the property-owners were allowed to vote. The same qualifications were required in Connecticut and Virginia. In South Carolina only the owner of 500 acres of land or at least 10 slaves could be elected to the "parliament." In North Carolina only the property owners were qualified to be elected to the assembly or to occupy any governmental position. In Georgia only the owners of 500 acres of land could be elected and only those who owned not less than 40 acres could vote.

As far as the struggles of the workers in the colonial period to improve their conditions are concerned, we have very little information. We have already seen that the slaves, both white and black, unable any longer to withstand the burden of toil and hardships, in many instances either tried to escape or revolted against their owners and masters and took revenge for their brutality and exploitation. But we find almost nothing of the kind in the ranks of these "free" workers. We know this at least, that before the Revolution they did not yet have any organization with which to fight their employers. There were no trade unions (Ely: *The Labor Movement in America*, p. 2).

Neither have we any knowledge of strikes conducted in the colonial period. Therefore, though the "free" workers may have felt the oppression and injustice inflicted upon them, they were not organized to carry on their struggle. Conditions were not ripe for concerted action. The workers were divided among themselves. Each one worked separately and with his lone hands and brain. The skill of the worker was his only means for bettering his conditions. He had to undergo many hardships to acquire this skill; he saw no other way of bringing a little bit of sunshine into his home and family than through its use; he defended it with all his energy and power against any encroachment by unskilled laborers.

Every wage earner sought to be an independent craftsman, an owner of the means of production and an employer. And there were many opportunities, as industry developed, for a dependent worker to become independent. On the other hand, even if he did not succeed in winning his independence through a lifetime of labor, even if he spent all of his days under the hand of another, that did not prevent him from hoping to win and get higher up on the ladder.

Before the Revolution there were no large factories in which hundreds or thousands of workers were employed. Only with the rise of the large factories and the development of industry on a vast scale did the working class organizations and the labor movement itself become possible. "The trade unions in this country appeared about the end of the eighteenth and the beginning of the nineteenth century" (Hoxie: *Trade Unionism in the United States*, p. 78).

In the Colonial period there was another class of poor and exploited people who, driven to despair, sometimes dared to take up arms and openly fight the large land-owners and their government. This class was composed of poor farmers, known in American history as "pioneers," who moved from the Atlantic coast deeper into the continent, felling forests and establishing new tracts of habitable lands. These pioneers were "forgotten" and neglected by the government. Many of them lost their lives in the struggle with the Indians who by bitter experience soon came to look upon the whites as their mortal enemies.

The large land-owners and the government did not approve the efforts of these pioneers in pushing deeper and deeper into the continent.

The land-owners had large tracts of land which had to be cultivated. They themselves, of course, would not till the soil, they needed workers who would toil for them. Continuous penetration further and further west into the continent absorbed labor-power. Thousands of the poor and oppressed people were ready to face the greatest hazards, to go through untold hardships of pioneer life, in order to become independent and own their own homes. Government officials and politicians also held back from supporting the efforts of the pioneers because the officials were carrying on very profitable business with the Indians through graft and crime, exchanging powder and guns for furs. Pushing further inland injured their business and profits. Governor Berkeley of Virginia was entirely absorbed in this graft with the Indians. He refused any assistance to the pioneers in his colony. The pioneers' condition became so unbearable that finally in 1676 they were forced to take up arms under the leadership of Nathan Bacon.

Bacon was only 28 years old and came from a well-to-do family. He also had a large tract of land upon which peaceful living was impossible on account of continuous attacks by the Indians. Therefore he was greatly interested in repulsing the Indians and protecting himself from their raids. On the other hand, Bacon sympathized with the poor farmers. Finally he demanded from Governor Berkeley permission to organize a military force against the Indians. The governor refused. Bacon thereupon disregarded the governor and undertook to lead the pioneers in their struggle against the Indians. After defeating the Indians he marched his army on Jamestown and forced the election of a new parliament.

In view of the fact that Bacon called the aristocrats of Virginia "parasites," and the poor farmers were following him, very soon the better-to-do elements deserted his army and joined the government forces. His ranks were weakened, and his fight against the authorities took on the appearance of a class struggle. Bacon with his small army proceeded farther north, but here the rebels sustained a terrible loss: their leader took ill and died. The ranks of the revolted farmers disintegrated and the rapacious governor of Virginia, rejoicing in his "victory," began a bloody revenge. Fearing that the grand jury would not impose death sentences upon the rebels, Berkeley instituted courts-martial and slaughtered his victims mercilessly. He murdered so many people that even the king of England, Charles II, exclaimed: "The old fool has put to death more people in that naked country than I did here for the murder of my father." And the assembly was forced to protest against the governor's bloody work and accepted a resolution "that the governor would spill no more blood."

Such was the answer of the ruling class, at the head of which stood bloody Berkeley, to those who dared raise their hand against its power and authority.

That "Bacon's Rebellion" was really a revolt of the oppressed against their oppressors can be seen from the way his followers were described by one of the members of the Council of Virginia. He says:

"Bacon gathers about him a rabble of the basest sort of people, whose condition was such, as by a change could not admit of worse . . . who for ye ease of the poore will have noe taxes paied . . . but would have all magistracie and Governm'nt taken away & sett up on themselves, & to make their Good Intentions more manifest stick not to talk openly of sharing men's estates among themselves."

And William Sherwood referred to the rebels as "ye scum of ye country" (Oneal: *Loc. cit.*, pp. 78-82).

There were also similar revolts, though on a narrower basis, of the farmers in other colonies. In North Carolina the population revolted against their tyrants. They were led by John Culpepper, who deserved, according to the ruling class, "hanging for endeavoring to set the poor to plundering the rich."

Another revolt occurred in New York, known as "Leisler's Rebellion," after Jacob Leisler, its leader. New York was ruled by two powerful classes—the rich landlords and the traders. Under their control was a great mass of common people, the working class population—small farmers, sailors, shipwrights and other artisans. The rebellion broke out in 1689. Leisler defeated the English governor and for a while ruled in his place. But additional troops from England overthrew him, and he was executed.

The colonial aristocracy kept the masses of common people in total darkness and ignorance. The wealthy and their government officials knew perfectly well that the more ignorant the workers were, the more easily they could be kept down. And for the ignorance of the workers the masters never failed to thank their god with whose help they could more easily maintain their power and privileges. In 1670 Governor Berkeley wrote to the authorities in England:

"But, I thank God, there are no free schools, nor printing, and I hope we shall not have them these hundred years; for learning has brought disobedience and heresy and sects into the world, and printing has divulged them, and libels against the best government. God keep us from bothe!" (Simons: *Loc. cit.*, p. 48).

CHAPTER V

WORKERS AND THE AMERICAN REVOLUTION

ON April 19, 1775, occurred the first armed conflict between England and America. British troops attempted to capture the arsenals at Lexington and Concord, but the American militia defended them and won the first victory. That was the beginning of war between England and America, or the American Revolution. On October 19, 1781, at Yorktown, the English army surrendered to the Americans. In March, 1782, England officially ended the war and admitted its defeat. From the American colonies arose the United States.

What was this American Revolution? How was it brought about? Who led it and to whom did it mean a real victory? Who bled and died for it? Was it a direct revolt of the working masses against their oppressors and exploiters?

The answer is "No." The American Revolution of 1775-1781 was primarily a conflict of the interests of the American ruling class with the interests of the ruling class of England.

It is true that, as in all other capitalist countries, it was the workers, the slaves, and the poor farmers who did the actual fighting. It was they who overthrew English rule, and with their blood and lives established the United States of America. On one hand, they were pushed into the army by force and violence; on the other hand, the ruling class of the colonies induced them to join the fight by promising them many good things if the enemy were defeated. Others were led to believe that by overthrowing foreign oppression they would win freedom for themselves. Nevertheless, the American Revolution was not a direct struggle of the working class against the capitalist class. It was rather a colonial revolt against foreign rule.

The ruling class of England wanted the American colonies to belong forever to them—to be a means of increasing their wealth and profits. But the ruling class of the colonies wanted America for themselves only. They asked themselves: Why should this great continent with all its wealth and people be the property of England? Why cannot the Washingtons, Franklins, Adamses, and Hancocks be the masters of America? What we need is unity and guns and ammunition, and our slogan "America for the Americans" will become a real and living thing!

Commerce played an important rôle from the very beginning of

American society. The merchants of New England, New York, and Philadelphia in a short period became a powerful section of the ruling class. Even the great masters of land and slaves to a very large degree were dependent on these merchant capitalists. Without their ships and their help it would have been impossible to import Negroes from Africa, or to export rice, tobacco, and cotton, on which the South depended.

Another section of the American ruling class came into existence a little later, but from year to year it grew in prestige and influence and soon developed into a powerful factor in the life of the colonies. This was the industrialists—the employer-capitalists. The middle colonies, such as New York and Pennsylvania, were considered the industrial colonies. With the constant increase of population there also increased the demand for better means of communication, for more clothes, shoes, homes, light, and other necessaries of life. This demand, in turn, compelled an extension of industry. But the ruling class of England hindered the growth and development of industry in America. The masters of England wanted the profits, derived from the toil of the American working class, to fall into their hands only. They demanded that the colonists buy all factory products in England and from English factories. For instance, the colonists raised cotton. They were required to export this cotton to England where it was made into cloth; then the colonists imported that cloth for making their clothes. They had to do the same thing with other raw material and manufactured products. The British Parliament forbade them to erect factories in America and to make the finished products themselves. In 1764 Parliament enacted further laws restricting American industry and commerce. It laid heavy tariffs on all products exported to the colonies from England. Then the American merchants, seeing the possibility of large profits, imported products from other countries illegally. For instance, the colonists consumed a great quantity of tea. The West Indies Company of England had a monopoly on tea. As England levied a high tariff, the price of tea in America was high and, therefore, the American merchants smuggled it in from England. "Nine-tenths of the merchants of New England were smugglers," says David H. Wells. "One-fourth of those who signed the Declaration of Independence were raised in commerce, navigation, and contraband" (Wells: *Encyclopedia of Political and Social Science*, p. 61).

Here they found a very important source of profit. At the same time the West Indies Company had 17,000,000 pounds of tea rotting in the storehouses of England. The English Parliament came to the assistance of the West Indies Company by reducing taxes on tea, thus making it possible for the company to ship its tea to the colonies and sell it cheaper than the colonial smugglers. The profiteers—Trumbull, Hancock, etc.,—saw this cheap tea of England seriously threatening their profits. Therefore, they organized the "Boston Tea Party." When the tea arrived from

England, they attacked the ships at night and threw the tea into the water. This act is painted as a revolt of the people to whom "the duty (taxes) was nothing, the principle everything" (James and Sanford: *American History*, p. 152). This boycott and destruction of English goods on the part of Boston merchants was motivated by selfish ends. It was, however, a revolutionary act, in that it was an act of protest against a foreign oppressor.

Finally, in 1764, the British Parliament levied special taxes on sugar and molasses. Immediately the ruling class of New England made a strong protest. As has been pointed out, the New England colonists imported sugar and molasses from Haiti, Cuba, and Porto Rico, and turned them into rum with which they bought Negroes in Africa, carried them into the southern states, and sold them to the land-owners. Therefore, these special taxes on molasses dealt a blow to the whole ruling class of the colonies.

There were other reasons why the southern planters and their agents were ready to fight for the separation of America from England. Some of them owed money to British merchants, and saw in the struggle an opportunity to annul their debts. Others were engaged in land speculation. George Washington, Hamilton, and other leaders of the American Revolution were the greatest land speculators of the time. They were interested in taking land from the Indians and selling it to newcomers from Europe. But in 1763 by a declaration of the crown it was strictly forbidden to survey and colonize lands further inland than the sources of the rivers which empty into the Atlantic. Washington was appointed surveyor and secretly surveyed for himself large tracts of land beyond the demarcation line set by the crown. Any attempt to prevent speculation or the grabbing of new lands struck directly at the pockets of the slave-owners and land speculators. Therefore, they were the first to take the leadership of the Revolution.

That George Washington was a great land speculator we learn from his letter to his agent William Crawford, written on September 21, 1787, in which he instructs this agent to find out "who aims to grab 1,500, or 2,000, or more acres of land in Pennsylvania," and to make every effort to get this land for Washington himself. Washington was also a large slave-owner and one of the richest colonists. Through marriage with Mrs. Martha Curtis he received as dowry from her 15,000 acres of land, £30,000, and 300 slaves.

The owners of the white slaves also were vitally affected by the law passed by the English Parliament in 1765, which laid taxes on all legal papers. This law demanded that the sum of money appearing on the contracts entered into by the masters and their "servants" (slaves) be clearly stated. According to this law, the slave might also bring charges in court against his master in case the latter did not live up to the agreement or attempted to evade it. It is well known that the masters were very clever in violating their contracts in various ways, making the temporary bondage of their slaves permanent. This section of the ruling class of the colonies was very numerous and very important and the law of 1765 directly attacked their economic interests. Wendell Phillips correctly declared:

"Northern merchants fretted at England's refusal to allow them direct trade with Holland and the West Indies. Virginia planters, heavily mortgaged, welcomed anything that would postpone payment of their debts. . . . To merchant, independence meant only direct trade—to planter, cheating his creditors" (Phillips: *Speeches, Lectures and Addresses*, Vol. I, p. 373).

There was another group of property owners who favored the Revolution—the petty bourgeoisie. Almost every colony had its own paper money which was nearly worthless. These small business men were very heavily indebted to the rich merchant capitalists of England and wanted to pay their debts in this depreciated paper money. But the English merchants would not accept scraps of paper. Parliament came to the merchants' assistance by forbidding the colonists to issue paper money. This law meant a great blow to the debtor business men of America. Hence like the debtor land-owners they saw in the possible separation from England a way of getting rid of their obligations (Simons: *Loc. cit.*, p. 66).

Thus all the measures of the ruling class of England were enacted in order to maintain America for its own benefit and were in direct conflict with the interests of all of the sections of the master class of America. Clearly the American Revolution was fundamentally a conflict between the interests of the ruling class of America and those of the ruling class of England.

"At every point the industrial life of the colonies had reached the stage where it was hampered and restricted by its connection with England. Large classes of the population required an independent government to further their interests. Evolution along the lines already drawn could proceed only with independence. Those who stood for independence were the most energetic and far-sighted among the colonists. In these great basic facts and fundamental conflicts of interests do we find the causes of the Revolution, and not in petty quarrels over insignificant taxes and abstract principles of politics" (*Ibid.*, p. 69).

Along with this economic development of the American ruling class there grew up political institutions which were to lead this class in its struggle with England for the independence of the colonies. It has already been pointed out that the colonial legislatures and governmental officials were elected by the property-owning class. And as the conflict between the colonies and England developed, these colonial institutions became more and more dominated by that part of the ruling class of America which opposed English rule. In New England these institutions were by the middle of the eighteenth century in the hands of merchant-smugglers; in Pennsylvania and other middle colonies they were in the hands of industrialists; in Virginia and similar tobacco and cotton-growing colonies they were in the hands of those planters who were debtors to England and dreamed that with separation from England they would be freed from the necessity of paying their debts. The institutions were also in the hands of powerful land speculators such as George Washington. The controversies between these political organs of the bourgeoisie of America and governors and other officials who represented the crown and defended the interests of the ruling class of England on this side of the water strengthened the colonial organs, made them militant, united and cemented them.

This development of America created the political organs of the ruling class not only in the various colonies. As the time for an open and armed conflict approached, the colonial masters clearly saw the necessity of establishing a national power also, and they were not afraid to take concrete steps to accomplish this important end. For some time there had been a great deal of agitation about getting the colonies to meet in a national congress for the establishment of a government which would bring the colonies nearer together. Their daily life, the most common commercial and industrial interests, led in such a direction. When it appeared that an armed conflict with England was inevitable and the only question to be decided was when it would take place, a call was sent from Massachusetts for the first general Continental Congress to meet in Philadelphia on August 1, 1774. With the exception of Georgia all colonies sent delegates. The first act of the Congress was a decision to defend Boston which had raised its hand against England and was to be punished for its act. Unity was established between the various colonies, and every colony pledged itself not to import or consume any English products after December, 1774, and not to export any American products to England or to her colonies after September, 1775. Further, this first Continental Congress drew up a declaration of rights in which the colonies recounted their grievances and told how unbearable English tyranny was becoming. This was the most daring step yet taken by the American ruling class against England, but it was inevitable and necessary for the further development of the economic and political interests of that class. The second Continental Congress assembled May 10, 1775, but the first battle between the American and British forces had already taken place. There was nothing else for Congress to do but to approve the accomplished fact at Lexington and Concord and take up energetically the work of mobilizing an army for war with England. It immediately appropriated $2,000,000 for war purposes and George Washington, "king" of the land speculators, was appointed commander-in-chief of the colonial troops.

The ruling class of America was now prepared economically, politically, and in a military way to overthrow English rule and take into its own hands the affairs and the wealth of the country. It was ready to take possession not by begging and praying, but by an open, armed struggle. No one stopped to consider how many lives and how much wealth the struggle would cost. This is one more proof that no class ever stops to think about the price when it struggles for power. Then the question is not one of "human sentiment," not how many lives will be destroyed, how much blood and tears will be shed, or how many hearts will be broken and how much suffering will be brought about, but how to win the fight and capture the power with all means at their disposal, regardless of how stern and how "inhuman" they may be.

The revolutionary bourgeoisie of the colonies not only captured the colonial parliaments and city councils, but also organized effective militant illegal secret revolutionary organizations under various names, such as "committees of correspondence," "committees of safety," "committees of observation," and the like. The main rôle of these underground revolutionary organizations was fourfold: to terrorize and crush active opponents of the Revolution; to whip into line for the Revolution the indifferent masses; to help the colonial armies; and to form a basis for the new state power.

"To establish a political machine of this character, extraneous to and unrecognized by any legal sanction, was difficult and dangerous as well. So dangerous was this that the Boston committee felt it wise to bind its members by oath not to divulge its proceedings. . . .

"This bold questioning of Britain's authority met with most enthusiastic support; Virginia's ringing call to action echoed up and down the Atlantic coast and before two months had passed the New England colonies were solidly organized into committee groups, with rumors of like activity coming in steadily from the southward. . . .

"It was this group organization that controlled at the outbreak of the hostilities of the Revolutionary War, and it held steady the reins of governmental power and authority until the Royalists' machinery was shaken loose and democratic governments set up and set in motion. . . .

"It is impossible to withhold admiration from action such as this. It was sabotage; but sabotage boldly and publicly recommended in the face of the bayonet. . . . It was plainly evident that the committees were engines of power and accomplishment sufficient in themselves to overturn the royal Government in the colonies. . . .

"The central Committees of Safety became, from their composition and character, the most important and powerful of all the committees. During the transition period before the royal Government fell to pieces and before the Revolutionary legislatures could begin to function, they held, for a time being, almost dictatorial power. But it was always wisely used and quietly wielded in coöperation with the local town and county committees. Together these committees held firm to the heavy, everyday work of massing the resources of the country behind the fighting forces. It was not spectacular work, but exacting and unceasing. A break in the lines of supplies, a check or delay of men or equipment, a need for wagons, for arms, for blankets, for animals and fodder, and the Committee of Safety was appealed to for aid. It called out the militia, collected arms and accouterments, handled deserters, received, managed, and guarded prisoners of war, arrested Tories, adjusted accounts, settled claims, and performed hundreds of other tasks of a minor nature, but none the less necessary, which, unattended to, would have increased immeasurably the burdens and difficulties of the war" (John C. Fitzpatrick: *The Spirit of the Revolution*, pp. 100-116).

The working class of the United States in its struggle for power can learn a very important lesson from these "underground" revolutionary committees of the first American Revolution. First of all they show that a class struggling for power uses illegal as well as legal means to fight the enemy. Second, they confirm the Marxian conclusion that as the American bourgeoisie could not take over and use for its own purposes the old state machinery, so the American proletariat will not be able to "simply lay hold of the ready-made state machinery and wield it for its own purposes." It will have to destroy the bourgeois state machinery and in its place establish its own state, that is, a *proletarian state* which will be the organ of its rule during the transition period from capitalism to the new society.

Only a minority of workers and poor farmers actively and enthusiastically supported the Revolution. They were attracted to the cause by their deep-rooted hatred of the English tyranny in the colonies, by the unbearable conditions under which they lived, by the business depression as a result of various restrictive measures adopted by the English parliament against the colonies, and also by glittering promises of the Declaration of Independence. In fact, these workers began an open fight against the government even before the War of Independence started, and went much further in their struggle than the colonial bourgeoisie wanted them to go.

"Artisans and laborers, hundreds of them rendered idle by business depression, formed themselves into societies known as 'Sons of Liberty.' Feeling their way toward that political power which was to come in the early nineteenth century, they leaped over the boundaries of polite ceremony. They broke out in rioting in Boston, New York, Philadelphia, and Charleston; they assailed the houses of the royal officers; in Boston the residence of the lieutenant governor was pried open, his chambers sacked, and his property pitched out into the streets. In fact, their agitation, contrary to the intent of the merchants and lawyers, got quite beyond the bounds of law and order. As Gouverneur Morris remarked, 'the heads of the mobility grow dangerous to the gentry, and how to keep them down is the question'" (Charles A. Beard and Mary B. Beard: *The Rise of American Civilization*, Vol. I, pp. 212-213).

And when on April 19, 1775, the news of the dispatch of British troops to Concord to capture the military stores had spread through New England, the revolutionary farmers left their homes by the thousands and swarmed to the scene of action. They had no military supplies nor military organization, but they were ready to give their all to the Revolution.

However, the large masses of the working men and women (wage-workers, artisans, white and black slaves, poor farmers) were mainly indifferent toward the War of Independence. This is plainly shown by the fact that it was impossible to get enough volunteers to join the revolutionary army. According to the historian Edward Chaning, "in the first flush of resentment at the attempt to disarm the New Englanders and to the first burst of enthusiasm after Bunker Hill, it might have been possible to raise a volunteer army of 30,000 men or even 50,000 for war. After 1776 this was impossible. As the years went on, the difficulty of getting men became greater and greater" (Edward Chaning: *History of the United States*, Vol. II, pp. 217-218).

The revolutionaries had to employ fair and foul means to swing the masses behind the Revolution. It must not be concluded, however, that these masses were militant supporters, nor were they supporters of English tyranny. They simply could not be moved by the high-sounding phrases of the revolutionary bourgeoisie of the colonies. They could not see the difference between the merchants, the manufacturers and land-owners of the colonies and those of England.

One should not think for a moment that all of the ruling class of the colonies was in favor of the Revolution, and that it had no active enemies behind the lines. The large land-owners of the coast and many slave-owners of the South who were in various ways connected with the government and the ruling class of England, actively opposed the Revolution. A powerful element composed of various agents and their hangers-on, appointed by the governors of the colonies, whose life depended upon the English rule in the colonies, fought against the Revolution very bitterly. The clergy of the Church of England, the more eminent lawyers and physicians, the merchants who did no smuggling, were active royalists. Against all of these enemies of the Revolution and the pillars of the old system, the revolutionaries waged a most determined and relentless war, not stopping for a single moment before the use of revolutionary terror. They were tarred and feathered, their homes were sacked and razed, they were whipped and beaten, and executed without trial. Thousands of them fled to Canada and other parts of the British empire, like so many rats from a sinking ship. When our reactionary bourgeoisie to-day refers to the revolutionary terror in the French and Russian revolutions with righteous indignation and scorn, we can only remind them of the terror employed by the American revolutionaries of 1776. A revolution can be successful only when it is ready to use all means at its disposal against its enemies.

"The proportion of the population of the thirteen original colonies," says Fitzpatrick, "who were loyalists during the Revolutionary War is not realized as generally as it should be. Our school histories have carelessly or intentionally ignored the facts, for the preponderance of the patriotic feeling was

WORKERS AND THE AMERICAN REVOLUTION 47

not as great as we have been led to believe. It is doubtful if a referendum in all the colonies on the question of independence, during the winter of 1777-78, would have shown a healthy majority in its favor."

"When the statement is made that only a minority of the population were revolutionists," says Simons, "the question naturally arises as to how this minority was able to win out. The answer is found in the fact noted by every writer who has studied this period that the revolutionists were much more active, efficient, cohesive, and belligerent, more conscious of their aims and more determined in their pursuit than any other portion of society. This is an invariable characteristic of a rising social class. The capitalist class was then the coming class. It was the class to whom the future belonged. It was the class whose victory was essential to progress. The Tories, with their adherence to the royal governors and to the old system of social castes and legal privileges, were harking back to an already dead society. They had neither ideas nor ideals to inspire them. The economic system to which they belonged was already crumbling into the dust of history" (Simons: *Loc. cit.*, p. 75).

When the war began, the life of the working masses became still harder. Many could not make ends meet. This condition not only "inspired" many to join the army, but forced them into service in order to avoid death by starvation. They expected that at least they would get something to eat in the army.

In the army itself the leaders of the ruling class and the Revolution treated the common soldiers with extreme cruelty. The generals and officers were not interested in the welfare of the masses of the soldiers. A soldier who violated army discipline or disobeyed the instructions of his superior was whipped and tortured. The whipping often was so severe that the victim died in agony after long suffering from infected wounds (A. B. Hart: *American History Told by Contemporaries*, Vol. IX, pp. 493-494).

Of course, the Revolution did not bring these hardships and suffering to everybody. To those in whose interests it was primarily fought it brought great opportunities and promises. Some adventurers and careerists joined the army and were given positions of leadership and esteem. They were many miles behind the battle, lived in luxury, and became rich through graft and robbery. They not only paid their debts, but made thousands of dollars in cold cash.

Other war patriots sat at home and robbed the common people. Depreciated paper money gave them an unrestricted opportunity to cheat their townsfolk of the last penny or even the last piece of bread. Others made contracts with the government to furnish ammunition, clothes, shoes, and other necessaries to the army for unheard-of prices. These goods were produced by the hands of the working masses, but the profit went into the hands of capitalists and parasites. Still others appeared before the people as great patriots and revolutionists while at the same time they maintained relations with the English army and the enemies of the Revolution and received splendid remuneration. The historian Lecky points out that at least 20,000 persons dropped their every-day occupation and took up the business of graft and smuggling (Lecky: *The American Revolution*, pp. 292-293).

Thus the American Revolution was in its essence a capitalist revolution, initiated and led by the bourgeoisie. Nevertheless, it was a revolution, a struggle fought and won by revolutionary means and organizations. It was a revolt of the colonial peoples against the imperialists of England. At that time the American bourgeoisie was revolutionary and its fight with England was a step forward, its victory meant progress and laid the foundation for the most powerful capitalist nation in the world. Today the American bourgeoisie is frankly reactionary. It rejects the Declaration of Independence and fights with all the means at its disposal against the very idea of revolution. The American working class is the only inheritor of the revolutionary methods and traditions of 1776.

CHAPTER VI

Life of the Working Masses After the Revolution

The Revolution was victorious, the tyranny of England was overthrown, for the first time America was a "free" and independent country. But for whom did that new sun of freedom rise?

"Washington's fortune," says Myers, "amounting at his death to $530,000, was one of the largest in the country and consisted mainly in land. He owned 9,744 acres, valued at $10 an acre, on the Ohio River in Virginia, 3,075 acres, worth $200,000, on the Great Kenawa, and also land elsewhere in Virginia and in Maryland, Pennsylvania, New York, Kentucky, the City of Washington and other places" (Myers: *Loc. cit.*, Vol. I, p. 43).

In a letter to one of his agents by the name of Crawford, Washington instructs him to acquire a large tract of land in Pennsylvania through the legislators. If the laws of the state made it impossible to get the land on a single name, Crawford was told to use several names, but he must get it at all costs. Washington further told his agents to keep this matter in great secrecy. And in his letter of June 16, 1794, Washington stated that he owned 32,373 acres of land by the Ohio and Kenawa Rivers (*The Daily Worker*, February 24, 1925).

Another well-known name in American history is that of Benjamin Franklin.

"After a long career, Benjamin Franklin acquired what was considered a large fortune. But it did not come from manufacture or invention, which he did so much to encourage, but from land. His estate in 1788, two years before his death, was estimated to be worth $150,000" (Myers: Vol. I, p. 43).

Washington and Franklin were not the only ones of their kind. They are cited only as examples to show that even those who wrote or signed the Declaration of Independence and on whose lips such high-sounding phrases as "all men are created equal" were ever present—even those exploited the masses without giving any consideration to their suffering, and amassed for themselves enormous wealth. Many of the biggest patriots of the Revolution appeared as the richest men in the country after the Revolution. The conflict brought them a real victory, economically as well as politically.

But how about those who had bled and died on the battlefields and suffered at their work-benches? How about the wage-workers, the handicraftsmen, and the small farmers? Their victory was taken away from them by the land-owners, the merchants, smugglers, grafters, employers, and bankers.

"What wealth there was lay in the hands of a few score men. The disparity of conditions between a laborer and Charles Carroll or George Washington was probably greater than exists to-day between a laborer and Carnegie. Employment was scarce; the circulating medium fluctuated in value; the workman had no security for his pay, and was frequently defrauded. Wages were paid quarterly, semi-annually, or annually. If the workman bought goods on credit, the debtors' prison yawned for him; and, if he was imprisoned, his food and comforts had to be supplied by private charity" (McLaughlin: *The Confederation and the Constitution*, p. 150).

For a long day's work, from sunrise to sunset, a worker received only 50 cents.

"On such a pittance," says McMaster, "it was only by the strictest economy that a mechanic kept his children from starvation and himself from jail . . ." (McMaster: *History of the People of the United States*, Vol. I, pp. 96-98).

Such were the conditions, after the Revolution, of the so-called free worker, the mechanic. We can image what hardships had to be confronted by one who worked for somebody else as a hired laborer or as a slave.

For those among the poor classes who fell into debt to their storekeepers, or merchants, or landlords, fate was hard indeed. McMaster describes very vividly the imprisonments which followed:

"No crime known to law brought so many to the jails and prisons as the crime of debt, and the class most likely to get into debt was the most defenseless and dependent, the great body of servants, of artisans and of laborers, those, in short, who depended on their daily wages for their daily bread. One hundred years ago the laborer who fell from a scaffolding or lay sick of a fever was sure to be seized by the sheriff the moment he recovered, and be carried to jail for the bill of a few dollars which had been run up during his illness at the huckster's or the tavern.

"For more than 50 years after the peace there was in Connecticut an underground prison which surpassed in horrors the Black Hole of Calcutta. This den, known as the Newgate prison, was an old worked out copper mine in the hills near Granby. The only entrance to it was by means of a ladder down a shaft which led to the caverns underground. There, in little pens of wood, from 30 to 100 culprits were immured, their feet made fast to iron bars, and their necks chained to beams in the roof. The darkness was intense; the caves reeked with filth; vermin abounded; water trickled from the roof and oozed from the sides of the caverns; huge masses of earth were perpetually falling off. In the dampness and the filth the clothing of the prisoners grew moldy and rotted away, and their limbs became stiff with rheumatism. The Newgate prison was perhaps the worst in the country, yet in every county were jails such as would now be thought unfit places of habitation for the vilest and most loathsome of beasts. . . .

"The misery of the unfortunate creatures cooped up in the cells, even of the most humanely kept prisons, surpasses in horror anything ever recorded in fiction. No attendance was provided for the sick. No clothes were distributed to the naked. Such a thing as a bed was rarely seen, and this soon became so foul with insects that the owner dispensed with it gladly. Many of the inmates of the prisons passed years without so much as washing themselves. Their hair grew long. Their bodies were covered with scabs and lice, and emitted a horrible stench. Their clothing rotted from their backs and exposed their bodies tormented with all manner of skin diseases and yellow flesh cracking open with filth . . ." (*Ibid.*, pp. 98-102).

Rich grafters, smugglers, and speculators never went to these horrible dungeons, nor to any other prison. This was their regular occupation; they were recognized as the best sons of America, as the finest patriots and the real heroes of the Revolution.

Imprisonment for debt affected a great many of those who made their living from their own work. McMaster points out that in New Hampshire in the fall of 1785 two-thirds of the population could have been sent to prison for debt if the law had been strictly enforced (*Ibid.*, p. 343). Similar conditions prevailed in other states also.

There was no escaping these conditions for the masses, except through open, armed struggle. But there was no organization to lead them in their struggles. There was no homogeneous class which would consciously fight for power. The working masses were composed of many different strata. As we have already seen, there were black slaves, whites in temporary slavery, a rather small number of proletarians, a larger number of handicraftsmen, a large number of apprentices, and a very numerous stratum of poor farmers. It is true that fundamentally their interests were common and their enemy also was common, namely, the bourgeoisie, which had rapidly risen to power, and the land-owners. But it is also true that we cannot very well expect a concerted, disciplined struggle on the part of such masses. Only the most unbearable economic conditions forced them into an open conflict with their exploiters. But their struggle had no definite and conscious goal. It was rather an unconscious, planless revolt against their nearest enemy institutions—the courts, the government officials, and the state legislatures. It was a revolt arising from the desperate conditions of the masses, an attempt to save themselves from starvation, at least for the time being.

"From Massachusetts, Rhode Island, Vermont, New Hampshire and other states, alarming news came of the growing restlessness among the poor. Mass meetings were being held, petitions circulated and demands made to legislatures for measures of relief. Debts had been contracted in depreciated currency and the wealthy classes were demanding payment in gold. Naturally, the poor debtors demanded paper currency and just as naturally their exploiters opposed it. The more paper was issued the more demoralized the currency became. . . .

"In some states men were on the march to the seats of the county or state governments, many of them armed and determined that the glorious promises should be in some measure fulfilled. Lawyers were hated and despised for their part in confiscating wealth in payment of debts. They were overwhelmed with cases and the courts could not try half of them . . ." (*Ibid.*, p. 343).

In New Hampshire and Vermont short-lived revolts were dispersed by the troops.

"But the most alarming rebellion took place in Massachusetts, a revolt that took six months to suppress and one that sobered the ruling classes in their scramble for wealth. . . . The Courts were invaded by large bodies of armed men and forced to suspend. Daniel Shays . . . was chosen leader and the revolt grew to large proportions. The legislature was not in session; there were no funds to pay troops to put down the revolt, but 'a number of wealthy gentlemen' advanced sufficient funds for the purpose.

" . . . Congress feared that the insurgents would capture the national arsenal at Springfield. . . . Secretary of War Knox was directed by Congress to go to Springfield and take such measures as he might deem necessary to protect it. Before he arrived the rebels had already confronted Major General Shepard's troops, 'many of them men of much substance both in wealth and character. . . .' The insurgents, though not active, were masters of the situation.

"Knox reported the situation to Congress and the matter was referred to a committee. The committee recommended an increase in the army of 1,340 non-commissioned officers and privates. This would make the total force 2,040. The report, and resolutions accompanying it, was adopted. One would expect that the resolutions would refer to the trouble in Massachusetts, but instead of this they were filled with startling reports of alleged preparations for war being made by several Indian nations. This report was intended for popular consumption and a shield to cover the real intentions of Congress.

"The following day a secret report was presented by the same committee and adopted by Congress. This one dealt frankly with Shays' rebellion, mentioned the perilous position of the arsenal, stated that 'particular circumstances' prevented governor and council from asking for aid in a formal manner, that troops must be raised, but that the insurrection must not be mentioned as a reason for raising them and that the Indians would serve as a pretext.

"Congress unanimously adopted a proposal of the treasury department that a requisition of $530,000 in specie be laid in due quotas on the states. 'On the credit of this requisition a loan of $500,000, bearing interest at 6 per cent, might be at once opened.' To stimulate subscriptions to the loan Congress 'warned the wealthy men of New England to contribute generously, unless they wished to see the recruits mutiny for lack of pay and go over to the insurgents.' General Lincoln personally solicited subscriptions from wealthy men of Boston and other towns, 'telling the contributors that it was simply a question of advancing a part of their property in order to save the rest.'

"On October 22nd, Knox notified Governor Bowdoin of the quota of troops required of Massachusetts and the governor, in transmitting the information to the general court, enlarged on the dangers of an Indian war. But the followers of Shays throughout the state suspected the troops were meant for them and not the Indians. . . . However, the troops were secured by the money advanced by rich men, some of whom enlisted to crush the rebellion. Attacks and counter attacks were made extending over six months before the revolt was crushed. The rebels had no funds or provisions and in the final rout some were frozen to death and others died of hunger and exposure. A price was placed on Shays' head and a large number arrested, of whom 300 were pardoned, 14 sentenced to death, eight of these being pardoned and the remainder reprieved conditionally . . ." (Oneal: *Loc. cit.*, pp. 127-131).

Thus ended this very important period in American history. Oppressed masses here and there attempted to raise their heads, but in every instance

WORKERS AFTER THE REVOLUTION

they were crushed. The same guns that the workers and farmers had used in the war with England now were turned against them by the ruling class of America.

Nevertheless these revolts of the poor did not pass without leaving their impress on those in power. The ruling class trembled with fear lest the exploited masses rise and take away from them the wealth which they had accumulated during the War of Independence. Therefore the bourgeois historians named this period "the critical period in American history" (For more information about this period *see* McLaughlin: *The Confederation and the Constitution;* Fiske: *Critical Period of American History;* McMaster: *History,* etc., Vol. I).

CHAPTER VII

THE BOURGEOISIE CAPTURES THE STATE POWER

WE have already seen how even before the Revolution the American bourgeoisie was moving carefully and systematically toward the conquest of the state power. First of all it captured the legislatures of various colonies, the courts, the city councils. Then, on the eve of Revolution, on August 1, 1774, it convened the First Continental Congress and laid down a national foundation for its political power. During the war, and after the war during the revolts of the poor, these political organs of the bourgeoisie became crystallized and perfected. With the adoption of the federal constitution by the various states in 1788 the bourgeois state of America was fully and firmly established.

The capitalist class of America understood perfectly well that without the state power in its hands, its economic domination would remain in constant danger. Without having in its hands the militia, the army, the courts, the entire governmental apparatus, it would not be able to withstand the working masses. Therefore it seized every opportunity, not shrinking from force, terrorism, graft and cheating, to gain control of the political power, and to eliminate the influence of the workers, the slaves, and the handicraftsmen from this power as far as possible. Even the right to vote was barred from the masses by the great wall of property qualifications.

The king of England was overthrown in America. Every state was left free to organize its own government. On May 15, 1776, the Continental Congress decided to "recommend to the assemblies and conventions of the United Colonies where no government sufficient for the exigencies of their affairs has been established, to adopt such government as shall in the opinion of the representatives of the people best conduce to the happiness of their constituents in particular and Americans in general."

The states at once began to build up their governments. In spite of the fact that in the Declaration of Independence they loftily proclaimed that "all men are created equal," that "all have been endowed with certain inalienable rights of which they cannot be stripped by any power," and that "among these rights are life, liberty, and the pursuit of happiness," the master class saw to it that this declaration was not taken literally and applied in practice by the workers and slaves. Women were not permitted to participate in elections. Neither were slaves.

THE BOURGEOISIE CAPTURES STATE POWER

Masses of poor people were excluded from voting and holding office by difficult property qualifications. As soon as the masters came to the point where political power must be organized, they were very careful to take it for themselves, to create democracy—for the ruling class only.

At that time the bourgeoisie was not yet trained in the art of securing the votes of the workers and slaves through corruption and high-sounding promises. Therefore, they were afraid to allow the workers and the slaves the right to vote at all. They thought that universal suffrage would endanger their property interests. That is why they allowed the vote only to the propertied classes.

"In New Hampshire the voter must be a Protestant and a taxpayer. Massachusetts required him to be possessed of a freehold estate yielding an income of three pounds a year, or to have personal estate worth £60. In Connecticut the requirement was an annual income of $7 from a freehold estate, or real estate rated on the tax list as worth $134. New York required a freehold estate of £30, or a house rent of 40 shillings. . . . In South Carolina the voter must be a free white man, acknowledging the being of a God and believing in a future state of reward and punishment, and must have lived one year in the state, have a freehold of 50 acres or own a town lot or has paid a tax equal to the tax on 50 acres of land. In Georgia any mechanic, any white male inhabitant owning £10 of property and paying a tax, not only might but must vote under a penalty of £5" (McMaster: *The Acquisition of Political, Social and Industrial Rights of Men in America*, pp. 17-20).

For holding office the property qualifications were still greater.

"To be eligible to the lower house of the legislature the voter must be a Protestant and have an estate worth £100 in New Hampshire. One must have a freehold of £300, or personal estate of £200, and must swear that he believes in the Old and New Testaments and divine inspiration in order to be a member of the lower house in Massachusetts. A freehold of £100 above all debts was required in New York; a belief in some Protestant creed and a personal estate was required in New Jersey; while in Delaware he must not only have the proper qualifications, but he must subscribe to this oath: 'I, A. B., do profess faith in God the Father, and in Jesus Christ, and in the Holy Ghost, one God blessed evermore, and I do acknowledge the Holy Scriptures of the Old and New Testaments, to be given by divine inspiration.' Maryland required each member of her assembly to own a freehold of £500 and subscribe in his belief in the Christian religion. . . .

"For membership in the upper house the qualifications were the same in kind as for membership in the lower house, but twice as great in quantity. The basis of office holding was property. The man of small means might vote, but none save the well-to-do Christians could legislate, and in many states none but the rich Christian could be a governor. No Hebrew, no atheist, no Roman Catholic could be a governor of New Hampshire, nor of New Jersey, nor of South Carolina, and none but a Christian in Massachusetts, Pennsylvania, Delaware, Maryland, and North Carolina. Nor were religious qualifications deemed enough. Heavy property qualifications were added, for the governor must be not only pious but rich. In one state he must own property worth £100, in another £500, in another £5,000, and in South Carolina £10,000. It was indeed true that all governments derived their just powers from the consent of the governed; yet under these early state constitutions, none but taxpaying, property-owning men could give that consent from which the government derives its just powers.

". . . The poor man counted for nothing. He was governed, but not with his consent, by his property-owning Christian neighbors. He was one of the people, but he did not count as such in the apportionment of representation. In short, the broad doctrine that governments derived their just powers from the consent of the governed, was not accepted by the Fathers" (*Ibid.*, pp. 19-21.)

Property was the foundation of every political institution. Only those who owned property were rulers and only these had voice and power. The greater one's property the higher the position he could get, and the more influence could he wield. In view of these property qualifications, the masses of slaves, workers, and handicraftsmen were separated from the state apparatus entirely. In theory it was claimed that "all men are created equal," that all have "certain inalienable rights," but in practice, in social and economic life itself, great masses of the people had no such rights.

Of course, even if everybody had been allowed to vote and to hold office, the mass of the people would not have been saved from the system of exploitation by their votes alone. But these property qualifications at the time the government was created made it in the very beginning an open political organ of the property-owning class. They clearly show how well the bourgeoisie, even then, understood the importance and necessity of having the state power in its hands.

Along with the building of the political organs of bourgeois rule in various states, went the building of the national state power. If the ruling class of each separate state was careful not to admit the masses to a position of influence in the government, in building up a federal régime it was on guard against the working class with even greater energy. Immediately after the Revolution it was found that the protection and safe-guarding of the general interests of the ruling class needed a strong, centralized national government. This national government must be stronger than the governments of the various states; it must have an army which would protect the interests of the master class from both inside and outside.

What did the revolts of the masses of New Hampshire, Vermont, and Massachusetts show? They showed that separate states were unable to put down these revolts. Especially Shays' rebellion in Massachusetts convinced the bourgeoisie that only the national government with a large army and a sufficient supply of guns and ammunition could quell these armed revolts of the masses and keep the latter under the yoke of the bourgeoisie. If there were any sentimentalists in the property-owning class who would worship the rights of the various states, then the actual life and growth of the bourgeoisie and the concrete facts accompanying it scattered this sentimentalism to the winds and showed the absolute and

THE BOURGEOISIE CAPTURES STATE POWER

immediate necessity of powerful centralized and armed state power for the further growth of the bourgeoisie.

In the midst of such a situation and under such conditions a Constitutional Convention was called on May 25, 1787, in Philadelphia. "This convention was simply a committee representing the commercial and manufacturing class of the northern and middle states and the southern plantation interests" (Simons: *Class Struggle in America*, p. 13).

These representatives of the ruling class met and discussed the constitution of the United States behind closed doors, in absolute secrecy. They knew the discontent of the masses and were afraid that these masses, discovering the conspiracy of the bourgeoisie and slave-owners, might take up arms and destroy their nest. Not in vain did George Washington, in mortal fear, write to his friend, Knox, Secretary of War: "There are combustibles in every state to which a spark may set fire" (Von Holst: *Constitutional History of the United States*, Vol. I, p. 46).

The dread that the masses might revolt had a tremendous hold on the secretly assembled representatives of the ruling class. A motion was made that the minutes of the convention be destroyed, but finally it was decided to turn them over to George Washington. And for fifty years the people of the United States did not know what the participants of the convention had talked about. Only when the bourgeoisie was firmly in the saddle, and when many of the makers of the constitution were in their graves, did James Madison, who had taken notes for himself on the proceedings of the convention, publish its secrets in his *Journal of the Constitutional Convention*.

"A government of property, for property, and by property," was the slogan of the bourgeoisie.

One after another the delegates openly and with brutal frankness defended the interests of property and of the exploiters of workers. Roger Sherman of Connecticut is quoted by Madison in his *Journal of the Constitutional Convention* as follows: "The people," he said, "immediately should have as little to do as may be about the government" (p. 78). Elbridge of Massachusetts said that "the evils we experience flow from the excess of democracy," and that he "had been taught by experience the danger of the leveling spirit" (p. 78).

Charles Pinckney of South Carolina declared that "an election of either branch by the people was totally impracticable" (p. 120). Gouverneur Morris, of Pennsylvania, said: "Give the votes to the people who have not property and they will sell them to the rich. . . . The ignorant and the dependent can be as little trusted with the public interest" as a child (p. 468).

Dickenson of Delaware exclaimed that property owners "are the best guardians of liberty; and the restriction of the right [of suffrage] to them as a necessary defence against the dangerous influence of those multitudes without principles, with which our country, like others, will in time abound" (p. 448).

Madison found that there were only three classes of citizens who must be the rulers of the country, that is, the land-owners, the commercial capitalist, and the industrial capitalists. In greatest alarm he said: "In future, a great majority will not only be without landed but any sort of property. These . . . will combine under the influence of their common situation—in which case the rights of property and the public liberty will not be secure in their hands" (p. 470).

Alexander Hamilton, of New York, was an outspoken advocate of a monarchy. He praised the government of England as "the only government in the world 'which united public strength with individual security.' In every community where industry is encouraged, there will be a division of it into the few and the many. Hence, separate interests will arise. There will be debtors and creditors, etc. Give all power to the many, they will oppress the few. Give all power to the few, they will oppress the many." Hence, Hamilton proposed to give all power to a single individual. "An executive for life," he said, "has not this motive for forgetting his fidelity, and will therefore be a safer depository of power" (pp. 182-184).

George Mason, of Virginia, could stand the speeches of the other delegates no longer and warned them: "We are, Mr. Chairman, going very far in this business. . . . Do the gentlemen mean to pave the way to hereditary monarchy? Do they flatter themselves that the people will ever consent to such an innovation? If they do, I venture to tell them, they are mistaken. The people will never consent" (p. 105).

After this secret convention of the ruling class had made the constitution it was clear why the gathering had been held and in whose interests it labored. The commercial and industrial interests demanded a strongly centralized government and they got it. According to the new constitution the federal government had the sole right to organize and maintain an army and navy, to levy taxes, to regulate tariff, and to declare war and make peace with other countries. The legislative body was to be composed of two branches—the House of Representatives and the Senate; the Senate could reject the demands of the House of Representatives and the President by his veto could reject the demands of both the House of Representatives and the Senate. On top of all this there was to be a Supreme Court composed of nine lawyers appointed by the President for life to interpret the laws. Under the leadership of Chief Justice Marshall this court usurped the power to declare unconstitutional any law passed by both branches of Congress and signed by the President.

The basis for election to Congress and to the Presidency was left the same as the basis of election to the legislatures of the various states. And as we have seen, these property qualifications for voters wrought havoc with the distressed masses. McMaster says that the "masses of the

THE BOURGEOISIE CAPTURES STATE POWER 59

unskilled workers had hardly ever had a chance to vote in their lives" (McMaster: *With the Fathers,* pp. 163-164). Even Woodrow Wilson admits that of a population of 4,000,000 in 1790, only about 120,000 had a right to vote (Wilson: *History of the American People,* Vol. III, pp. 120-121).

In this constitution there is not a word for the workers. But in order to satisfy the land-owners and planters of the southern states the consitution expressly approved slavery and forbade Congress to interfere with it.

The constitution answered another question vitally affecting both black and white slaves. As we have already seen, the temporary white slaves and the permanent black slaves often tried to run away from their masters. The slave-owners of various states feared that the new government might protect these fugitives. Therefore, the constitution provided the following in Article IV, Section 2, Paragraph 3:

"No person held at service or labor in one state, under the laws thereof, escaping into another, shall, in consequence of any law or regulation therein be discharged from such service or labor, but shall be delivered up on claim of the party to whom such services or labor may be due."

Therefore the constitution officially approved slavery and sought to make it impossible for the slaves to escape. If a slave or a servant ran away from his master into another state, the government of that state had to capture him and return him to his master.

The industrial and commercial interests did not oppose this approval of slavery. First, they were interested in having the slave-owners support the constitution, and second, they foresaw that in time the proletariat would take the place of the slaves. Representative Ellsworth of Connecticut expressed the opinion of the bourgeoisie of all of New England and of the middle states when he said: "Let us not intermeddle. As population increases poor laborers will be so plenty as to render slaves useless" (Simons: *Loc. cit.,* p. 96).

With such a constitution these conspirators and representatives of the ruling class of America emerged from secrecy, announced the results of their labor, and demanded the approval of the various states. In every state a struggle began for and against the adoption of this constitution. The authors of the constitution, Washington, Hamilton, Madison, and others, worked day and night for its acceptance. They not only wrote articles for its adoption, but also bribed newspapers and voters.

"A very little study of long forgotten politics," says McMaster, "will suffice to show that in filibustering and gerrymandering, in stealing governorships and legislatures, in using force at the polls, in colonizing and distributing patronage . . . in all the frauds and tricks that go to make up the worst form of politics, the men who founded our state and national governments were always our equals and often our masters" (McMaster: *With the Fathers,* p. 71).

The authors of the constitution did not lack money for bribing politicians, hiring gangsters, and buying votes. Behind them was a powerful property-owning class. In every state the masters—the commercial and industrial interests—were for the adoption of the constitution. The citizens of Virginia who had a right to vote were opposed to adoption, but their voices meant very little. Great masses of the poor had no say in the matter. Frances Norton Thorpe says that "a hundred years ago in America the free people made up only about one-fifteenth of the population" (Thorpe: *Magazine of History*, Vol. XVIII, p. 131).

Having built up a powerful state-machine, the ruling class was now standing on both feet and began to breathe more easily. Its rule was secure. It had all the power. The toiling masses were under its heel economically and politically. Through the mouth of Fisher Ames the bourgeoisie rejoiced as follows in the first session of Congress after the adoption of the constitution:

"I understand, sirs, that the present constitution is born from commercial causes more than from any other causes. Wise people foresaw long ago and the patriots who were interested in the general welfare pointed out that it is necessary to have a government which would protect the industrial interests and increase our commerce."

From this time on the working class of America was confronted with a powerful, well-organized ruling class, ready at all times to thwart any attempt of the poor to gain power or even to better their position.

CHAPTER VIII

INDUSTRIAL DEVELOPMENT, 1783-1860

AFTER the Revolution the American ruling class was the overlord of the country. It had defeated England in the open struggle and had taken possession of the land. It had separated the working masses from the state power very cleverly and effectively. It was now free to build America in its own image. However, our ship-owners, merchants, and manufacturers found themselves economically in a very critical situation. After concluding peace with England, they had to compete with other countries in commerce and industry and this was, in view of the youth of the country, not an easy task for them. Their only salvation was in the state which, as was pointed out, had been established to protect commercial and industrial interests. The merchants and ship-owners were the first to demand from the state a protective tariff. The commercial interests of Baltimore made an appeal to Congress, saying that "among the advantages looked for from the national government is the increase of the shipping and the maritime strength of the United States of America by laws similar in their nature and operation to the British Navigation Acts." Then followed the merchants of Charleston and Philadelphia.

The government, of course, immediately came to the assistance of these interests. In 1789 Congress enacted a law requiring all foreign vessels doing business with this country to pay a special tariff of 50 cents a ton. In 1792 a law was enacted excluding foreign-built vessels from American registry. In 1817 an even more restrictive act was passed which practically prohibited foreign vessels from entering American ports.

The effect of discriminating duties was soon evident. The number of vessels flying the American flag increased rapidly. The shipyards were busy building craft for ocean trade. The foreigners engaged in commerce with America took out citizenship papers so that they might enjoy the privileges of the American shipmasters. The tonnage of the foreign trade rose from 123,893 in 1789 to 981,019 in 1810, and the proportion of foreign trade carried in American vessels increased from 24 to 92 per cent during the same period. By 1860 the total tonnage of United States vessels had reached 2,807,000.

In value foreign commerce rose from $48,000,000 in 1791 to $205,000,000 in 1801. During the same interval exports increased from $19,000,000 to $94,000,000. With 1807 foreign commerce reached $247,000,000—exports $108,000,000, imports $138,000,000. In 1860 total exports reached $316,242,000.

At the end of the eighteenth century Evans, Rumsey, and Fitch developed the steamship. The work of clearing rivers for navigation, and digging canals for communication, was pushed forward with great energy. The opening of the Erie Canal in 1825 moved other states to connect their rivers by canals and open their doors for commerce. In 1830 the United States had 1,270 miles of canals; in 1840, 3,320 miles; and in 1850, 3,700.

Railroad building did not lag behind in this period either. Communication by water could not satisfy the commercial interests of the country. In 1830 there were in the United States only 73 miles of railroad, while in 1840 there were already 2,800 miles; in 1850 9,020 miles, and in 1860 there were 30,600.

As Isaac Lippincott correctly remarks, "no period of equal duration has witnessed such a remarkable commercial development as the one from 1790 to 1860" (Lippincott: *Economic Development of the United States*, p. 263).

The history of industrial development is the same. After the Revolution the competition between the manufactured goods of the United States and those of England became very acute. English manufacturers had an accumulated stock of woolens, cotton cloths and ironware which had to be disposed of, therefore they were ready to sell them at 25 per cent below London prices. In 1790 our imports exceeded our exports by $53,992,655. American manufacturers could not compete with their English rivals in an open market and demanded protection from the government. They pointed out the dangers to the industrial interests of the country and said that from the "supreme legislature of the United States as the guardian of the whole empire . . . they expect to derive that aid and assistance." In one of their declarations they accused the government of faithfully helping commerce while at the same time entirely neglecting the manufacturing interests. The reason for this state of affairs, they said, lay in the fact that the "commercial interests have always good representation in Congress while the industrial interests never have been represented" (*Niles' Weekly Registry*, July 17, 1819, p. 351).

But the voice of the fast-rising industrial bourgeoisie was hearkened to by Congress and a helping hand was extended. A tariff was levied on all imported industrial products, from steel and iron to fish and salt. In 1791 as much as $4,000,000 was collected through this protective tariff, and soon the revenue it provided covered all ordinary expenses of the government.

INDUSTRIAL DEVELOPMENT 68

The industry of the country, thus protected and assisted by the government, developed very rapidly, and soon it was found that industry was a more profitable place for the investment of capital than commerce. In 1807 there were only 15 cotton mills running 8,000 spindles and producing 300,000 pounds of cotton yarn annually; in 1811 there were already 87 mills operating 80,000 spindles, producing 2,880,000 pounds of yarn annually, and employing 4,000 workers, mostly women and children; by 1815 there were 500,000 spindles and the number of workers employed reached 76,000.

PROGRESS OF THE COTTON INDUSTRY

Year	Number of Spindles	Pounds of Cotton Consumed
1830	1,246,000	155,000
1840	2,285,000	237,000
1850	3,998,000	575,000
1860	5,236,000	845,000

Great development took place not in the cotton industry alone. In 1840 there were 1,420 woolen factories, which produced goods worth $20,696,000; while in 1860 woolen products reached $68,000,000 annually.

Steel and iron did not lag behind other industries. The huge resources of iron ore and coal made production of iron a very successful and profitable enterprise.

IRON PRODUCTION, 1810-1860

Year	Tons
1810	53,908
1830	165,000
1840	286,900
1850	563,700
1860	821,200

The growth of manufacturing in this period can be judged also from the following general statistics. The number of workers employed in factories which annually produced goods worth $500 or more was in 1820, 349,000; in 1840, 791,000; and in 1860, 1,311,000. Value of product rose from $483,278,000 in 1840 to $1,019,106,000 in 1850, and to $1,885,861,000 in 1860.

"America" wrote Engels in 1844, "with its inexhaustible resources, with its unmeasured coal and iron fields, with its unexampled wealth of water power and its navigable rivers, but especially with its energetic, active population . . . America has in less than ten years created a manufacture which already competes with England in the coarser cotton goods, has excluded the English from the markets of North and South America, and holds its own in China, side by side with England. If any country is adapted to holding a monopoly of manufacture, it is America" (Engels: *Condition*, etc., p. 295).

The growth of the population of the country was as fast as the development of commerce and industry.

POPULATION OF THE UNITED STATES, 1790-1860

Year	Population	Year	Population
1790	3,929,214	1830	12,866,020
1800	5,308,483	1840	17,069,453
1810	7,239,881	1850	23,191,876
1820	9,638,547	1860	31,443,321

The growth of industry meant also growth of the city population. In 1790 there was no city having over 50,000 population. New York had 49,400, Philadelphia was next with 28,522, Boston had 18,320, and Baltimore 13,503. But by 1860 the appearance and size of the cities had entirely changed. By that time New York had 1,174,700, Philadelphia 565,520, Chicago rose from 4,470 in 1840 to 109,260 in 1860, Baltimore reached the 212,000 mark, and New Orleans was next with 168,670.

At the end of this period of rapid growth of capitalism in the United States attention was turned from agriculture to industry, from the farm to the city. In the large cities where hundreds of thousands of men and women were sweating at the machines, where smoke from the factory chimneys hid the horizon, where the streets were packed with human beings almost every minute of the twenty-four hours—in these large cities the heart of the country's life was now beating.

Not satisfied with commerce and industry, the bourgeoisie stretched out its mighty hands and ruthlessly acquired for itself the land of the country also. One detachment of the capitalist class was active in towns and cities, another detachment enlarged its wealth and power on the seas, while another seized rivers, forests, and fields. And the government was always their ally, assistant and protector. The land laws were enacted to discriminate against the poor settlers; they made it possible for the capitalist companies as well as individual capitalists to secure vast tracts for trivial sums and later force the actual settlers to pay exorbitant prices for small plots. Absentee landlordism became an important factor. Speculation in land soon became the main occupation of a great portion of the master class.

For example, by act of Congress, passed in 1792, the Ohio Land Company received 100,000 acres, and in the same year it bought 892,000 acres for $642,856.66, but this sum was not paid in money. In 1795 the legislature of Georgia, by special act, sold millions of acres in the state to four land companies for a trivial sum and everybody was convinced that this purchase was obtained through bribery and graft. Then came the railroad companies and corporations. From 1850 to 1872 Congress donated over 155,000,000 acres of the public domain either directly to the railroad companies or to the various states which transferred them

INDUSTRIAL DEVELOPMENT

to these corporations. Powerful canal companies were not to be forgotten. It is estimated that up to 1860 the government had donated to them over 4,000,000 acres of the public lands in various states.

What Marx and Engels said about the bourgeoisie of Europe in 1844 was also true of the American bourgeoisie in 1860:

"It has agglomerated population, centralized means of production, and has concentrated property into a few hands ... created more massive and more colossal productive forces than have all preceding generations together. Subjection of nature's forces to man, machinery, application of chemistry to industry and agriculture, steam-navigation, railways, electric telegraphs, clearing of whole continents for cultivation, canalization of rivers, whole populations conjured out of the ground—what earlier century had even a presentiment that such productive forces slumbered in the lap of social labor?" (Marx and Engels: *Communist Manifesto*, pp. 18-19).

But this growth of the bourgeois system did not proceed without disastrous economic crises. The first crisis occurred in 1819. It was a result of "overproduction." The capitalists were competing with one another, getting control of everything, investing their money everywhere, stealing everything that they could lay hands on; new factories, new canals, new railroads, new enterprises of all sorts, new banks, paper money flooded the country! A crash had to come and it did come. Hundreds of enterprises were prostrated, factories closed, thousands of workers thrown out of employment, the streets of the industrial cities became crowded with destitute men and women.

Then the storm began to recede and the sky became brighter once more. Industry and commerce again became active and once more the country entered a period of speculation and "prosperity." Capital again spread its wings far and wide, new investments, new enterprises everywhere! But this prosperity could not last very long, the speculation and expansion had gone beyond safe limits, and by 1837 again the country was plunged into economic crisis. Business went to pieces, factories closed, and hundreds of thousands of workers were thrown on the streets. And the cause of all this was another "overproduction." Too many factories, too many machines, too much cotton and wool, too much bread and clothing! At the same time thousands of people in every city could not find work, hungry and in rags. This crisis lasted for five years, until 1842.

CHAPTER IX

DEVELOPMENT OF THE WORKING CLASS, 1783-1860

WHILE the capitalist class was thus putting itself solidly in possession of the resources and the industries of the country, what was happening to the workers?

The American bourgeoisie had never been seriously confronted with the problem of shortage of labor power. It is true that hundreds of thousands of workers from the eastern and northern industrial states every year emigrated to the West, but the industrial capitalists discovered two inexhaustible sources of labor power: immigrants, and women and children. We must not forget that America in the eyes of the European poor still remained a paradise and, therefore, millions of Europeans considered that to reach America was to attain the highest goal in life. Here they dreamed of mountains of gold and unlimited liberty. Only those remained in Europe who had no chance of raising the money necessary to come to America, or who were leading an easy life in their own country. During the period from 1840 to 1860, 2,000,000 came from Germany alone, while during the 10 years from 1850 to 1860, 740,000 "souls" emigrated to America from little Ireland.

IMMIGRATION, 1820-1860

Period	Number of Immigrants
1821-1830	151,824
1831-1840	599,125
1841-1850	1,713,251
1851-1860	2,598,214

These millions of Europeans who came to this country were not white-collar "gentlemen." Almost all of them were workers, "beasts of burden."

"These immigrants," says Lippincott, "were a most important factor in the industrial upbuilding of the country. Coming at a time when there was the most urgent demand for labor, they performed indispensable work in building canals and railroads, in opening up the new country, and in adding to the necessary labor supply of the new factories. The largest number were undoubtedly unskilled laborers, but workmen of this kind were sorely needed in the new country where there was much hard work to be done. But thousands were artisans of all descriptions, including mechanics, manufacturers, musicians, painters, engineers, and these contributed new knowledge and skill which was greatly needed in the development of industry" (Lippincott: *Loc. cit.*, pp. 137-138).

DEVELOPMENT OF THE WORKING CLASS

The second almost inexhaustible source of labor power for American industry was woman, and child labor. The ruling class of America saw how the capitalists of England exploited women and children in the factories, mills and mines, and they were jealous. They asked themselves, why should they have a man operate the machine when a woman could do the same work for half the pay, or when a child could do it for still less? Labor-saving machinery made it possible to displace more expensive labor-power by cheaper labor-power. In his report to Congress on the situation of American industries, Alexander Hamilton pointed out that:

"Women and children are rendered more useful, and the latter more early useful, by manufacturing establishments, than they would otherwise be. Of the number of persons employed in the cotton manufactories of Great Britain, it is computed that four-sevenths, nearly, are women and children; of whom the greatest proportion are children and many of them of a tender age" (Coman: *Industrial History of the United States*, p. 147).

Weaving and spinning were taken from the homes of the people and carried into factories and mills. Thousands of women were left without occupation. Therefore they were forced to leave their homes and enter the factories and the proletarian army. We often hear it said that our mothers and daughters leave their homes and go to work in factories, mills, offices and laundries for the sake of making money to spend on luxuries and for "good times." But the actual facts tell an entirely different story. Various searching investigations have proven that most women in industry left their homes and entered the ranks of the gainfully occupied, sometimes for the smallest remuneration, because of the necessity of supporting themselves and in many instances of supporting their families.

The textile industry was in the beginning and to a very great extent still remains the stronghold of our women workers. In 1814 there were 30,000 working women in this industry, while in 1848 their number increased to 78,000.

How important a rôle was played by women and children in industry can be seen from the fact that

"in 1831, in the six New England states and in New York, New Jersey, Pennsylvania, Maryland, and Virginia, 58.1 per cent of all the employees, including hand weavers, in cotton mills, were women and 7 per cent were children under 12 years of age. In Lowell in 1833 the factories are said to have employed only 1,200 males and 3,800 females, and in 1834, 4,500 females out of a total of 6,000 employees; while in Paterson, N. J., where the Fall River system was in force, the proportion in 1830 was 2,000 males to 3,000 females, and in 1835 it was said that out of 1,900 to 2,000 factory operatives, not including hand weavers, about 600, or nearly one-third, were under 16 years of age. Even in New England in 1832 a committee of the New England Association of Farmers, Mechanics, and Other Working Men estimated that two-fifths of the whole number of persons employed in all the factories were children under 16 years of age. And in some states it was said that, as in England, apprentices were taken from the poorhouses to work in factories" (Commons: *History*, etc., Vol. I, pp. 173-174).

But the textile industry was not the only one in which we find women toiling side by side with men.

"In 1837 there were about 100 occupations in which women were engaged, usually for small wages and long hours. About the same time it was shown that there were more than 15,000 women in the shoe industry of Massachusetts, hundreds of them earning only from 8 or 10 cents a day to 40 or 50" (Mary Beard: *A Short History of the American Labor Movement*, pp. 47-48).

"Yes, savagery, barbarism, civilization called upon woman and child to share in life's struggles, but it remained for the age of machinery, the age of 'society,' the age of the billionaire, the age of general suffrage and democratic governments, the age of triumphant science and free schools, the age of marvelous inventions—marvelous means of production—to enslave body and soul. It remained for this age of progress to reduce millions of them to a servitude in which they may well envy the condition of the medieval serf or the black slave of the southland" (N. A. Richardson: *Industrial Problems*, p. 110).

In other words, it remained for the age of capitalism to enslave the body and soul of women and children as well as of the whole working class. The capitalist system of production mercilessly dragged women and children from the fireside into the factories and made them wage slaves, part and parcel of the machine.

Capitalism has taken out of their homes children of five, six and seven years of age and made of them fodder for capitalist industry. The most horrible abuses of child labor in England were transplanted bodily to America as soon as the rise of industry and commerce made it possible to put the children of the poor at the machines. It is also interesting to observe that the labor struggles of the last century for the betterment of the worker's status affected the horrible conditions of child labor very little. Industry even to-day remains an inferno for the health and lives of the toiling and suffering little ones of the working class.

The age of machine and factory brought no paradise on earth to those who make their living with their own hands—the working masses. The ruling class increased its power and wealth, industry developed by leaps and bounds, the bourgeoisie systematically, step by step, conquered and enslaved in its service all public institutions, extended its roots to every joint of society, pushed into the background the decaying aristocracy with all its servants and slaves attached to the cultivation of the land. Modern industry with its machinery and division of labor rapidly swept aside the handicraftsman with his primitive tools of production. The machine defeated the spinning wheel, the productivity of labor increased many fold, men, women, and children left their benches and their homes and went into the factories, but the sun shone no brighter for those who had to make their own living. The life of the proletarians, of the working class, who are entirely and completely separated from the ownership of

DEVELOPMENT OF THE WORKING CLASS

the means of production and who have nothing else to sell but their labor power, failed to improve with the expansion of industry. They had no political rights, socially they were outcasts, the wealth that they produced with the help of machinery in the factories and mills was taken away from them by their masters, their work was hard and monotonous, their hours of labor were unending.

"The social and economic conditions of working people in the cities," says McMaster . . . "did indeed call loudly for reform. . . . The influx of paupers . . . the overcrowded labor market; the steadily increasing number of unemployed; the housing of the poor; the rise of the tenement house; the congestion of population . . . and all its attendant vice and crime; and the destitution produced by low wages and lack of employment became a matter for serious consideration. An unskilled laborer was fortunate if he received 75 cents for 12 hours' work. . . . Hundreds were glad to work for 35 cents and even 25 cents a day in winter. . . . In truth, it was not uncommon during the winter for men to work for their board. . . . But the earnings of women were lower yet . . ." (McMaster: *History*, etc., Vol. V, p. 121).

The hours of labor in Lowell, Mass., "varied from 11 hours and 24 minutes in December and January, to 13 hours and 31 minutes in April, the average for the year being 12 hours and 13 minutes per day, or about 73 hours and 30 minutes per week. In many, and perhaps the majority, of the middle and southern states . . . the average was even higher, being about 13¾ hours per day, or 82½ hours per week in summer, and about 75½ hours per week throughout the year" (Commons: *History*, etc., Vol. I, p. 172).

The employers knew well the art of chaining the workers to their factories. The "homes," the churches and the stores for the workers were built by the companies. The workers were compelled to eat in the company lunchrooms, to live in the company houses, to buy their goods in the company stores, to pay from their meager wages to the company for the church and other "benefits." The Lowell Manufacturing Company compelled its workers to attend church services, and they were not allowed to leave their jobs without notifying the company two weeks in advance. The Cocheo Manufacturing Company of Dover, N. H., had a similar system. The workers of this company were forced to sign an agreement that they would work under stipulated conditions and for the wages given by the company, that they would not belong to or join any labor organization, and that they would not leave their jobs without notifying the company two weeks in advance under pain of losing two weeks' pay.

About the wages of the workers of this period we find ample information in Mathew Carey's booklet, *The Public Charities of Philadelphia*, issued in 1829. He points out that thousands of workers were willing to go hundreds of miles from their homes and work on railroads or canals for from 62 to 87 cents a day, paying from $1.50 to $2 a week for board, working under the most horrible conditions. They came back home broken in health and spirit. In the cities there was always a sufficient number of wage slaves willing to chop wood 12 or 14 hours a day, for from 35 to 50 cents. Carey estimated that a woman without children, in New England, could earn in the needle trades no more than $58.50 a year and a woman with children no more than $36.40 a year (Mary Beard: *Loc. cit.*, p. 48).

Such was the life of the workers of this country before the Civil War.

Branding, whipping at the post, imprisonment for debt, did not disappear from American soil with the advance of the nineteenth century and the rise of the machine age. On the contrary, it seems that imprisonment and torture for debt, or, rather, for poverty, gained new impetus and increased in severity and cruelty with the advance of the century and the appearance of large cities and tall buildings, with narrow streets and hell-holes of so-called "homes," and their armies of proletarians.

It was estimated in 1833 that in the United States 75,000 persons were sent to jail each year for debt—in New York, 10,000; in Pennsylvania, 7,000; in Massachusetts and Maryland, 3,000 each (McMaster: *History*, etc., Vol. VI, p. 99).

In their greed for more profits the capitalists even developed a theory that low wages are beneficial to the workers themselves. The upper classes openly proclaimed that the more the worker gets for his work the less inclined will he be to work, the more leisure time he will have, the more opportunities will he use for developing bad habits. Starvation wages, long working hours, savage oppression in the factory, were the best medicine the ruling class could use to save workers from going "astray." The church enthusiastically approved this theory, proclaiming that only those who worked hard and suffered greatly would enter the "Kingdom of Heaven." "He who does not work neither shall he eat," became the masters' favorite slogan in relation to the workers. That they themselves did not work, and led a parasitic life, did not worry them in the least.

Just as the southern planters looked upon their black slaves as beasts of burden, the northern capitalists looked upon their wage slaves with the utmost contempt. They held it as a "self-evident truth" that the workers of their mills had been sent to them by their god to increase their profits and make their life on earth easy and happy.

CHAPTER X

LABOR ORGANIZATIONS AND LABOR STRUGGLES, 1783-1819

From the foregoing description of factory and working class life it would seem that in these very factories and among these proletarian masses the forerunners of the trade unions and other labor organizations of to-day should have been born. But it was not so. Apparently these thousands of wage workers were too exhausted, too young in their new environment, too greatly oppressed to have a class consciousness crystallized in organization. The great proletarian element which arose in the beginning of the nineteenth century, along with the development of capitalist production, remained for some time a blind, helpless mass in the hands of the bourgeoisie.

The beginning of the trade unions, or the predecessors of the trade unions, we find, therefore, among the skilled laborers—mechanics, handicraftsmen, or journeymen, who still remained outside of the factories and looked upon the rising modern industry with great disdain. They still held some of the tools of production which the capitalist system threatened to take from them. These masses of unskilled workers—men, women, and children,—these great factories, which, it seemed, had sprung from nowhere almost overnight, were snatching away from the tailors the sewing of clothes, from the shoemakers the making of shoes. On the other hand, the master-mechanics or "employers" were always ready to cut down the wages of their employees or journeymen, in order to increase their profits or to undersell their rivals on the market.

In the early stages of economic development, of course, the employers endeavored to persuade the journeymen that their interests were the same as those of the masters, that their wages had been reduced only because the owner of raw material and of the warehouse had refused to pay sufficiently for the products. And in some instances they were successful in convincing the journeymen that their interests were identical. Thus, for example, in Philadelphia among the cordwainers (shoemakers) a benevolent society included both journeymen and masters. But, "on the whole the journeymen established separate mutual aid societies" (Commons: *History*, etc., Vol. I, p. 85).

As to the aims of these "benevolent" societies of the journeymen there is a disagreement between McMaster and David J. Saposs. The former says that at least in some of the trades these organizations "were almost invariably for the purpose of regulating wages" (McMaster: *History*, etc., Vol. III, p. 511), while the latter maintains that "on the contrary, the acts of incorporation of the journeymen societies enumerated by him (McMaster), as well as others, clearly indicate that they were purely beneficial, and were distinctly forbidden to use the organization for the purpose of regulating wages" (Commons: *Ibid.*, Vol. I, p. 86).

Whatever the articles of incorporation were, it was inevitable that these working class societies should often be used in the fight against reduction of wages. This was especially true in the later stage of development, when the class division between the masters and the journeymen became more definite and the class struggle between them became more intense.

These benevolent societies of journeymen were really the forerunners of the trade unions. Some of them developed directly into trade unions; others dissolved or were destroyed by the employers and the government, leaving only the material for future trade unions.

"The origin of trade unions," says Saposs, "can, in many cases, be definitely traced to the encroachments of the merchant-capitalist upon the standard of life of the mechanics. The early grievances of the trade unionists were based on the sweatshop practices injected by him.

"To offset his encroachments the workingmen demanded a minimum wage below which none were to work irrespective of the quality of the product. Those who did better work could demand higher wages. To further safeguard their standard of life they also demanded a strict observance of apprenticeship rules, which would automatically eliminate the competition of woman, child, unskilled and convict labor.

"Our researches led us to conclude that it was not, as many believe, the lack of opportunity to become independent producers that actuated the mechanics to form trade unions. On the contrary, it seems that their only motive for organizing was to protect their standard of life as skilled mechanics. . . . Thus the early unions were composed exclusively of skilled workers like printers, shoemakers, tailors, carpenters, and so on. Some of these even excluded the less proficient of their trade.

"On the other hand no traces of organization can be found among the unskilled, especially the cotton-mill operatives who numbered 100,000 in 1815."

And this situation is explained, Saposs thinks,

"by the fact that the wages of the unskilled were going up while those of the skilled were kept down by the merchant-capitalist. In 1784 common laborers were paid less than $4 a week, while in 1810 they were receiving close to $7 or $8 per week. At the same time the wages of skilled workers remained stationary, or actually declined, although the cost of living was constantly mounting" (*Ibid.*, pp. 104-105).

That there is some truth in this statement, there can be no doubt, but there were other factors also responsible for the situation. Among these, as has been mentioned, were the ease with which unskilled factory workers were replaced, the mixed composition of the army of factory hands, women

LABOR ORGANIZATIONS AND LABOR STRUGGLES

and children making up a large percentage of it, the careful attachment of the workers to the factory and to their jobs, the division of work in such a way that the more efficient workers could be pitted against less efficient, and the exhaustion due to laboring long hours under the most oppressive conditions. We have no reason to assume, therefore, that only those organize into trade unions who are paid least. The history of American trade unionism shows quite the contrary. As a rule, skilled workers have better jobs and get higher wages than unskilled, but even to-day skilled workers are the leaders of the trade unions in America. On the other hand, it would be a great mistake to jump at the conclusion that only skilled workers organize and maintain permanent proletarian organizations; for the fact is that some of the largest trade unions of this country are composed mainly of unskilled or half-skilled workers.

The shoemakers of Philadelphia were the craftsmen who in 1792 organized the first trade society in this country which had as its aim the maintenance or the raising of wages. It existed for only one year. In 1794 they again organized under the name of the Federal Society of Journeymen Cordwainers which, it is said, lived till 1806 when it was tried for "conspiracy to raise wages for its members." In 1794 the printers of New York organized the Typographical Society, which lived only two years and six months. In 1809 the New York Typographical Society was founded, which remained an active trade union until 1818 (*Ibid.*, p. 109). Similar was the story of all other societies or trade unions in the early development of the labor movement in this country. They were only local organizations and short-lived.

How rapidly the idea was developed in the minds of the workers that they could not remain in the same organizations and work in harmony with their employers, and that their interests were opposed, we see from the action of the New York printers. In 1809 they declared that "between employers and employed there are mutual interests," while in 1817 they expelled an employer from their society and loudly proclaimed the following principle:

"Experience teaches us that the actions of men are influenced almost wholly by their interests, and that it is almost impossible that a Society can be well regulated and useful when its members are actuated by opposite motives, and separate interests. This society is a society of journeymen printers; and as the interests of the journeymen are *separate* and in some respect *opposite* to those of the employers, we deem it improper that they should have any voice or influence in our deliberations. . . ."

The Philadelphia Typographical Society in 1802 firmly believed that the interests of employees and employers are mutual, for they declared:

"Indeed, we cherish a hope that the time is not far distant when the employer and employed will vie with each other, the one, in allowing a competent salary, the other, deserving it."

On the other hand the cordwainers of New York as early as 1805 advanced the following principle for a separate journeymen's society:

"Impressed with the sense of our just rights, and to guard against the intrigue or artifices that may at any time be used by our employers to reduce our wages lower than what we deem an adequate reward for our labor, we have unanimously agreed to the following articles as the constitution of our society" (*Ibid.*, pp. 119-120).

As soon as these trade societies began to spread their roots among the mechanics, the first industrial crisis—that of 1819—swept through the United States, bringing in its wake widespread unemployment. In Philadelphia alone there were 20,000 unemployed; in New York about the same number; in Baltimore, 10,000. The industrial depression was a death-blow to these trade societies. Some of them disappeared, others were greatly reduced in membership, still others became narrow benevolent circles.

Beginning with the crisis of 1819, for several decades after that date every industrial depression either entirely destroyed the trade unions or disrupted them to such an extent that it took a number of years to revive them. Trade unions rose in strength and influence during the periods of so-called prosperity, but as soon as the depression set in, the streets of the cities became congested with unemployed workers, despair overtook those who were organized, confidence in their efforts was lost, and the trade unions dissolved.

Trade unions are not intellectual inventions. They are the product of certain economic conditions. Division among the workers proved to them concretely that singly they were helpless in the hands of their masters. They learned from actual life that competition among themselves only strengthens their enemy.

"What gives unions and the strikes arising from them real importance," says Engels, "is this, that they are the first attempt of the workers to abolish competition. They imply the recognition of the fact that the supremacy of the bourgeoisie is based wholly upon the competition of the workers among themselves; i. e., upon their want of cohesion. And precisely because the unions direct themselves against the vital nerve of the present social order, however one-sidedly, in however narrow a way, are they so dangerous to this social order. The workingmen cannot attack the bourgeoisie, and with it the whole existing order of society, at any sorer point than this. If the competition of the workers among themselves is destroyed, if all determine not to be further exploited by the bourgeoisie, the rule of property is at an end" (Engels: *Condition of the Working Class in England in 1844*, pp. 218-219).

Along with the growth of industry and the rise of the bourgeoisie, came the development of the class struggle, an ever-increasing resistance of the workers against their employers. In 1791 the first strike occurred in Philadelphia among the carpenters. The conditions of work became unbearable, and in order to frustrate an attempt of the contractors to

LABOR ORGANIZATIONS AND LABOR STRUGGLES

reduce their already very low wages, the carpenters stopped work completely and declared a war against their masters. In their declaration they complained that they had

"heretofore been obliged to toil through the whole course of the longest summer's day, and that, too, in many instances, without even the consolation of having our labor sweetened by the reviving hope of an immediate reward."

They also enlarged their demands by asking for shorter hours and "bound" themselves

"by the sacred ties of honor to abide by the following resolution: That, in future, a day's work, amongst us, shall be deemed to commence at 6 o'clock in the morning, and terminate, at 6 in the evening of each day" (Commons: *History*, etc., Vol. I, pp. 69-70).

How this first strike in the United States ended, we do not know. No records are left.

Not all strikes are won by the workers. In fact, only a very few strikes are successful in immediate results. Nevertheless, strikes under the present system rise one after another; sometimes their number becomes so great and their size so large that they involve thousands of workers.

If these strikes do not always assure the workers the success of even their petty, immediate demands, why do the workers strike at all, and why are strikes considered an indispensable weapon of the workers in their struggle against the employers?

"Simply because they must," says Engels, "protest against every reduction, even if dictated by necessity; because they feel bound to proclaim that they, as human beings, shall not be made to bow to social circumstances, but social conditions ought to yield to them as human beings; because silence on their part would be a recognition of these social conditions, an admission of the right of the bourgeoisie to exploit the workers in good times and let them starve in bad ones. Against this the workingmen must rebel so long as they have not lost all human feeling. . . . These strikes, at first skirmishes, sometimes result in weighty struggles; they decide nothing, it is true, but they are the strongest proof that the decisive battle between the bourgeoisie and the proletariat is approaching. They are the military school of the workingmen in which they prepare themselves for the great struggle which cannot be avoided; they are the pronunciamentos of single branches of industry that these, too, have joined the labor movement" (Engels: *Condition*, etc., pp. 218 and 224).

Strikes are an outcome of economic relations. They are part of the class struggle which is inevitable and unavoidable in the capitalist system of production.

"The very development of modern industry," says Karl Marx, "must progressively turn the scale in favor of the capitalist against the working man, and consequently the general tendency of the capitalist production is not to raise, but to sink the average standard of wages, or to push the value of labor more or less to its minimum limit. Such being the tendency of things in this system, is this saying that the working class ought to renounce their resistance against the encroachments of capital, and abandon their attempts at making the best of the occasional chances for their temporary improvement? If they did, they would be degraded to one level mass of broken wretches past salvation. . . . their struggles for the standard of wages are incidents inseparable from the whole wages system, that in 99 cases out of 100 their efforts at maintaining the given value of labor, and that the necessity of debating their price with the capitalist is inherent to their condition of having to sell themselves as commodities. By cowardly giving way in their every-day conflict with capital, they would certainly disqualify themselves for the initiating of any larger movement.

"At the same time, and quite apart from the general servitude involved in the wages system, the working class ought not to exaggerate to themselves the ultimate working of these everyday struggles. They ought not to forget that they are fighting with effects, but not with the causes of those effects; that they are retarding the downward movement, but not changing its direction; that they are applying palliatives, not curing the malady. They, ought, therefore, not to be exclusively absorbed in these unavoidable guerilla fights incessantly springing up from the never-ceasing encroachments of capital or changes of the market. They ought to understand that, with all the miseries it imposes upon them, the present system simultaneously engenders the material conditions and the social forms necessary for an economical reconstruction of society. Instead of the conservative motto, 'A fair day's wages for a fair day's work,' they ought to inscribe on their banner the revolutionary watchword 'Abolition of the wages system!'" (Marx: *Value, Price and Profit*, pp. 124-127).

Every-day struggles of the workers with the employers are inevitable and necessary, but the working class should not satisfy itself with these struggles. Its mission is to overthrow and destroy the wage system and to establish a communist society in its place. The development of humanity tends in that direction and the proletariat marches toward that goal.

Strikes are the means the workers employ to defend their wages from the attacks of the employers; they are also a means of struggle for a shorter working day and for better working conditions. The workers cannot renounce this means of their struggle unless they would at the same time renounce every struggle with their oppressors and exploiters. And this would mean their gradual degradation into a mass of "broken wretches past salvation."

On the other hand, strikes are a training school for the workers. Here they are taught how to fight their enemy. Here they develop courage; here they find that their interests as workers are mutual and the outcome—class solidarity. All of this is absolutely necessary in the preparation for the final struggle which will bring them victory over capital and place them on the road to abolition of the wage system.

Saposs tells us that the first organized strike in this country occurred in 1799. It was a strike of the shoemakers of Philadelphia who were organized into the Federal Society of Journeymen Cordwainers. It seems that the strike was a serious one and the conflict lasted for 9 or 10 weeks (Commons: *History*, etc., Vol. I, p. 109).

The tailors of Baltimore led a series of strikes in 1795, 1805, and

LABOR ORGANIZATIONS AND LABOR STRUGGLES

1807. But it seems that these struggles were unorganized outbreaks, for there are no records of the existence of any labor organization at that time in Baltimore.

Several sailors' and ship-builders' strikes of 1817 at Medford, Mass., were vigorous replies of the workers to the attacks of their employers. The sailors' strike in New York on March 26, 1800, resulted in an open clash with the forces of oppression. Thus the Baltimore *Federal Gazette*, a labor-hating sheet, of April 11, 1800, had the following to say about this militant struggle of the sailors:

"A large mob of sailors who had turned out for higher wages, and were parading the streets of Fell's Pt., on Monday, in riotous confusion, made an attempt after dark to board and rifle a vessel belonging to Messrs. David Steward and Sons, on board of which it was said, men had entered at $18 per month. Their design being learnt, several citizens put themselves on board, to defend her in case of necessity, from the ravages of the mob, who seemed bent on mischief, and approached with drums and fife, and colors flying. As they attempted to get on board they were opposed, when a severe conflict ensued, and notwithstanding the vessel lay close alongside the wharf, they were three times repulsed, with broken heads and bloody noses. Mr. David Steward, Mr. J. Beeman, and several others who were on board, we learn, were very considerably wounded,—but fortunately no lives were lost" (*Ibid.*, pp. 110-111).

The tone of this report on the sailors' strike tells us the attitude of the bourgeois press toward the struggling workers. It shows only contempt for those who dared fight for higher pay and better conditions.

In 1802 the New York sailors struck again for higher wages. Instead of the $10 they were receiving they demanded $14. They arranged a demonstration and persuaded others not to take their places. But their struggle was short-lived, for the state militia was called out and crushed the revolt. The leaders of the strike were arrested and imprisoned. The workers now learned a lesson as to whose interests the "democratic" government protects. They saw with their own eyes how the government had hastened with its armed forces to assist the employers (McMaster: *History*, etc., Vol. II, p. 618).

The shoemakers' strike of Philadelphia, in 1806, was marked by demonstrations and militancy of the workers. Enraged strikers beat the scabs and smashed the windows of the factories (*Documentary History*, Vol. III, pp. 95-101).

In 1809, the New York shoemakers conducted a general strike. The walk-out started in the Corwin and Aimes shops, but the employers attempted to break it up by giving their work out to other shops. The general strike resulted (*Ibid.*, pp. 369-370). As to its outcome we have no records.

This period before the crisis of 1819 was also marked by a conflict of the American workers with the courts, whose whole history shows loyalty to the propertied classes. In their struggle with the workers the capitalists found in the courts a very effective means for breaking up the efforts of their employees to improve their conditions. Behind the courts there stands a powerful bourgeois state with its police, militia and army. Their decisions are carried into effect not by empty phrases but with the help of the armed state power. Herein lies the importance of the stand of the courts against the working class.

As soon as the workers began to organize and to defend their interests against the employers by united efforts, they found themselves defendants before the bourgeois court. And what were the charges against them? They were charged with organizing their force for the purpose of raising wages. Such action was considered at that time a conspiracy against the existing economic and political system.

Before the crisis of 1819 the shoemakers of this country were brought at least six times before the courts as criminals. Once in 1806 and twice in 1809 the shoemakers of Philadelphia were indicted on the charge of being conspirators; once in 1809 their fellow craftsmen in New York were brought before the court; and twice those in Pittsburgh faced trial, once in 1814 and again in 1815. In four cases the verdict of the court was against the workers and only in two cases were they found not guilty. In all these trials the local courts, in their desire to serve the employers and to prevent the workers from organizing into trade unions, employed the laws of England, which had been passed against the interests of the poor and imported into this country before the Revolution.

In all these cases the workers were charged with criminal conspiracy for the purpose of raising their wages. For centuries the ruling class had looked upon the workers as slaves having no other reason for existence but to toil for the profits of their masters. But now the workers of Philadelphia, Baltimore, Pittsburgh, and other cities were organizing societies and with united efforts attempting to lighten their burden. Therefore the main question on the order of business of the ruling class was to destroy these organizations root and branch.

In the 1806 case the Philadelphia shoemakers were charged with unlawfully assembling to "unjustly and corruptly conspire, combine, confederate and agree together that none of them, the said conspirators, . . . would work for any master . . . who would employ any artificer, workman or journeyman . . . who should thereafter infringe or break" the unlawul rules and orders of the boot and shoemakers (Oneal: *Loc. cit.,* p. 160).

In instructing the jury the judge declared: "A combination of workmen to raise their wages may be considered in a twofold point of view: one is benefit to themselves . . . the other is to injure those who do not join the society. The rule of the law condemns both" (*Documentary History,* etc., Vol. III, p. 233). The verdict of the jury was: "We find defendants guilty of a combination to raise wages." And, as has

LABOR ORGANIZATIONS AND LABOR STRUGGLES

already been pointed out, "a combination to raise wages" was a "criminal conspiracy" against both the system and the state. This decision of the court made trade unions illegal organizations.

Before the verdict was rendered the workers decided to appeal to the people and explain the situation to them. This appeal was published in the *Aurora,* in November, 1806, and reads in part:

"In the constitution of this state, it is declared . . . 'that the citizens have a right in a peaceable manner to assemble together for the common good.' . . . These masters, as they are called, and who would be masters and tyrants if they could, or the law would allow them, have their associations, their meetings, and they pass their resolutions; but as they are rich and we are poor—they seem to think that we are not protected by the constitution in meeting peaceably together and pursuing our own business. They suppose that they have a right to limit us at all times, and whatever may be the misfortune of society, the changes in the value of necessaries, the increase or the decrease of trade, they think they have the right to determine for us the value of our labor; but that we have no right to determine for ourselves, what we will or what we will not take in exchange for our labor. . . . If the association of men to regulate the price of their own labor is to be converted into a crime and libeled with the same reproachful terms as a design against the freedom of the nation, the prospect is a very sad one for Pennsylvania. . . . What we have here said, will inform the public of our conduct, and will show that under whatever pretences the thing is done, the name of freedom is but a shadow, if for doing what the laws of our country authorize, we are to have taskmasters to measure our pittance of subsistence—if we are to be torn from our fireside for endeavoring to obtain a fair and just support for our families, and if we are to be treated as felons and murderers only for asserting the right to take or refuse what we deem an adequate reward for our labor."

The appeal of the shoemakers, of course, was in vain. Their words about their rights guaranteed by the constitution fell on the rocks and were lost. The workers did not yet know that their rights were guaranteed on paper only and remained so while the ruling class moved forward over the body of the constitution and the constitutional rights of the workers.

Other fights of the workers occurred in the bourgeois courts in those days, but all of them were alike and in four cases out of ten the results were the same—the workers were found guilty and their organizations were declared illegal. The charges against the workers were preferred by the employers and the expenses of the prosecution were almost entirely paid directly from the latters' pockets. And how they rejoiced when the courts convicted the workers as "criminal conspirators"! For instance, a certain "Obedient Servant" of the manufacturers writes about the Pittsburgh case of 1815, in which the workers were convicted as "conspirators" because they "combined to raise wages," as follows:

"The verdict of that jury is most important to the manufacturing interests of the community; it puts an end to those associations which have been so prejudicial to the successful enterprise of the capitalists of the western country. But this case is not important to this country alone; it proves beyond any possibility of doubt, that notwithstanding the adjudications in New York and Philadelphia, there still exist in those cities, combinations which extend their deleterious influence to every part of the union. The inhabitants of those cities, the manufacturers particularly, are bound by their interests, as well as the duties they owe the community, to watch those combinations with a jealous eye, and to prosecute to conviction, and subject to the penalties of the law, conspiracies so subversive to the best interests of the country" (*Documentary History*, etc., Vol. III, pp. 15-16).

The workers spoke about "freedom" and "love," and appealed to the sentiments of bourgeois society, while the capitalist class coolly and openly defended its economic interests. The capitalists came out victorious from almost every battle because they had in their hands the state power.

"With the precedent of the English laws as an example," says Myers, "they held that it devolved upon government to keep the workers sternly within the bounds established by employers. In plain words, this meant that the capitalist was to be allowed to run his business as he desired. He could overwork his employees, pay them the lowest wages, and kill them off by forcing them to work under conditions in which the sacrifice of human life was held subordinate to the gathering of profits, or by forcing them to work or live in disease-breeding places. The law, which was the distinct expression of the interests of the capitalist, upheld his right to do all this. Yet if the workers protested, if they sought to improve their condition by joining in that community of action called a strike, the same code of law, with its police, military, and judges, descended upon them, and either drove them back to their task or consigned them to prison" (Myers: *Loc. cit.*, Vol. II, pp. 56-57).

CHAPTER XI

LABOR ORGANIZATIONS AND THEIR STRUGGLES, 1819-1837

THE crisis of 1819 reached its worst point in 1820. From that time on the situation began to improve, and aggressive organizations of wage-earners were formed in many industries. With the revival of industrial activity, the employers began to search for cheap labor, first to withstand competition, second—to increase profits. They even opened prison doors and put the prisoners to work without compensating them for their labor. In 1823 the journeymen cabinetmakers of New York called a mass meeting and adopted a strong protest against convict labor which the employers were using to cut down the wages of the "free" workers.

As the demand for labor-power increased, the workers took advantage of the situation to get something for themselves also. Besides the spread of unionism among the skilled craftsmen, "other signs of awakening are the organizations of factory and women workers. Previous to this time only the handicraft workers were organized. . . . The factory workers were the first to use the word 'union' in the name of their organization." For instance, "we find in New York in 1825 a Nailers' Union and a Weavers' Union joining with a number of journeymen societies in the celebration of the opening of the Erie Canal" (Commons: *History*, etc., Vol. I, p. 156).

Before this period there were only local labor organizations, having no connection with one another, struggling separately, and leading a precarious existence. But in 1827, in Philadelphia, "as a result of a strike of building trades workmen for a 10-hour day, there was formed the first effective city central organization of wage-earners in the world—the Mechanics' Union of Trade Associations." All labor organizations in the city were invited to send delegates to this central organization, and those workers who were still unorganized were called upon to organize and join hands with the rest of their fellows. In their constitution these workers protested against exploitation and social inequality. They pointed out that they were compelled to work hard, and for long hours, for the handful of those who did not produce anything useful in this world, but who were nevertheless living in plenty and luxury.

"The real object, therefore, of this association," they declared, "is to avert, if possible, the desolating evils which must inevitably arise from a depreciation of the intrinsic value of human labor; to raise the mechanical and productive classes to that condition of true independence and equality (sic!) which their practical skill and ingenuity, their immense utility to the nation, and their intelligence are beginning imperiously to demand; to promote, equally, the happiness, prosperity and welfare of the whole community . . . and to assist . . . in establishing a just balance of power, both mental, moral, political and scientific, between all the various classes and individuals which constitute society at large" (*Ibid.*, p. 190).

We see from this declaration of principles of the Mechanics' Union of Trade Associations that there were elements in that organization entirely foreign to the workers. Their protest ended with efforts to bring together the opposing interests of various classes and to avoid the class struggle which was rising higher and higher. But in spite of their inconsistency and their futile efforts, the establishment of the Mechanics' Union of Trade Associations was an important step forward in comparison with the former organizations of the workers, which had no common bond of unity whatever. In 1828 the Mechanics' Union participated in the state and city elections. At the beginning it had under its flag about 14 societies, but it immediately began to decline and by 1829 there were only four of these societies left affiliated with the city central body. Finally the Mechanics' Union itself was dissolved.

But in November, 1833, in Philadelphia the General Trades' Union was organized to continue the work of the Mechanics' Union. Because there was a general opinion that the Mechanics' Union had died on account of participation in elections, the General Trades' Union declared in its constitution that "no party, political, or religious questions shall at any time be agitated in or acted upon in the union." Its official organ, the *National Laborer,* declared that "the Trades' Union never will be political because its members have learned from experience that the introduction of politics into their societies has thwarted every effort to ameliorate their conditions" (Perlman: *History of Trade Unionism in the United States,* p. 21).

City central bodies of trade unions were formed also in many other cities. In 1836 there were at least 13 such city centrals.

It is hard to tell how many local trade unions were organized during the "prosperity" period from 1821 to 1837. Their number constantly increased until

"in 1833 there were in New York 29 organized trades; in Philadelphia, 21; and in Baltimore, 17. Among those organized in Philadelphia were hand-loom weavers, plasterers, bricklayers, blacksmiths, cigar makers, plumbers. and women workers, including tailoresses. . . . Several trades, such as the printers and tailors in New York and the Philadelphia carpenters, which formerly were organized upon the benevolent basis, were now organized as trade societies. . . ." (Perlman: *Loc. cit.,* p. 19).

But the greatest number of trade unions appeared between 1835 and 1837. "The factor that compelled labor to organize on a much larger

LABOR ORGANIZATIONS AND THEIR STRUGGLES 83

scale was the remarkable rise in prices" in that period. The "cost of living having doubled, the subject of wages became a burning issue." Such conditions made fertile soil for the growth of trade unionism. "In 1836 there were in Philadelphia 58 trade unions; in Newark, N. J., 16; in New York, 52; in Pittsburgh, 13; in Cincinnati, 14; and in Louisville, 7. In Buffalo the journeymen builders' association included all the building trades" (*Ibid.*, p. 19).

The wave of organization in this period did not leave women workers untouched. The first working women's organization on record was formed in Lowell, Mass., when after the great strike of 1834 about 2,500 of them joined the Factory Girls' Association.

"In New York there was in 1835 a Female Union Association, in Baltimore a United Seamstresses' Society, and in Philadelphia probably the first federation of women workers in this industry. In Lynn, Mass., a 'Female Society of Lynn and Vicinity for the Protection and Promotion of Female Industry' operated during 1833 and 1834 among the shoe binders and had at one time 1,000 members" (*Ibid.*, p. 20).

It is estimated that in 1836 union membership in the seaboard cities amounted to 300,000.

In view of the great development of industry and the ever-increasing conflict between the interests of the workers and those of the employers, these local trade unions and the city central organizations were not sufficient to cope with the situation. By this time the employers of one city were able, without great difficulty, to get in touch with the employers of other cities and unite their forces against the workers. Therefore the unity of the workers was compelled to reach further than the boundaries of a single city, and they also began a move to unite their efforts nationally in the same trade. It is true that these efforts were not as yet general. Nevertheless, they did affect quite a number of branches of industry. During 1835-1836, no less than five separate crafts or trades held national conventions of their own. These were the cordwainers, printers, comb makers, carpenters, and hand loom weavers.

Still another important step was made toward a greater unity of the workers in this period when in 1834 the National Trades' Union was organized. This was the first serious attempt to unite the workers of all occupations into a national body.

The initiative to form a national organization came from the General Trades' Union of New York. In the convention call the aims of the gathering were stated as follows:

"To advance the moral and intellectual condition and pecuniary interests of the laboring classes, promote the establishment of trades' unions in every section of the United States; and also to publish and disseminate such information as may be useful to mechanics and working men generally; and to unite and harmonize the efforts of all the productive classes of the country" (Commons: *History*, etc., Vol. I, p. 425).

We see from this declaration that the aim of the convention was not very clear. Nevertheless, the delegates, once they came together, did not leave the assemblage without accomplishing something. At the convention were represented the city central organizations of New York, Brooklyn, Boston, Newark, Poughkeepsie, and Philadelphia. The result was the birth of the National Trades' Union.

At this first convention of the National Trades' Union there occurred an intense discussion on political action. The Philadelphia delegates pointed out that the Mechanics' Union of Philadelphia in 1828 had merged with the Working Men's Party and "both were now extinct." The majority of delegates feared that their organization might fall under the control of some one of the existing political organizations, and therefore decided to strike from the constitution the word "political" and to substitute the world "intellectual."

The convention adopted several resolutions on various important questions of the time. In one of them the workers were urged to organize so "that they may by these means be enabled effectively to make common cause with their oppressed brethren." In another the educational system of the country was condemned for drawing "a line of demarkation between the producers of the wealth, and the other portions of society which subsist upon the fruits of the working men's industry," and the demand was raised for an "equal, universal, republican system of education." The convention also advanced a demand that land should belong to those who work on it. It called for the repeal of the laws which held trade unions illegal.

The question of woman and child labor in the factories was always an important one at labor gatherings. At the convention of the National Trades' Union it again came up for serious consideration. Charles Douglass, president of the New England Association of Farmers, Mechanics, and Other Working Men, pictured the conditions of the women workers in Lowell, Mass. He told the delegates that in the factories of that city there were about 4,000 females of various ages

"now dragging out a life of slavery and wretchedness." He pointed out how distressing it was "to behold these degraded females as they pass out of the factory—to watch their wan countenances—their woe-stricken appearance. These establishments are the present abode of wretchedness, disease, and misery; and are inevitably calculated to perpetuate them—if not to destroy liberty itself!" He says that "the sons of our farmers, as soon as they are of sufficient age, have been induced to hasten off to the factory, where for a few pence more than they could get at home, they are taught to become the willing servants, the servile instruments of their employers' oppression and extortion!"

Douglass proposed, as a remedy for these evils, to demand from the legislature a law compelling the employers to shut their factories at a given hour each day, "so that all may have an opportunity to rest their weary limbs, and to enjoy free and wholesome air."

But John Commerford, of New York, was of a different opinion and turned the discussion into a new channel. He condemned the entire factory system. He pointed to the great development of that system in England, and said:

"It is true, sir, that her wealth has arisen from these sources; but it is equally true, that the moral degradation of her people may be attributed to her manufacturing system. No one will dispute that the same causes produce the like effects."

And the discussion at the convention ended with the hope that "every individual would feel himself obligated . . . to use all diligence for the entire reformation of this system" (*Ibid.*, pp. 428-430).

The third and last convention of the National Trades' Union was held in October, 1836, in Philadelphia. Only 35 delegates were present. The convention went on record for entering the field of coöperatives as a remedy for the evils of the factory system which divided the "workingmen into employers and journeymen." Coöperation would restore to the laborer the disposal of his own products! And in order to make the road for the disintegration of the union more slippery the convention declared that "if trade unions and trades societies were to apply their funds to the establishing of coöperation in societies suffering aggression, instead of exhausting their funds by supporting strikes, a much more permanent benefit would be rendered." In other words, the convention adopted as a policy for the union, not to fight back against the onslaughts of the employers, but to run away from them! Such a policy was the last nail in the coffin of the National Trades' Union, as far as the proletariat was concerned.

The aims and principles of the trade unions of this period were well expressed by Ely Moore, president of the New York General Trades' Union, in his speech of October 2, 1833. They were: To protect themselves from the attacks of the aristocracy, to maintain the natural and political rights of the workers, to improve their moral and intellectual condition, to improve their material interests, to narrow the line separating employers from the workers, to establish their trades on a firmer and more secure foundation, and to assist those who were in distress (Ely: *Loc. cit.*, pp. 43-44).

And the leaders of the trade unions did their utmost to restrict the movement to these narrow limits; they fought against the principle that trade unions should increase the number of strikes and sharpen the class struggle. On the contrary, it was maintained that the trade unions should lessen the number of strikes and lessen the class struggle by acquainting the workers with their employers and bringing both sides nearer to each other.

In this period we also meet the first attempts of the American workers in the field of the parliamentary (political) action. Three main factors led in this direction—first, inability of the trade unions to improve labor conditions; then the idea that it was possible for the workers, through elections, to take over the government and use it in their own interests; and finally the continuous use of the government by the capitalist class to fight the workers. These early efforts, of course, were feeble. They had no definite goal and they accomplished no substantial results. Nevertheless, the workers from time to time would show such courage and such class consciousness that the majority of the present-day labor leaders would do well to pattern after the workers of that early period.

The first political party of labor in the world was organized in Philadelphia in May, 1828, under the name of the Working Men's Party, when the Mechanics' Union of Trade Associations sent out a call to all trade unions and trade societies of the city to come to a meeting at which nominations were to be made for the state and city elections. It was proposed to name candidates who would "represent the interests of the working classes." Various trade unions and societies responded favorably to this call and the meeting was held in July of the same year. A resolution was adopted urging the "working classes" to enter upon independent political action.

It is true that the Working Men's Party of Philadelphia was composed mainly of workers. Nevertheless, it seems, the bourgeoisie, especially the petty bourgeoisie, found a place there too. And here it is necessary to emphasize the fact that the intrusion of the bourgeoisie into working class parties has been the main reason for the disruption of these parties. At the first meeting of the Philadelphia Working Men's Party the question was raised whether the employers should be allowed to participate in the convention and in the party. It was decided that they should, because at that time the idea prevailed, especially among the skilled workers, that the employers were also "working people." The *Mechanics' Free Press,* considered the first working-class paper in America, in an editorial in 1829 made the following declaration on this question:

"If an employer superintends his own business (still more if he works with his own hands) he is a working man and has an interest on the side of the remuneration of labor. . . . If this view of things be correct, shall we look with a jealous eye on those employers who prefer being considered working men, who are willing to join us in obtaining our objects, who wish to see production attended with respectability, comfort, and intelligence?"

And these employers, after joining the working men's parties, and in accordance with their economic and political interests which are opposed to the interests of the working class, knew well how to destroy these parties by disrupting them from within or by attaching them to one or another of the capitalist parties.

As soon as the Working Men's Party of Philadelphia was organized the bourgeoisie raised the cry that the party was propagating infidelity and the division of property. The workers through their organ, the *Mechanics' Free Press,* again and again denied these accusations. But the bourgeoisie had better means with which to scare the workers, whose minds were poisoned by religious teachings and the bourgeois conception of the sacredness of property. Those workers who in the beginning had joined the party with great enthusiasm now began to desert it. The year 1831 was the last in which the Working Men's Party participated in elections.

Another serious attempt of the workers in the parliamentary field was made in New York City, where in 1829 the New York Working Men's Party was organized. Robert Dale Owen and Frances Wright were its first leaders. Owen was outspoken in his condemnation of capitalism, religion, and marriage based on material considerations. Hence, as soon as the Working Men's Party was organized it was condemned by the bourgeoisie as an enemy of church and property. The Working Men's Party of New York differed from the Working Men's Party of Philadelphia in that it was much more radical. It distinguished itself by stormy factional struggles and splits within. It gained wide influence and won enthusiastic support throughout the state. Frances Wright wrote in 1830:

"What distinguishes the present from every other struggle in which the human race has been engaged, is that the present is, evidently, openly and acknowledgedly, a war of class, and that this war is universal."

And the *Working Men's Advocate* declared:

"Your fathers of the Revolution secured to you a form of government which guarantees to you, almost universally, the elective franchise. . . . If you possess the rights of freemen, you have exercised them as the privileges of slaves. . . . Awake then, from your slumbers; and insult not the memories of the heroes of '76, by exhibiting to the world, that what they risked their lives, their fortunes, and their sacred honor to obtain, you do not think worth preserving."

With what contempt the bourgeoisie looked upon this attempt of the workers of New York in the parliamentary field we may judge from *The Commercial Advertiser* which called them "poor and deluded followers of a crazy atheistical woman." And further:

"Lost to society, to earth and to heaven, godless and hopeless, clothed and fed by stealing and blasphemy . . . such are the apostles who are trying to induce a number of able bodied men in this city to follow in their own course . . . to disturb the peace of the community for a time; go to prison and have the mark of Cain impressed upon them; betake themselves to incest, robbery, and murder; die like ravenous wild beasts, hunted down without pity; and go to render their account before God, whose existence they believed in their miserable hearts, even while they were blaspheming him in their ignorant, snivelling, puerile speculations. Such is too true a picture in all its parts of some of the leaders of the new political party, which is emerging from the slime of this community, and which is more beastly and terrible than the Egyptian Typhon" (Commons: *History*, etc., Vol. I, pp. 272-73).

But the bourgeoisie did not have to fear the Working Men's Party very long. In its very bosom there was a cancer spreading—a suicidal internal struggle. At first there appeared two different camps, and later three, led and developed by bourgeois newspapers such as the *Evening Journal* and the *Morning Herald*, which in the beginning supported the movement, but later on did everything in their power to destroy it. On the other hand, the bourgeoisie by sending its agents into the Working Men's Party and corrupting the leaders of the various factions successfully disrupted the organization. In 1832 the *Working Men's Advocate* came out openly and urged the workers to vote for the candidates of Tammany Hall, composed of the most corrupt bourgeois politicians.

Gustavus Myers speaks enthusiastically about this Working Men's Party of New York, and mercilessly condemns the leaders who split it to pieces and sold it to the bourgeoisie. He says:

"By 1831, however, it had gone out of existence. The reason was that it allowed itself to be betrayed by the supineness, incompetence, and as some said, the treachery, of its leaders, who were content to accept from a legislature controlled by the propertied interests various mollifying sops which slightly altered certain laws, but which in no great degree redounded to the benefit of the working class. For a few bits of counterfeit, this splendid proletarian uprising, glowing with energy, enthusiasm, and hope, allowed itself to be snuffed out of existence" (Myers: *Loc. cit.*, Vol. I, pp. 172-174).

The temporary success of the Working Men's Party of New York, its militancy and enthusiasm, reached other cities and states. Everywhere the workers raised the slogan of separation from the capitalist parties in parliamentary action.

"In at least 15 states local labor parties were formed; at least 50 labor papers were founded to voice the aims and demands of labor; political organizations along the old, familiar lines of county and ward committees and conventions were established; and radical agitators demanding revolutionary changes came to the front" (Mary Beard, *Loc. cit.*, p. 36).

Space does not permit us to deal with the principles of all of these parties. One will suffice. The Working Men's Republican Political Association of Penn Township, Pa., stated its principles as follows:

"There appear to exist two distinct classes, the rich and the poor; the oppressor and the oppressed; those that live by their own labor, and they that live by the labor of others; the aristocratic, and the democratic; the despotic, and republican, who are in direct opposition to one another in their objects and pursuits; the one aspiring to dignified stations, and office of power, the other seeking for an equality of state and advantage; the one apparently desirous and determined to keep the people in ignorance of their rights and privileges, that they may live in ease and opulence at the expense of the labor and industry of the others; the other showing that they are acquainted with the nature of their rights, and are determined to maintain and possess them; the one seeking to introduce and perpetuate amongst us invidious and artificial distinctions, unnatural and unjust inequalities, while the other party declare that all men are created free and equal, enjoying a perfect uniformity of rights and privileges, and that unnatural and artificial distinctions, independent of merit, are pernicious in their effects and deleterious in their consequences" (Commons, *History*, etc., Vol. I, p. 193).

Thus the Working Men's Republican Political Association sought to abolish social inequalities while at the same time it said nothing about the struggle for the abolition of the system which causes these inequalities. None of these parties stated the problem of overthrowing the bourgeoisie and the reconstruction of society on a new basis squarely. They did not and could not raise this problem in this way because they were not revolutionary parties. They were not free from bourgeois elements and influence; they did not draw a clear line between the exploiters and exploited, between the workers and capitalists.

The immediate demands of the workers of that period were serious and far reaching. Trade unions as well as political parties raised these demands and fought for them. At this time we do not find that sharp division by which trade unions raise only economic demands, and political parties only political demands. The most important of these demands were the following:

1. Free public schools; 2. Ten-hour work day; 3. Mechanics' lien law; 4. Abolition of banks issuing paper money; 5. Abolition of the militia system; 6. Abolition of imprisonment for debt; 7. Abolition of chartered monopolies; 8. Limitation of woman and child labor; 9. Universal suffrage.

In the period we are discussing the demand for establishment of free public schools was one of the most important. The workers of New York in 1830 declared that after life and liberty the next most important thing is education. And the workers of Pennsylvania pointed out:

"All history corroborates the melancholy fact, that in proportion as the mass of the people becomes ignorant, misrule and anarchy ensue—their liberties are subverted, and tyrannic ambition has never failed to take advantage of their helpless condition. . . . Let the productive classes, then, unite for the preservation of free institutions, and by procuring for all the children in the commonwealth republican education, preserve our liberties from the dangers of foreign invasion or domestic infringement. . . . Our government is republican; our education should be equally so" (Mary Beard: *Loc. cit.*, p. 41).

At that time many workers looked upon the establishment of the public school system as a cure for all social ills. It is true that even then there were so-called "free" schools maintained at the expense of the state treasury, but they were conducted only for children whose parents had not sufficient means to send them to private schools. They were pauper institutions. In Philadelphia, for instance, the parents had openly to declare themselves "too poor to pay for the education of their children before they were allowed the questionable privileges of the public schools so much odium was attached to these schools that they were practically useless." Thousands of parents preferred to leave their children without any education, rather than to put the stamp of pauperism on them. A decent education could be had only by the children of those who had money to send their offspring to private schools.

The result of such a system of education was as might be expected. The number of illiterates continuously increased. In 1820 in New York City there were 24,200 illiterate children; 10,000 attended the so-called "public" schools, and 17,000 children of the well-to-do were in private schools. As late as 1837 in Pennsylvania out of 400,000 children, 250,000 did not attend any school. In New Jersey in 1835, out of a child population of 200,000, 15,000 were illiterates, 12,000 did not attend school.

"In 1833 it was estimated that in the entire United States 1,000,000 children between the ages of 5 and 15 were not in any school, and that out of these 80,000 were in the state of New York. The next year the number of illiterate children in the United States was placed at 1,250,000" (Commons: *History*, etc., Vol. I, p. 182).

This great mass of illiterate children came entirely from the working classes, from the poor and exploited.

The ruling class was strongly opposed to the establishment of free public schools. It was dangerous for its rule to have such a system of education. "Who will till the soil, who will build the railroads, who will sweat in the factories, if all people are educated?" shouted the bourgeoisie and the masters of the land. The ruling class argued openly and shamelessly that their class alone had been chosen to think for the world and to rule it, while, on the other hand, the farmers and the workers had been condemned to ignorance and slavery.

"The peasant," argues the *National Gazette*, of Philadelphia, "must labor during those hours of the day which his wealthy neighbor can give to abstract culture of his mind; otherwise, the earth would not yield enough for the subsistence of all; the mechanic cannot abandon the operations of his trade for general studies; if he should, most of the conveniences of life and objects of exchange would be wanting; languor, decay, poverty, discontent would soon be visible among all classes. No government, no statesmen, no philanthropists, can furnish what is incompatible with the very organization and being of civil society."

A little later the same paper exclaimed:

"The scheme of universal equal education at the expense of the state, is virtually agrarianism. It would be a compulsory application of the means of the richer for the direct use of the poorer classes; and so far an arbitrary division of property among them" (*Documentary History*, Vol. V., pp. 108-110).

But later the ruling class changed its attitude in regard to free public schools—partly because of the strong demand by the labor movement, and partly because of its realization that it could turn the public schools into effective machines for providing itself with mental slaves. To poi-

LABOR ORGANIZATIONS AND THEIR STRUGGLES 91

son the minds of the toilers' children with the opium of patriotism, of loyalty to the system of private property, appeared to be a practical and necessary step in the further development of the capitalist system. "Enslavement of science, and through it of the minds of the working class" became the slogan of the class conscious section of the rising capitalist class.

The ruling class, therefore, yielded to the demand of the working class for free public schools, but only in its own interests. The workers struggled and won the schools "free for all," but the bourgeoisie took them over and used them for their own purposes. To-day the bourgeoisie do not complain that they have to contribute a few dollars in taxes for the maintenance of the public schools. In 1920 the public schools of America were worth $2,500,000,000, and during the same year they spent $1,000,000,000. The boards of education which control our lower schools as well as the boards of trustees of higher educational institutions, are completely in the hands of the bourgeoisie.

More important than the issue of the public schools, at this period, was the demand for shorter hours. Daily toil from sunrise to sunset, or from 14 to 15 hours in every 24, became a heavy burden upon the mechanic as well as the factory slave. A 10-hour day slogan was raised by the labor movement. The carpenters of Boston struck for a 10-hour day in 1825. They were defeated, but in 1830 they united with the bricklayers and again started the fight. And again they were defeated. Nevertheless, the 10-hour day movement continuously spread, not only in Boston, but through all New England. In November, 1831, the mechanics and machinists of Providence, R. I., decided not to work more than 10 hours a day beginning with March, 1832. During the same year there was a convention held by farmers, mechanics, and other workers of New England at which a resolution was accepted "to reduce the hours of labor to 10 hours per day, after the 20th of March next."

"The year 1835 was the banner year of the 10-hour movement. It started in Boston, and from there spread as far south as Baltimore, including in its sweep Philadelphia and seven other smaller places—Salem, Mass., Hartford, Conn., Batavia, Seneca Falls and Albany, N. Y., and Paterson and New Brunswick, N. J." (Commons: *History*, etc., Vol. I., p. 387).

"The politicians," says Myers, "denounced the movement; the cultured classes frowned upon it; the newspapers alternately ridiculed and abused it; the officials prepared to take summary action to put it down. As for the capitalists—the shipping merchants, the boot and shoe manufacturers, the iron masters and others—they not only denied the right of the workers to organize, while insisting that they themselves were entitled to combine, but they inveighed against the 10-hour demand as 'unreasonable conditions which the folly and caprice of a few journeymen mechanics may dictate.' 'A very large sum of money,' says McNeill, 'was subscribed by the merchants to defeat the 10-hour movement.' And as an evidence of the intense opposition to the workers' demands for a change from a 14 to a 10-hour day, McNeill quotes from a Boston newspaper of 1832: 'Had this unlawful combination had for its object the enhancement of daily wages, it would have been left to its own care; but it now strikes the very nerve of industry and good morals by dictating the hours of labor, abrogating the good old rule of our fathers and pointing out the most direct course to poverty; for to be idle several of the most useful hours of the morning and evening will surely lead to intemperance and ruin'" (Myers: *Loc. cit.*, Vol. II, pp. 59-61).

The trade unions of Baltimore petitioned Congress for the establishment of the 10-hour day by legislation, but Congress after a short discussion tabled the petition.

The fights against shorter hours on the part of the employers were always resolute and systematic. The newspapers of the country exclaimed that the 10-hour day would be a source of degradation and vice for the workers. They maintained that the longer the worker toils the less time he has to spend on "sinful" temptations.

But, of course, this argument was used only as a smoke screen. Fundamentally the demand of the workers for shorter hours attacked the most vital nerve of the profit system. The less hours the worker spends at the machine the less surplus value he produces and therefore so much less profit does he make for the capitalists. This was the reason that the employers resorted to all means at their disposal to crush any attempt on the part of the workers to gain the 10-hour day.

The militia system was also pressing hard on the shoulders of the laboring masses. Free men of a certain age were required to spend a few days each year in military training. Each had to have his own arms and other necessaries for military service. Nobody paid for the time lost during such service. Those who failed to perform this duty were fined, and those who had no money to pay the fine were sent to jail. In New York, for instance, for every failure to attend military training the fine was $12; and while this $12 was of no account to the rich employer or his sons, it meant a great deal to the worker. The rich paid the fine and in that way escaped military service. The workers went to prison. The labor movement of the time fought against such a military system and emphatically demanded its abolition.

Child and woman labor in the factories was another weighty issue. It loomed large, first, because such labor was detrimental to the skilled workers, and second, because the horrible conditions in the factories, the long hours of labor, and the crushing of the health of women and children aroused widespread sympathy among the men wage-earners. They therefore demanded the abolition of this vicious exploitation.

The right to vote was also given serious attention. As has already been pointed out, in every state the right of suffrage was kept from the masses by a barrier of property qualifications. Millions of poor workers could not vote. On the other hand the workers strongly believed in the possibility of improving their conditions by their votes. It appeared to

LABOR ORGANIZATIONS AND THEIR STRUGGLES 93

them that they could eliminate the conditions which oppressed them by electing officials who would defend their interests. Of course, this conception was wrong, for it is impossible to emancipate the masses from the capitalist system through parliamentary action alone. Nevertheless, universal suffrage was vital to the workers, and the labor movement rightly struggled to attain it.

While the struggle for these demands was being waged, the employers again turned to the courts to suppress the labor movement. They knew that by declaring the trade unions illegal, and using the state power to crush them, sure death could be brought upon the workers' militant organizations. The courts were always ready to serve the propertied class. At least 11 times during the period 1819 to 1837 the workers' organizations were brought before the bar. The New York hatters were attacked in 1823; the Buffalo tailors in 1824; the Philadelphia tailors in 1827; the spinners of Philadelphia, the weavers of Baltimore, and the shoemakers of Chambersburg, Pa., in 1829; the carpet weavers of Thompsonville, Conn., were sued in 1834; the shoemakers of Geneva, N. Y., in 1835; the tailors of New York, the shoemakers of Hudson, N. Y., and the plasterers of Philadelphia in 1836.

In every instance the workers were charged with conspiring to hinder commerce and production or with trying to win higher wages through their organizations. On both counts the employers and the government considered the workers conspirators and traitors to the country.

Let us take only two examples, the shoemakers of Geneva and the tailors of New York.

In 1835 the Geneva shoe workers organized and decided that they would work only for certain wages and would not work with shoemakers who accepted lower wages. A fine of $10 was to be imposed by the union upon members who violated this rule. They were at once arrested, and when put on trial Judge Savage found them guilty and told them that it was forbidden for workers to attempt to stop others from working for smaller wages.

"If the defendants cannot make coarse boots for less than $1 per pair," Judge Savage declared, "let them refuse to do so; but let them not directly or indirectly undertake to say that others shall not do the work for a less price" (Commons: *History*, etc., Vol. I, p. 407).

In New York it was the employers who organized, in 1836, and decided to cut down the wages of the tailors. The latter struck. The employers hired scabs, and the workers answered this challenge by picketing. Then the employers invited the government and the court to their assistance. Twenty strikers were arrested and imprisoned. They were found guilty of being conspirators, and their union was declared illegal. But sentence was delayed for a week. The workers were aroused by the court's action and issued an appeal in which they said:

"On Monday, June 6, 1836, these freemen are to receive their sentence, to gratify the hellish appetites of the aristocracy. On Monday, the liberty of the workingmen will be interred! Judge Edwards is to chant the requiem! Go! Go! Go! every freeman, every workingman, and hear the melancholy sound of the earth on the coffin of equality! Let the courtroom, the city hall, yea, the whole park, be filled with mourners! But remember, offer no violence to Judge Edwards! Bend meekly, and receive the chains wherewith you are to be bound! Keep the peace! Above all things keep the peace!" (*Ibid.*, p. 409).

The president of the union was fined $150; another member who had been active during the strike was fined $100, and the rest $50 each. In sentencing the workers the judge once more emphasized that "in this favored land of law and liberty, the road to advancement is open to all and the journeymen may through their skill and industry, and moral worth, soon become flourishing master mechanics." He also announced that the trade unions were injurious not only to employers but also to the workers; and finally that the unions "are mainly upheld by foreigners."

We must not think that only the workers were organizing during that period and that the employers were not forming their own organizations. Employers' associations were flourishing at the very moment when the trade unions were declared illegal and when the state power was being used to crush them. Neither the courts nor the government dared to raise a voice or a finger against these associations.

These employers' associations were militant organizations and established for the sole purpose of waging war on the workers. In this war they used every effort and every means. The slogan of the bourgeoisie was "to destroy every labor organization root and branch." In this endeavor they were assisted by the government and the courts, the bourgeois press faithfully defended their interests, and the clergy of the country fought on their side.

While labor organizations during this period were few in number, and the whole bourgeoisie was against them, the workers showed great militancy and much energy and perseverance. This is shown by the numerous strikes, revolts, and demonstrations.

"Most of the strikes, as in the preceding periods, centered around the question of wages," reports Commons. Low wages meant great suffering to the families of the workers and, therefore, they struggled for a larger piece of bread. In addition, strikes were very often caused by attempts of the employers to reduce wages even below the existing low levels.

In 1824 the textile workers of Pawtucket, R. I., declared a strike against a wage cut and the lengthening of working hours. This is believed to be the first strike in which women workers took part, and they showed great bravery in the struggle. In 1825 the women tailors of New York City struck against wage cuts.

The stone cutters of New York went on strike for the establishment of a uniform wage scale of $1.62 a day. The hat makers of Philadelphia quit their jobs in 1825 in order to establish a uniform wage system.

"Beginning with 1824 and running through 1825, the year which saw the culmination of a period of high prices, a number of strikes occurred in the important industrial centers. The majority were called to enforce higher wages. In 1824, the Buffalo tailors, Philadelphia ship carpenters, the New York journeymen house painters, and others struck for increases in wages. In 1825 there were strikes of tailors, stonecutters, riggers, stevedores, and common laborers in New York City; hand loom weavers in Philadelphia; and cabinetmakers in Baltimore and Philadelphia. The New York tailors are said to have asked 'for what is equivalent to about $3 advance a week on previous wages.' The stonecutters won their strike for $2 a day; and the riggers asked $1.50 and the stevedores and common laborers $1.25 per day; in Philadelphia 2,900 weavers out of about 4,500 in the city went on strike early in April for higher wages; the Baltimore cabinetmakers in May asked for an increase of 25 per cent on existing prices; and a month later the Philadelphia cabinetmakers presented the same demand" (Commons: *History,* etc., Vol. I., p. 157).

In the same year, 1825, began a struggle for shorter hours. The first step was taken by the carpenters of Boston. The employers refused to yield to their demands and they went on strike; this involved about 600 carpenters. They resolved: "that 10 hours' faithful labor shall hereafter constitute a day's work." The employers, on the other hand, in the name of "morality and the welfare of society" declared that the hours of work from sunrise to sunset were recognized from time immemorial and must remain so forever. They maintained that in this struggle against the demand of the carpenters all the employers must be united, for if the carpenters were to win, the workers of all other industries throughout the United States would present the same demands. And the results, of course, would be "horrible." "Laziness" and "moral degradation" would immediately sweep the nation!

The carpenters lost the fight. Their efforts were crushed by the united power of the employers. But the 10-hour day slogan resounded in all corners of the country and gained new impetus. In 1827 the carpenters of Philadelphia went out for the 10-hour day. They appealed to the people, declaring that during the winter they had to go without work while in summer when the days were long they had to sweat in the heat of the sun 15 hours a day. This strike was a serious affair. About 600 carpenters were involved. A committee was elected to take care of the relief work. The employers advertised in the newspapers of other cities for scabs, promising them good jobs and good pay. The workers were again defeated, but the 10-hour movement did not end. On the contrary, it continued to spread, embracing ever larger and larger masses of skilled workers.

In 1832, in Boston, we come to another serious attempt to shorten the hours of work. This time the ship-carpenters were affected. They belonged to the Association of Mechanics, Farmers, and Other Workers of

New England, of which the Boston branch, in March of that year, adopted a resolution for the 10-hour day. In their demands the carpenters pointed out that they would agree to work longer hours, if the employers would pay them extra for the work done above 10 hours a day. Again the workers were confronted with the united power of the ruling class—merchants, shipowners, and contractors were as one in their efforts to crush the workers. The masters openly declared that they would use every possible means to crush the strike, which, they said, was directed against a century-old system of work—from sunrise to sunset. They raised a fund of $20,000, and also decided not to give work to any man who belonged to a trade union. They advertised in the newspapers for scabs, promising to pay them from $2 to $3 a day for three months, and to pay their railroad expenses to Boston and back home.

Once more the bourgeoisie was successful. The workers now realized with what powerful forces they had to contend in order to achieve their goal.

Beginning with 1835 a further wave of strikes for a 10-hour day swept the country. Although the Boston carpenters had been twice defeated in their efforts to shorten working hours, in 1835 they again declared a fight to attain their aim. The masons and stonecutters now also joined with them in appealing to the skilled workers of all other industries. They declared:

"We have been too long subjected to the odious, cruel, unjust and tyrannical system which compels the operative mechanic to exhaust his physical and mental powers. . . . We have rights, and we have duties to perform as American citizens and members of society, which forbids us to dispose of more than 10 hours for a day's work" (Commons: *History*, etc., Vol. I, p. 388).

The strikers elected a committee which visited Philadelphia, Newark and Paterson, N. J., and other cities. The committee was received with great enthusiasm in all the industrial centers; the workers promised them support and urged them to continue their struggle to a victorious conclusion. But after about seven months the strike was once more lost. "It is probable," writes Commons, "that the lack of a clearcut division between journeyman and master was responsible for its defeat."

We must not omit the fact that the clergy went hand in hand with the employers in crushing the efforts of the workers to improve their condition. Their work in the interests of the ruling class was habitually so open that in 1834 a trade union committee in Boston declared at a mass-meeting:

"The committee of arrangements have an apology to make to their fellow citizens. We regret to say that no one of our respected clergy are present. Applications having been made to 22 different societies for the use of a meeting-house on this day for trades unions, the doors of all were shut against us, and under the circumstances your committee felt a delicacy to apply to any clergyman to officiate at the table, lest he might consider it an affront" (Geo. E. McNeill: *The Labor Movement*, etc., p. 83).

In Philadelphia the movement for the 10-hour day ended with a *general* strike and victory for the workers. We may say that this was the first general strike in the United States. It was started by the coal heavers of Schuylkill Docks. The employers attempted to defeat the walk-out with the help of strikebreakers. There were open clashes between the workers and the strikebreakers. The bourgeoisie condemned the strikers but the workers supported them.

"Within the next few days most of the building trades, carpenters, bricklayers, plasterers, masons, hod-carriers and painters declared that they would not work more than 10 hours . . . then followed the leather dressers, blacksmiths, and plumbers with a similar declaration. The cordwainers, who were pieceworkers and who were among the first to strike, but for higher wages, now argued that they wanted higher rates so that they might be able to work fewer hours. The cigar makers, saddlers, and printers, who also were pieceworkers, advanced the same argument and presently declared their intentions to strike. The bakers joined in by demanding that baking on Saturday night and Sunday be discontinued, and the clerks asked that the stores be closed at early candlelight" (Commons: *History*, etc., Vol. I, p. 390).

A great demonstration was organized. Thousands of workers marched through the streets with fife, drum, and flags bearing the inscription "From 6 to 6."

"We marched to the public works," recorded John Ferral, "and the workmen joined in with us. . . . Employment ceased, business was at a standstill, shirt sleeves were rolled up, apron on, working tools in hand were the orders of the day. Had the cannon of an invading enemy belched forth its challenge on our soil, the freemen of Philadelphia could not have shown a greater ardor for the contest; the blood-sucking aristocracy, they alone stood aghast; terror stricken, they thought the day of retribution was come, but no vengeance was sought or inflicted by the people for the wrongs they had suffered from their enemies" (*Ibid.*, Vol. I, p. 391).

The Philadelphia *Gazette*, organ of the capitalists, wailed that "the times are completely out of joint . . . our streets and squares are crowded with an idle population. Some manifestations of violence have already taken place; and if the difference be not accommodated the excitement will probably be increased. Our buildings are at a stand, and business generally is considerably impeded" (*Ibid.*, Vol. I, pp. 390-391).

An organ of the New York plutocracy, the *Journal of Commerce*, hypocritically said that "what we object to is not the thing sought . . . but the means of attaining it." Of course, the capitalists would not have objected if the workers had been satisfied with talking about shorter hours and asking their employers for mercy. But as soon as they rose and declared themselves ready to enter a general struggle for their rights, the whole capitalist world condemned them and opened war upon them.

In spite of all difficulties, the workers of Philadelphia won their fight. They won, in the words of John Ferral, because they "were united and acted militantly." The victory of the Philadelphians gave a new impetus to the movement for shorter hours and soon it reached the smaller cities also, but we have no information as to its success in other places.

If 1835 was a banner year in the struggle for the 10-hour day, 1836 was noted for its great struggles for higher wages. Of the 69 strikes occurring in the latter year, only one was for a 10-hour day. The demand for higher wages was a daily question before the labor movement. Prices of food had almost doubled, while wages remained the same. A mass meeting held in New York on February 25, 1836, declared:

"It is evident to every intelligent person that for several years past, such has been the enormous increase in the rent of houses, and the extraordinary rise in the price of all the necessaries of life, that it is morally impossible for any honest mechanic or laborer . . . to support himself and family creditably" (*Ibid.*, p. 396).

As prices continued to go up, "the demand for higher wages came to be considered so much a matter of course," reports Edward B. Mittelman, "that when employers attempted to reduce them they precipitated the most bitter strikes of the time. Such was the tailors' strike in New York City out of which the General Trades' Union itself emerged badly crippled. Such also was the bookbinders' strike in Philadelphia, which won the support, not only of the union of which the society was a member, but of the working population throughout the country" (*Ibid.*, p. 399).

So far, we have spoken exclusively of the movement of the skilled workers, but we must not forget the strikes and revolts of the factory workers, the canal diggers, and railroad laborers.

"The movement among factory workers really dates from the summer of 1829, the first recorded strike of factory operatives having occurred at Paterson, N. J., in 1828" (*Ibid.*, p. 418).

The strikers showed great unity but they were crushed by the militia.

In the fall of 1829 the textile workers of Philadelphia and vicinity went out. They revolted against a wage cut of 28 per cent. The workers of other industries collected money for their relief. Nevertheless, the strikers were defeated.

In the period between 1829 and 1836 we find many strikes among the cotton mill workers along the Atlantic coast, especially in Pennsylvania and New Jersey. The majority of these strikes were only defensive. For instance, in March, 1835, in Schuylkill, Pa., the owners of one factory closed it and later reopened it inviting the workers back at a wage reduction of 25 per cent. The weavers refused the offer. The company brought in scabs under police protection, and the strike was lost.

LABOR ORGANIZATIONS AND THEIR STRUGGLES

The textile strike in Paterson, N. J., in 1835, was called mainly to shorten hours from 13 to 12 a day. The workers organized into the Paterson Association for the Protection of the Laboring Classes, and sent a committee to the employers for negotiations. But the latter refused to have anything to do with them. The strike followed. Two thousand wage workers, in 20 factories, left their jobs. Workers of other cities were appealed to for support.

"Two-thirds of the hands returned to work on factory time, not at 13½ hours a day as before, but at 12 hours for five days in the week and nine hours on Saturday. The employers yielded to a reduction of one and a half hours per day, and in doing so, broke the strike. Some still continued to hold out for an 11-hour day. But so far as the strike was concerned, it was practically over. Those that did not return to work were blacklisted, especially the children of the leaders" (*Ibid.,* p. 421).

The factory workers of New England also conducted serious fights with their employers. Strikes on a large scale occurred in Dover, N. H., and Lowell, Mass., attracting the attention of the whole labor movement. In December, 1828, 400 women workers of Dover left their jobs to defeat the efforts of the employers to reduce wages by 10 per cent. They also demanded a 10-hour day. We do not know how the strike ended; but five years later, in 1833, the women workers of Dover again walked out, and this time their army was composed of 800 operatives. This strike ended with the workers organizing a union. The employers saw the solidarity of their slaves and in taking them back they forced each applicant to sign an individual contract according to which she promised not to belong to any labor organization and agreed to work under such conditions and for such wages as the employer saw fit to grant.

The echo of the struggle of the Dover women reached the workers of Lowell, Mass., and in 1834 they also went out. Over 2,000 girls of the textile factories paraded through the streets and held mass meetings.

They formed a union which 2,500 of them joined. In the morning they issued an appeal in which they invited the workers of other industries to join them in the common struggle. On their part they promised not to go back to work until the reduction of wages was revoked and until every one of them was reinstated.

We cannot leave unmentioned the struggles of the workers on the railroads and canals. They were the most unskilled and most exploited section of the working class. Their army was composed almost exclusively of foreign-born, mainly Irishmen, who at that time were considered the most hard-worked slaves in America. The bourgeoisie liked to call the resistance of the workers "uprisings," and the press of the country called such workers "the dregs and scum of the old world."

These unskilled workers made from $10 to $12 a month during the summer, and during the winter they were glad to work for as little as

$5 a month. Others worked only for their board. We can imagine under what conditions those who had families to support were forced to live. They had no organization and the only means of defense accessible to them were "revolts" or strikes. In 1829 the workers on the Pennsylvania canal demanded a raise to $1 a day. When the employers refused, a clash occurred, and only the police were successful in vanquishing the enraged workers. In August of the same year the workers on the Baltimore and Ohio railroad revolted; one man was killed and a few wounded, and one building was destroyed. The militia was called to suppress the revolt. The railroad workers of Boston and Providence revolted in April, 1834, demanding higher wages. This strike was crushed by the army and many strikers were arrested. In the fall of the same year 300 Irish workers of the Washington railroad went on strike and it was said that a few of the contractors met their deaths in the course of the struggle. When 1,000 workers of the Chesapeake and Ohio canal quit their jobs in February, 1835, they were crushed by the army. The dock workers of New York struck for higher wages in 1836; as the police were not able to suppress the strikers, the cossacks were called in to do the job.

The end of the period of "prosperity" and great speculation was rapidly approaching. In 1837 a great economic crisis, much more widespread and severe than the crisis of 1819, descended upon the country. It was a panic in the real sense of the word.

"With the first descent of the panic the labor movement was crushed out of existence. The local societies, the city assemblies, the national federation of assemblies and locals, and the national trade unions disappeared. With them went their official organs, the newspapers they had started for purposes of agitation and for carrying news of interest to their members.

"It is hard to estimate how much the labor movement of this period really achieved. Nevertheless, it did leave footprints in the sand. After the disruption of the movement with the panic of 1837, the face of society had been largely transformed. Imprisonment for debt was no more. A mechanics' lien law was in existence in nearly every state in the union.... The common school was an established institution in nearly every state. The grotesque militia system had been abolished.... Property qualifications for voting and for office had almost completely disappeared...."

Of course, these great changes had not been brought about directly by the labor movement alone. There had also been very important economic, social and political factors working in the same direction.

"But the organized workers were the only ones that were publicly and energetically demanding these steps. They were strong enough to exert a great influence. No other force can begin to compete with the labor movement as a direct cause of these important steps. Is it, then, too much to say that this movement of the workers, measured by the impress it left, was the most important event in American history?" (Simons: *Loc. cit.*, pp. 186-188).

CHAPTER XII

The Labor Movement from 1837 to 1860

AFTER the panic of 1837 followed 15 years of hard times. With the revival of industry the prices of the necessaries of life rapidly increased but the employers did not hasten to raise the wages of the workers accordingly. This resulted in a new wave of trade union organization.

Immediately after the panic a new question confronted the American workers, the question of immigration. As soon as the army of unemployed in this country had disappeared, thousands of Europeans began to immigrate. During the 55 years from 1790 to 1845, only 1,000,000 "foreigners" came to this country, but in the 10 years between 1845 and 1855, about 3,000,000 entered. The previous immigrants had consisted mainly of farmers, who tried to secure land here, but after the crisis of 1837 the newcomers were mostly workers. Instead of scattering throughout the country, the majority of them settled in the industrial cities on the Atlantic coast. They were mostly unskilled laborers, cheap and appropriate raw material for the rapidly developing industry of the country.

The American-born workers began to look upon this rising tide of immigration with fear. The employers lured the Europeans here with promises of good jobs and good pay. But when they arrived, they were often used by the employers to reduce the wages of the American workers and to neutralize their struggles for better conditions. Often these unorganized immigrants, driven by starvation, agreed to work for less than the American-born workers. The Americans were therefore opposed to the importation of cheap labor and did their best to stop immigration. It is true that they struggled in vain. But they struggled, nevertheless, for it appeared to them that the foundation of all their troubles was these foreign-born workers. They failed to understand the capitalist system; they did not realize that these "foreigners" were absolutely necessary to the development of capitalism in America and that in spite of all opposition on the part of the skilled workers, immigration would continue. This opposition of the American-born workers to immigration has been an important factor in the whole history of the class struggle in America, beginning with the fifties of the nineteenth century. Even now a great section of American workers, because they have comparatively better positions than the foreign workers and are **members of the American Federation of Labor, are emphatically opposed** to immigration. In fact the craft unions of this country have never ceased to struggle against it.

The crisis of 1837 brought about a dissolution of some of the trade unions. Others turned to the coöperative movement to improve their conditions. First of all they formed coöperatives in the production field, and when these failed they started to work in the field of distribution. What was left of the labor movement after the crisis of 1837 up to 1850 lost all hope of gaining anything through militant trade unionism. It adopted the slogan that the worker must at the same time be an employer.

But after this great crisis began to fade from the horizon of American industry, at the end of the forties, the workers began again to form trade societies and trade unions for the defense of their daily interests.

"In the latter part of 1845 and the spring of 1846, immense mass meetings were held in Massachusetts, New York, and Pennsylvania. In Lowell, Mass., and Manchester, N. H., the town halls were crowded to their utmost capacity. The people seemed to be aroused from their apathy. . . . The papers made an active canvass of the towns for subscribers, publishing letters in which the conditions of labor were described . . ." (McNeill: *The Labor Movement: the Problem of To-day*, p. 105).

That the workers in this period faced great hardships we can see from the declaration of 20 New York mechanics, calling a mass meeting for July 16, 1845. We read in this declaration that in New York City alone there were 65,000 paupers, and in the entire state of New York one-sixth of the population was living on charity. The authors of the declaration emphasized the point that the wages of the workers were being continuously reduced, that thousands of workers were on the edge of starvation, and that the free workers of the northern states were living under far worse conditions than the Negro slaves of the South (*Ibid.*, p. 102).

It is hard to tell how widely the workers were organized in this period (1837 to 1860), but in every industrial center there were a number of fraternal and protective societies and local trade unions. For instance, when on June 6, 1850, the "industrial congress" met in New York there were 110 delegates from 55 trade societies and local unions.

The unions of the time were very careful in accepting new members. They protected their trades as they would their property. The constitutions of some of these organizations forbade the admission of any one who had not worked at the trade for at last three years. It is also important to point out that the unions of this period denied membership to women. True, not many unions were confronted with this problem in 1850, but those which included the printers, waiters, tailors, and shoemakers. In some of the constitutions there was a paragraph openly forbidding women workers to join the organization, with the exception of the members' wives or daughters.

The most important step made by the labor movement of the period was the formation of the New England Workingmen's Association, composed mainly of the unskilled and women workers. This association was a sort of continuation of the Association of Farmers, Mechanics, and Other Workers of New England which had existed before the crisis of 1837. The first convention of the New England Workingmen's Association was held on May 28, 1845. The preamble to its constitution pointed out that in the present system of society, labor is and must be a slave of capital, and that abolition of this inequality belongs to the worker and the worker alone. It declared that in association lay the strength of the workers, and that "the aim of our association is strength, strength for the benefit of humanity" (McNeill: *Loc. cit.,* p. 102).

Though this New England Workingmen's Association promised to accomplish a great deal, from the practical standpoint it achieved very little. At first it was hoped that the association would be an all-embracing organization and would undertake to defend the interests of the workers on the economic as well as on the political field. The convention of October 29, 1845, showed the organization in its true colors. The most important resolution it adopted declared that "the ballot box is the only effective means of defending the rights of the workers."

The trade unions of the fifties were mainly local organizations. Formation of national unions was slow. Such national unions as existed were founded rather to discuss trade questions than to unite the local unions for action. Struggles with the employers were left to the local organization. The Typographical Union was organized in 1850, the United Cigar Makers' Union in 1856. In the latter year also was launched the National Protective Association of the United States, composed of railroad workers. Other national unions which existed before the Civil War were the Hat Finishers' Association, Upholsterers' National Union, Plumbers' National Union, National Union of Building Trades, Mechanics' Trades Union of the United States, Lithographers' National Union, Painters' National Union, Cordwainers' National Union, and the National Union of Iron Molders. As to the activities of these unions very little information remains. Many of them existed only in name.

About this time there was an extensive movement toward the formation of "industrial congresses" on a national as well as on a state and local basis. The first of these "industrial congresses" was called jointly by the New England Workingmen's Association and the National Reform Association of New York. Even before the congress opened there appeared two different viewpoints. One was represented by Evans, Masquerier, and Bovay, who proposed to solve all problems through land reform, by taking the land out of the hands of speculators and capitalist companies and transferring it to those who worked on it. Another viewpoint was represented by well-known utopians such as Albert Brisbane,

Horace Greeley, and Robert Owen. The latter looked upon the congress as the beginning of the end of the class struggle. They were enthusiastic about the gathering and declared that at last the workers and the employers would join hands and thus usher in a new era of love and brotherhood. The employer would receive what "justly" belonged to him, and the worker would not be wronged because the employer would "justly" pay him for his honest labor!

But the followers of Owen and Brisbane were sadly disappointed when they saw, on one hand, that the congress was controlled by the exponents of land reform, and on the other—that the employers did not take part in the congress at all. Greeley lamented the fact, saying that the meeting was not a real "industrial congress" and that it represented only "the employed class, or those who labor for others" (Commons: *History*, etc., Vol. I, p. 549).

The congress took upon itself to unite "the farmers, workers, and mechanics" in order that these might be in a position to resist the united forces of the "rich, capitalists, and non-workers" who through their organization strive to get the fruits of the labor of others. It also condemned the factory system which undermines the energy of the workers from their very childhood and produces physical and mental wrecks.

In 1851 the industrial congress nominated a candidate for the presidency of the United States. In 1856 only 11 delegates attended its meeting. This meant that the congress was practically dead.

In the New York City industrial congress which first met in 1845, a heated discussion took place over the declaration of principles and constitution. The congress declared itself against the control of the government by capital, against monopolies, banking institutions, convict labor, and bourgeois newspapers. In the declaration of principles the delegates complained "that the hostility of the relations which now exist and of the constant tendency of these relations to increase the evils complained of" bring upon the "laboring classes" great "privations and sufferings," therefore, "we do hereby form ourselves into a permanent organization for *the purpose of devising means to reconcile the interests of labor and capital*—to secure to the laborer the full product of his toil—to promote *union,* harmony and brotherly feeling among all the workmen of whatever occupation—and to use all available means to promote their moral, intellectual and social elevation" (Commons: *History*, etc., Vol. I, p. 554).

A movement which had as its aim the establishment of harmony between the interests of labor and capital, interests that are opposed to each other, could have no future, and it soon dissolved in the class struggle. Nevertheless, these industrial congresses were quite an important phase of the labor movement in this period. They expressed, in a certain form, the efforts of the downtrodden class to get away from their burdensome conditions. Their significance lay also in the fact that they showed how hopeless must be the efforts of those who try to harmonize the interests of the oppressed with the interests of the oppressors, who instead of following the road of struggle run away from it and sing the song of class coöperation and community of class interests.

As always, the clergy of the period were on the side of the capitalists and exploiters and against the workers. Their loyalty to the ruling class was so brazen that it exhausted the patience of even religious workers. In the second New York industrial congress, which was held in 1847, the following resolution was proposed against the clergy:

"Resolved, that while we fully appreciate the labors of all in behalf of suffering humanity, we are constrained to declare, more in sorrow than in anger, that the great body of so-called Christian church and clergy of the present day are fearfully recreant to the high and responsible duties upon them. That they sustain the bloodstained banner of capital and are proud in their crusade against labor, and have themselves become the fiercest of the vampire brood that gorge upon the veins of honest industry and justice; therefore we warn them that . . . they must infuse into their preachings and practice more truth, justice, and regard for the rights of humanity" (McNeill: *Loc. cit.,* p. 116).

This resolution was rejected by a small majority only, after a long and heated discussion.

The 10-hour day remained one of the main demands of the labor movement of the forties and fifties. All attempts to shorten the hours of work through the legislatures brought no results. Begging for shorter hours failed absolutely. Then began anew the organized movement to gain the 10-hour day. The Association of Fall River Mechanics called a convention of all mechanics of New England to work out a plan for winning shorter hours. The meeting was held in October, 1844, and resulted in the formation of the Mechanics' Association of New England. In January, 1845, the Lowell Female Labor Reform Association was organized, which worked for the 10-hour day together with the New England Workingmen's Association.

On June 10, 1845, a great mass meeting was held in Pittsburgh, Pa., at which about 5,000 working people participated, among whom were many women. Soon after this meeting a great strike took place in which, it is said, 4,000 workers took part. The strike lasted for five weeks. The workers were defeated and compelled to go back under the old conditions.

The bourgeois politicians, on one hand frightened by the labor movement, and on the other hand anxious to get the votes of the workers, now began to give the wage-earners small crumbs from their well laden tables.

"That adroit master of political chicanery, President Van Buren," says Myers, "hastened to issue an executive order on April 10, 1840, directing the establishment of a 10-hour day, between April and September, in the navy yards. From the first day of October, until March 31st, the 'working hours will be from the rising to the setting of the sun'" (Myers: *History*, etc., Vol. II, p. 66).

The legislature of New Hampshire passed a 10-hour law in 1847, but allowed employers to make special contracts with the workers who agreed to work longer hours. The employers knew how to use this privilege, and practically nullified the 10-hour law, forcing the workers to work as before, 12½ hours daily.

In March, 1848, the Pennsylvania legislature adopted a 10-hour law for cotton, wool, paper, and flax factories. The employers immediately declared a lock-out and about 2,000 workers found themselves on the streets idle. The masters yielded only when the workers agreed to take a 19 per cent reduction in wages. In several other states 10-hour laws were passed, but they did little good. Hours were actually shortened only where the workers were strongly unionized and could compel the employers to yield to their demands.

It would be hard to find a branch of industry in which there were no strikes during this period. As the years 1853-1854 were years of so-called "prosperity" many of these strikes were successful. The workers succeeded in winning higher wages.

Once more, also, the workers had to face prosecution in the bourgeois courts. Just as in the thirties, the employers again in the fifties used every agency they could lay hands on to annihilate the trade unions on the grounds that they were conspiracies against society, the established order, and the church.

The employers of Baltimore appealed to the most prominent lawyers in the city for an opinion on whether the trade unions were not really conspiracies against society. These faithful agents of the bourgeoisie found, of course, that unions for the purpose of raising wages or improving the conditions of their members were conspiracies against social welfare. This declaration was effectively used by the employers to frighten the workers away from unionism and to defeat their efforts to improve conditions. On July 10, 1854, four compositors of the Philadelphia *Register* were brought before the court, charged with conspiracy to raise their wages by picketing and persuading other workers not to take their places. In 1859, four glass workers were arrested in Glassboro, N. J., for going on strike. They also were charged with conspiracy to raise their wages (*Ibid.*, pp. 611-612).

The era of prosperity was coming to an end, and with it the end of the labor movement of the period from 1837 to 1860. The crisis of 1857 was casting its shadow ahead, and by the end of 1854 from one-half to two-thirds of the mechanics in the different trades were unemployed. With the setting in of the crisis, strikes disappeared also. Only the unemployed formed some sort of weak labor movement. Driven by starvation in large cities, they held demonstrations and threatened their

THE LABOR MOVEMENT

enemies whom they accused of having seized all the wealth of the country and of throwing them out of the factories.

"Mass meetings and parades of the unemployed became common. Banners bearing such legends as the following were displayed: 'Political knaves and speculators have robbed us of our bread. They offer us soup. Behold your work! This you have done in the name of God and Liberty. We have borne the stripes of men, we now claim the stars'" (Commons: *History,* etc., Vol. I, p. 619).

Hardly had this third severe industrial depression passed when a new storm arose in the country, the Civil War. With the beginning of the Civil War in 1861 this period of American labor was closed.

CHAPTER XIII

Era of Utopian Socialism

WHILE the mechanics and workers were organizing into trade unions and fighting the employers for the necessaries of life, there were people who did not belong to the working class, but who prophesied a new and better life. These were the utopian socialists or "dreamers." Their minds were with the bourgeoisie, but their hearts were with the workers. They declared themselves new Messiahs, possessed of great wisdom, who would lead not only the workers but all classes out of hardship and travail. They said that it was only necessary that their gospel be accepted—by the workers as well as by the employers—and a new sun would shine upon the world; the struggle between the workers and capitalists would disappear, and without any pain or suffering, we would step into a paradise on earth!

Owen Greeley, and Brisbane were the main apostles of this new "gospel" in America. Let us see who furnished these people with such "high" ideas and such "great" wisdom.

Utopian socialism, as well as scientific socialism or communism, had its beginning in Europe and only later was transferred to the American continent. It was a product of the development of capitalism of those days. The walls of feudalism had in some places already been destroyed, in other places they were shaking. The population was being concentrated into cities and towns; factories were being constructed one after another. A new age was dawning—an age of machinery and mass production. Agriculture was being pushed into the background, the city was conquering the village.

"With constantly increasing swiftness," says Engels, "the splitting-up of society into large capitalists and non-possessing proletarians went on. Between these, instead of the former stable middleclass, an unstable mass of artisans and small shopkeepers, the most fluctuating portion of the population, now led a precarious existence.

"The new mode of production was, as yet, only at the beginning of its period of ascent; as yet it was the normal, regular method of production—the only one possible under existing conditions. Nevertheless, even then it was producing crying social abuses—the herding together of a homeless population in the worst quarters of the large towns; the loosening of all traditional moral bonds, of patriarchal subordination, of family relations; overwork, especially of women and children, to a frightful extent; complete demoralization of the working-class, suddenly flung into altogether new conditions, from the country into the town, from agriculture into modern industry, from stable conditions of existence into insecure ones that changed from day to day" (Engels: *Socialism, Utopian and Scientific*, pp. 66-67).

These distressing social conditions could not continue without arousing a deal of sympathy in the hearts of "enlightened" men and women of the middle or petty bourgeois class. They were shocked at the state of affairs and decried them as leading humanity to destruction. Therefore, they sought means of remedying the evils they condemned. There appeared in Europe three great "apostles," noble in their desires and full of the milk of human kindness; their feelings were much more exalted than their knowledge of the situation. These "apostles" were Saint-Simon, Charles Fourier, and Robert Owen. Although they did not reach their goal and although their efforts proved futile, these men nevertheless left their impress on the history of humanity. Their names will always remain connected with the efforts of the masses to emancipate themselves from oppression and exploitation—not as having given a plan by which this emancipation may be brought about, but as a warning to the masses not to follow their plan, for their idea can lead the working class only to defeat and hopelessness.

Saint-Simon was a whole-hearted exponent of the new bourgeois order. From the bottom of his heart he hated the old aristocracy—the feudal lords, the lackeys of monarchy, those who lived on rents. He called them parasites who fed on the products of others. Saint-Simon condemned them and declared them ineligible to rule humanity. He saw salvation in a new society composed of "working people," but these "working people," in his mind, were far from being the workers and handicraftsmen alone. The bankers, merchants, and manufacturers, that is, all of the capitalist class, were also considered by Saint-Simon as part of the working people. Upon poor people he looked with contempt and, therefore, he would not even entertain the idea that these people would save humanity. He pointed to the French Revolution as an example of the rule of the poor, where in order to protect themselves from their enemies the workers (the poor) had been compelled to employ terror.

"Then, who was to lead and command? According to Saint-Simon, science and industry, both united by a new religious bond, destined to restore that unity of religious ideas which had been lost since the time of the Reformation—a necessarily mystic and rigidly hierarchic 'new Christianity.' But science, that was the scholars; and industry, that was in the first place, the working bourgeois, manufacturers, merchants, bankers. These bourgeois were, certainly, intended by Saint Simon to transform themselves into a kind of public officials, of social trustees; but they were still to hold, vis-a-vis of the workers, a commanding and economically privileged position. The bankers especially were to be called upon to direct the whole of social production by the regulation of credit" (*Ibid.*, pp. 60-61).

The workers were and must remain only workers and the bourgeoisie must be the leaders and rulers of society. Therefore, this new order of

Saint-Simon was a pure and simple capitalist order. What he wanted was that in this system there should be no fights and struggles. The workers and the capitalists should be imbued with the spirit of a "new religion" or "reconstructed" Christianity, which had been "toned down" to a certain extent by the era of the Reformation. Then—according to Saint-Simon—peace and brotherhood would dawn between the classes; there would be plenty of everything for all and want and hardship would be ended. The capitalists would not take everything for themselves; they would not forget the poor under their heel. But the latter would also not seek too much for themselves; they would love and respect their rulers and their leaders from the bottom of their hearts. Such was the system developed by that great utopian, Saint-Simon.

Another great utopian of the period was Charles Fourier, born in 1772 in the little town of Besançon, France. With his literary work and with his ideas for the salvation of humanity, Fourier came into notice at the beginning of the nineteenth century, about 1808. He was much farther advanced than Saint-Simon, as far as knowledge and criticism of the capitalist system was concerned.

But did Fourier advocate the class struggle, the victory of the workers over the capitalists, the abolition of all classes? No, he also advocated social peace, peace of all people and of all classes. It appeared to him that classes are necessary, that they always have been and always will remain. The task is not to abolish the classes, but to establish order in production. The class struggle does not lead toward such order. Therefore Fourier invents, and in detail develops, a plan according to which society should be organized. That plan is as follows: Let us say that there are 2,000 people (we are not interested in their social divisions or in their class standing, for we need all of them). They form an association or "phalanx." This phalanx is a social unit. It occupies a large tract of land, constructs for itself factories, dwellings, and various other buildings. However, this phalanx is not a commune. The composition of its membership is as follows:

"Seven-eighths of the members of a phalanx are farmers and mechanics, the balance being composed of capitalists, men of science, and artists. The property of the phalanx is represented by shares of stock, but it is not necessary for every member to hold stock, nor need a stockholder be a member. The phalanx keeps accounts with every member, crediting him for his services at rates fixed by the council. . . . At the end of the year an inventory is taken, and the profits are divided as follows:

"Five-twelfths to labor.
"Four-twelfths to capital.
"Three-twelfths to skill or talent.

"No jealousy or antagonism is created by this division of profits, as there are no fixed classes in the phalanx. The same member holds one or more shares in the phalanx, does work in one or more groups, and develops special skill in one or more branches of industry, and thus shares in all these classes of profits.

On the other hand, the capitalist is either satisfied with the mere dividends on his investment, or he adds to it such income as he may earn by applying his labor or talents to any useful pursuit, while the poor man works and earns more or less according to his preference for leisure or enjoyment" (Hillquit: *History of Socialism in the United States*, p. 84).

We see, then, that there would be classes, there would be workers who would live by their labor, and capitalists who would live on their income from invested capital. But, of course, there would be no class struggle! In other words, there would be a bourgeois society, but a harmonious one. Fourier thought that the people would accept this idea, that it was only necessary to make a beginning, to establish one phalanx, the example of which would spread over the world and everybody would organize phalanxes on the same basis. Thus would society be reorganized and an end put to all the horrible conditions produced by the present lack of order.

The third great utopian was Robert Owen, who was born in 1771 in Scotland. He was a highly talented man. He even succeeded in becoming rich. At the age of 30 he was a manufacturer.

"Robert Owen had adopted the teaching of the materialistic philosophers: that man's character is the product, on the one hand, of heredity, on the other, of the environment of the individual during his lifetime, and especially during his period of development" (Engels: *Socialism*, etc., pp. 67-68).

What we need, therefore, is to make good conditions and we will have good people. But how can we attain this goal? We have a certain society composed of certain classes; on one hand, we have hardships and lack of necessaries of life, while on the other hand we have wealth and an oversupply of everything. On one hand we have workers, and on the other we have—employers.

Did Robert Owen advocate for the workers the road of the class struggle to overthrow the rule of the bourgeoisie, to establish themselves as a ruling class? No. Owen also advocated class solidarity. According to his idea, if only all of the people of all classes would understand the importance of the brotherhood of the classes, it would be very easy peacefully to reconstruct society on a communist basis and the classes and the class struggle would peacefully disappear. We needed only an example and the mass would, of course, understand and follow. Therefore Owen took upon himself the responsibility of furnishing such an example to the world in order to teach them by practical means how to administer their affairs and live in peace and happiness.

His first experiment was made in Scotland. In 1800 we find him in a little village called New Lanark, where there was one large cotton mill and about 2,500 workers and their families.

"The work was so hard, and the pay so small, that none but the lowest stratum of adult workingmen would take employment at the mills. The village was dirty and the population given to brutality, drunkenness, thievery, and sexual excesses, and was deep in debt to the petty village usurer, the tavern-keeper, and storekeeper" (Morris Hillquit: *Loc. cit.,* p. 53).

Owen went into partnership with a few other stockholders and bought the factory from its owner, Dale, for £60,000.

Then he began to put his theory into practice. He eliminated all the old store-keepers and established his own stores where goods were sold at cost. Breweries and saloons were moved outside of the town; the streets were cleaned and new homes were built for the workers. He did away with punishment, replacing it with friendly advice. He shortened working hours and raised wages. He abolished child labor and established free public schools, and thus

"a population, originally consisting of the most diverse and, for the most part, very demoralized elements, a population that gradually grew to 2,500, he turned into a model colony, in which drunkenness, police, magistrates, lawsuits, poor laws, charity, were unknown. And all this simply by placing the people in conditions worthy of human beings, and especially by carefully bringing up the rising generation" (Engels: *Socialism,* etc., pp. 68-69).

But Owen was still dissatisfied. It appeared to him that the workers were still his slaves and did not yet enjoy conditions under which they could fully develop.

"'And yet, the working part of this population of 2,500 persons was daily producing as much real wealth for society as, less than half a century before, it would have required the working part of a population of 600,000 to create. I asked myself what became of the difference between the wealth consumed by 2,500 persons and that which would have been consumed by 600,000?'

"The answer was clear. It had been used to pay the proprietors of the establishment 5 per cent on the capital they had laid out, in addition to over £300,000 clear profit. . . . 'And yet this new power was the creation of the working-classes.' To them, therefore, the fruits of this new power belonged. The newly-created gigantic productive forces, hitherto used only to enrich individuals and to enslave the masses, offered to Owen the foundations for a reconstruction of society; they were destined, as the common property of all, to be worked for the common good of all" (*Ibid.,* pp. 70-71).

As a philanthropist, Owen became well-known throughout Europe. But as soon as he began to advance the theory of communism, everything changed. He found the whole capitalist world against him. Finally his efforts in New Lanark failed. In 1824 he came to America and began to organize communes in the middle west. But even here his efforts were futile. He lost his wealth and did not succeed in convincing society to follow his lead. The class struggle did not disappear and his lofty dreams came to an end. Finally, Owen himself saw the truth.

"Banished from official society, with a conspiracy of silence against him in the press, ruined by his unsuccessful communist experiments in America, in which he sacrificed all his fortune, he turned directly to the working-class and continued working in their midst for 30 years. Every social movement, every real advance in England on behalf of the workers links itself on to the name of Robert Owen" (*Ibid.*, pp. 72-73).

As these utopian dreams of improving the world reached the shores of America, attempts were made to give them root on this soil. Here were great tracts of land where it was possible to put into practice all the dreams and ideas of the great utopians of the age. Most far-reaching of these attempts were those by the followers of Fourier and Owen. Though these efforts did not play a very great rôle, the agitation for their ideas was extensive before the Civil War. When Owen himself came to America, in 1824, he bought a tract of 30,000 acres in Indiana along with the necessary buildings and invited to his assistance William Mac-Lure, a very rich man. The latter was considered a scientist and brought with him many well-known educators. Owen appealed to the people of all classes to join his commune. Within six weeks after the appeal was made, 800 persons had responded. Many of them were workers, but the leading rôle was played by intellectuals who were caught by the high-sounding ideas on the reconstruction of mankind. The name given this colony was New Harmony.

Toward the end of 1824 Owen went to Cincinnati and made a great impression upon the followers of the Swedenborgian church and their spiritual leader, Daniel Roe. About 100 families accepted Owen's ideas and decided to put into practice his widely advertised "communism." A large plot of land was acquired at Yellow Springs and a colony was established. The majority of its members came from the well-to-do.

The leader of the third colony of Owenites was Frances Wright. This colony was established near Memphis, Tenn., under the name of Nashoba. The members were mainly Negro slaves purchased by Frances Wright herself. There were also a few whites. She dreamed of establishing a school in which the children of the blacks and whites would study happily together. The affairs of the colony would be conducted by philanthropists who joined her in her efforts to "save" the Negro race. The Nashoba colony existed for only one year.

There were other Owenite colonies, the majority of which were organized between 1825 and 1830. The life of most of them was very short, from one to three years.

The ideas of Fourier were put into practice in America by such utopians as Albert Brisbane, son of a rich landowner, and Horace Greeley, editor of the *New Yorker* and later of the *Tribune*. Thus the ideas of Fourier found support amongst well-to-do intellectuals, saturated to the marrow with bourgeois ideology, but in their hearts sympathizing with the poor and oppressed. An extensive discussion was carried on over Fourierism and the defenders of the system proved themselves well fitted for their rôle. Brisbane and Greeley immediately gained many recruits in the ranks of the intellectuals. In 1834 Brisbane established a monthly journal, *Phalanx,* and when that magazine died the *Harbinger* was born, the pages of which were filled with articles by utopian intellectuals.

Many of these colonies or phalanxes of the Fourierists were established in New York, Massachusetts, New Jersey, Pennsylvania, Ohio, Illinois, Indiana, Wisconsin, and Michigan. A wide-spread and enthusiastic movement developed. But the life of these settlements was just as short and as tragic as the life of the Owenite communes.

The causes of the failure of utopian socialism are not far to seek. First of all, it was based on the wrong idea. Second, it was led by people for whom socialism was not necessary because they had a comfortable life without it. If they made these attempts, they did so either out of curiosity or because they sympathized with the poor and wanted to help them in their own way. Instead of propagating the idea that the workers should conquer the world and its wealth, science, and inventions, they offered the workers the delusion of running away from this world by forming separate groups and sects. According to their philosophy these groups, separately and independently of one another, composed of various classes of people, would establish a new order, a new life, a new economic, political, and social system. The result was that these dreams of the utopians dashed themselves against the wall of reality and broke.

Though the utopian movement was not a strictly working class development, nevertheless it left its mark on the workers. The labor movement of this period had accepted the capitalist system and sought only to improve the conditions of the poor through strikes, trade unions, begging, and protesting. Utopian socialism proposed to "reconstruct" society, leaving it with exploiters and exploited, capitalists and proletarians, with various classes, but without a class struggle.

CHAPTER XIV

THE WORKERS IN THE CIVIL WAR

THE tradition still prevails in this country that the Civil War was waged only in behalf of emancipation of the slaves, that the North fought only to liberate the Negroes, that the Republican Party advocated emancipation while the Democratic Party stood for the maintenance of slavery, and that Abraham Lincoln desired only freedom for the black man. Such explanations of the Civil War are false and misleading. The causes of the American Civil War were economic and political—a conflict between the interests of the northern capitalists and the interests of the land and slave owners of the South. It was a struggle between two social systems, one based on slavery and the other on free labor.

We have already seen that chattel slavery did not become firmly established in the northern states because there was no fertile soil for its existence. The labor of chattel slaves was not needed by industry and commerce. The capitalist industrial system required a different kind of slavery, namely, wage slavery—it required "free" laborers. Negro slavery fitted the needs of the South in raising cotton, rice, and tobacco. Therefore, as far back as the eighteenth century Negro slavery was concentrated in the South, in the agricultural states of the country, while wage slavery arose and developed in the industrial and commercial states, in the North. Both of these forms of slavery responded very well to the economic interests of these two sections of the ruling class.

There was no conflict between North and South over chattel slavery for a long time, because there was a sufficient field for all. There was not even any talk in either section of the country about the abolition of slavery. The bourgeoisie of New England whole-heartedly approved slavery in the South. If there were any organized opponents of chattel slavery they were found mainly in the South itself. In Boston, for instance, mobs infuriated by the bourgeois newspapers and agitators often attacked and sometimes murdered speakers against slavery.

But, as we have seen, with the nineteenth century the age of machinery and invention advanced. In the northern states industry developed, capitalism spread its wings ever wider and wider, conquering new territories. About the middle of the nineteenth century the northern and middle states were one powerful social unit, having fully developed organs of bourgeois rule.

116   HISTORY OF THE AMERICAN WORKING CLASS

On the other hand, the invention of the cotton gin had made cotton growing a very profitable occupation. The southern planters therefore industriously increased their land, pushing farther and farther north, seizing new territories, extending the production of cotton, and also slavery.

Sooner or later these two economic systems had to clash, regardless of the welfare of the Negro slaves of the South or the wage slaves of the North. A struggle developed for state power. The northern capitalists wanted to have the state power in their hands in order to protect their class interests—to defend manufactures by raising the tariff on imported goods. At the same time the southern masters saw that a high tariff was against their own best interests, and they were therefore opposed to any tariff. For half a century the struggle between the North and South for state power went on. The United States Senate became the center of that struggle for the reason that in the upper house of Congress, which is composed of two senators from each state, a balance of forces was to be maintained. Before a new state entered the union there was always a bitter struggle as to whether it would be a slave or a free state. Vermont was accepted into the union in 1791 as a free state; Kentucky in 1792 as a slave state; Tennessee in 1796 as a slave state; Ohio in 1802 as a free state; Louisiana in 1812 as a slave state; Indiana, 1816, free state; Mississippi, 1817, slave; Illinois, 1818, free; Alabama, 1819, slave; Missouri, 1819, slave; Maine, 1819, free; Arkansas, 1836, slave; and Michigan, 1837, free. Thus in the Senate there was continuously maintained an exact balance of forces, until there were 13 free states and 13 slave-holding states.

"Then the South woke up in wild alarm," says Newton. "The slave territory was becoming exhausted, whilst the North had still immense tracts stretching away to the Northwest, out of which it could carve new states, and so obtain the preponderance of power. To prevent this the southerners assisted Texas to shake off the Spanish dominion and to establish itself as an independent republic. Then they demanded its admission to the union. Eight months after the admission of Florida as a slave state in 1845 they succeeded, and so obtained a decided advantage. Then the North was aroused and the Mexican war was provoked as a result. It ended in large accessions of territory to the United States, and eventually the organization of New Mexico and California as territories. Arizona, now lying exactly between them, was not then in existence as a separate state. In 1846 the free men secured the admission of Iowa to the union and Wisconsin in 1848, and so for a time once more restored the precarious balance of power" (Newton: *Captain John Brown of Harper's Ferry*, pp. 13-14).

But immediately a struggle developed over New Mexico and California. The North wanted to take them into the union as free states, while the South demanded that they be admitted as slave states. The question was solved by the 1850 agreement: California was accepted as a free state, New Mexico and Utah were left as territories, and a law was passed according to which the northern states agreed to help capture run-away slaves for the masters of the South and deliver them back to bondage. About 20,000 run-away Negroes in the North found themselves in danger of being hunted down and delivered to their owners.

In 1854 two new territories—Nebraska and Kansas—were organized and it was decided to leave it to the people of these territories to decide for themselves whether they wanted to join the union as free or as slave states. Agitation and organization were carried on in both North and South to send as many people as possible into the territories in order that they might have a majority when the vote was taken. This inevitably led to chaos and armed conflicts. Many lost their lives in the struggle. In the congressional elections of 1854 the Democratic party, representing the southern interests, was entirely defeated. The bourgeoisie of the North was convinced that the decisive hour had come. The ruling class of the South understood it as well.

In 1856 the northern bourgeoisie organized the Republican party, around which all the capitalist interests gathered. In the elections of 1860 the Republican party won and Abraham Lincoln was made president. The ruling class of the South now clearly saw that the governmental power had slipped completely from its hands. It was clear to that class that the final solution of the question depended upon the strength of arms: upon which section of the country or which group of the propertied class could win in open warfare. The attempt to solve the question by peaceful means came to an end. Now the cannon began to speak, and the Civil War had begun.

On February 4, 1861, the southern states held a convention at Montgomery, Alabama, at which it was decided to secede from the Union. The convention also laid a foundation for the government of the Confederate States by adopting a constitution which openly recognized slavery as an institution and forbade all legislation which might in any way impair the right of property in Negro slaves. This action of the South was an open challenge to the North.

"Already during 1856-1860," Marx wrote in 1861, "the political leaders, jurists, moralists and theologians of the slaveholder party, did not try so much to prove that Negro slavery is justified as rather that the color is immaterial in the matter and that the working class is everywhere created for slavery.

"Thus one sees that the war of the Southern Confederacy is, in the exact sense of the word, a war of conquest for the expansion and perpetuation of slavery. . . .

"With the relinquishing of its plan of conquest, the Southern Confederacy would renounce its vitality and the purpose of secession. Secession, to be sure, only took place because the transformation of border states and territories into slave states no longer seemed attainable within the Union. On the other hand, with a peaceful surrender of the disputed territory to the Southern Confederacy, the North would abandon more than three-fourths of the entire territory of the United States to the slave republic. The North would lose the Gulf of Mexico entirely, the Atlantic Ocean with the exception of the narrow strip of the Bay Penobscott up to the Bay of Delaware and would even cut itself off from the Pacific Ocean. Missouri, Kansas, New Mexico, Arkansas and Texas would draw California after them, the great agricultural states in the basin between the Rocky Mountains and the Alleghenies, in the valleys of the Mississippi, Missouri, and Ohio, incapable of wresting the mouth of the Mississippi from the hands of the stronger hostile slave republic in the South, would be forced by their economic interests to secede from the North and join the Southern Confederacy. These northwestern states would, in their turn, draw after them in the same whirlwind of secession all northern states situated further east with the exception of, let us say, the states of New England.

"Thus, in fact, no dissolution of the Union would take place but a *reorganization* of the same, *a reorganization on the basis of slavery*, under the acknowledged control of the slave-holding oligarchy. The plan of such a reorganization has been openly proclaimed at the Montgomery Convention by the leading speakers of the South, setting forth the paragraph of the new constitution which allows every state of the old Union to join the new Confederacy. The slave system would infect the entire Union. In the northern states, where Negro slavery is practically unfeasible, the white working class would gradually be pressed down to the level of helotism. This corresponds entirely to the loudly proclaimed principle that only certain races are capable of freedom; and just as the actual labor in the South is the lot of the Negro, so in the North it is the lot of the German and Irishman or of their direct descendants" (Karl Marx: *The Civil War in the United States*, reprinted in *The Communist*, May, 1927, from the *Presse*, Vienna, Nov. 7, 1861).

Was the Republican party fighting for the abolition of slavery? No. Until the middle of the war the Republican party never even mentioned a desire to abolish slavery.

Was Lincoln fighting for the abolition of slavery? No. The Republican party time and again had declared that it had no desire to abolish slavery, that it did not want to "mix" in the affairs of the South. Lincoln's position was the same. What he wanted was to leave slavery alone where it existed, but not to allow it to spread further North and so endanger the supremacy of the northern capitalists.

Away back in 1837, when Congress adopted a resolution on the slavery question, it had appeared to Lincoln that the resolution interfered with slavery to a certain extent. With his friend Stone, Lincoln emphatically protested against the resolution and against interference on the part of Congress. In their protest they declared that:

"They believe that the institution of slavery is founded on both injustice and bad policy, but that the promulgation of abolition doctrines tends rather to increase than abate its evils.

"They believe that the Congress of the United States has no power under the constitution to interfere with the institution of slavery in the different states" (Moore: *Lincoln—Addresses and Letters*, p. 15).

Coming nearer to the Civil War, in 1845 some of the members of the "Third Party" of Putnam County, Illinois, wanted to take a firmer stand against slavery than that taken by the party. On October 3 Lincoln wrote to his friend W. Durley, saying:

"I hold it to be a paramount duty of us in the free states, due to the union of the states, and perhaps to liberty itself (paradox though it may seem), to let the slavery of the other states alone; while, on the other hand, I hold it to be equally clear that we should never knowingly lend ourselves, directly or indirectly, to prevent that slavery from dying a natural death—to find new places for it to live in, when it can no longer exist in the old" (*Ibid.*, p. 37).

Here Lincoln clearly expressed the attitude of the northern bourgeoisie of not interfering with slavery where it already existed and of not allowing it to develop in any state where it did not already exist.

In his answer to Senator Douglas Lincoln wrote on October 16, 1854:

"Before proceeding let me say that I think I have no prejudice against the southern people. They are just what we would be in their situation. If slavery did not now exist among them, they would not introduce it. If slavery did now exist among us, we should not instantly give it up. This I believe of the masses north and south. . . .

"When southern people tell us they are no more responsible for the origin of slavery than we are, I acknowledge the fact. When it is said that the institution exists, and that it is very difficult to get rid of it in any satisfactory way, I can understand and appreciate the saying. I surely will not blame them for not doing what I should not know how to do myself. . . . Free them (slaves), and make them politically and socially our equals? My own feeling will not admit of this, and if mine would, we well know that those of the great mass of whites will not. . . . We cannot then make them (slaves) equals . . ." (*Ibid.*, pp. 56-57).

On August 24, 1855, Lincoln said: "I now do no more than oppose the extension of slavery . . ." (*Ibid.*, p. 63).

"I will say here . . . that I have no purpose, directly or indirectly, to interfere with the institution of slavery in the states where it exists. I believe I have no lawful right to do so, and I have no inclination to do so. I have no purpose to introduce political and social equality between the white and the black race. There is a physical difference between the two, which, in my judgment, will probably forever forbid their living together on the footing of perfect equality; and inasmuch as it becomes a necessity that there must be a difference, I, as well as Judge Douglas, am in favor of the race to which I belong, having the superior position" (*Ibid.*, p. 87).

Shortly before the war began Lincoln in his New York speech, on February 27, 1860, not only washed his hands of any desire to abolish slavery, but emphatically declared that the whole Republican party had nothing to do with the abolition movement or with the agitation amongst the slaves to revolt against their masters.

He said:

"You charge that we stir up insurrections among your slaves. We deny it; and what is your proof? Harper's Ferry! John Brown! John Brown was no Republican; and you have failed to implicate a single Republican in his Harper's Ferry enterprise. . . . Republican doctrines and declarations are accompanied with a continual protest against any interference whatever with your slaves, or with you about your slaves . . ." (*Ibid.*, pp. 127-128).

In his inauguration speech as President, on March 4, 1861, when the southern states had already decided to secede from the union and when the guns were already being prepared for open struggle, Lincoln once more expressed his attitude against the freeing of slaves in the southern states and swore that he would faithfully carry out the laws pertaining to capturing fugitive slaves and returning them to their masters. Citing the clause in the constitution which stated that a fugitive servant must be caught and sent back to his master, he pledged himself to carry out this clause with every means at his disposal (*Ibid.*, pp. 158-159).

As we have already seen, the main object of the bourgeoisie of the northern states was to maintain in their hands a strong federal government which would be able to protect their interests. In the midst of the Civil War Lincoln publicly declared that he was not interested in ending slavery, but that all of his efforts were directed towards the preservation of the Union. In his letter to Horace Greeley, who criticized him for catering to the slave-owners and for not making energetic enough efforts to carry on the war against them, Lincoln said on August 22, 1862:

"I would save the union. I would save it in the shortest way under the constitution. The sooner the national authority can be restored, the nearer the union will be 'the union as it was.' If there be those who would not save the union unless they could at the same time destroy slavery, I do not agree with them. My paramount object in this struggle is to save the union, and is not either to save or to destroy slavery. If I could save the union without freeing any slave, I would do it; if I could save it by freeing all the slaves, I would do it; if I could save it by freeing some and leaving others alone, I would also do that. What I do about slavery and the colored race, I do because I believe it helps to save the union; and what I forbear, I forbear because I do not believe it would help to save the union" (*Ibid.*, p. 173).

On August 30, 1861, General John Charles Fremont, who had been sent to Missouri, issued a proclamation, declaring that all the property of all Missourians who had taken up or would take up arms against the United States was or should be confiscated and their slaves declared freemen.

"On September 2 Lincoln wrote to Fremont that the confiscation of slaves would alarm the Southern Union men and, perhaps, ruin the Union prospects in Kentucky. He asked Fremont to modify his proclamation 'as of your own motion.' As Fremont refused to do this, Lincoln modified the proclamation himself on September 11, and some time thereafter removed Fremont to another sphere of activity" (Edward Channing: *Loc. cit.*, Vol. VI, p. 530).

On December 1, 1862, in the midst of the conflict, instead of issuing an emancipation proclamation, Lincoln urged Congress to propose to the masters of the southern states to accept "compensated emancipation" (Moore: *Loc. cit.*, pp. 178-182).

THE WORKERS IN THE CIVIL WAR

The emancipation proclamation was not issued by Lincoln or by his government at the outset of the war. It was delayed for two years. Only in September, 1862, did Lincoln declare that on February 1, 1863, he would free the slaves in those states which would not lay down their arms and submit to the northern army. In this way he gave the masters of the southern states an opportunity to accept peace and keep their Negroes in bondage. But as the slave-owners did not accept this proposal, the emancipation proclamation was issued on the date set. Only now were the Negroes invited to join the northern army. Thus for two years the blood of the workers and farmers was being shed on the field of battle and Lincoln did not invite the Negroes of the South to take up arms for their freedom, nor did he promise them that freedom. On the contrary, even in the emancipation proclamation itself Lincoln urged "the people so declared to be free to abstain from all violence, unless in necessary self-defense." And therefore "I recommend to them that in all cases when allowed they labor faithfully for reasonable wages" (*Ibid.*, pp. 184-186).

Undoubtedly, the freeing of the slaves stirred the masses of both the black and the white population, and the northern cause immediately won many new recruits for fighting the war until the southern ruling class was defeated. Many Negroes joined the northern army. This is admitted by Lincoln in a letter to James C. Conkling, August 26, 1863. In this letter Lincoln said that his generals stated that the issuance of the emancipation proclamation strengthened the front, and some of the battles would have been lost if the Negro soldiers had not flocked into the northern army (*Ibid.*, pp. 198-199).

Let Lincoln himself speak on the question. In a letter to A. G. Hodges, April 4, 1864, he declared:

"When, early in the war, General Fremont attempted military emancipation, I forbade it, because I did not then think it an indispensable necessity. When a little later, General Cameron, the Secretary of War, suggested the arming of the blacks, I objected because I did not think it an indispensable necessity. When, still later, General Hunter attempted military emancipation I again forbade it, because I did not yet think the indispensable necessity had come. When, in March and May and July, 1862, I made earnest and successive appeals to the border states to favor compensated emancipation, I believed the indispensable necessity for military emancipation and arming the blacks would come, unless averted by that measure. They declined the proposition, and I was, in my best judgment, driven to the alternative of either surrendering the Union, and with it the constitution, or laying strong hand upon the colored element. I chose the latter. In choosing it, I hoped for greater gain than loss; but of this I was not entirely confident. More than a year of trial now shows no loss by it in our foreign relations, none in our home popular sentiment, none in our white military force—no loss by it anyhow or anywhere. On the contrary, it shows a gain of quite 130,000 soldiers, seamen, and laborers.

These are palpable facts, about which, as facts, there can be no caviling. We have the men, and we could not have had them without the measure. I claim not to have controlled events, but confess plainly that events have controlled me (*Ibid.*, pp. 205-206).

We see therefore that Lincoln was emphatically opposed to emancipating the slaves and maintained this position until war strategy compelled him to change it. There can be no doubt that if the emancipation proclamation had been issued at the beginning of the war, and the Negroes had been called upon to join the northern army, the war would not have lasted so long or cost so much in human blood and life. But all during the first two years Lincoln was opposed to emancipation and told the Negroes to remain faithful to their masters. If any one was guilty of shedding so much innocent blood, and destroying so many lives of workers and farmers unnecessarily, it was the northern government under Lincoln.

We have dwelt extensively upon the attitude of Lincoln during the Civil War for the reason that the bourgeois historians and the trade union and socialist leaders almost worship Lincoln as the emancipator of the slaves. The Negro masses are made to believe that the representative of the northern bourgeoisie led them like a Moses, from the land of bondage to the land of freedom. But it is not so. If events had developed the way Lincoln desired the world would never have heard of the emancipation proclamation.

Without doubt Lincoln repeatedly declared that he was at heart opposed to Negro slavery. But that only makes matters worse. It shows that Lincoln acted not the way his conscience dictated, but the way the interests of the northern bourgeoisie directed.

Now, what was the attitude of the masses toward slavery and the Civil War?

First of all, let us consider the attitude of the Negroes themselves. On the eve of the Civil War there were in the United States 4,442,000 Negro slaves. The majority of them were so backward, so ignorant and so oppressed, that they did not even dream of living as free people. They worked hard and bowed low before their masters.

But every oppressed and enslaved class has its vanguard, its most advanced and class-conscious elements, who feel and understand the oppression, who see the injustice imposed upon their class, and therefore seek to bring about their own emancipation and that of their downtrodden brethren. The Negroes of the South also had their vanguard. There were slaves who waged both underground and open struggle with the slave-owners. In this struggle many of them lost their lives, others lost their health. New fighters took the place of the fallen. They communicated with the whites who were fighting slavery, and carried on a concerted struggle. Thousands of slaves ran away through secret

THE WORKERS IN THE CIVIL WAR

channels into the northern states or Canada. Some became desperate and attacked their masters unexpectedly and in this way gained their revenge. The masters, after crushing these revolts, mercilessly murdered the rebels. Here is one example:

"The leader of the insurrection was Nat Turner, a slave living in Southampton County, Va. Turner could read and write . . . on the night of August 22, 1831, just before the break of day Turner, with 20 or 30 followers, began an attack on the whites living near Cross Keys. The house of a widow was first visited, and the family of five whites murdered. A neighbor hearing screams hurried to the scene to find all five dead, and on his way home was met by his Negro boy, who told him that his own wife and child had been butchered. The family of Turner's master furnished the next victims, and ere the day closed 55 persons—men, women and children—had been killed.

". . . But he, too, was taken and executed. A hundred are said to have been shot and 19 executed.

"How far reaching the insurrection might be no one knew, and in the excited state of the people new plots and conspiracies were believed to exist in North Carolina. According to one rumor, credited for a while, Wilmington was burnt, half its inhabitants killed, and the Negroes of several counties were on the march for Raleigh. The wildest excitement prevailed. The people of Fayetteville and Raleigh flew to arms; troops were hurried to Newburne. Scores of free Negroes were arrested, examined and many ordered to leave the state, and numbers of slaves were executed or sold and sent south" (McMaster: *History*, etc., Vol. VI, pp. 73-74).

The ruling class was in continuous fear of such revolts. The masters felt guilty and feared that they might have to pay with their lives for the injustice done to their chattels. This was another important reason why the southern ruling class engaged in mortal combat for control of the federal government, for only a well-centralized national government, under its absolute control, would be able to hold millions of slaves under the iron heel of their masters.

When the war began only a limited number of the laboring people approved of it and sympathized with the northern cause. But toward the middle of the conflict, especially after the emancipation proclamation was issued in 1863, that number increased to a great army and turned the scales of war in favor of the North. Word of the freedom which was promised to the slaves by the northern bourgeoisie spread throughout the country, and as Lincoln reported, nearly 130,000 Negroes joined the northern ranks.

As to the white population of the South, not all of them made their living out of the sweat and blood of Negro slaves. Comparatively speaking, only a handful of slave-owners monopolized the labor of the Negroes. Not more than half a million out of the 9,000,000 whites in the South maintained slaves. Of this half a million many had from two to four slaves. Those who owned as many as 100 slaves each numbered only about 10,000 and were the real masters of the country. In 1850 the situation was as follows:

Owners having 1 slave each	68,820
Owners having 1 slave and less than 5	105,683
Owners having 5 slaves and less than 10	80,765
Owners having 10 slaves and less than 20	54,595
Owners having 20 slaves and less than 50	29,733
Owners having 50 slaves and less than 100	6,196
Owners having 100 slaves and less than 200	1,479
Owners having 200 slaves and less than 300	187
Owners having 300 slaves and less than 500	56
Owners having 500 slaves and less than 1,000	9
Owners having 1,000 and more	2

Total number of slaves 3,200,000; owners 347,525 (H. R. Helper: *The Impending Crisis*, p. 146).

The price of slaves increased from $150 in 1808 to $4,000 before the Civil War. Only the richest of the landowners were able to purchase them. This handful of powerful slave-owners was heart and soul for the war.

But what about the 8,000,000 or 9,000,000 whites who had no slaves, who were small farmers, handicraftsmen, small business men, or workers? The ruling class held them in such contempt that in its press or in conversation it forgot to consider them as part of the people of the South. Economically they were poor, politically they had no rights. Helper says:

". . . They have never yet had any part or lot in framing the laws under which they live. There is no legislation except for the benefit of slavery, and slaveholders. As a general rule, poor white persons are regarded with less esteem and attention than Negroes, and though the condition of the latter is wretched beyond description, vast numbers of the former are infinitely worse off. A cunningly devised mockery of freedom is guaranteed to them, and that is all. To all intents and purposes they are disfranchised, and outlawed, and the only privilege extended to them is a shallow and circumscribed participation in the political movements that usher slaveholders into office" (Helper: *Ibid.*, p. 42).

An attempt was made to introduce industry, to build railroads, in order to supply the poor with work. But it was impossible for industry to develop side by side with slavery. Hence the condition of the masses of the white people grew worse and worse. The ruling class of the South was afraid that the white masses, like the blacks, might revolt against their rule.

As far back as 1850 *De Bow's Review* pointed out that these masses of the poor were beginning to feel their burden of oppression and exploitation, and that they seriously threatened "our institutions" (*De Bow's Review* (1850), Vol. II, p. 25).

It is true that the majority of these millions of whites looked upon the Negroes with great contempt and hated them; but the fact remains that their economic interests were not connected with and did not depend

THE WORKERS IN THE CIVIL WAR

upon the maintenance of slavery. Therefore they did not consider the war as their own war. On the other hand, there were many whites in the South who understood the injustice of slavery and labored for its abolition. On the eve of the Civil War there were tens if not hundreds of anti-slavery societies. These opponents of slavery also carried on their work against the war of the ruling class.

This fundamental division, these differences in the economic interests of various classes and sections were, it seems, the main factor which brought about the defeat of the South in the Civil War. The longer the war lasted, the greater apathy toward it overtook these masses.

No more uniform was the attitude of the population of the northern and middle states toward the war. The bourgeoisie introduced terror against those who opposed it. Freedom of assembly and speech was abolished. The "loyal" citizens were only those who supported the war and kept their mouths shut about the graft and corruption of the bourgeoisie which through theft and cheating enriched itself enormously. Those who dared to criticize Lincoln's government paid dearly.

It is well to note that during the whole half century preceding the Civil War the northern bourgeoisie and its government persecuted and terrorized those who dared to criticize slavery either by written or spoken word. Especially did the ruling class of New England terrorize the opponents of slavery. The reason for this attitude of the bourgeoisie can be found in the fact that after the Revolution hundreds of textile factories were established in New England, the owners of which were anxious to get the cotton of the South raised by Negro slaves. In this instance the interests of the cotton manufacturers of the Norh coincided with the interests of the slave-owners of the South, and therefore both of these sections of the ruling class supported slavery. Only when the factory system reached a very high point of development, and besides the textile industry many other industries had developed in New England, did the interests of the bourgeoisie of New England begin to conflict with the interests of the southern masters. Only then did the northern bourgeoisie turn its back upon its former allies, the slave-owners of the South.

Anti-slavery societies were cruelly persecuted in the northern and middle states. Editors of anti-slavery newspapers were attacked by incited mobs; mass meetings against slavery were dispersed by government authorities; anti-slavery speakers were attacked and beaten. Lovejoy, that great opponent of slavery, was attacked and murdered in 1837 in St. Louis.

On the other hand, of course, there were men and women who hated slavery from the bottom of their hearts and worked faithfully for its abolition. People of this kind were found in both sections of the country—North and South. They organized anti-slavery societies, wrote to the newspapers against slavery, secretly helped the slaves to run away from their masters. One of the most noteworthy of these was John Brown.

John Brown was born at Torrington, Conn., May 9, 1800, and later moved to Ohio. He hated slavery intensely, and set for himself the aim of emancipation. In 1855, with four of his sons, Brown moved to Kansas territory and settled at Pottawattomie with the idea of carrying on a struggle against slavery and preventing its advocates from capturing the territory for the South. All who were sincere abolitionists rallied around John Brown as their leader.

The coming of John Brown to Pottawattomie aroused the ire of the anti-abolitionists and they decided immediately to get rid of him. But they knew that Brown and his followers kept their muskets always ready to repulse enemies Therefore, under the leadership of three of Brown's neighbors—Doyles, Wilkinson, and Sherman—the anti-abolitionists organized a gang on the Missouri boundary for the purpose of attacking and making an end of Brown and his plans. Brown called together his followers and decided at the least suspicion of danger to capture Doyles, Wilkinson, and Sherman, to try them by lynch law and, if necessary, execute them on the spot. A few days later the pro-slaveryites invaded Brown's home, insulted his daughter, and left the message with her: "Tell your men that if they do not get away from here immediately we will come to-morrow and kill them." That evening Brown and his followers captured the three conspirators and executed them.

From then on John Brown made energetic preparations for armed emancipation of the slaves. In 1858 he went to Canada with the idea of getting assistance from the fugitive Negroes who, it is said, numbered 40,000. In one of the Negro churches he called a secret meeting and there proposed a draft of the constitution according to which the freed Negroes would govern themselves. Newton says that Brown's "object was not to run away with slaves to the North, but to emancipate them in the slave-holding states, and by military organization and defensive operations in the mountains to maintain them in freedom until the United States legislature should repeal the slavery laws" (*Ibid.*, pp. 108-109).

John Brown opposed chattel slavery only. He was in full agreement with the system of wage slavery, which oppressed the workers of the northern states. The bourgeois state was his own state. In his proposed constitution he emphasized the following:

"The foregoing articles shall not be construed so as in any way to encourage the overthrow of any state government, or of the general government of the United States; and we look to no dissolution of the union, but simply to amendment and repeal; and our flag shall be the same that our fathers fought under in the Revolution" (*Ibid.*, p. 110).

THE WORKERS IN THE CIVIL WAR

For this armed emancipation of the slaves, John Brown prepared seriously, whole-heartedly, and with great pride. After the conference in Canada he wrote to his friend at Sanborn:

"I have only had this one opportunity in a life of nearly 60 years. . . . God has honored but comparatively a very small part of mankind with any possible chance for such mighty and soul-satisfying rewards. . . . I expect nothing but to endure hardness, but I expect to effect a mighty conquest, even though it be like the last victory of Samson" (*Ibid,* p. 111).

This victory was to begin at Harper's Ferry, a Virginia town lying near the boundary of Maryland, where the Potomac and Shannon Rivers meet. There the United States government had an arsenal, which Brown hoped to capture to supply arms for his further activity. Sunday night, October 16, 1859, Captain Brown, with 16 of his white followers and five Negroes, moved on Harper's Ferry. They captured the bridge and four of the buildings. At dawn the news spread that the town had been taken by armed abolitionists. Immediately the "loyal" citizens armed themselves, invited the state militia, and attacked the handful of abolitionists. A tragic struggle began. In a few hours about 1,500 anti-abolitionists were in action.

"Of Brown's total little force of 22 men 10 were killed, seven were captured, tried and hanged, and only five escaped. On the other side six were killed and eight wounded" (*Ibid.,* p. 163).

In the hands of his enemies Captain Brown exclaimed:

"I have failed. I have failed. You may dispose of me very easily—I am nearly disposed of now; but this question is still to be settled—this Negro question, I mean. The end of that is not yet" (*Ibid.,* pp. 163-164).

On the way to the gallows Brown did not show any distress or emotion and told his executioners:

"I, John Brown, am now quite *certain* that the crimes of this *guilty land* will never be purged away but with *blood.* I had, as I now think vainly, flattered myself that without very much bloodshed it might be done" (*Ibid.,* p. 261).

This deed of John Brown and his comrades did not achieve the desired result. They did not know how to analyze and weigh the conditions of the times. They based their hope on the assumption that millions of slaves, hearing that their emancipators were coming, would suddenly revolt against their masters, take up arms, and end their slavery. They also thought that thousands of fugitive Negroes from Canada and the northern states would come to their assistance. They believed that it was enough to make a beginning and the echo of the heroic struggle would reach every slave and make him fight for his freedom. This was a grave mistake. Brown and his followers did not understand that the southern masters had enslaved the Negroes not only physically but mentally as well.

Nevertheless, the struggle at Harper's Ferry struck great fear into the plutocracy of the South.

"Meanwhile all Virginia was in alarm. Her proud slave-holders and their boasted constitution had felt the impact of a handful of determined men, and both rocked under the blow. Business was suspended, 4,000 militia were kept under arms, slaves were sold 'South' in hundreds, at an estimated loss of $10,000,000, prominent slave-holders slept in fresh houses each night, and the whole state remained under a sense of insecurity, timorousness, and nervous dread until their few prisoners were no longer above ground" (*Ibid.*, p. 171).

The northern bourgeoisie, who were themselves ready to wrest state power by force of arms from the slave-owners of the South, condemned Captain Brown and called him a lunatic. They did not like him because he went directly to the slaves, and set for himself the goal of emancipating them.

What was the attitude of the workers of the North toward the Civil War? The great mass of factory hands, the unorganized, unskilled wage slaves, were indifferent to the conflict. But the skilled workers—the tailors, shoemakers, carpenters, blacksmiths—who were organized in trade societies or trade unions, were divided on the question. Some of them condemned slavery and the approaching conflict, while others condemned the abolitionists. As far back as 1846 a convention of workers of New England adopted the following resolution:

"Whereas there are at the present time 3,000,000 of our brothers and sisters groaning in chains on southern plantations; and whereas we wish not only to be consistent but to secure to all others those rights and privileges for which we are contending ourselves; therefore be it

"Resolved that while we honor and respect our forefathers for the noble manner in which they resisted British oppression, we, their descendants, will never be guilty of the glaring inconsistency of taking up arms to shoot and to stab those who use the same means to accomplish the same objects.

"Resolved that while we are willing to pledge ourselves to use all the means in our power, consistent with our principles, to put down wars, insurrections, and mobs, and to protect all men from the evils of the same, we will not take up arms to sustain the Southern slaveholder in robbing one-fifth of our countrymen of labor.

"Resolved, that we recommend our brethren to speak in thundered tones, both as associations and as individuals, and to let it no longer be said that northern laborers, while they are contending for their rights, are a standing army to keep three millions of their brethren and sisters in bondage at the point of the bayonet" (McNeill: *Loc. cit.*, p. 107).

The national convention of trade unions which met in Philadelphia in February, 1861, adopted a resolution supporting the northern cause. On the other hand, a mass meeting of workers in Boston condemned the abolitionists; they also urged "our brethren in the South to deal with their traitors at home." They said that the war was the work "of politicians and office seekers" who had "deceived and betrayed the people" (Oneal: *Loc. cit.*, p. 171).

As far as the socialist movement was concerned, which was very weak at that time and existed mostly among the German workers, it supported the abolition movement. When the war broke out, "each of the various groups of socialist organizations then in existence furnished its full quota of soldiers for the union army. . . . In fact, the war had thinned the ranks of the incipient socialist organizations to such an extent as to paralyze their activity, and it was not before 1867 that the movement commenced to recover" (Hillquit: *Loc. cit.,* pp. 171-172).

The ruling class of the South was very careful to protect their sons from losing their lives in the war. The Confederate Congress passed a law according to which a slave-owner who had 20 or more slaves was exempted from military service. Later the number of slaves which afforded exemption was reduced to 10 or more. Those who owned many slaves divided them among their sons and in this way protected the latter from war duty.

The northern bourgeoisie could not get sufficient volunteers, and a compulsory military service law was enacted. But, of course, this law did not affect the bourgeoisie, for the law exempted every one from military duties who could pay a $300 fine. The sons of the rich could easily pay these $300, while to the workers and poor farmers this sum was a wall over which they could not climb. In many places the masses of the poor saw this great injustice imposed upon them and revolted. Lincoln's government resorted to arms to put down the revolts. For instance, such an uprising took place in New York City.

"From the start the police had met the riotous masses with terrible brutality, using their clubs indiscriminately. The rage of the people would certainly not have reached the proportions it did if they had not been so fiendishly treated by the police. . . . But the terrible treatment of the masses, and the bloodshed, first by the police, then by the military summoned from Fort Hamilton, West Point, and other outlying garrisons, drove the masses far beyond the original scope of the movement. On the West Side barricades were erected, whereupon the soldiers fired volleys into the crowd and dispersed them by shells. The police ordered to attack the people were told to make no arrests; the military were under like instructions, whoever came in their way was clubbed or shot down. The soldiers fired so recklessly that they even hit policemen.

"The disturbance lasted from Monday until Friday. More than 50 buildings were burned. The loss in property was estimated at $1,200,000. The number of persons killed by the police and the militia was variously estimated at from 400 or 500 to 1,200. As the bodies of the dead were in most cases removed by their relatives, the exact number could not be ascertained" (Schlueter: *Lincoln, Labor and Slavery,* pp. 206-207).

On the other hand, to the northern bourgeoisie the Civil War opened a new era of unheard-of profits and graft.

"The capitalists abundantly proved their devout patriotism by making tremendous fortunes from the necessities of that great crisis. They unloaded upon the government at ten times the cost of manufacture quantities of munitions of war—munitions so frequently worthless that they often had to be thrown away after their purchase. They supplied shoddy uniforms and blankets and wretched shoes; food of so deleterious a quality that it was a fertile cause of epidemics of fevers and of numberless deaths; they impressed, by force of corruption, worn-out, disintegrating hulks into service as army and naval transports. Not a single possibility of profit was there in which the most glaring frauds were not committed. By a series of disingenuous measures the banks plundered the Treasury and people and caused their banknotes to be exempt from taxation. The merchants defrauded the government out of millions of dollars by bribing custom house officers to connive at undervaluations of imports."

Theft became so open and reached such a degree that Congress was forced to appoint an investigating committee.

"The chairman of this committee, Representative C. H. Van Wyck, of New York, after summarizing the testimony in a speech in the House on February 23, 1863, passionately exclaimed: 'The starving, penniless man who steals a loaf of bread to save life you incarcerate in a dungeon; but the army of magnificent highwaymen who steal by tens of thousands from the people, go unwhipped of justice and are suffered to enjoy the fruits of their crimes. It has been so with former administrations; unfortunately it is so with this'" (Myers: *History*, etc., Vol. II, pp. 127-130).

The capitalists found in Europe some old, useless "Hall's carbines." They brought them to this country and sold them to the government for $22.50 each. "It was found that their mechanism was so faulty that they would shoot off the thumbs of the very soldiers using them." This criminal theft was performed by the "patriots" of the North who organized so-called "defense committees" to fight "traitors" of the country! J. Pierpont Morgan was the "king" of this corruption, and the Civil War meant the beginning of his billions (*Ibid.*, pp. 295-296).

The merchants collected broken and useless ships and sold them to the government for army service at high prices. The investigation in 1863 showed that in this way the government was "cheated out of at least $25,000,000" (*Ibid.*, p. 293).

Government bonds were another great source of corruption and profits. Through influence of the banking interests laws were enacted which allowed the bankers

"to get an annual payment from the government of 6 per cent interest in gold on the government bonds that they bought. They could then deposit those same bonds with the government, and issue their own bank notes against 90 per cent of the bonds deposited. They drew interest from the government on the deposited bonds, and at the same time charged borrowers an exorbitant rate of interest for the use of the bank notes, which passed as currency.

"It is by this system of double interest that they were able to sweep into their coffers hundreds upon hundreds of millions of dollars, not a dollar of which did they earn, and all of which was sweated out of the adversities of the people of the United States. From 1863 to 1878 alone the government paid out to national banks as interest on bonds the enormous sum of $252,837,556.77. On the other hand, the banks were entirely relieved from paying taxes; they secured the passage of a law exempting government bonds from taxation. Armies were being slaughtered and legions of homes desolated, but it was a rich and safe time for the bankers; a very common occurrence was it for banks to declare dividends of 20, 40, and sometimes 100 per cent" (*Ibid.*, pp. 300-301).

"Never before," says Professor Ely, "was there in this country such a sharp contrast between wealth and poverty" (Ely: *Loc. cit.*, p. 61). To the bourgeoisie the war meant great prosperity while to the workers and farmers it brought only bloodshed and poverty.

The Civil War in America did not pass without making a great impression upon the workers of Europe also. They had heard of the millions of Negro slaves in America and of their sufferings. The struggle between South and North soon appeared to them as a war purely for the freedom of these slaves.

The attitude of the working class of England toward the northern cause will always remain as a wonderful example of class solidarity. The ruling class of England always sympathized with the South and when the Civil War cut down the importation of cotton from the South, forcing the British cotton factories to close, they openly began to talk about extending help to the Confederate States. By the end of 1862 recognition of the South was only a question of time. But suddenly a mighty voice of protest on the part of the workers swept over Great Britain against the contemplated assistance of the English ruling class to the southern slave-holders. The trade unions organized mighty protest meetings and demonstrations in all the industrial centers, condemning the attitude of the government and pledging their support to the North. When at the end of September, 1862, Lincoln announced that he would issue an emancipation proclamation in case the southern states would not lay down their arms, great mass meetings were held in London, Sheffield, Manchester and other cities to greet this announcement of the northern government and to denounce slavery as a greatest curse upon humanity.

The revolutionary communist movement of the entire world, led by Marx and Engels, sided with the northern cause, without, of course, approving the specific policies of Lincoln's government, which, especially in the beginning of the Civil War, were wavering and disgraceful. In fact, Marx repeatedly criticized the northern government for catering to the Southern slave-holders or to their sympathizers in the North and for not taking determined, energetic steps to crush the revolt, for not immediately freeing the slaves and thus enlisting them in the cause of the North. But this criticism of the vacillation of Lincoln's government would not deter the great communist leaders from whole-heartedly supporting the northern cause. On October 29, 1862, Marx wrote:

"Like others, I naturally see that which is repulsive in the form of the Yankee movement; but I find the reason for it in the nature of a 'bourgeois' democracy. Nevertheless, the events there are world upheaving. .... The anger with which the southerners receive Lincoln's acts proves their importance. Lincoln's acts all have the appearance of illiberal stipulated conditions which an attorney presents to an opponent. This, however, does not hinder their historic content."

The communists looked upon the Civil War as historically a great step forward. The victory of the bourgeois republic over the slave-oligarchy of the South, the destruction of the social system based upon slave labor, was a historical necessity to the forward march of the social revolution. Slave labor is not and cannot be the bearer of a new society, a society without classes, without exploitation and oppression. To bring about such a change is the mission of free labor, the proletariat.

In this great struggle of the northern bourgeois republic against the slave-oligarchy of the South no sincere opponent of slavery could remain neutral. Especially after the Emancipation Proclamation was issued and after about 150,000 Negroes had joined the northern army, the issue was a clear and definite class issue: If the South won, slavery would be perpetuated in the South and it would tend to reduce the standard of the proletariat of the North to the same level. On the other hand, if the North won, slavery would be abolished and the system based upon slavery would be destroyed root and branch. Therefore, the support of the North in its war against the slave-holders of the South did not in any way mean an endorsement of the bourgeois republic as a form of government acceptable by the working class as its own, or an endorsement of the bougeois system for which the North stood.

The most active element in the European labor movement, energetically stirring the masses in favor of the North, were the communists led by Marx and Engels. It was Marx and his comrades who started the movement of mobilizing a protest of the English working class against the attitude of the government. Marx called upon his friend, George Eccarius, the leading member of the London Trades Council, to make a motion in that body for the holding of a mass demonstration of organized workers of London and for issuing an appeal to the organized workers of other industrial centers to take similar steps.

The General Council of the First International sent congratulations to the American people upon the reëlection of President Lincoln, on December 23, 1864. This historic document, expressing the attitude of revolutionary section of the working class of Europe toward the Civil War, reads as follows:

"We congratulate the American people on your reëlection by a large majority. If resistance to the slave power were the reserved watchword upon your first election, the triumphant war-cry of your reëlection is 'death to slavery'. From the commencement of the titanic American strife the workingmen of Europe felt instinctively that the star-spangled banner carried the destiny of their class.

"The contest for the territories which opened the dire epopee, was it not to decide whether the virgin soil of immense tracts should be wedded to the labor of the emigrant, or prostituted by the tramp of the slave-holder? When an oligarchy of three hundred thousand slave-holders dare to inscribe, for the first time in the history of the world, slavery on the banner of armed revolt; when on the very spots where hardly a century ago the idea of one great republic had first sprung up, whence the first declaration of the rights of man were issued, and the first impulses given to the European revolution of the eighteenth century; when on those very spots counter-revolution, with systematic thoroughness gloried in rescinding 'the ideas entertained at the time of the formation of the Old Constitution' and maintained slavery to be a beneficent institution, indeed the only solution of the great problem of the relation of Capital to Labor and cynically proclaimed property in man the cornerstone of the new edifice; then the working classes of Europe understood at once, even before the frantic partisanship of the upper classes for the Confederate gentry had given its dismal warning, that the slave-holders' rebellion was to sound the tocsin for a general holy crusade of property against labor, and that for the men of labor, with their hopes for the future, even their past conquests were at stake in that tremendous conflict on the other side of the Atlantic.

"Everywhere they bore, therefore, patiently, the hardships imposed upon them by the cotton crisis, opposed enthusiastically the pro-slavery intervention importunities of their 'betters' and from most parts of Europe contributed their quota of blood to the good cause. While the workingmen, the true political power of the North, allowed slavery to defile their own republic, while before the Negro, mastered and sold without his concurrence, they boasted in the highest prerogative of the white-skinned laborer to sell himself and choose his own master, they were unable to attain the true freedom of labor, or to support their European brethren in their struggle for emancipation; but this barrier to progress has been swept off by the red sea of civil war.

"The workingmen of Europe feel sure that as the American war of Independence initiated a new era of ascendency for the middle class, so the American anti-slavery war will do for the working classes. They consider it an earnest of the epoch to come, that it fell to the lot of Abraham Lincoln, the single-minded son of the working class, to lead his country through the matchless struggle for the rescue of an enchained race and the reconstruction of a social work."

It seems that Marx, who wrote this letter to Lincoln, overestimated the immediate effects of the Civil War upon the working class. Later on he wrote:

"The American Civil War brought in its train a colossal national debt, and with it pressure of taxes, the rise of the vilest financial aristocracy, the squandering of a huge part of the public land on speculative companies for the exploitation of the railways, mines, and, in brief, the most rapid centralization of capital. The great republic has, therefore, ceased to be the promised land of the emigrant laborers (Marx: *Capital,* Vol. I, p. 847).

In the declaration of the General Council of the First International we also see that Lincoln is classed as a "son of the working class," which he was not. He was a "representative of the lower middle class, known in Europe as the petit bourgeoisie, which in conjunction with the farmers constituted the majority of the inhabitants of the United States at this time. He championed the interests of this class and could not rise above its opinions" (Schlueter: *Loc. cit.*, p. 11).

It was not a question of Lincoln personally or of his government. This was a question of a gigantic struggle of two different social systems and the victory of the North was in the line of progress, therefore the class conscious workers all over the world were on its side as against the cause of slave-holders of the South.

Those who to-day attempt to make Lincoln a great champion of freedom for the slaves or a defender of the rights of workers are misleading the workers. We saw that he issued the Emancipation Proclamation only when the strategy of the struggle with the South demanded it. And as for his attitude toward the workers, he did not defend their rights in the North. It is true that in his statement on March 21, 1864, in accepting membership in the Republican Workingmen's Club of New York, he condemned those who tried to "place capital on an equal footing with, if not above, labor, in the structure of government." It is also true that he praised the international solidarity of the workers, saying: "The strongest bond of sympathy, outside of the family relation, should be one uniting all working people, of all nations, tongues and kindred." But these expressions were only so many words having nothing to do with the actual treatment of the workers of the North in the hands of Lincoln's government. He, probably more than any other representative of the bourgeoisie, understood at that time the importance of the support of the workers for the cause of the North in the great conflict and therefore was ready to do his best to get this support. Similarly, Woodrow Wilson, in his efforts to draw the support of the workers to the World War, sent congratulations to the St. Paul convention of the American Federation of Labor, writing to Gompers:

"Please convey to the 38th annual convention of the American Federation of Labor my congratulations upon the patriotic support which the members of your organization have given to the war program of the nation in the past year, not only in the trenches, and on the battlefield where so many of our younger men are now in uniform, but equally in the factories and the shipyards and the workshops of the country where the army is supported and supplied by the loyal industry of your skilled craftsmen" (American Federation of Labor: *History, Encyclopedia, Reference Book*, Vol. I, p. 71).

And again in his message to the American Alliance for Labor and Democracy, a chauvinist organization formed by Gompers with the aid of pro-war socialists, he exclaimed:

"I myself have had sympathy with the fears of the workers of the United States; for the tendency of war is toward reaction, and too often military necessities have been made an excuse for the destruction of laboriously erected industrial and social standards" (*Ibid.*, p. 72).

Lincoln's bourgeois government did not shrink from using force and terror to crush the strikes of the workers or their protests against the increase of prices or against the draft law. Strikers were considered traitors. In the New York and Massachusetts legislatures it was proposed to make the trade unions illegal organizations. Only a strong protest on the part of the workers prevented the enactment of a law outlawing labor organizations.

CHAPTER XV

Economic Development After the Civil War

The southern states were defeated in the Civil War. Economic destruction in the South was so great that it took decades to recuperate. The mode of living had to be reconstructed on a new basis. In place of big plantations cultivated by slaves, came the bourgeois system in agriculture with its modern machinery driven by steam and electricity. The northern capitalists, victorious in the war, pressed the population of the South to the utmost, on one hand to increase their war spoils, and on the other to put fear into the hearts of their opponents and show the world that from then on they would rule supreme, unchallenged. In his book, *Reconstruction in Mississippi,* James W. Garner describes as follows the post-war conditions of that state:

"The people were generally impoverished, the farms had gone to waste, the fences having been destroyed by the armies, or having decayed from neglect; the fields were covered with weeds and bushes; farm implements and tools were gone, so that there were barely enough farm animals to meet the demands of agriculture; business was at a standstill; banks and commercial agencies had either suspended or closed on account of insolvency; the currency was in a wretched condition; . . . there was no railway or postal system worth speaking of; only here and there a newspaper running; the labor system in vogue since the establishment of the colonies was completely overturned; . . . worse than all this was the fact that about one-third of the white breadwinners of the state had either been sacrificed in the contest or were disabled for life, so that they could no longer be considered as factors in the work of economic organization. . . . The number of dependent orphans alone was estimated at 10,000" (p. 122).

There can be no doubt that the burden of this terrible destruction was thrown on the shoulders of the workers and poor farmers. None of the masters in whose interests the war was waged starved or went naked. They immediately came to an understanding with the capitalists of the North.

Economic conditions in the North after the war were entirely different from those in the South. Amid the war a great economic development was taking place—old enterprises increased enormously in value and in size, and new ones were born. The capitalist class grew in size and power.

The war ended officially in August, 1866. Now the northern bourgeoisie had the whole country in its hands. Now industry, commerce, banks, state power, press, schools, and churches—all were under its control. The bourgeoisie was at last "almighty."

"Indeed," says Lippincott, "the decade following the close of the Civil War marks the beginning of one of the greatest industrial eras of all times. Even the most enthusiastic word painters of former times failed to foresee the magnitude of coming economic achievements. With their limited vision it was not possible to forecast the rapid growth of population, the opening of many new resources, the appearance of hundreds of new industries, the unusual development of business enterprise, and the great increase of wealth. Nor was it possible to appreciate the significance of the powerful economic forces that lay beneath these changes" (Lippincott: *Loc. cit.*, p. 275).

The short period of the last four decades of the 19th century, 1860-1900, brought forth such great changes on this continent, the industrial development was so vast and so all-embracing, that it surprised the old world and the latter began to look with fear upon the rise of its new competitor.

There are two fundamental factors which determine the degree of economic development of every country; namely, the supply of cheap labor-power, and raw material. Cheap labor-power was supplied to the factories by women, children, and immigrants, and America has always had enormous and easily accessible deposits of raw materials. After the Civil War the extractive industries developed by leaps and bounds. In the five-year period from 1881 to 1885 the total yearly value of mineral products amounted to $426,175,600. During the five years from 1896 to 1900 the annual value of mineral products increased to $827,742,700.

The growth of manufactures is shown by the following table:

GROWTH OF MANUFACTURES, 1860-1900

Year	Number of Establishments	Number of Employees (in thousands)	Capital (in thousands)	Value of Products (in thousands)
1860	140,433	1,311	$1,000,856	$1,885,862
1870	252,148	2,054	1,694,567	3,385,860
1880	253,852	2,733	2,790,274	5,369,579
1890	355,405	4,252	6,525,051	9,372,379
1900	207,514	4,713	8,975,256	11,406,927

We see that the value of manufactured products increased from $1,885,862,000 in 1860 to $11,406,927,000 in 1900. In 1860 there were only 30,626 miles of railroads and by 1910 the mileage reached 242,107.

The rise of industry also brought about a revolution in agriculture. The invention of machinery for sowing and harvesting, and finally the introduction of tractors, changed agriculture into a more profitable business by enabling the farmer to raise wheat, oats, and corn on a much more extensive scale. Now the same capitalists or capitalist corporations appropriated great tracts of land for themselves and transformed agriculture into a source of enormous profits. In other words, agriculture was reorganized on the bourgeois basis of production. The small farmer whose little piece of land did not permit the introduction of machinery was pushed more and more into the background as time went on. The value of agricultural products increased from $1,958,030,927 in 1870 to $4,717,069,973 in 1900. And the value of agricultural implements rose from $246,118,141 in 1860 to $749,775,970 in 1900.

In connection with the increase of production it is also necessary to point out the following: At the close of the nineteenth century a process of concentration and centralization of industry began to take place. In place of small workshops, gigantic factories sprang up; in place of scattered production in hundreds of thousands of different localities, manufacture began to flourish in a few great centers. In place of individual manufacturers, there appeared large companies and corporations and finally gigantic trusts.

Let us take only two evidences of that process of centralization. In 1890 there were 355,405 industrial establishments, while by 1900 the number fell to 207,514. Production during the 10-year period from 1890 to 1900 increased from $9,372,378,842 to $11,406,926,701, while at the same time the number of establishments responsible for that production decreased by about 150,000. Especially noticeable concentration of production is found in the agricultural implement line. In 1860 there were 2,116 establishments producing such implements; by 1900 there remained only 715. During the same period agriculture increased many fold and the demand for agricultural implements grew in proportion. Yet the number of factories was cut to less than half, while production was four times as great—$20,831,000 in 1860 and $81,271,000 in 1900.

Concentration of capital had its effect upon the labor movement. At the time of the Civil War the workers were scattered through many small workshops, divided into many small groups. After the war they were massed in ever larger factories and recruited into ever greater industrial armies. Slowly but inevitably class-consciousness began to develop among them as well as class solidarity.

The growth of industry also strengthened the rule of the bourgeoisie in all spheres of life, especially in its state power. Before the Civil War the federal government was looked upon merely as the "supervisor" of the relations between the different states or between groups of states with divergent interests. After the war the government became "omnipotent" —a strong and well-organized instrument in the hands of the bourgeoisie, and all talk of withdrawal from the union disappeared. By the end of the nineteenth century the United States was one powerful bourgeois state or "nation," with one tariff wall, with one army and navy. For practical purposes, state boundaries almost completely disappeared.

The population of the United States during this forty-year period more than doubled. From 31,443,321 in 1860 it reached 75,994,575 in 1900.

The rise of industry concentrated the population into large cities, great industrial and commercial centers. The urban population increased much faster than the rural population. For instance, in 1880 the city population numbered 14,772,438 and by 1900 it reached 30,797,185. Thus it more than doubled during the period of 20 years. On the other hand, the rural population, from 35,383,345 in 1880 increased to only 45,197,390 in 1900.

The growth of large cities after the Civil War was remarkable. New York's population increased from 1,174,779 in 1860 to 3,437,202 in 1900; Chicago, from 109,260 to 1,698,575; Brooklyn, from 279,122 to 1,166,582; Philadelphia from 565,529 to 1,293,697; St. Louis, from 160,773 to 575,238; Boston, from 177,840 to 560,892.

All these facts indicate that by the end of the nineteenth century the city had conquered the village. The struggles of the oppressed against their oppressors were transferred to the cities, the industrial centers. The bourgeoisie became the only ruling class and the proletariat of the cities its only direct and serious opponent.

The question of immigration again came to the fore with the Civil War. About 1,000,000 American workers had enlisted in the army and their places had to be filled; industry expanded and demanded new labor-power; those workers who remained at home and saw that the oversupply of labor-power was disappearing began to put forth demands for higher wages and better conditions. The constant rise of prices made it impossible for the workers to make both ends meet, and therefore they were forced to struggle for higher pay. To satisfy the demand of expanded industry for labor-power, to fill the places of those who were taken into the army and to effectively defeat the demands of the workers, there was only one way open to the employers and their government. There were always millions of workers and peasants in Europe anxious to come to America. It was only necessary to open the gates of this country and help the immigrants financially and in a very short time the problem of shortage of labor would be solved. Therefore, on December 8, 1863, Lincoln in his presidential address to Congress complained that in our cities there was a great shortage of labor while at the same time the United States consulates in European countries were being besieged day and night by men and women seeking an opportunity to come to America. The only thing that prevented them from coming to this country was lack of money to pay for their passage. Therefore Lincoln urged Congress to pass a law which would permit the consulates in Europe and the agents of the American capitalists to assist these Europeans to come here by making a contract with them that they would, during a certain period after being brought to America, work in places assigned to them to pay back their traveling expenses. In 1864 Congress accepted Lincoln's proposal and allowed the agents of American manufacturers to gather these Europeans, make contracts with them, and bring them to America

But this looked too much like reëstablishing the white slavery of the seventeenth century. Therefore Congress limited such contracts with immigrants to 12 months. During these 12 months the immigrant was bound to toil for his master like a slave. "Such contracts were held valid in law and might be enforced in the courts" (*Ibid*, p. 317).

The American workers objected very strongly to these efforts of the government and employers. It appeared to them—and justly so—that the employers were bringing these contract workers from Europe for the purpose of cutting down the wages of the American workers, breaking their strikes, and lowering their standard of living. But, of course, the government and the employers did not pay any attention to the protest of the workers, for they were interested only in getting cheap labor power for industry and thus increasing the profits of the capitalist class.

Under the influence of this contract labor law, immigration expanded rapidly:

IMMIGRATION TO THE UNITED STATES, 1861-1900

1861-1870	2,314,824	1881-1890	5,246,613
1871-1880	2,812,191	1891-1900	3,844,420

This great army of immigrants came mainly into the large cities and took up the hardest, the most dangerous, and the lowest paid jobs in industry and on the railroads. On the other hand, they brought with them radical-revolutionary ideas which had drawn a much greater army of discontented workers under their influence in Europe than in America. Thus the revolutionary movement in this country got its footing first among the foreign-born workers.

The great economic progress which was ushered in by the Civil War in the North and henceforth continued through the whole United States did not create an earthly paradise. It did not bring with it a better and easier life for the toiling masses. The workers and farmers had suffered and bled in the war, but when they came back home they found that hard work and great hardships stared them in the face.

It is true that the Emancipation Proclamation had made the Negroes free men and women politically. Economically, also, they no longer were considered the property of their masters. Like the workers of the North, now they could work if they desired, or not work if they did not desire. But during the time that they were slaves and belonged to their masters "soul and body," they had been supplied with shelter, food, and clothes. Now being "free" they had to shift for themselves. They had been passed from one economic system into another, from chattel slavery into wage slavery. This transformation thrust the Negro masses into an abyss of untold hardships of which they had never dreamed. Many of them would have gladly exchanged their new slavery for the old, provided they had been able to get food and clothing. For example, near the town of Mobile, Ala.,

"Nine hundred (Negroes) assembled to consider their conditions, their rights and their duties under the new state of existence upon which they have been so suddenly launched. . . . After long talk and careful deliberation, this meeting resolved, by a vote of 700 to 200, that they had made a practical trial for three months of their freedom which the war had bequeathed to them; that its realities were far from being so flattering as their imagination had painted it . . . and finally that their last state was worse than their first, and it was their deliberate conclusion that their true happiness and well-being required them to return to the homes which they had abandoned in the moment of excitement, and go to work again under their old masters" (*Documentary History of Reconstruction,* Vol. I, p. 89).

Now they had to hire themselves to the same master and toil for him for the most meager compensation. Others rented a piece of land and sweated away on it in abject want. The economic condition of the Negro masses was indeed miserable.

Politically, in the eyes of the law, Negroes were declared free citizens. For the first 10 years, during which the South was under the military rule of the northern bourgeoisie, the Negroes with their right to vote were made an instrument in the hands of the capitalist politicians of the North. After the military rule was lifted, the ruling class of the South very easily and effectively took away from the Negroes practically all of their political rights through state legislatures and secret terroristic organizations such as the Ku Klux Klan. Even to-day the Negroes of the South are allowed to use their political rights only to a limited extent.

Socially, even to-day, Negroes in the South are persecuted and oppressed. The southern capitalists do not consider them human beings. They are segregated from the whites in schools, in churches, in residential districts, on street cars and railroads. Even in the ranks of the white workers of the South there is considerable antagonism toward the Negroes. Of course, this condition is most harmful to the labor movement and therefore is intentionally developed and stirred up by the bourgeoisie.

The condition of the white workers after the Civil War was likewise far from enviable. The report of the New York City Health Department for 1866 and 1867 states that:

"The first and at all times the most prolific cause of disease was found to be the very insalubrious condition of most of the tenement houses in the cities of New York and Brooklyn. They are almost invariably overcrowded, and ill ventilated to such a degree as to render the air within them constantly impure and offensive.

"The halls and stairways are usually filthy and dark, and the walls and banisters foul and damp, while the floors were not infrequently used . . . (for the purposes of nature) . . . for lack of other provisions . . . many of the sleeping rooms are simply closets without light or ventilation save by means of a single door" (Myers: *Loc. cit.,* Vol. I, pp. 218-219).

The conditions of the unskilled workers were also very hard. The Eight Hour Day League of Boston at its convention in 1872 declared of the factory system:

"It employs tens of thousands of women and children 11 and 12 hours a day; owns or controls in its own selfish interest the pulpit and the press; prevents the operative classes from making themselves felt in behalf of less hours, through remorseless exercise of the power of discharge; and is rearing a population of children and youth of sickly appearance and scanty or utterly neglected schooling . . ." (Myers: *Loc. cit.*, Vol. II, pp. 181-182).

Here again economic conditions took the women and children from their homes and placed them at monotonous and hard work in the factories. It was estimated that in 1870 not less than 700,000 children were toiling in the workshops of the country. And at the end of the Civil War over 1,000,000 women were making their own living in various branches of industry. Their number continuously increased and by 1880 it rose to 2,647,151.

CHAPTER XVI

Labor Organizations and Struggles, 1860-1873

ONLY two national trade unions showed any activity worth mentioning immediately before the Civil War, and even they disappeared in the crisis of 1861 and 1862. These were the Moulders' International Union and the National Union of Machinists and Blacksmiths. Both of them were founded in 1859. William H. Sylvis was the leader of the moulders. His death on July 27, 1869, while still a young man, deprived him of the opportunity to devote all his energies and enthusiasm to the cause of labor. Sylvis had at one time established connections with the leaders of the First International, Marx and Engels. When the news of his untimely death reached London the International issued the following statement:

"That the American labor movement does not depend on the life of a single individual is certain, but not less certain is the fact that the loss sustained by the present labor convention through the death of Sylvis cannot be compensated. The eyes of all were turned on Sylvis, who, as a general of the proletarian army, had an experience of 10 years outside of his great abilities—and Sylvis is dead" (Hillquit: *Loc. cit.,* p. 172).

The Moulders' Union conducted many strikes and showed great militancy.

The Machinists' and Blacksmiths' Union boasted in 1860 of 87 affiliated local unions, but the fall convention in 1861 was attended by only a few delegates from no more than four states.

Only at the end of 1862 did the trade unions again begin to appear. There were two main reasons for this awakening: the disappearance of the army of unemployed with the advance of the war, and the rise of prices. In 1862 the government issued paper money ("greenbacks") to the amount of $300,000,000, and in 1863 to the amount of $750,000,000. A great era of speculation set in, the wheels of industry began to turn, the bourgeoisie was stuffing into its pockets unheard-of profits in the very midst of the Civil War. On the other hand, the prices of the necessaries of life advanced by leaps and bounds. The cost of living was 70 per cent higher and wages had increased only 30 per cent. Therefore, the worker, try as he would, could not make a living. Conditions opened his eyes and taught him that only through united action with his fellow workers could he lighten his burden.

The skilled workers' organizations began to pick up rapidly. *Fincher's Trade Review,* a weekly paper supporting the interests of labor, reported that by December of 1863 there were 79 local unions embracing 20 different industries, and by December of 1864 their number had increased to 270, embracing 53 different trades and 16 states. In November, 1865, there were nearly 300 local trade unions, in 61 different trades.

It is impossible to tell how many unionists there really were at that time, but "it would not be far from the truth to put the membership during 1870-1872 at about 300,000." Some labor leaders, however, claimed that the total was as high as 600,000.

The necessity for greater unity compelled the local trade unions to combine into national trade organizations. Following are some of the national unions organized in this period: the Grand National Division of Locomotive Engineers, organized in 1863; the Plasterers' National Union, the Ship Carpenters' and Caulkers' International, and the National Union of Cigar Makers, 1864; the Coach Makers' International Union, the Journeymen Painters' National Union, the Tailors' National Union, the Carpenters' and Joiners' International Union, and the Bricklayers' and Masons' International Union, 1865; the Knights of St. Crispin and the Grand Division of the Order of Railway Conductors, 1868; the Daughters of St. Crispin, organized in 1869. In the four years 1870-1873 nine national organizations were formed. The leading ones were the International Coopers' Union of North America, 1870, and the Miners' National Association and the Brotherhood of Locomotive Firemen, 1873. By the close of 1873 there were 22 national and international unions (Commons: *History,* etc., Vol. II, pp. 45-47).

As to the aims of the trade unions of this period, it will suffice to take two or three of them. The Brotherhood of Locomotive Engineers was organized on a militant basis, but remained so only for one year. Then it fell into the hands of the reactionary Charles Wilson, and from then on "the policy of the union was to win the good graces of the employers through elevating the character of its members and thus raising their efficiency as workmen. The employer would be so well pleased with their work that he would of his own free will provide better recognition of labor and higher pay" (*Ibid.,* p. 63).

On January 18, 1866, the engineers and firemen of the Michigan Southern and Northern Indiana Railway went on strike against the introduction of a new system of work and the reduction of wages. The strike was long drawn out. The employers immediately hired scabs and blacklisted their old employees. On June 22, 1866, a special convention of the brotherhood was held to discuss the strike situation. Reactionaries were in full control of the convention. They passed a resolution begging the other companies not to mistreat the workers who had been blacklisted, and declared, concerning the strikebreakers who had been hired:

LABOR ORGANIZATIONS AND STRUGGLES

"We do not wish to be understood as claiming the right to dictate who shall be hired by any company. ... If the Michigan Southern Railroad Company thinks it to their advantage to employ such men to run their engines they have the right to employ them" (*Ibid.*, p. 65).

Wilson again and again declared that the interests of employers and workers were the same, and that they should not fight each other, but must live in peace and harmony. Later the brotherhood was incorporated. It also organized an insurance company, and to-day it still exists mainly as an insurance institution for its membership and an instrument in the hands of the reactionary officials for carrying out a policy of class collaboration.

The National Union of Cigar Makers was organized June 21, 1864, as a pure and simple trade union and remained as such. It led several important strikes and showed some militancy, and its leaders played an important rôle in the formation of the American Federation of Labor.

The Knights of St. Crispin, organized March 7, 1867, at Milwaukee, was a secret organization. Its fundamental aim was to fight against the employment of unskilled shoemakers. Especially in Massachusetts the new organization was met enthusiastically by the craftsmen. Membership grew rapidly, until it was estimated that by 1870 it had 50,000 in its ranks. At first the Knights of St. Crispin were militant also, but this militancy did not last long. The leaders of the organization dragged it into the establishment of coöperative shoe stores; at one time there were 10 such stores in various cities. These enterprises went to pieces and the once flourishing union of the shoemakers lost its influence.

In this period we also find efforts to establish one national union embracing under its banner all existing unions in the United States.

On August 20, 1866, 77 delegates from 50 trade unions and 13 trades' assemblies met at Baltimore, Md., and organized the National Labor Union.

"It is more than a coincidence," says John B. Andrews, "that the famed international . . . should have risen and disappeared in the same years as the attempted national organization of all labor in the United States. The year 1864, which witnessed the meeting at Louisville of the Industrial Assembly of North America, witnessed at London the preliminary Conference of the International Workingmen's Association. In the year 1866 the National Labor Union was organized at Baltimore and the International held its first meeting of delegates from different countries at Geneva. In 1867 the American organization met at Chicago, the European at Lausanne; in 1868 the one met at New York, the other, at Brussels. In 1869 the one that met at Philadelphia was represented by a delegate to the other at Basle. In 1870 the Franco-Prussian War interrupted the European congress, and the next two years witnessed the dissolution of both organizations through similar internal dissensions —the American organization through the antagonism of 'political actionists' and trade unionists, the European through the antagonism of socialists and anarchists" (*Ibid.*, pp. 86-87).

It must be added that external factors, the economic and political situation in Europe, helped to bring about the dissolution of the International.

At its first convention the National Labor Union made several important decisions. A resolution was adopted urging the unskilled workers to organize into general workingmen's associations which, later, would directly affiliate with the National Union. The question of independent political action by the workers gave rise to a lengthy discussion. Even at that time a controversy was going on in the ranks of labor over this important matter. Some argued for remaining in the old capitalist parties, while others agitated for the establishment of a labor party, separate and independent from the old parties. At this first convention of the National Labor Union the exponents of independent political action won. In the proposed resolution we read:

"The history and legislation of the past had demonstrated that no confidence whatever can be placed in the pledges of existing political parties so far as the interests of the industrial classes are concerned. *The time has come when the workingmen of the United States should cut themselves aloof from party ties and predilections, and organize themselves into a National Labor Party,* the object of which shall be to secure the enactment of a law making eight hours a legal day's work by the national Congress and the several state legislatures, and the election of men pledged to sustain and represent the interests of the industrial classes" (*Ibid.*, pp. 99-100).

The opponents of a labor party immediately revolted against this resolution and threatened to disrupt the convention. A compromise was reached and a resolution was finally accepted supporting the idea of independent political action, but as far as the actual organization of the labor party was concerned, it should be done "as soon as possible." The convention itself did not take any concrete steps toward the formation of such a party. And so the resolution remained on paper only.

The question of land distribution also came up. The delegates adopted a resolution declaring as their motto: "The tools to those that have the ability and skill to use them, and the land to those that have the will and heart to cultivate it."

In still another resolution the convention pledged itself whole-heartedly to help the women factory workers to better their conditions.

The eight-hour day was another outstanding question of the convention. The arguments for the eight-hour day were based not on the ground that it would lessen the exploitation of the workers by the capitalists but that shorter hours are necessary for the moral, political, and cultural development of the workers.

The convention failed miserably on two most vital problems, and these failures finally led to the dissolution of the union itself. First of all, it did nothing toward establishing a permanent organization which would withstand the attacks of the capitalist class and successfully defend the interests of the workers. The convention was satisfied with the decision to hold annual congresses, passed a series of resolutions, and adjourned.

The second great blunder was made in the matter of strikes. The convention went so far in its anti-strike policy as publicly to criticize strikes as detrimental to the workers themselves! It is evident that the workers, and especially their leaders, had not learned anything from the history of the class struggle. They still believed in the good-heartedness of their enemies—the employers—and therefore openly threw aside the most important weapon of the proletariat in its every-day struggle with the capitalist class. The convention even failed to understand that the capitalists after the Civil War were systematically organizing powerful associations of their own for the sole purpose of mercilessly smashing every organization of the workers. The employers openly spoke about destroying the labor organizations, while the latter continued blindly without a definite plan and threw away their most important weapon—the strike.

At its second convention, in 1867, the National Labor Union went still further afield and lost itself in the money reform wilderness. This was the beginning of the end of the National Labor Union.

By 1868 the union was at the height of its career. In its New York congress of that year it was claimed that representatives of 600,000 organized workers participated.

At the congress of 1869 the Negro problem was discussed. A committee was elected to carry on work among the Negro masses and it was decided to invite Negro organizations to send delegates to the next convention. But these efforts to unite the white and black workers failed. Constantly stirred up by the bourgeoisie, the antagonism between whites and blacks continued to grow, especially among the skilled white workers who were afraid that the unskilled Negroes might take away their jobs, and therefore refused to admit Negroes to any of their meetings or conventions. Often the Negroes were forced to organize into separate bodies.

By 1870 the National Labor Union started to go down. Various national trade bodies began to withdraw. The work of the union was now almost entirely limited to money reform schemes. In 1872 it attempted to organize a labor party, but in that very year it died of degeneration.

It is necessary to mention here the birth of one more organization which played an important rôle in the labor movement of America. Under the leadership of Uriah Smith Stephens and James L. Wright a handful of Philadelphia garment cutters organized a secret society under the name of the Knights of Labor. This secrecy of the Knights of Labor was maintained until 1878. As the Knights became an important factor in the labor movement after the period we are now discussing, we shall deal with it later.

In this period few large strikes occurred. As already pointed out, almost all of the important unions either entirely rejected strikes or considered them unimportant as weapons in the struggle to improve the conditions of the workers or to defend them against attack by the employers. Besides, the unions of this period were composed almost exclusively of skilled workers or craftsmen who were incapable at such an early date of developing a serious mass labor movement. We can mention the cigar makers' strike which started in October, 1869, for an increase in wages, and which lasted 18 weeks. The strike was won by the workers, but only on paper, for "the victory soon turned into failure. At the end of the strike the employers introduced the mould, and the union, foreseeing a reduction in wages and fearing another struggle, voluntarily reduced the price it had thus secured after a long fight" (Commons: *History*, etc., Vol. II, p. 72).

In San Francisco in 1869, and in Philadelphia and Worcester in 1870, a series of strikes occurred, led by the Knights of St. Crispin. The shoemakers' strike of 1872, in Lynn, Mass., failed and the local organization was disrupted.

The most important walk-out of this period was that of the workers of New York City, mostly among the building trades, for the eight-hour day, in which about 100,000 participated.

"The strike lasted three months and ended very successfully. The eight-hour day was gained by the bricklayers, carpenters, plasterers, plumbers, painters, brown and blue stone cutters, stone-masons, masons' laborers, paper hangers, and plate printers" (*Ibid.*, p. 151).

As far as the unskilled workers were concerned we do not find evidence of any important struggles or organization on their part. Almost all of the unions that appeared after the Civil War were composed exclusively of skilled men. The same was true of the strikes: those that did take place in this period were conducted by the upper strata of the working class.

The movement for independent political action of labor was started. As already indicated, the National Labor Union attempted to form a labor party, but failed. Here and there local "workers' parties" sprang up and led a precarious existence for a time, but did not play an important rôle.

The revolutionary socialist movement was also very weak. It is true that some connections with the International were maintained and even an American section of the International was established, but there was no mass revolutionary movement of any kind. Mention has already been made of the forming of the First International in London in 1864. It declared that the "emancipation of the workers must be brought about by the workers themselves," and set for itself the goal of uniting the workers on an international scale to bring about this emancipation. Its leaders were Marx and Engels, the greatest revolutionists of the world and the founders of scientific socialism or communism.

LABOR ORGANIZATIONS AND STRUGGLES 149

The first American organization to make connection with the International was the National Labor Union. William Sylvis, its leader, worked hard to make these connections firmer and closer, but his early death prevented him from achieving this aim. At the Chicago convention of the union, in 1867, the question of contact with the International was raised. The session decided not to affiliate, but adopted the following resolution:

"Whereas, the efforts of the working classes in Europe to acquire political power, to improve their social conditions, and to emancipate themselves from the bondage under which they were and still are, are gratifying proof of the progress of justice, enlightenment, and civilization;

"Resolved, that the National Labor convention hereby declares its sympathy, and promises its coöperation to the organized working men of Europe in their struggle against political and social injustice" (Hillquit: *Loc. cit.*, p. 188).

At its convention in Philadelphia, 1869, the union decided to send a delegate to the international congress at Basle, and elected A. C. Cameron for the honor.

When war threatened between the United States and England, the International appealed to the National Labor Union for united efforts to prevent the conflict. In his answer to the International Sylvis declared:

"Our cause is a common one. It is war between poverty and wealth. . . . This monied power is fast eating up the substance of the people. We have made war upon it, and we mean to win it. If we can, we will win through the ballot box; if not, then we shall resort to sterner means. A little bloodletting is sometimes necessary in desperate cases" (Commons: *History*, etc., Vol. II, p. 132).

But it was left to other labor organizations to make direct contact with the international revolutionary movement.

"The first organizations directly affiliated with the International appeared in the United States around the year 1868. They were small societies in New York, Chicago, and San Francisco, composed almost exclusively of German socialists, and styled 'sections' of the International."

In 1871 the Paris Commune was crushed and many radical Frenchmen were driven out of the country. Later these came to America and "were cordially welcomed by the International; and finally the organization succeeded in reaching the ranks of American labor by its active support in the numerous strikes of that year." Especially in the demonstrations of the unemployed the International sections everywhere stood in the front ranks.

"The total number of enrolled membership was about 5,000, and they were composed of Americans, Irishmen, Germans, Frenchmen, Scandinavians, and Bohemians . . . the first national convention of the International was held on the 6th day of July, 1872, at the city of New York. Twenty-two sections were represented. The convention assumed the official name of North American Federation of the International Working Men's Association, and adopted a set of rules and regulations for the government of its affairs," which "provided that in every section to be formed in the future, at least three-fourths of the

150   HISTORY OF THE AMERICAN WORKING CLASS

members should be wage-workers, and enjoined upon all sections 'to entertain good relations with the trade unions and to promote their formation' " (Hillquit: *Loc. cit.,* pp. 194-206).

But the era of "prosperity" was fast coming to an end. With it the end of this period of the labor movement was also approaching.

"The panic of 1873 swept over the country, opening a six-year period of industrial distress, strikes, labor disorders, and disasters to unionism. With the paralysis of industry employers began to reduce wages and these reductions were followed by prolonged and desperate strikes. Within seven years, between 1873 and 1880, wages in the textile districts were cut to almost one-half the former standard. Similar action was taken in other industries. Unemployment became so widespread that strikes to maintain wages were perilous; where they were attempted, lockouts usually followed. Blacklists and prosecutions intimidated labor leaders. A successful national organization was out of the question. The number of effective national craft unions fell from about 30 to eight or nine and even they were in dire financial straits. Where the national union did not vanish, its membership declined; the machinists lost two-thirds of their members; the cigar makers, four-fifths; and the coopers nearly six-sevenths. It is estimated that the trade union membership in New York City fell from 44,000 to 5,000. In Cincinnati it dropped to about 1,000" (Mary Beard: *Loc. cit.,* pp. 81-82).

The crisis which thus shattered the labor movement also brought distressing conditions to the masses of the workers. Tens of thousands in every industrial center were thrown out of work and were left on the streets to starve.

"The winter of 1873-4," says McNeill, "was one of extreme suffering, especially in large cities. Midwinter found tens of thousands of people on the verge of starvation, suffering for food, for the need of proper clothing, and for medical attendance. Meetings of the unemployed were held in many places, and public attention called to the needs of the poor. . . . Men asked for work and found it not, and children cried for bread.

"On the announcement of public meetings of the unemployed, the conscience-pricked communities took alarm and feared that the bringing together of so many heretofore patient sufferers might imperil their lives and property. . . .

"The unemployed and suffering poor of New York City determined to hold a meeting and appeal to the public by bringing to their attention the spectacle of their poverty. They gained permission from the board of police to parade the streets and hold a meeting on Tompkins Square, on the 13th of January, 1874, but on the 12th of January the board of police and board of parks revoked the order and prohibited the meeting. It was impossible to notify the scattered army of the order, and at the meeting the people marched through the gates of Tompkins Square . . . when the square was completely filled with men, women, and children, without a moment's warning, the police closed upon them on all sides.

"One of the daily papers of the city confessed that the scene could not be described. People rushed from the gates and through the streets, followed by the mounted officers at full speed, charging upon them without provocation. Screams of women and children rent the air, and the blood of many stained the streets, and to the further shame of this outrage is to be added that when the attention of the general assembly of New York state was called to this matter, they took testimony, but made no sign" (McNeill: *Loc. cit.*, pp. 147-148).

They could not do anything, for the state legislatures under the capitalist system are composed of the representatives of the capitalist class.

The police force is also an instrument of the bourgeois class to suppress the workers. The fact that the police on this occasion appeared more vicious than usual was only because the working class was becoming stronger, better organized, more class-conscious and therefore more dangerous to the interests of the capitalist class.

These events in New York City on January 13, 1874, again unmasked the bourgeois state as an instrument of the capitalist class to maintain the system of exploitation on the backs of the workers. None of the organs of the bourgeois state would defend the unemployed and starving workers. None of the bourgeois institutions would sympathize with those who only yesterday were creating wealth for the master class and now found themselves without a roof over their heads and without bread.

Similar demonstrations took place in other industrial cities, for unemployment was wide-spread throughout the country. And everywhere the workers were met with clubs and bullets!

CHAPTER XVII

PERIOD OF MILITANT LABOR STRUGGLES, 1873-1880

THE seven-year period from 1873 to 1880 may properly be called a period of industrial depression. As in all depressions the working masses carried the load. They had to suffer and starve; they had to bear the attacks of the capitalist class and its armed forces, the state.

The trade union movement received a set back. Some of the craft unions disappeared entirely, others were rendered helpless, though some of them heroically and desperately remained on the battle field till the very end. The Cigar Makers' Union fell from 5,800 members in 1869 to 1,016 by 1877; the Coopers' Union was reduced from 7,000 in 1872 to 1,500 in 1878; the Knights of St. Crispin which in 1871 had about 50,000 members disappeared almost entirely by 1878; the Bricklayers' Union with 43 locals and 5,332 members in 1873 was left with three locals by 1880; the Typographical Union was reduced from 9,797 members in 1873 to 4,260 in 1878.

In spite of their previous failures, the trade unions again made efforts to combine into a national body even during this period. These efforts show that the labor movement, in spite of almost insurmountable difficulties, and often against the will of its leadership, continually strove for greater and lasting unity. Life itself, the development of the capitalist system of production, compels the workers to strive for more power, compels them to make more concerted efforts, to defend themselves against their class enemies or to attack them, to win from them more bread and butter and to lighten the burden of toil in the factories.

As we have already seen, the National Labor Union disappeared before the dawn of 1873. But it had not lived in vain: it left behind it the idea that the unity of all trade unions on a national scale is important and necessary. And this idea received concrete expression even in the midst of great industrial crisis.

On May 3, 1873, a convention call appeared in the *Workingmen's Advocate,* signed by William Saffin, president of the Moulders' International Union; Fehrenbath, president of the Machinists' and Blacksmiths' International Union; Foran, president of the Coopers' International Union; and John Collins, secretary of the Typographical Union. The aim of the convention, as stated by the authors of the call, was as follows: Capital

PERIOD OF MILITANT LABOR STRUGGLES

has been very rapidly and very highly concentrated; the laws of the land serve only this concentrated capital; the farmers are shamefully exploited; the capitalists have organized powerful state associations of their own; at the same time the labor unions still remain separated from one another and therefore are helpless before the mighty power of the capitalists; the failure of all efforts to unite the labor organizations on a national scale in the past must not stand in the way of unity in the present and in the future. The convention was to meet on July 15, 1873, at Cleveland, Ohio, and all labor unions, anti-monopoly coöperatives, and any other associations were invited to send delegates. On their part, the authors of the call pledged themselves "that the organization, when consummated, shall not, so far as in our power to prevent, ever deteriorate into a political party, or become the tail to the kite of any political party, or a refuge for played-out politicians, but shall to all intents and purposes remain a purely industrial association, having for its sole and only object the securing to the producer his full share of all he produces."

In another circular the same trade union officials swore that "we desire it distinctly understood that we have no agrarian ideas, we neither believe nor preach the doctrine that capital is robbery." They also stated that they had no connection whatsoever with the "Commune," that is, with the revolutionary movement of the proletariat. They pointed out that the government treated the trade unions as conspiracies and that the country was being overrun by imported Chinamen (Commons: *History*, etc.. Vol. II, pp. 157-158).

The convention assembled on the appointed date with 70 delegates present. Six national trade unions were represented. Two momentous errors paved the way for the death of the movement: first, failure to get rid of all elements foreign to the working class, and, second, rejection of the strike as a workers' weapon against the employers.

At the convention there was a lot of talk about the "producers," but nothing was said to the effect that the new organization must be a purely proletarian movement. Among the "producers" were included the small manufacturers. This section of the bourgeoisie was, then as now, united in various organizations having nothing to do with the trade unions. These petty bourgeois organizations repeatedly injected themselves into the early efforts to establish a National Labor Union, and did great harm to the movement. On one hand, they were always opposed to militant tactics; on the other, they did not allow the workers definitely and clearly to separate themselves from the influence of the capitalist class.

Instead of strikes and struggles, the 1873 convention accepted arbitration as the means of settling disputes between the workers and their enemies. Therefore the movement was based not on the class struggle but on class collaboration. Such a movement could not live for any length of time in the face of an ever-sharpening class struggle. Never before had the employers attacked the labor organizations and the wages of the workers with such ferocity, while the organized workers continued their idle talk about the uselessness of active struggle—the strike!

On the question of independent political action by the workers, no decision was reached. The eight-hour day was approved, but nothing was said as to the means by which this goal was to be attained.

The second convention was held on April 14, 1874, at Rochester, N. Y., and the name "Industrial Brotherhood" was given to the movement. Heated controversy developed over the constitution. Some demanded that the organization should get rid of the non-labor elements and that it be a strictly secret body. Others defended the old constitution, but did not oppose making the organization secret. Finally a committee was elected to draft a new constitution and present it to the next convention. The Rochester gathering again condemned strikes and affirmed its stand for arbitration. The eight-hour day was again approved. On the question of independent political action the convention decided to have nothing to do with any of the political parties and to vote "only for those persons who agree with us in our principles."

The third and the last convention of the Industrial Brotherhood was held on April 13, 1875, at Indianapolis, with only 20 delegates present; with the exception of the International Typographical Union, none of the national unions sent delegates. It was more than clear that the brotherhood was on the verge of extinction. The convention itself "found" that "a unification of the existing labor organizations was an impossibility." Several resolutions were adopted, the most important being that which designated July 4, 1876, as the date for the eight-hour day to be introduced by a "united movement on the part of the working masses of the United States." None of the decisions of the convention was carried out, and the Industrial Brotherhood itself disappeared.

In the steel and iron industry in 1876 two national unions combined into one—the Amalgamated Association of Iron and Steel Workers. At first the association had only 3,755 members, but by 1882 it had increased to 20,000. It seems that this union was the first in the country to sign a permanent contract with the employers, and its members were chained to this contract for a quarter of a century. The efforts of the leaders to avoid any struggle with the employers continues to date, and the organization to-day plays a very small part in the industry.

In the bituminous coal fields a national organization was formed in 1873 under the leadership of John Siney. One year later it had 21,000 members. This union also was based not on the class struggle but on peaceful collaboration with the employers. The leaders were so anxious to maintain peace that in 1874 they peacefully accepted a wage reduction of 19 cents a ton. The membership revolted against the leaders, and compelled them to abrogate the contract and demand a raise in wages.

PERIOD OF MILITANT LABOR STRUGGLES

John Siney was forced to summon a special convention, which left it to the members to disregard the contract with their employers (*Ibid.*, pp. 179-180).

We come now to a period of militant struggles. The great wave of unemployment that swept the country gave the capitalist class an opportunity to reduce wages, and to provoke the workers and their organizations into hasty clashes in order once for all to destroy every vestige of organized resistance on their part.

The anthracite coal miners had a bitter seven-months' strike in 1874-1875 which resulted in the workers being crushed into submission. The coal owners now attacked them with even greater ferocity. Open organization was impossible. Secret action was all that remained. For the Irish miners of that time a secret organization was no new experience. In the old country many of them had belonged to the Ancient Order of Hibernians which had been formed to fight the landlords. After the great defeat of 1874-1875 the miners united in a secret organization known as the "Molly Maguires." The new order developed rapidly and reached every center of the coal industry. At one time it counted 6,000 local units.

The coal barons immediately scented danger, and determined more than ever to crush all organized resistance on the part of the miners. As usual in such cases, they sent their spies and provocateurs into the Molly Maguires to learn the plans of the workers and to commit crimes in their name in order to hunt them down later as criminals. It was openly admitted that the coal barons hired the well-known Pinkerton spy agency for this business. The provocateurs played their part cleverly, and murders in the coal fields became so numerous that by 1875 the time was ripe for striking a final blow at the miners' organization. The bourgeois newspapers, the politicians, the clergymen created the opinion throughout the country that the Molly Maguires was established for criminal purposes and consisted of criminals only. At the same time the spies knew by heart all the connections of the secret organization and its most active members and officials. It is possible that the provocateurs may have succeeded in drawing some members into criminal acts, but nothing could be farther from the truth than the accusation that the aim of the organization was criminal.

In the fall of 1875 the government made a general attack upon the Molly Maguires; many of the officials and members of the order were arrested and tried as criminals. Spies and provocateurs were the only witnesses against the accused. The capitalist courts paid no attention to the defense; everything was set in advance to get rid of the miners. The result was that "fourteen were committed to prison for terms varying from two to seven years and 10 were executed" (Commons: *History*, etc., Vol. II, p. 185).

"They all protested their innocence and all died game," says Eugene V. Debs. "Not one of them betrayed the slightest evidence of fear or weakening. Not one of them was a murderer at heart. All were ignorant, rough and uncouth, born of poverty and buffeted by the merciless tides of fate and chance.

"To resist the wrongs of which they and their fellow workers were victims and to protect themselves against the brutality of their bosses, according to their own crude notions, was the prime object of the organization of the 'Mollie Maguires.' Nothing could have been farther from their intention than murder or crime. It is true that their methods were drastic, but it must be remembered that their lot was hard and brutalizing; that they were the neglected children of poverty, the products of a wretched environment. . . .

"June 21, 1877, the curtain fell upon the last mournful act in this tragedy of toil. The executioner did his bidding and the gallows-tree claimed its victims. On that day history turned harlot and the fair face of truth was covered with the hideous mask of falsehood. The men who perished upon the scaffold as felons were labor leaders, the first martyrs to the class struggle in the United States" (*Appeal to Reason*, November 23, 1907).

When the working class conquers power in the United States and the workers write the history of the country with their own hands, the Molly Maguires will be vindicated. A monument will be erected to the leaders who fell as martyrs in the class struggle, while those who condemned and executed them will be reviled.

The most important battles in the textile industry were fought in Fall River, Mass. At the end of the Civil War, Fall River had 265,238 spindles and a population of 17,525. In 1874 the population increased to 43,289 and the total number of spindles to 1,256,508. Fall River thus became the most important center of the textile industry of New England.

As soon as the industrial crisis overtook the country, the mill owners started a campaign to reduce wages. In the fall of 1874 the workers took a cut of 10 per cent, and a little later another reduction was announced. Mass meetings were held in protest. In the same year a conference of spinners and weavers was held, which decided to unite forces against the attacks of the employers. As a result, the Weavers' Protective Association was formed, composed almost entirely of women workers. In 1875 the association had 5,000 members.

In February, 1875, from 3,000 to 4,000 textile workers struck. In March negotiations began and the employers agreed to restore the old wages which had been reduced by 10 per cent. But in August the employers again slashed wages 10 per cent. The workers answered with another walk-out. It was a general strike in the real sense of the word: 15,000 workers left their jobs and silenced 30,000 looms. After three weeks the strikers were beginning to lose hope, and talked of going back to work. Encouraged by such reports, the employers announced that they would accept the workers on one condition: that they would sign individual contracts pledging themselves never to go on strike or belong to a union again. This proposal was emphatically rejected, the strike took on

PERIOD OF MILITANT LABOR STRUGGLES 157

new life. But after eight weeks of struggle, sheer starvation forced the workers into submission. They lost a great fight: they were compelled to accept the 10 per cent reduction and sign the "yellow dog" contract. The Weavers' Protective Association was entirely demoralized.

In 1876 a further reduction of 10 per cent took place. In 1878 the wages of the textile workers in Fall River were 30 per cent lower than in 1873. But that fact did not satisfy the victorious textile barons, and on March 15, 1878, they announced another cut of 15 per cent. In May the workers held a great protest demonstration in which about 20,000 participated. On June 26, 1879, 1,000 spinners, and 100 children working in the same department, went out. The employers decided to crush the strike at any cost. They brought scabs from as far as Canada, armed them with revolvers, and instructed them to shoot down any striker who tried to approach them. A relief campaign was organized in other New England cities. But after 16 weeks the strikers had to yield to starvation and mass arrests (McNeill: *Loc. cit.,* pp. 221-233).

By 1877 the crisis had driven the working class into abject misery. There were about 3,000,000 unemployed. Thousands of families were starving.

"In the great industrial cities cases of death from starvation, not only of single individuals but of entire families, were reported by the police every week. During the winter of 1877, the police stations were filled every night with crowds of working men and their families seeking shelter from the cold of the streets, and the police courts were besieged by men, women, and children imploring to be committed to the workhouse" (Hillquit: *History,* etc., p. 219).

The wages of those who still remained in jobs were continuously being reduced. It was not sufficient for the railroad magnates that during the period 1873-1877 the wages of railroad employees had been reduced by 25 per cent; in June, 1877, another 10 per cent cut was declared. This was too much for the patience of the workers and they revolted. It was a spontaneous, unprepared uprising. Nevertheless, it was a mass struggle. For the first time in its history the proletariat of the United States showed the world its power, and through its class solidarity it struck fear into the hearts of the ruling class.

The great railroad strike of 1877 started at Martinsburg, W. Va., on July 17, one day after the wage reduction went into effect. The workers refused to move freight trains. The company called for the state militia, but soon learned that it could not rely on the militia alone, for there were men in its ranks who sympathized with the workers' cause. The governor of the state therefore appealed to President Hayes for federal troops. That faithful servant of the capitalist class gladly complied, and sent into the town 200 soldiers, armed to the teeth. After two days the strike was suppressed and trains began to operate.

But the powder magazine lay ready, and the events at Martinsburg were only the spark needed for an explosion. The strike spread like wildfire to other centers on the Baltimore and Ohio Railroad. In many places, especially at Cumberland, Md., the strikers gained the upper hand. One full militia regiment and part of another were ordered from Baltimore to crush them. As the troops were marching to the railroad station, part of them were engulfed by the masses of the workers and were forced to flee from a shower of rocks and bricks. The bulk of the militiamen took refuge in the station, whence they commenced shooting at the workers, who in turn attempted to set the station on fire. Police finally dispersed the people. After the fight was over 10 workers were found dead and many more were wounded. In the morning the federal army reached the city and other railroad centers and suppressed all resistance on the Baltimore and Ohio.

But now the workers on the Pennsylvania Railroad rose. This strike started on July 19, in Pittsburgh and vicinity. By evening all freight trains were stopped and the walkout was spreading rapidly. Most of the people in the city sympathized with the strikers. The militia was called out, but neither the employers nor the government had much faith in it, hence the governor despatched 800 troopers from Philadelphia. The soldiers arrived at Pittsburgh on July 21. It was a Saturday afternoon, when many of the factories were closed. Thousands of other workers joined with the strikers in a great mass demonstration. It seemed as if all the people of the city were on the side of the railroad men.

As had been expected, the Pittsburgh militia fraternized with the strikers, but the troopers from Philadelphia attacked them mercilessly. Twenty-six workers were murdered. The masses became enraged and began to move forward to avenge the murders. Seeing that they could not suppress the "mob," the troopers decided to retreat, and ran into the railroad shops. The local militia were told to go home as they were of no use anyhow, and the troopers from Philadelphia were left to defend themselves alone. About 10 o'clock in the evening the cars and the shops were in flames. The struggle lasted till 7 in the morning. At last the troopers saw that there was no hope of withstanding the workers. They retreated from the city, pursued with stones, bricks and guns, leaving the workers victorious. It is said that about $5,000,000 worth of property was destroyed during the struggle. Of course, all the blame was thrown on the workers, though later it was proved that agents of the company had themselves set fire to useless cars in the barns in order to claim indemnity from the state for losses incurred in the strike.

In Reading, Pa., 13 workers were killed on the spot and 22 were wounded in a clash between a great strike demonstration and the militia. The workers became enraged and fought the murderers so hard that they were forced to flee the city in civilian clothes.

PERIOD OF MILITANT LABOR STRUGGLES

In St. Louis the workers became masters of the city and for two weeks held the reins in their hands. Additional vigorous uprisings against the armed forces of the ruling class took place in New York, New Jersey, Ohio, Indiana, Illinois, and other states (Commons: *History*, etc., Vol. II, pp. 185-190).

Although the workers fought bravely and with remarkable solidarity, they were at length crushed by the united efforts of the ruling class and its government. Once more the wage workers were forced to submission at the point of a gun.

In this period a peculiar movement developed in California. Instead of carrying on a struggle with the bourgeoisie, the labor movement turned its face against the Chinese. During the crisis of 1873 thousands of workers could not find employment, while during the following three years about 150,000 immigrants arrived in California from Asia, most of them from China. The workers of California thought that all their troubles were due to these immigrants and they directed their movement against the latter. Doubtless the agents of that section of the bourgeoisie which could not profit by the Chinese also helped stir up the movement against them.

In San Francisco a mob attacked the Chinese section on the evening of July 23, 1877, and the fight lasted for two days. Four were killed. The local members of the socialistic Workingmen's Party of the United States did not join in this attack. But a certain individual by the name of Denis Kearney, who had openly defended the capitalists not so very long before, suddenly appeared as a friend of the workers and assumed the leadership of the anti-Chinese movement. He gained influence and formed an organization of his own, the "Workingmen's Party of California," with a violent anti-Chinese platform. Among other things, the platform declared:

"We propose to rid the country of cheap Chinese labor as soon as possible, and by all means in our power, because it tends still more to degrade labor and aggrandize capital.

"When we have 10,000 members we shall have the sympathy and support of 20,000 other workingmen.

"The party will then wait upon all who employ Chinese and ask for their discharge, and it will mark as public enemies those who refuse to comply with their request.

"This party will exhaust all peaceable means of attaining its end, but it will not be denied justice when it has the power to enforce it . . ." (*Ibid.*, p. 255).

This anti-Chinese party gained great influence. Later on even some of the socialists joined its ranks. It developed into a real mass movement, and held many large demonstrations in San Francisco.

On January 3, 1878, Kearney with about 800 unemployed marched to the city hall and demanded that the mayor give them either work or bread.

The mayor answered that he could do nothing to help them. Kearney made a speech against the government and immediately he and four of his friends were arrested and charged with inciting rebellion. Meetings were forbidden and the city police were called upon to suppress any movement on the part of the workers.

On January 21 a secret convention of the party was held with 140 delegates present. The platform it adopted declared that the government of the United States had fallen completely into the hands of the capitalists; that it was necessary to rid the country of cheap Chinese labor; that the land should belong to those who work on it; that the financial system should be such as would satisfy the needs of industry and commerce and not be in the hands of a few bankers; that the eight-hour day should be established by law; that prison labor should be eliminated; and that an end should be put to the growth of millionaires and monopolists through taxation upon their wealth.

The party's agitation spread rapidly through the state and it became a real factor in the local elections. For example, the candidates of the Workingmen's Party for mayor in Oakland and Sacramento won against the united forces of Republicans and Democrats. However, the party soon began to disintegrate. It was not composed of workers alone: small capitalists were an important element in it, and the candidates of the party for political offices were almost exclusively manufacturers. Furthermore, a factional struggle developed, and resulted in a split. In 1880 the Workingmen's Party failed to nominate its own candidates, and cast its lot with the Democratic Party. Yet the violent anti-Chinese agitation which it set on foot resulted in 1886 in the passage of a law forbidding the immigration of Chinese into California.

John B. Andrews gives the following notable summary of the labor struggles of 1877:

"The strikes failed in every case, but the moral effect was enormous. For the first time a general strike movement swept the country. Heretofore, the general eight-hour movement in New York City in the spring of 1872 had been the largest strike on record. But now labor became a matter of nation-wide and serious interest to the general public. Fundamental changes followed. The inefficiency of the militia showed the need of a reliable basis of operation for the troops, and the construction of numerous and strong armories in the large cities dates from 1877. The courts began to change their attitude toward labor unions; the strikes and riots brought back from oblivion the doctrine of malicious conspiracy as applied to labor combinations. The legislatures in many states enacted conspiracy laws directed against labor. But the strongest moral effect was upon the wage-earning class. The spirit of labor solidarity was strengthened and made national. This was the first time in the history of the American labor movement that federal troops were called out in time of peace to suppress strikes. Nor had the state militia ever been used for the same purpose on so large a scale. The feeling of resentment engendered thereby began to assume a political aspect, and during the next two years the territory covered by the strike wave became a most

PERIOD OF MILITANT LABOR STRUGGLES 161

promising field for labor parties of all kinds and descriptions. On the side of trade union organization, the effect of the strike appears to have been more remote. Nevertheless, it can safely be stated that there was a direct connection between the active coming forth of the unskilled during the strike and the attempts, so largely secret, that were made immediately after to organize this class of labor" (*Ibid.*, pp. 190-191).

On one hand, the strikes and uprisings of 1877 taught the bourgeoisie that in the struggle with the proletariat it needed a stronger and better equipped state power. In every important industrial center it built great armories and stationed federal troops so that they might be ready to serve the capitalist class.

On the other hand, the struggles of 1877 showed the great class solidarity and militancy of the proletariat. The workers had had a wonderful opportunity to learn the lesson that the bourgeois state is only an instrument in the hands of their enemies. Bourgeois democracy is only a masked dictatorship of the capitalist class. Finally, they saw the crying need of greater unity and that the masses of unskilled factory slaves could not be neglected.

Another prominent psychological reason for the cruelty of the American bourgeoisie in its struggle with the workers was the memory of the Paris Commune. In 1871 the working class of Paris defeated the ruling class and conquered the state power for themselves. It is true that the Communards, after three months, were defeated by the bourgeoisie. But the uprising showed the workers of the whole world that they can emancipate themselves only through revolution. The bourgeoisie of this country remembered the Paris Commune with fear and trembling. The master class dreaded the possibility of the strikes and uprisings of the workers of this country developing into a real revolution, and did not hesitate to use the most drastic means to suppress them. With every defeat of the workers, with every crushing of a strike, the capitalist class sought to prove to the working class how strong its state power was, how deeply rooted the capitalist system was, and how hopeless was the struggle of the proletariat against it.

Failure of strikes, disruption of trade unions, state interference in the struggle between labor and capital, turned the labor movement of America in another direction. Especially the leaders of the movement who had been frightened by the strength and aggressiveness of the workers now began to see the real labor movement only in political parties and in parliamentary action. They loudly proclaimed that there was only one way left for the workers to fight their exploiters—the ballot box. They argued as follows: If the militia and army murder workers during strikes, if there is an industrial and financial crisis, those who are responsible are the officials who are elected by the people. You cannot remove them by strikes and revolts. You must have a party whose representatives, elected to various governmental positions, will serve the workers and not their masters. In other words, in the eyes of their leadership, bourgeois democracy became the only hope and salvation of the workers. The labor movement swung from one extreme to the other. Previously the workers looked upon the craft unions as their only salvation, now their entire hope was placed in parliamentary action. They could not understand that the working class must be united on both the economic and the political fields.

The so-called Greenback Party was the main parliamentary expression of the workers of this period. Especially in the beginning, greenbackism was purely a petty bourgeois and farmers' movement having for its aim some financial reforms. The Greenback Party held its first convention in 1874 and presented the following demands:

"1. The withdrawal of national bank-notes.

"2. That the only currency should be paper, and that such currency be exchangeable for United States interest-bearing bonds.

"3. That coin be used only for the payment of such bonds as called expressly for payment in coin" (Hillquit: *Loc. cit.*, p. 266).

"'Greenbackism' was" says Perlman, "in substance, a plan to give the man without capital an equal opportunity in business with his rich competitor" (Perlman: *Loc. cit.*, p. 51).

In 1876 the Greenback Party participated in the presidential elections and its candidate, Peter Cooper, a manufacturer, received only 100,000 votes.

In 1877 the fortunes of the Greenback Party changed. The failure of the workers' struggles on the industrial field threw them into parliamentary action. Workers' parties sprang up everywhere, and later joined hands with the Greenbackers. The workers were convinced by their leaders that through the financial reform propagated by the Greenback Party they would attain their goal—through the coöperatives backed by government paper they would become the masters of production!

This happy situation was to be brought about in the following manner: Before the crisis of 1873 there had been an extensive consumers' coöperative movement. It was bankrupted by the crisis. Now the exponents of the consumers' coöperative movement "grasped" the idea that all the evil of the times came directly from production, and not from the distribution of the products. And the way to conquer production was as follows: The government was to aid the coöperatives by giving them credit at 3 per cent instead of the 12 per cent that they had to pay before. The coöperatives, by getting cheap credit, would prosper. In this way the workers, especially the handicraftsmen and mechanics who were being constantly pushed further and further into the ranks of the proletarian army by the development of capitalist production, would become independent producers themselves! In other words, the coöperatives would

PERIOD OF MILITANT LABOR STRUGGLES 163

eliminate the bourgeoisie from production. The wage slaves would escape from wage slavery, not through fights, not by overthrowing the bourgeoisie by revolution, but by a peaceful process of the development of coöperatives.

In 1878 a national convention of the Greenback Party was held at Toledo, Ohio, at which leaders of the trade unions and various "Workingmen's Parties" participated. Its most important act was to change the name of the Greenback Party to the "Greenback Labor Party." This was a sign of the unity of workers, petty bourgeoisie, and farmers. Though this joint convention showed great enthusiasm for the movement, the presidential candidate of the Greenback Labor Party, James Weaver, attracted only 300,000 votes in the 1880 elections. From that time on the party slowly disintegrated or, rather, dissolved into the Republican and Democratic Parties.

The Greenback Labor Party lacked a clear working-class program, and it was not rooted in a social class with a future. For although the workers supported it in 1878, the party was not a party of the working class, and did not represent the real interests of that class. It was led by petty bourgeois politicians and the bureaucrats of the farmers' and trade union movements. As soon as the industrial crisis disappeared and "prosperity" dawned on America again, the varying elements of the Greenback Labor Party each went its own way and the fate of the organization was sealed forever.

The socialist movement of this period had as its aim not the improvement of the capitalist system, but the substitution for it of a new system of production. The second convention of the American section of the First International was held in Philadelphia on April 11, 1874. But this convention took place under such conditions that it could not benefit the movement. Even before the meeting a controversy developed in the ranks of the Internationalists on the question of tactics to be pursued in the future. One side contended that in view of the changed conditions after the crisis of 1873 the socialist movement should change its tactics too, while the other side maintained that its former methods were still correct. This controversy went so far that in Chicago the Socialistic Labor Party of Illinois was organized and a few of the sections withdrew from the International and formed the Social Democratic Workingmen's Party of North America.

The Philadelphia convention was, therefore, very poorly attended, only 23 branches sending representatives. The convention declared that:

"The North American Federation rejects all coöperation and connection with the political parties formed by the possessing classes. . . . Consequently, no member of the Federation can belong any longer to such a party." The Federation agreed not to enter "into a truly political campaign or election movement before being strong enough to exercise a perceptible influence."

While the American section was torn by this factional controversy the crisis in the International was rapidly developing. On one hand the struggle between the Marxists and anarchists, on the other the bloody reaction which swept the European continent after the defeat of the Paris Commune, were rapidly leading the First International to its grave. In 1876 the last convention of the International was held in Philadelphia. Only the American branches were represented, with the exception of the German Internationalists, who sent one delegate. The convention decided to disband the International, but its declaration to the workers of the world was full of hope that the time would come when the great work which had been started by the First International would be taken up again by the proletariat and continued. The authors of the declaration proclaimed:

"Fellow Workingmen:

" 'The International is dead,' the bourgeoisie of all countries will again exclaim, and with ridicule and joy it will point to the proceedings of this convention as documentary proof of the defeat of the labor movement of the world. Let us not be influenced by the cry of our enemies! We have abandoned the organization of the International for reasons arising from the present political situation of Europe, but as a compensation for it we see the principles of the organization recognized and defended by the progressive workingmen of the entire civilized world. Let us give our fellow-workers in Europe a little time to strengthen their national affairs, and they will surely soon be in a position to remove the barriers between themselves and the workingmen of other parts of the world.

". . . the comrades in America promise you that they will faithfully guard and cherish the acquisitions of the International in this country until more favorable conditions will again bring together the workingmen of all countries to a common struggle, and the cry will resound again louder than ever:

" 'Proletarians of all countries, unite!' "

Further development of the American socialist movement proceeded from the Social Democratic Workingmen's Party of North America, which had been organized in July, 1874, by the split-off sections of the International. In its declaration of principles the party stated that it sought "to establish a free state founded upon labor." Following are the principles:

"1. Abolition of the present unjust political and social conditions.

"2. Discontinuance of all class rule and class privileges.

"3. Abolition of workingmen's dependence upon the capitalists by introduction of coöperative labor in place of the wage system, so that every laborer will get the full value of his work.

"4. Obtaining possession of the political power as a prerequisite for the solution of the labor question.

"5. United struggle, united organization of all workingmen. . . .

"6. Sympathy with the workingmen of all countries who strive to attain the same object."

PERIOD OF MILITANT LABOR STRUGGLES

From this declaration, with its talk about "a free state" and "full value of his work," it can easily be seen that the party stood much nearer to the German Lassalleanism than to the revolutionary Marxism.

The second convention of the party took place on July 22, 1876, at Philadelphia. Other socialist groups participated. In fact, the convention was summoned as a unity convention. The result was that all the groups joined hands and formed the so-called Working Men's Party of the United States. And at the second convention of the latter, which was held in Newark, N. J., in December, 1877, the name of the Socialist Labor Party of America was adopted.

Ninety per cent of the membership of the party was made up of foreign-born workers. In spite of this serious shortcoming, the party's strength, numerically and in influence among the workers, progressed rapidly. By 1879 it had 10,000 members.

The position of the socialist movement of this period, and especially during the militant labor struggles of 1877, was queer and non-revolutionary.

"They had no part in the instigation of the labor troubles of 1877," says Hillquit (who, by the way, even to-day maintains the same position on the labor fights and revolts as the socialists of the seventies held), "but, on the other hand, they did not neglect the excellent opportunity to propagate their theories among the excited masses. They did not overestimate the significance of the strikes, and realized at the very outset that the movement is but a passing phase in the struggle between capital and labor. They were opposed to unnecessary acts of violence, and at the numerous mass meetings called by them, they dwelt almost uniformly on the futility of planless revolts, and the necessity of organized and intelligent action of the working class.

"In Philadelphia the party decided to hold two mass meetings 'to discuss in a quiet and moderate manner the pending dispute between capital and labor, to express sympathy with the strikers, but to declare energetically against any destruction of property" (Hillquit: *Loc. cit.*, pp. 223-224).

In other words, at the time when the masses of the workers were forced into the struggle with the ruling class by economic conditions and the attacks of the bourgeoisie, when the latter were using the most violent and bloody methods to fight the masses, and workers were dying almost daily at the hands of cold-blooded murderers—at that time the socialists preached the uselessness of force and the sacredness of the property of the ruling class.

CHAPTER XVIII

AWAKENING OF THE LABOR MOVEMENT, 1880-1886

AFTER the struggle of 1877 the American labor movement was exhausted and the bourgeoisie loudly celebrated its complete victory. The ruling class saw prostrated beneath its feet the giant which had so recently been militantly fighting for the most elementary necessaries of life.

But with the year 1879 the wheels of industry again began to turn, and the country entered another period of "prosperity." Revival of industry carried with it an era of big profits to the capitalists, but the latter did not hasten to increase the wages of the workers proportionally, even though these had been greatly reduced during the crisis. The capitalists never raise the wages of the workers voluntarily. In order to improve their conditions with the revival of industry, and to meet the rising cost of living at least partially, the workers had to revive their organizations and use them in their struggle against the master class. The year 1879 witnessed new efforts of the workers again to build up their trade unions.

GROWTH OF TRADE UNION MEMBERSHIP, 1880-1883

	1880	1881	1882	1883
Bricklayers	303	1,558	6,848	9,139
Printers	6,520	7,931	10,439	12,273
Cigar Makers	4,409	12,000	11,430	13,314
Carpenters		2,042	3,780	3,293
Knights of Labor	28,136	19,422	42,517	51,914

"The total trade union membership in the country," says Perlman, "counting the three railway organizations and those organized only locally, amounted to between 200,000 and 225,000 in 1883 and probably was not below 300,000 in the beginning of 1885" (Commons: *History*, etc., Vol. II, p. 314).

The revival of organizing efforts by the workers could be seen also in the beginning, in 1879, of city central bodies, which occupy a very important position in the movement. At the beginning of the eighties they existed in almost every important industrial center. A city central union unites, though sometimes very loosely, the local unions in a particular locality and thus establishes greater unity among the workers and renders their efforts more powerful. This period also witnessed the birth of many national trade organizations embracing all the local unions of a particular trade or craft.

The trade union movement of this period may be divided in two parts: first, the organization of the skilled workers into craft unions, and second, the development of the Knights of Labor, embracing all of the workers, unskilled as well as skilled, in a particular territory.

Real trade unionism, in its present form and ideology, began in this country only about 1879, and the Cigarmakers' National Union (whose national president at that time was Strasser and whose New York president was Samuel Gompers) was its pioneer. Strasser and Gompers not only worked out for their union a peculiar form of organization but they also furnished a peculiar philosophy for it, which still flourishes in the American Federation of Labor. First of all, their trade unionism rejected all efforts to overthrow the capitalist system of production and emphatically declared against joining any movement seeking to substitute any other order for the present order of society. In other words, this unionism recognized the present social system as permanent.

The sole aim of Gompers trade unionism was to make the workers of a certain craft sufficiently strong so that they could, in their bargain with the employers, maintain the balance of power—the employers were to get "fair" profits for their invested capital and the workers were to receive wages which would enable them to make a decent living. It absolutely rejected the revolutionary goal of the working class.

As one of the founders of this trade unionism, Strasser, in his testimony before the United States Senate Committee on Education and Labor, in 1883, clearly stated its philosophy and its object:

"Q. You are seeking to improve home matters first?

"A. Yes, sir, I look first to the trade I represent; I look first to the cigar makers, to the interest of men who employ me to represent their interest.

"Chairman: I was only asking you in regard to your ultimate ends.

"Witness: We have no ultimate ends. We are going on from day to day. We are fighting only for immediate objects—objects that can be realized in a few years." And again: "we say in our constitution that we are opposed to theorists. . . . We are all practical men" (*Ibid.,* p. 309).

This balance of power between labor and capital at the bargaining table was intended to establish an "ideal" system, in which there would be no class struggle, no strikes, and no antagonism between the two classes, though the classes would still exist; a system in which the worker and the employer would live in peace and brotherhood, and neither would think of harming the other, for each would receive his proper share! The employing class would not attempt to squeeze the workers too much because it would know that the workers were organized into craft unions and would not stand for it.

But why craft unions? We do not have to go very far to find an answer to this question also. First of all let us ask ourselves: What was nearest to the heart of the worker, especially the skilled man, back in the eighties when the skilled worker still had a few privileges and his skill still meant higher pay? It was easy for Strasser and Gompers to answer this simple question. They knew from experience that the nearest thing to the heart of the skilled worker was his skill, his trade. Therefore the form of trade union organization had to be such as to be nearest to the heart of the skilled worker too, and that form was the *craft form*. The worker was not interested, or at least was very little interested—so thought Strasser and Gompers—in what was going on outside of his narrow craft world. Primarily, directly, and immediately he was interested in what was going on in his shop, in his home, and about the money in his pocket. This peculiar conception of the needs, desires, and ideas of the worker on the part of the founders of modern trade unionism in America gave rise to the craft form of organization.

Furthermore, in order that this national craft union should be strong enough to maintain the balance of power in its negotiations with the employers, it had to be centralized and supplied with sufficient funds. It was inconceivable that one local should be allowed to do as it pleased and that the national union should remain the head of the organization in name only and have no disciplinary powers.

At the convention of the Cigarmakers' Union in 1879 the Strasser-Gompers plans were adopted in their entirety. The national committee was given complete power over the local unions, membership dues were increased in order to supply funds for the national organization, the national officials were authorized to compel the rich locals to contribute from their treasury for the maintenance of the weaker locals.

We have dwelt extensively upon the philosophy of the Cigarmakers' Union and its officials for the reason that the same form of organization and the same conception of the aim and object of trade unionism were adopted by all other unions and by the American Federation of Labor which was organized later. The only exceptions were the independent railroad brotherhoods, which have remained until to-day more as insurance societies than organizations to defend the wages of the workers. This was probably one of the reasons why the railroad brotherhoods remained outside of the American Federation of Labor, which in its early stages, as we shall see, represented a militant trade unionism as far as defense of the immediate interests of the workers was concerned.

Now as to the rise of the American Federation of Labor. On August 2, 1881, at Terre Haute, Ind., the officials of a few national trade unions met and issued an appeal to the organized workers requesting them to send delegates to a convention which was to take place November 15, 1881, at Pittsburgh, Pa. The appeal stated that the object of the convention was to try to bring all trade unions and labor organizations into a single federation. They also pointed out the aims of such a federation, "*which will be to work for the benefit of all of the industrial classes.*"

AWAKENING OF THE LABOR MOVEMENT   169

Its conventions would discuss the needs of the workers of various occupations separately and then through united efforts it would be so much easier to "secure that justice which isolated and separated trade and labor unions can never fully command." Secondly, such conventions "can prepare labor measures and agree upon laws they desire passed by the Congress of the United States." Thirdly, they "could organize a systematic agitation to propagate trade union principles, and to impress the necessity of protective trade and labor organizations, and to encourage the formation of such unions and their amalgamation in trades assemblies."

The convention assembled as called. One hundred and four delegates, representing eight national trade unions, 11 city central bodies, 42 local unions, and three districts, and 46 locals of the Knights of Labor, were present. The Knights of Labor were well represented at the convention for another very important reason: they feared that it might set up an organization in competition with their own. And there is no doubt that the authors of the call did really have the idea of accomplishing something of that kind.

Two groups, a conservative and a radical, became manifest at the convention. They divided clearly on the election of a president. The so-called radical group nominated Samuel Gompers, while the choice of the conservative group was Richard Powers. The newspapers immediately spread the news that an intense fight was going on between the two elements and that Gompers had been nominated by the socialists who were seeking to "capture the convention." But an open clash was avoided when both nominees "voluntarily" withdrew their candidacies. John Jarett, president of the Amalgamated Iron and Steel Workers, was then elected.

Another controversy arose over the name. The constitution committee suggested as a title the Federation of Organized Trades Unions of the United States of America and Canada. The representatives of the Knights of Labor strongly objected on the ground that such a name could be interpreted as restricting membership to the trade unions only, and as the Knights of Labor was not at that time considered a trade union, there would be no place for them in the federation. Gompers and others assured them that their organization would never be barred from the federation even if the suggested name were adopted. But the representatives of the K. of L. stood firm, and the name as finally chosen was the Federation of Organized Trades and Labor Unions of the United States of America and Canada.

There was also a clash over the composition of future conventions. Some delegates fought for the idea that the basis of representation should be the local union, declaring that only such conventions would truly express the will of the rank and file. Others demanded that the national organizations be made the basis for representation. The latter won, and it was decided that at future conventions the local unions should have no representation whatsoever, every city central body should have one representative, and every national organization should have one representative for every 1,000 members.

The following demands were incorporated in the program of the Federation:

"Legal incorporation for trade unions, compulsory education for children, the prohibition of child labor before 14, uniform apprentice laws, the enforcement of the national eight-hour law, prison labor reform, abolition of the 'truck' and 'order' system, mechanics' lien, abolition of the conspiracy laws as applied to labor organizations, a national bureau of labor statistics, a protective tariff for American labor, and an anti-contract immigrant law; and recommend 'all trades and labor organizations to secure proper representation in all law-making bodies by means of the ballot, and to use all honorable measures by which this result can be accomplished'" (*Ibid.*, p. 324).

The most peculiar demand of the convention was that on incorporation of trade unions. An argument was advanced that such incorporation was necessary to safeguard the funds of the organizations. Later this viewpoint was emphatically rejected and to-day the trade unions of the country are bitterly fighting this very idea of incorporation.

The second convention of the Federation met in Cleveland, November 21, 1882, with only 19 delegates. The Knights of Labor failed to send their delegation.

The third convention was held in New York, August 21, 1883, with 27 delegates present. The question of attempting to unite all organized workers under the single banner of the Federation was thoroughly discussed. A motion was made to elect a special committee to "confer with the Knights of Labor, and other kindred labor organizations, with a view to a thorough unification and consolidation of the working people throughout the country." Gompers strongly opposed this proposition and made a motion that the legislative committee be instructed to confer with officials of all organizations on the question of the unification of the labor movement and report back to the next convention of the Federation. Gompers' motion was adopted.

Meanwhile the controversy between the Federation and the Knights of Labor was becoming constantly sharper. On the other hand, many of the national trade unions were dissatisfied with the political stand of the Federation and refused to participate in its conventions.

The fourth convention met in Chicago, in October, 1884, with 25 delegates. The fifth convention was held in December, 1885, at Washington, D. C., with only 18 delegates. It was apparent to every one that the Federation was doomed to die, that it had not attained its object, and was unable to unite all of the unionists under its flag. Indeed, none of the conventions of the Federation represented more than one-fourth of the organized workers of the country. On the other hand, the quarrel between the Federation and the Knights of Labor by this time had grown into open warfare.

On December 8, 1886, at Columbus, Ohio, a convention was called by the national trade unions which belonged neither to the Federation nor to the K. of L. The leaders of the Federation immediately grasped the importance of this meeting and hurriedly called a convention of their own on the same date and in the same city. After negotiations, these two bodies combined. The old Federation was dissolved and in its place the present American Federation of Labor was formed. The leaders of the united convention claimed that they represented 316,468 members.

Parallel to the efforts of Strasser and Gompers to unite the skilled workers into trade unions an attempt was made toward the end of the seventies to organize also the unskilled workers whose army was daily growing larger with the rapidly developing industry of the country. In 1878 the International Labor Union was launched, led by the well-known labor leaders of that period, McDonnell, McNeill, Parsons, Schilling, Weydemeyer, Sorge, and Ira Steward, who formed a provisional committee, drew up a platform, and called the first convention on December 28, 1878, at Paterson, N. J. The craft unions recognized the capitalist system as a permanent order of society and were opposed to any revolutionary movement, but the International Labor Union, on the contrary, proposed to get rid of this system and to emancipate the proletariat. But the theory of the leaders as to how to bring about this great change was odd and utopian. Here is the nucleus of the theory as we find it in their platform:

"The wage system is a despotism under which the wage-worker is forced to sell his labor at such price and such conditions as the employer of labor shall dictate. . . . That as the wealth of the world is distributed through the wage system, its better distribution must come through higher wages and better opportunities, until wages shall represent the earnings and not the necessities of labor; thus melting profit upon labor out of existence, and making co-operation, or self-employed labor, the natural and logical step from wage slavery to free labor. . . . The first step toward the emancipation of labor is a reduction of the hours of labor. . . ."

The provisional committee set for itself the following objects:

"The reduction of the hours of labor; higher wages; factory, mine and works inspection; abolition of the contract convict labor and truck system; employers to be held responsible for accidents by neglected machinery; prohibition of child labor; the establishment of labor bureaus; labor propaganda by means of a labor press, labor lectures, the employment of a general organizer, and the final abolition of the wage system. . . ."

The practical methods by which these things were to be attained were:

"1. The formation of an amalgamated union of laborers so that members of any calling can combine under a central head, and form a part of the amalgamated trades unions.

"2. The establishment of a general fund for benefit and protective purposes.

"3. The organization of all workingmen in their trade unions, and the creation of such unions where none exist.

"4. The national and international amalgamation of all labor unions" (*Ibid.*, pp. 303-304).

The practical methods, steps, and demands of the International Labor Union were serious and fitted the needs of the times, but their theory on the abolition of the capitalist system was ridiculous. In the first place, the union demanded shorter hours because "the added leisure produced by a reduction of the hours of labor will operate upon the natural causes that affect the habits and customs of the people, enlarging wants, stimulating ambition, decreasing idleness, and increasing wages." Secondly, the union was to demand higher and higher wages until all the profits of the employers would be absorbed into the wages of the workers. In this way, step by step, gradually, the capitalist system would be pushed to the wall and would have to disappear! The owners of the factories—since profits would no longer be coming to them!—would turn the factories over to the workers. In the same way all other capitalist institutions would disappear! It seems that the authors of the platform entirely forgot even the experience of the Paris Commune which had proved that the bourgeoisie would never voluntarily abandon its privileges and property in favor of the workers or society as a whole, but, on the contrary, would fight to the bitter end until routed by the mighty forces of the working class in open battle.

There can be no doubt that the leaders of the union had lofty intentions and sought their ends conscientiously. In their organization they saw salvation for the great masses of unskilled workers. McNeill, its president, declared at the first convention:

"Not only are the skilled mechanics concentrating their numbers but the unskilled, the manual laborers who heretofore have been without hope and without organization, are fast learning from the experience of the past the necessity of combination. The International Labor Union presents a plan by which the unorganized masses and local unions can become affiliated."

The Paterson convention was almost entirely composed of representatives of the textile workers of Paterson and Fall River. They decided that the local unions and the organizations of the unskilled workers should affiliate. But in spite of the zeal and the enthusiasm of the leaders of the new movement, efforts to attract the masses failed, and a rapid decline set in. By 1880 the membership of the union amounted only to about 1,500, and after one more year it went to pieces.

The Knights of Labor, which attracted into its ranks hundreds of thousands of workers, occupied an outstanding position in the labor movement of the period. As has already been pointed out, the Order of the

AWAKENING OF THE LABOR MOVEMENT

Knights of Labor was formed in 1869 as a secret organization. For a few years it remained numerically a small sect and did not show any important activity. Even in the great struggles of 1877 the Knights of Labor were not prominent. Powderly, the grand chief of the order, tells us that it did not participate in the strikes of that year. On the contrary, the national leaders of the order even helped to prevent the workers from attacking the ruling class. The rank and file, and local organizations, did take part in these struggles, even though against the will of their leaders (Powderly: *Thirty Years of Labor*, pp. 207-219).

For a long time the Knights of Labor remained a decentralized organization. The local units did as they pleased. Only at the Reading convention, on January 1, 1878, was a highly centralized form of organization established. The basic unit was the local, which might be composed of people either of a single trade or occupation, or of various callings, but not less than three-fourths of them must be wage-earners. The delegates from five or more locals formed a district assembly, and the representatives of the various district assemblies made up the general assembly. The general assembly was the highest institution in the order, and had complete power over all lower units.

From the beginning the Knights of Labor was not a purely working-class organization, and it remained in that condition for some time. The constitution adopted at the Reading convention provided that any person over 18 years of age *"working for wages, or who at any time worked for wages,"* could become a member. But "no person who either sells, or makes his living by the sale of, intoxicating drink, can be admitted, and no lawyer, doctor, or banker can be admitted."

The coming of the order out into the open was also a long process. The bourgeoisie and the church had begun a most violent and slanderous attack upon it. On the other hand, the labor movement was developing rapidly, the membership of the order increased by leaps and bounds, and the question arose whether it was worth while keeping the affairs of the organization an absolute secret. A special convention was held in June, 1878, at Philadelphia, to discuss this important question. The exponents of "legalization," or coming into the open, did not get the required two-thirds majority, and the question was referred to the membership. The vote was against dropping secrecy. But it seems that the leadership of the order was in favor of ending secrecy, and the general assembly decided to leave the question to the various districts with the right to declare their name openly by two-thirds vote. Only in 1881 did the general assembly decide by 28 votes against 6 to declare the name of the order openly.

The aims of the Knights of Labor were not revolutionary. On the contrary, they meant *"no conflict with legitimate enterprise, no antagonism to necessary capital."* Further:

"We mean to create a healthy public opinion on the subject of labor (the only creator of values or capital) and the justice of its receiving a full, just share of the values of capital it has created."

They would have nothing to do with the class struggle. On the contrary,

"We shall, with all our strength, support laws made to harmonize the interests of labor and capital, for labor alone gives life and value to capital, and also those laws which tend to lighten the exhaustiveness of toil" (*Documentary History,* etc., Vol. X, pp. 23-24).

The main field of the order's activity was to be the coöperative movement, which was to emancipate the worker by opening to him an escape to self-employment. Its motto was "Coöperation of the order, by the order, and for the order." Parliamentary action was another field of its activity. The order was opposed to strikes and boycotts and demanded a law for compulsory arbitration of labor disputes. Other demands of the Knights of Labor were similar to those of the trade unions: insurance, incorporation of labor organizations, prohibition of child labor, compulsory education, and abolition of such laws as make distinctions between the rich and poor.

Nevertheless, the Knights of Labor led many militant strikes. Its militancy was the main reason for its growth numerically and in influence. But this militancy, of course, did not come from the constitution or the leadership of the order. The constitution pointed out the futility of strikes and boycotts, the leaders preached the solidarity of the interests of labor and capital, but the rank and file marched into the struggle, carried on war against their enemies, and compelled their leaders to stand, at least for a time, in the forefront of the battle. District Master Workman Thomson in his report of District Assembly 1, writes:

"Am sorry to say that I found very few of the principles of our order in practice. In fact, there seems to be a general ignorance, or disregard of the principles of our organization. The older ideas of former trade organizations seem to predominate and control the actions of the locals generally."

The growth of the Knights of Labor was unusual. In a very short time it became the largest and the strongest union of the unskilled and semiskilled workers in the United States. In 1879 it had only 20,151 members; in 1880, 28,136; in 1883, 51,914. But from then on the order increased tremendously. In 1885 it had reached 104,066 and in 1886 the membership mounted to 702,924. During the period of one year, 1885-1886, about 600,000 joined. This, however, marked the peak of its development. From then on it declined as rapidly as it had risen.

The constitution of the Knights of Labor provided that trade unions could affiliate with it. And it really was to the advantage of the unions to join. Many of the national trade unions were very poor and could not send organizers into the different parts of the country. But this deficiency could easily be overcome by joining the K. of L., which was organized on the basis of districts including the workers of all trades. One organizer of the order could assist at the same time all trades where there was not a sufficient number of workers of a particular trade to form a local. Those who sympathized with unionism could be combined into a mixed local of the order till such time as their number would permit them to form a trade union local. Such a form of organization helped the development of the order and attracted many trade unions to it.

At the beginning of the eighties there was no conflict between the Knights of Labor and the trade unions. The fight developed only when both of these movements increased in strength, when the present American Federation of Labor was formed, and the question of jurisdiction and leadership of the labor movement came up. Finally, the fight developed into a life and death struggle. The K. of L. was defeated and disappeared from the scene.

CHAPTER XIX

STRIKES, KNIGHTS OF LABOR, TRADE UNIONS, AND ANARCHISTS, 1880-1886

THE first strike openly led by the Knights of Labor was that of the telegraph operators in 1883. The year before the telegraphers had organized a national trade union and affiliated with the K. of L. as District 45. The general strike was declared on June 18, 1883. The workers demanded one day of rest in seven, an eight-hour day and seven hours for night workers, and a 15 per cent increase in wages. The walkout started successfully, but ended in a great defeat for the workers. At the end of July they went back to work; the most active lost their jobs and were blacklisted. After this defeat the Telegraphers' National Union, with a membership of 3,561, withdrew from the order.

There were also a few smaller strikes in 1882, mostly of semi-skilled and unskilled workers. The most important was the strike of the freight-handlers on the railroads centering in New York City. It was an unorganized strike and the railroad companies easily broke it.

A great wave of strikes swept the country beginning with the end of 1885 and through the whole of 1886. During the years 1883-1885 there was an economic crisis, though not so severe as that of 1873. According to *Bradstreet's* only about 168,000 workers were unemployed. Nevertheless, the depression reduced wages from 15 to 40 per cent. The wave of revolts followed (*Bradstreet's,* December 20, 1884).

A textile strike in Fall River, Mass., which affected 10 factories and 5,000 workers, was crushed in 1884. The fight lasted 18 weeks. The companies brought in scabs from other cities and the workers were beaten into submission. Again those who had been active in the strike were blacklisted.

Four hundred stove mounters of Troy, N. Y., went on strike against a 20 per cent reduction of wages and against an attempt of the employers to compel the men to desert their union. The struggle lasted from May till September; the workers were defeated and their organization went to pieces.

In Cincinnati, Ohio, the members of the Cigar Makers' Union were locked out in March, 1884. A bitter struggle ensued, which lasted until April, 1885. The national union was strong and gave effective financial assistance. From the beginning of the conflict until November, 1884,

$140,000 was spent for the relief of the workers. Nevertheless they lost.

But the most bitter strike of 1884 was the coal miners' strike in Hocking Valley, Ohio. The coal companies decided to reduce wages 10 cents a ton. The Ohio state miners' union took up the fight and on June 28, 1884, 4,000 miners were called out. The companies decided to crush the resistance at any cost and declared another reduction of wages by 10 cents a ton. They also demanded that the miners sign a contract promising to leave the union. They hired spies and gangsters of the Pinkerton agency and also asked the state militia to assist them.

"The strike was one of the longest in the mining industry. Expressions of sympathy and pecuniary aid came to the starving miners from many parts of the country, but, in view of the falling market, the companies could not be forced to surrender. After six months, having expended over $100,000 for strike benefits, the union ordered the men back to work upon the drastic conditions offered at the beginning of the strike" (Commons: *History*, etc., Vol. II, p. 364).

After the failure of these strikes the workers took up the boycott, or the "strike on the job," as a means of defense. It is estimated that in 1885 there were 196 boycotts. Of course, not all were successful. The majority of the boycotts were conducted by the members of the Knights of Labor, almost always without the knowledge of their leaders.

Another strike in 1885 which attracted much attention was the effort of the unorganized, unskilled workers of Saginaw Valley, Mich. On July 6 the men in the lumber and shingle mills left their jobs and demanded an immediate 10-hour day with no reduction in pay. The strikers arranged a great demonstration and marched from mill to mill asking the other workers to join them. The army of strikers increased to 5,500 and affected the entire lumber industry, embracing 17 shingle mills, 61 lumber mills, and 58 salt blocks attached to the latter. The workers soon found out that they could not win without an organization and they invited T. B. Barry, a member of the general assembly of the Knights of Labor, to lead them. The employers imported 150 gangsters from the Pinkerton agency and mobilized the state militia. The strike lasted for two months—July and August. The impregnable solidarity of the workers compelled the employers to grant their demands. The strikers in this case were almost entirely foreign-born, mainly Poles.

Two thousand stonecutters of Lemon and Joliet, Ill., went out for a 50 per cent raise in wages. All were foreign-born. The employers brought in scabs, whites as well as Negroes. A wave of indignation swept the ranks of the workers. The governor of the state called out the militia. When the battle was over four strikers and a woman were found dead. Such was the treatment accorded the unorganized workers at the hands of the bourgeois state.

Many struggles occurred on the railroads. The shopmen of the Union Pacific Railroad, at Denver, Colo., went out on May 4, 1884, against a 10 per cent wage reduction. They invited J. R. Buchanan, a well known member of the Knights of Labor, to lead their fight. The main question was that of organization, for the workers were not unionized. In two days every shop from Omaha to Ogden was organized, and the strike spread through all branches of the railroad. After three days the company gave in and recalled the wage reduction. This victory increased the prestige of the Knights of Labor amongst the masses and was the beginning of the growth of the order on the railroads.

But the Union Pacific submitted to the workers only temporarily. In the rise of the Knights of Labor it saw a danger to its profits and in August of the same year it again declared a reduction of wages against the machinists of Ellis, Kan. At the same time 20 members of the order were thrown out of work at Denver. This trial of strength between the organized employers and the organized workers ended with a victory for the railroad hands.

In October of 1884 the wages of the Missouri, Kansas, and Texas Railroad shopmen were cut, and on February 26, 1885, a 10 per cent reduction was declared for the Wabash Railroad shopmen. The workers on the latter line struck on February 27, while those on the former went out on March 9. Later the shopmen on the Missouri Pacific Railroad joined them. All three of these railroads belonged to the famous Gould interests. The strike affected 4,500 workers. It was also supported by other railroad crafts such as the engineers, conductors, and switchmen. The Knights of Labor organization on the Union Pacific Railroad sent Buchanan to lead the strike and gave $30,000 to finance it. From now on the influence of the Knights rapidly increased.

But very soon the same companies, under the leadership of Gould, saw the danger in the Knights of Labor amongst the unskilled workers of the railroads and decided to crush the organization. On August 18, 1885, the owners of the Wabash Railroad decided to reduce the number of shopmen at Moberly, Mo., to the lowest possible figure. This meant that many of the members of the Knights of Labor would be dismissed from their jobs. The general assembly of the Knights decided that all members of the order working on the Union Pacific, as well on Gould's Southwestern system, should refuse to handle any work connected with the Wabash Railroad. If this strike had been declared, it would have affected 20,000 workers. Gould thereupon decided to head off the strike, and persuaded his colleagues that it would be better to yield to the demands of the workers than to have a strike on their hands, in all probability as militant as that of 1877. The Knights demanded that all men who had been dismissed from their jobs since the beginning of the lockout be reinstated and that persecution of its members be stopped. The strike was won even before it started. This victory naturally brought still further prestige to the Knights of Labor among the unskilled railroad workers. In this dispute the skilled railroad workers, such as the engineers and conductors, declined in any way to support the struggle led by the Knights. This was probably the first sharp division in the ranks of the railroad men, which gave rise to separate organizations for the skilled and unskilled, the shopmen's unions affiliating with the American Federation of Labor, while the brotherhoods remained independent, conservative, semi-insurance organizations.

Now the Order of the Knights of Labor appeared in the eyes of the bourgeoisie a terrible force which threatened the very foundations of the capitalist system. The bourgeois press began to tell the world how dangerous the order was, and that it had millions of men in its ranks. It said that this army was under the command of a few leaders, totalling not more than five men. In 1885 the New York *Sun* sent a reporter to investigate the order, and he reported:

"Five men in this country control the chief interests of 500,000 working men, and can at any moment take the means of livelihood from 2,500,000 souls. These men compose the executive board of the Noble Order of the Knights of Labor of America. The ability of the President and cabinet to turn out all the men in the civil service, and to shift from one post to another the duties of the men in the army and navy, is a petty authority compared with that of these five Knights. The authority of the late cardinal was, and that of the bishops of the Methodist church is, narrow and prescribed, so far as material affairs are concerned, in comparison with that of these five rulers.

"They can stay the nimble touch of almost every telegraph operator; can shut up most of the mills and factories, and can disable the railroads. They can issue an edict against any manufactured goods so as to make their subjects cease buying them, and the tradesmen stop selling them.

"They can array labor against capital, putting labor on the offensive or defensive, for quiet and stubborn self-protection, or for angry, organized assault, as they will" (Powderly: *Thirty Years of Labor,* p. 494).

This story was reprinted by all the bourgeois press and the name of the Knights of Labor resounded in every nook and corner of the continent. The secretary of the order began to receive letters from Florida, Alabama, and other far-away states requesting information on how to organize sections.

Another important strike led by the Knights took place in 1886. As has already been pointed out, the Gould railroad companies in 1885 promised not to persecute the members of the order. But they violated this promise and finally, on March 1, 1886, the controversy developed into a strike, when a member of the order was discharged at Marshall, Tex. The workers presented a demand for recognition of the order and a day's pay of $1.50; 9,000 were affected. In this struggle the workers resorted to sabotage, taking out parts of the engines so that they could not run. The engineers, firemen, switchmen, and conductors refused to come out, and the strikers were sometimes compelled to use force against them. The leader of the order, Terrence V. Powderly, was really hamstringing the strike by starting negotiations with Jay Gould, the owner of the railroad, to settle the controversy through arbitration, instead of leading the workers in the fight. The negotiations failed because the workers soon learned of the scheme of their leader and emphatically rejected it. For two months they carried on the struggle, but finally were defeated. The treachery of Powderly in this strike is clearly established.

While the Knights were thus struggling, how fared it with the crafts in the Federation of Organized Trades and Labor Unions of the United States and Canada? Their most important action was preparation for the great strike of 1886, to establish the eight-hour day. This strike was important not only because it attracted into the struggle the lowest strata of the working class, but also because it laid the foundation for the later growth of the American Federation of Labor, and delivered a blow to the Knights of Labor from which it never recovered.

The convention of the Federation, held on October 7, 1884, at Chicago, adopted the following resolution on the eight-hour day:

"Resolved, by the Federation of Organized Trades and Labor Unions of the United States and Canada, that eight hours shall constitute a legal day's labor from and after May 1, 1886, and that we recommend to labor organizations throughout this jurisdiction that they so direct their laws as to conform to this resolution by the time named."

The Federation further made a step forward by officially inviting the Knights of Labor "to coöperate in the general movement to establish the eight-hour day."

The Federation at the time was still weak, having only about 50,000 members. The decision to set the date for a struggle to establish an eight-hour day was a daring step, and showed its militancy. The national trade unions received this decision of the Federation very indifferently. Only two of them, the Cigar Makers and the Carpenters, had decided before the 1885 convention of the Federation to support the eight-hour strike financially. In spite of this lack of backing, the convention of 1885 reaffirmed its former stand for the strike on May 1, 1886. It again appealed to all trade unions to join the walkout on May 1, even though they did not give financial assistance. Despite the coolness of the national unions toward the general strike, their ranks increased substantially during the last half of 1885 and the first half of 1886.

But it was apparent to everybody that the success or the failure of the movement would, to a very great extent, depend upon the attitude of the Knights of Labor, which was much stronger than the Federation and which had conducted a number of successful strikes. But the leaders of the order did not support the movement. Instead they practically declared war against it. At a meeting of the general assembly in 1885, a resolution was submitted to support the general strike.

"On the eve of the eight-hour strike the general officers of the Knights adopted an attitude of hostility toward the movement. On March 13, 1886, Grand Master Workman Powderly issued a secret circular in which he advised the Knights not to rush into the eight-hour movement" (Commons: *History*, Vol. II, p. 378).

In order to justify his anti-labor position toward the movement, Powderly invented a peculiar "philosophy." This is what he said:

"To talk of reducing the hours of labor without reducing the power of the machinery to oppress instead of to benefit, is a waste of energy. What men gain through a reduction of hours will be taken from them in another way while the rule of iron continues. . . . The advocate of the eight-hour system must go beyond a reduction of the number of hours a man must work and must labor for the establishment of a just and humane system of land ownership, control of machinery, railroads, and telegraphs as well as equitable currency system before he will be able to retain the vantage ground gained when the hours of labor are reduced to eight per day" (Powderly: *Loc. cit.*, p. 514).

On the surface it would seem that Powderly was much more revolutionary than those who were fighting for shorter hours of labor. He spoke of necessary reforms before the time would be ripe to demand shorter hours. But the demand for shorter hours always was and will remain, as long as wage slavery exists, a revolutionary demand, much more important than the demand for a few cents' addition to the wages of the workers. It was perfectly clear that Powderly was not so much interested in whether the workers would be able to maintain the eight-hour day after they had won it, as he was afraid of the mass movement of the workers, and desired not to antagonize the bourgeoisie. His rôle was that of a faithful agent of the bourgeoisie in the ranks of the workers, regardless of all his philosophical justifications for his stand.

Despite the opposition of the leaders of the Knights of Labor to the eight-hour strike on May 1, the rank and file of the order joined the movement with the greatest enthusiasm. About 340,000 workers participated, of whom nearly 200,000 won their demand. Though not all of them won directly through the strike, their success was nevertheless a result of the movement which the Federation had originated. After this strike the rôles of the Federation and the Knights of Labor changed. Slowly the star of the order began to descend. The working class lost confidence in an organization which had failed them in the most important hour of their struggles. On the other hand, the trade unions which had begun the strike came out victorious. For many years they were able to point with pride to their militant record of 1886.

The labor struggles of the last half of 1886 ended in defeats for the workers in nearly all cases. In the first half of the year the workers were on the offensive against the employers, demanding higher wages and shorter hours. In the second half the tables were turned and the employers made militant and successful attacks upon the workers. There were many lockouts, affecting 75,000 men.

The most important lockout of the period occurred in the Chicago packing industry when on October 8, 1886, 20,000 butchers were locked out in order to reëstablish the 10-hour instead of the eight-hour day. The employers formed a packers' association. The governor sent two regiments of militia in addition to the several hundred Pinkerton agents and provocateurs employed by the association. But the solidarity of the workers, who were organized in District Assemblies 27 and 54 of the K. of L., was unbreakable and the ranks of their enemies gradually weakened. In order to get their men to work, the latter rescinded their decision not to hire members of the K. of L., but the workers remained unmoved by this trick and demanded a return of the eight-hour day which they had won on May 1. On the eve of victory for the workers,

"suddenly on November 15, like a thunderbolt out of a clear sky, a telegram arrived from Powderly ordering the men back to work. Powderly had refused to consider the reports from Barry and Carlton, the members of the general executive board who were on the ground, but, as charged by Barry, was guided instead by the advice of a priest who had appealed to him to call off the strike and thus put an end to the suffering of the men and their families" (Perlman: *Loc. cit.*, p. 98).

This treachery of Powderly demoralized the ranks of the strikers and they were compelled to submit to the packers' association. Again its own leader had dealt the Knights of Labor a grievous blow.

The militant labor movement of 1886 is characterized by Perlman as follows:

"This upheaval meant more than the mere quickening of the pace of the movement begun in preceding years and decades. It signalled the appearance on the scene of a new class which had not hitherto found a place in the labor movement, namely, the unskilled. All the peculiar characteristics of the dramatic events in 1886 and 1887, the highly feverish pace at which organizations grew, the nation-wide wave of strikes, particularly sympathetic strikes, the wide use of the boycott, the obliteration, apparently complete, of all lines that divided the laboring class, whether geographic or trade, the violence and turbulence which accompanied the movement—all of these were the signs of a great movement by the class of the unskilled, which had finally risen in rebellion. This movement, rising as an elemental protest against oppression and degradation, could be feebly restrained by any considerations of expediency and prudence; nor, of course, could it be restrained by any lessons from experience. The movement bore in every way the aspect of a social war. A frenzied hatred of labor for capital was shown in every important strike . . ." (*Ibid.*, p. 90).

This mass rising on the part of the unskilled workers could not even be stopped by the labor leaders. "Whenever the leaders undertook to hold it within bounds they were generally discarded by their followers, and others who would lead as directed were placed in charge." At the beginning of 1886 Powderly wrote about the militancy of the rank and file of the K. of L.:

"In some places where our order is strong, the members refuse to arbitrate, simply because they *are strong*. Such course is not in keeping with plank XXII of the declaration of principles of the Knights of Labor. One of the causes for complaint against employers has been that they refused to recognize the employees in the field of arbitration. Now that we are becoming powerful, we should not adopt the vices which organized labor has forced the employer to discard" (*Ibid.*, p. 374).

The militant labor struggles of 1886 ended in a great tragedy which was prepared for the workers by the bourgeoisie. This was the bloody event in Chicago for which the bourgeoisie blamed the "anarchists," though the bourgeoisie itself was responsible for it.

As has already been pointed out, a struggle was going on in the First International between the communists and anarchists. The former were led by Marx and Engels, and the latter by Bakunin. The followers of Marx won, and the office of the International was transferred to America. The International formally ceased to exist in 1872.

In America, anarchistic tendencies began to appear in the Socialist Labor Party at its convention in 1879. There were two factions, "right" and "left." The main controversy developed over the question of organizing military fighting organizations. Hillquit speaks bitterly against the anarchist movement. On developments at the S. L. P. convention he says:

"Shortly before, the socialists of Chicago and Cincinnati had organized some military organizations of working men under the name of 'Educational and Defensive Societies.' The national executive committee of the party was opposed to these organizations, on the ground that they tended to create a false impression of the aims and character of the socialist movement. 'As they carried the red flag and acknowledged their socialistic tendencies, the public were informed that the socialists were determined to accomplish by force what they could not obtain by the ballot,' Van Patten reported to the convention. The national committee publicly disavowed any connection with the military organizations, and requested all party members to withdraw from them.
"The sponsors of the military labor organizations resented the interference of the executive committee, and when the convention assembled they moved for a vote of censure against the latter. The motion was adopted by a small majority after a heated debate" (Hillquit: *Loc. cit.*, pp. 234-235).

It is really very hard to see much of anarchism in the "left wing" of the convention. Its stand for the workers' fighting organizations to defend themselves against the brutal attacks of the bourgeoisie cannot be construed as a real replica of Bakuninism. Only later the anarchistic tendencies began to shape themselves into a definite movement.

On the other hand, the "right wing" of the convention, led by the executive committee, took a very definite opportunistic position by rejecting in principle the use of force and advancing the idea that through the ballot alone the working class will overthrow capitalism and establish socialism.

Some of the "left wingers" left the Socialist Labor Party and formed "revolutionary clubs" in various cities. At the head of the movement stood such well-known leaders as Most, Spies, Parsons, and Grottkau. In October, 1883, these "social revolutionists" had a convention at Pittsburgh and formed the "International Working People's Association." They adopted a manifesto in which, on the question of force, they declared: "Destruction of the existing class rule, by all means, i.e., by energetic, relentless, revolutionary, and international action."

This statement of the "social revolutionists" was heralded by the opportunists as pure and simple anarchism. It is true that it spoke of the use of force or energetic, militant action on the part of the workers, but this cannot be in any way interpreted as anarchism as developed in Europe by Bakunin and his followers. Even some of the prominent leaders of the Socialist Labor Party of that time could not see any anarchism in the manifesto of the Internationalists and demanded unity with them. On their part, the Internationalists were ready to unite with the S. L. P. and even invited the latter to their Pittsburgh convention. But "the executive committee of the party declined the invitation, declaring that there could be no common ground between social democrats and anarchists" (*Ibid.*, pp. 239-240).

But as time went on and the great labor struggles of 1886 approached, in which the Internationalists took a most active part, some actual anarchistic tendencies began to be shown by Most, Spies, Parsons, Schwab, Grottkau, and other leaders. These tendencies appeared in the fact that the Internationalists were not able to analyze and understand the conditions under which the working class will have to employ force against their enemies. The leaders of the movement began to speak more often about the necessity of taking up arms against the bourgeoisie, though the conditions for such action were far from ripe.

To do justice to the "anarchist" movement of America it is necessary to distinguish it from European anarchism. One of the characteristics of anarchists is belief in the action of small, isolated groups, devoted to the cause. But this was not true of the American anarchists of this period. They believed in mass proletarian action. They paid special attention to the trade union movement and by all means endeavored to draw the trade unions into action along with them. They believed in a general revolt of the proletariat. In July, 1884, at the meeting of the Progressive Cigar Makers' Union, the "anarchists," Spies and Grottkau, fought for and succeeded in passing a resolution which declared:

"That the only means whereby the emancipation of mankind can be brought about is the open rebellion of the robbed *class in all parts of the country* against the existing economic and political institution."

They also actively participated in and succeeded in organizing the Central Labor Union of Chicago, which for the time being exerted a great influence on the labor movement of that city.

Thus the leaders of the American anarchist movement neither believed in nor advocated the assassination of individual oppressors of the workers, as was the case with many extreme anarchists in Europe. If they appealed to the workers to arm themselves, they always had in mind, and clearly pointed out that they meant, the arming of the workers as a class and not as individuals. Therefore the American anarchists of that period must be clearly distinguished from the anarchists of Europe who in July, 1881, in London organized the so-called "Black International," at least as far as their "propaganda of the deed" was concerned. It is true that they maintained connections with the "Black International," and their groups were called "sections of the Black International" which in Chicago alone had a membership of about 3,000. Nevertheless they did not pursue the tactics of the "Black International" nor did they live up to its principles.

The anarchist movement was the most active section of the labor movement prior to and during the struggles of 1886, and it exerted a great influence on the whole working class in Chicago. The previously mentioned Cigar Makers' Union led by Spies, Grottkau, and others issued an appeal to all labor unions in Chicago, in June, 1884, asking them to withdraw from the conservative Amalgamated Trades and Labor Assembly and to organize a new, progressive central union. Many unions responded to this appeal and organized the Central Labor Union of Chicago. By June, 1886, the new union was larger than the conservative central union, having 22 affiliated unions, among which were 11 of the largest locals in Chicago.

In October, 1885, the Central Labor Union issued a program in which it declared that land is a social heritage, that labor creates all wealth, that there can be no harmony between capital and labor, that strikes as then conducted by trade unions were doomed to fail, and that therefore it was "the sacred duty of every workingman to cut loose from all capitalist political parties and to devote his entire energy to his trades or labor union . . . in order to stand ready to resist the encroachment by the ruling class upon our liberties."

In this declaration we really see the syndicalist tendencies of the anarchists. They reject all political parties, including the necessary revolutionary party of the proletariat, and urge their followers to devote their entire energy to industrial action.

The official organs of the "syndico-anarchists" were the *Alarm* in English and the *Arbeiter-Zeitung* in German. Around them were gathered the best literary forces of the movement.

On Thanksgiving Day of 1884, Parsons and others organized a demonstration of the unemployed in which about 5,000 participated. The demonstration culminated in a mass meeting in Haymarket Square and was addressed by Parsons, Spies, Griffin, and Schwab. The anarchist press spoke enthusiastically about this demonstration as a new page in the history of the American labor movement. For instance, the *Arbeiter-Zeitung* declared:

"Yesterday took place the birth of a new phase in the social struggle. Hitherto the revolutionary movement has been restricted to the better situated and the more intelligent German, Bohemian, and Danish workingmen.... Since yesterday this is no longer the case. Yesterday, the typically American working class carried the red flag through the streets and thereby proclaimed its solidarity with the international proletariat."

As soon as the agitation for the eight-hour day was started the Chicago Central Labor Union took up the slogan and actively participated in the movement. There can be no doubt that due to this activity the eight-hour movement in Chicago was much more successful than in any other industrial center. However, the Central Labor Union did not consider the eight-hour movement an end in itself. Its leaders constantly emphasized the fact that the working class can emancipate itself from capitalism only through the forcible overthrow of bourgeois rule. They looked upon the conquest of the eight-hour day only as a battle in the general struggle in which every class-conscious and sincere worker must participate. This attitude of the Central Labor Union was clearly stated in a resolution submitted by Spies and adopted in October, 1885. The resolution declared:

"Be it resolved, that we urgently call upon the wage-earning class to arm itself in order to be able to put forth against their exploiters such an argument which alone can be effective: Violence; and further be it resolved, that notwithstanding that we expect very little from the introduction of the eight-hour day, we firmly promise to assist our more backward brethren in this class struggle with all means and power at our disposal, so long as they will continue to show an open and resolute front to our common oppressors, the aristocratic vagabonds and the exploiters. Our war-cry is 'Death to the foes of the human race.'"

Here again we see that the anarcho-syndicalists were not concerned with arming a few individuals or small groups, or with getting rid of individuals. They called to action the whole proletariat. They condemned as parasites, exploiters, and enemies of the human race not the individual capitalists, but all their class.

The strike for the eight-hour day on May 1, 1886, aroused great enthusiasm among great masses of the workers of Chicago. On the second day of the general strike about 80,000 were involved. The struggle was peaceful and the workers' solidarity was remarkable.

KNIGHTS OF LABOR AND ANARCHISTS

But just before May 1 a strike had broken out at the McCormick Harvester Works. The employers imported scabs and sluggers. The Internationalists Parsons, Spies, Fielden, and Schwab were active in the strike, and raised a protest against the use of strikebreakers. On May 3 the McCormick strikers held a large mass meeting at which Spies spoke. During the meeting they noticed the scabs coming out of the factory, and some of the strikers advanced upon them. Immediately the police appeared and began to shoot at the crowd without warning. Six workers were murdered on the spot and many were wounded. A flood of indignation against the bloody attack swept over the workers of Chicago. The Internationalists decided to stage a protest meeting against the brutality of the police. On May 4, at 7:30 P.M., about 3,000 workers massed at the protest meeting in Haymarket Square. Fearing that trouble might develop, Mayor Harrison came to the meeting. Spies spoke first, Parsons second, and Fielden last. The meeting was absolutely peaceful; the speakers did not urge the workers to use violence or to take up arms. They condemned the brutality of the police and pointed out how the capitalists exploit the workers. Harrison himself admitted that there was nothing in the speeches which could in any way be construed as inciting to violence. He left the meeting at 10 P.M. But suddenly about 180 policemen surrounded the crowd. Fielden, who was concluding his address, appealed to the captain, saying that the meeting was peaceful and should not be broken up. But the command was given to attack the meeting. At this moment a bomb was hurled at the police, killing a sergeant. The police immediately opened fire and bullets began to fly on both sides. When the onslaught was over seven policemen and four workers were dead, and several were wounded. Next day Spies, Schwab, Fielden, Parsons, Fischer, Engel, Lingg, Neebe, Schnaubelt, and Seligeri were arrested and charged with first degree murder. Schnaubelt escaped, and Seligeri was freed for turning state's witness and thus betraying his comrades.

The trial of the other victims started on June 21, 1886. Judge Gary presided. Not a single worker was on the jury. The state did not attempt to prove that a worker had thrown the bomb. There was no doubt that the bomb-throwing was the work of a provocateur. It was a prearranged plan of the employers and police department to get rid of the most active leaders of the Chicago labor movement. No charge was made at the trial that any one of the accused either at the mass meeting on May 4 or at any other time or place had actually killed anybody. The only charge against them was that their speeches and their writings were indirectly responsible for the tragedy. It was proved that it was the police who had attacked, not the workers. The whole trial was a nasty hypocrisy, a prearranged conspiracy against the labor movement. The jury "found" the defendants "guilty." Spies, Fielden, Schwab, Parsons, Fischer, Engel, and Lingg were condemned to death, and Neebe was sentenced to the penitentiary for 15 years. All appeals to the higher courts failed. The bourgeoisie were thirsty for the blood of the workers' leaders.

A "Citizens' Association," composed of manufacturers and bankers, was formed to prosecute the Internationalists. In a few short hours $100,000 was collected among the members of the association for this purpose.

Some of the condemned asked the governor for pardon; their sentences were commuted to life imprisonment, and later they were given their freedom. But Spies, Parsons, Fischer, and Engel refused to pray for mercy and died courageously. On November 11, 1887, they were hanged. Even on the gallows, facing death, they continued war upon the capitalist class. As the noose was placed about Spies' neck, he declared: *"The time will come when our silence in the grave will be more eloquent than our speeches."* Parsons' last words were: *"Let the voice of the people be heard."* Fischer, as he ascended the scaffold with his head erect, exclaimed: *"This is the happiest moment of my life."*

Labor organizations throughout the country expressed sympathy with the martyrs of the working class. The American Federation of Labor passed a resolution demanding their pardon. The rank and file of the Knights of Labor also were on the side of the Internationalists, but their leader, or rather, traitor, Powderly prevented the general assembly from passing a resolution demanding their freedom.

The first point on the program of the capitalists was to get rid of the loyal labor leaders, to cut off the head of the revolutionary labor movement that was beginning to be an inspiration and encouragement to the workers. To attain their end this class did not shrink from using any means at its command, heeding not the cost, not only to the working class, but even to its own servants—the police. Provocation was organized, the workers were attacked, the bright lights of the labor movement were extinguished, and with them the promising, militant movement of the eighties was temporarily put down. It was long before labor again rallied its shattered ranks.

Parsons, Spies, Fischer and their comrades, who fell at the hands of the merciless bourgeoisie, will always be remembered as martyrs of the class struggle who gave their all for the emancipation of the working class.

CHAPTER XX

THE STRUGGLE BETWEEN THE KNIGHTS AND THE FEDERATION, 1886-1900

THE Knights of Labor reached its highest development in 1886. From that time on the organization rapidly disintegrated, and declined continuously in importance until it entirely disappeared.

KNIGHTS OF LABOR MEMBERSHIP, 1886-1893

Year	Members	Year	Members
1886	700,000	1889	220,607
1887	500,000	1890	100,000
1888	259,758	1893	74,635

There were many causes for the fall of the Knights of Labor. Foremost, probably, was the treachery of the leaders of the order. Their stand against strikes, the continuous complaint of Powderly and other leaders that the membership was waging war against the capitalists in defiance of their orders, shattered the militant spirit which the organization had developed during the great upheaval of 1886. Their refusal to participate in the struggle for the eight-hour day, and Powderly's desertion of the packing-house workers in the same year, cooled the enthusiasm of the masses toward the movement.

The composition of the membership of the Knights also helped to bring about its disintegration. From its very inception the order had accepted into its ranks elements entirely foreign to the working class—the petty bourgeoisie and well-to-do farmers. It is true that in the long run the proletarian element outweighed these foreign elements; nevertheless the latter systematically undermined the organization from within. There was no strike, or struggle, or uprising in which the members of the order participated, which was not compelled to face opposition by these elements. The leadership was clearly under the influence of the petty bourgeoisie. They considered that strikes were something to be avoided at all costs, and that if they did take place in spite of all attempts to avoid them, they must be ended as soon as possible. Their policy was a policy of class collaboration.

Lack of a clear economic, as well as political, program hindered the work of the organization at every step. One of its fundamental aims was to improve the conditions of the members "morally, socially, and financially," but when these members attempted to better their conditions through struggle the leaders of the order tried to hold them back and told them to be at peace with their enemies. The constitution approved and whole-heartedly supported the coöperative movement, but experience proved that coöperatives could not improve the condition of the great mass of the members, who were being oppressed and exploited in the factories by the capitalists. Still worse, the industry of the country was completely in the hands of a comparatively few big companies, corporations, and trusts with billions of dollars of capital. In spite of this gigantic concentration and centralization of industry, the order or, rather, its leaders continued to talk about getting rid of the industrial capitalists, not through struggle, but by establishing producers' coöperatives with a few hundred thousand dollars gathered from half-starved workers! This "philosophy" was absolutely false. It appealed only to the bourgeois element of the order, and hindered its development into a compact, militant army of the working class capable of repulsing the attacks of its enemies.

The wrong attitude of the leaders toward the trade unions which took hold of the labor movement of the country also inevitably assisted in the downfall of the Knights of Labor. No efforts were made to come to an understanding with the trade unions for the purpose of bringing about united action between the two movements. On the contrary, Powderly and his colleagues refused to accept the hand of the trade unions even when the latter made advances of friendship to them. The struggle between the Federation and the Knights did great harm to the entire labor movement, but the Knights, who were composed mainly of unskilled workers, received the severest blow.

Then, of course, the savage attack of the capitalist class upon the order was another reason for its downfall. As has been pointed out, in spite of the stand of the leaders against strikes, the rank and file had time and again shown such militancy that it made the bourgeoisie of the country shake in its boots. Almost all of the great and militant strikes, with the exception of the eight-hour strike of 1886—and even in that the rank and file participated very actively—were carried on under the flag of the Knights. The participation of the great mass of the unskilled in the struggles demonstrated to the capitalists of America as never before that the order was their most dangerous enemy. Therefore the war-cry of the entire capitalist class, of the entire bourgeois world, was "Death to the Knights of Labor." The employers organized into local and national associations for the struggle. The government and courts were on their side. Nor was there any trouble in financing the assault on the Knights. One after another, blows were delivered. Members of the order were thrown out of work and blacklisted. The entire organization was made practically illegal, persecuted and hunted down by the capitalist class. The bourgeois press and church, day in and day out, poisoned the minds of the masses with lies about the order, while the latter, in view of the suddenness of its development and its lack of experience and revolutionary leadership, had no means of defending its ideas and actions. Terrorized by unemployment and imprisonment, the workers themselves began to desert their organization.

The trade unions, organized into the American Federation of Labor, were at this time in much better condition. It is hard to estimate the actual membership of the trade unions in 1886, but 250,000 (A. F. of L.: *History*, etc., Vol. I, p. 63) is considered to be a fair figure, including also the membership of the railroad brotherhoods which did not belong to the Federation.

Trade union membership increased considerably during this period but not without difficulty and not as rapidly as the membership of the Knights. Indeed, to the very end of the nineteenth century and for a number of years in the beginning of the twentieth century the growth of the American trade unions was gradual and painful. For example, the cigar makers had 20,566 members in 1887, 17,555 in 1888, 24,624 in 1890; the printers had 19,190 in 1887, 17,491 in 1888 and 21,120 in 1889; the bricklayers had 16,489 in 1887, 20,110 in 1888, 21,348 in 1889, and 24,423 in 1890. The carpenters had 5,879 in 1885, 21,423 in 1886, and 63,769 in 1890.

A. F. OF L. MEMBERSHIP, 1882-1900

Year	Members	Year	Members
1882	50,000	1892	250,000
1884	100,000	1898	300,000
1887	150,000	1900	775,000
1889	200,000		

Thus with the crisis of 1893 the growth of the trade unions stopped and for the following five or six years it was at a standstill. Only in the second half of 1899, after the crisis of 1893-1894 had entirely disappeared, did the trade union movement again awaken and its army begin to grow. It is important to point out that with the fall of the Knights of Labor the movement of the unskilled workers temporarily disintegrated almost entirely, and the field of action was left to the skilled workers organized in the trade unions.

A few important reasons, which remain to a certain extent to-day, hindered the growth of the trade unions. The main reason, of course, was the organization of the American bourgeoisie for the struggle against the labor movement. The manufacturers' associations, which grew much faster than the trade unions, were established for the sole purpose of fighting the workers. In their struggle with the labor movement, the employers do not shrink from using any means at their disposal. The state power is in their hands, therefore they can use it effectively to crush the efforts of the workers. None of the more important strikes of this period ended without bloodshed.

Bourgeois psychology among the workers was also an important factor against the success of the labor movement. In large sections of the working class, individualism still flourished. Many were convinced that a worker could become rich and escape from his class into the beautiful palace of the bourgeoisie. Such opportunities of escape were becoming scarcer and scarcer, the industrial proletarian army was becoming more and more stabilized. Nevertheless the psychology of individual advancement remained among the workers and hindered the establishment of labor organizations. As long as the worker thinks that he can leave the factory and become either an employer or a shopkeeper, so long will he be unable to see the necessity for belonging to a class organization and fighting to improve the conditions of his whole class.

Also the division of the workers into Americans and foreign-born, and then into various nationalities among the foreign-born, to a certain extent hampered the work of labor organization. National or racial antagonism amongst the workers is always a barrier over which it is difficult for an organization to climb.

Last and not least important among the reasons for the slow growth of the trade unions was the lack of devoted and militant leaders. Gompers and his coterie were coming step by step nearer to the bourgeoisie. Ever louder did they urge peaceful collaboration with the capitalist class. They were not concerned with the interests of the proletariat as a whole, though they repeatedly professed to be. Instead, they worked primarily on those who occupied strategical positions in industry and who could be organized without great difficulty—the skilled workers.

Between these two movements—the Knights of Labor and the American Federation of Labor—arose that detrimental clash which ended with complete annihilation of the Knights and for many years hindered the development of the labor movement as a whole. Had that suicidal struggle not taken place, if work between the Knights and the Federation had been properly coördinated, the American labor movement to-day would be entirely different in nature and in a vastly stronger position.

Probably the most important factor which led to the clash between the Knights and the Federation was the division between skilled and unskilled workers. The Knights comprised mainly unskilled, common, hardworking workers, while the Federation was made up almost entirely of skilled workers who occupied strategic positions in industry. As time went on the Knights became convinced that only the united efforts of the skilled and unskilled workers could successfully withstand the employers. This was especially clearly demonstrated by the railroaders' strike. The shopmen and unskilled laborers went out, while the skilled men—engineers, conductors, and others—remained at their jobs. It is easy for the employers to replace unskilled workers with men who can always be found at the factory gates waiting for a chance to work. But it is difficult to get a substitute for an engineer. Therefore, it was the desire of the Knights of Labor to organize under its flag both sections of the working class, unskilled as well as skilled, and to improve the conditions of both.

The skilled workers, however, who were organized into trade unions, looked upon this question from an entirely different standpoint. They were afraid to get together with the unskilled workers because the latter might take away from them their skill or their trade. They began to look on their union as a trade monopoly. Especially in the eighties, it appeared to them that they would better protect their craft interests through their narrow craft organizations. They looked upon this attempt of the Knights to attract the skilled workers into its ranks as a means of using them for the benefit of the unskilled workers. And it was easy for such trade union leaders as Gompers to appeal to the narrow psychology of the skilled workers and to convince them that they could raise their wages more easily and quickly through their own craft organizations than if they amalgamated with the millions of the unskilled.

Different forms of organization also added to the sharpness of the struggle. The Federation was composed of national craft unions. These craft unions were made up of craft locals. On the other hand, the form of organization of the Knights was twofold. On one side, there were mixed locals, districts, and assemblies; on the other, there were trade organizations similar to those of the national trade unions, which called themselves national trade assemblies. As time went on efforts were made to get the national trade unions into the Knights. A controversy developed between the Federation and the Knights over jurisdiction. The order thought that the Federation was seeking to destroy it by getting its members into the national unions. Indeed, the Federation had been established as a competing organization to the order. The founders of the Federation in 1881 were opposed to the order and therefore wanted to organize a parallel organization. On the other hand, an organization of the national craft organizations within the order appeared gravely dangerous to the Federation, composed of national craft unions.

A third reason for the struggle was the treachery of the leadership of both organizations. The leaders began to fight amongst themselves for their own individual careers. The leaders of the Knights of Labor, especially, were opposed to dealing with the Federation. As if drunk with the success of their organization in 1886, they rejected coöperation with the Federation even when the latter was ready to deal with them.

The feud between the Knights and Federation appeared in the middle of the eighties. As already shown, the Knights of Labor were invited to send delegates to the first convention of the Federation in 1881. This invitation was accepted and the Knights were well represented. Only later they withdrew from the Federation. We have also seen that even as late as 1884 the Federation invited the Knights to join hands in a common struggle for the eight-hour day. In 1882 the Knights, in turn, informed the Amalgamated Association of Iron and Steel Workers that they would not accept into their ranks individual members of that union. In 1883 the Knights rejected a proposal to organize a district assembly of printers for the reason that the latter already had their national union. In the same year the general assembly of the Knights appointed a committee to work out a plan for unity between the order and the existing trade unions. In 1884 the general assembly adopted a resolution urging the members and units of the order not to quarrel with those workers who belonged to craft unions. We see, then, that friendly relations between the two organizations did exist for a few years.

But beginning with 1885 complaints began to be made by the national trade unions that in spite of the resolutions of the general assembly of the Knights, the locals of the order in many places were recruiting into their ranks the members of the national unions. And when by 1886 the influence of the order had become very great there did really exist a danger of the trade unions being absorbed into the order.

The first open clash occurred in New York, where District Assembly 49 of the Knights was located. The fight took place over the cigar makers. At that time the cigar makers had two unions, the International Cigar Makers' Union and the Progressive Cigar Makers' Union. The Knights decided to support the latter. In 1886 the Progressive Union decided to affiliate with the order. Thereupon the International Cigar Makers' Union declared war against the Knights. Similar clashes occurred in other cities. Soon the struggle reached other trade unions. It was reported at a special meeting of the general assembly that there were from 150 to 160 complaints of the trade unions against the order.

On May 17, 1886, a special general conference of trade unions was called in Philadelphia to which delegates were sent by almost all the national unions, as though preparing for action. They were brought together by a common aim: to defend themselves against the Knights of Labor. It appeared to the leaders of these unions that the order would absorb all their members and thus make of them generals without an army. Indeed, they were not far from the truth. In 1886, at the time of the militant struggle, it looked as if the class solidarity of the workers, which was represented by the Knights of Labor, would really bring into their ranks the entire working class, and that of the trade unions which represented the division of the workers into skilled and unskilled, there would be left only a handful of stubborn leaders.

The conference declared that the trade unions have their historical basis, that they had effectively defended the interests of their members in the past, and that they must therefore remain independent. The conference did not deem it "advisable for any trade union to be controlled by or to join the Knights of Labor in a body, believing that trade unions are

THE KNIGHTS AND THE FEDERATION 195

best qualified to regulate their own internal trade affairs. Nevertheless, we recognize the solidarity of all labor interests." But it was apparent that the leaders of the trade unions were not sincere in this declaration about the "solidarity of all labor interests." They represented skilled workers; one of the reasons for establishing craft unions was to protect the immediate, narrow interests of these skilled workers, to separate them from the masses of the unskilled, and to save their positions. Later the same union leaders issued a declaration to all trade unions in which they openly exposed their real aim in the struggle with the Knights. They pointed out that as industry develops the tendency is to displace skilled workers by unskilled, men by women and children,

"So that the skilled trades were rapidly sinking to the level of pauper labor. To protect the skilled labor of America from being reduced to beggary, and to sustain the standard of American workmanship and skill, the trade unions of America have been established. . . . When they are founded on such grounds, there need be no fear of their destruction, nor need there be any antagonism between them and the Knights of Labor."

Therefore, the leaders of the trade unions declared that the Knights of Labor must take care only of the unskilled masses and must leave the skilled workers entirely to the trade unions. This, of course, was an impossibility. Such division in the working class is detrimental to its interests. The unskilled workers alone cannot win against the powerful capitalist class. Neither can the skilled workers succeed permanently in their struggle with the capitalists, since the development of industry renders skill more and more unnecessary and the market for skilled labor is always overflowing. This narrow, sectarian attitude of the trade unions, which characterized the whole policy of Gompers, has injured the trade unions themselves. Such a wrong conception of the rôle of trade unions, rejecting the class solidarity of the proletariat in view of the united front of the capitalist class is one of the most important causes of the backwardness of the American working class.

Finally, the conference adopted the following points for negotiation with the Knights:

"First, that in any branch of labor having a national or international organization, the K. of L. shall not initiate any person or form any assembly of persons following said organized craft or calling without the consent of the nearest national or international union affected.

"Second, that no person shall be admitted to the K. of L. who works for less than the regular scale of wages fixed by the union of his craft.

"Third, that the charter of any K. of L. assembly of any trade having a national or international union shall be revoked and the members of the same be requested to join a mixed assembly or form a local union under the jurisdiction of their respective national or international trade unions.

"Fourth, that any organizer of the K. of L. who endeavors to induce trade unions to disband, or tampers with their growth or privileges, shall have his commission forthwith revoked.

"Fifth, that whenever a strike or lockout of any trade unionists is in progress no assembly or district assembly of the K. of L. shall interfere until the difficulty is settled to the satisfaction of the trade unions affected.

"Sixth, that the K. of L. shall not establish nor issue any trade mark or label in competition with any trade mark or label now issued or that may hereafter be issued by any national or international trade union."

The general assembly, at its session on May 25, 1886, rejected the proposition of the trade unions and issued a friendly and conciliatory appeal addressed to all trade unions. It said in part:

"We recognize the service rendered to humanity and the cause of labor by trade union organizations, but believe that the time has come, or is fast approaching, when all who earn their bread by the sweat of their brow shall be enrolled under one general head, as we are controlled by one common law—the law of our necessities; and we will gladly welcome to our ranks or to our protection under our banner any organization requesting admission. And to such organizations as believe that their craftsmen are better protected under their present form of government, we pledge ourselves, as members of the great army of labor, to coöperate with them in every honorable effort to achieve the success which we are unitedly organized to obtain; and to this end we have appointed a special committee to confer with a like committee of any national or international trades union which shall desire to confer with us on the settlement of any difficulties that may occur between the members of the several organizations."

But it seems that this appeal was not adopted in good faith, for the same meeting of the general assembly also adopted an address to the Amalgamated Association of Iron and Steel Workers calling upon it "to annex your grand powerful corps to the main army that we may fight the battle under one flag." This proposition of the Knights was emphatically rejected by the association as well as by other trade unions which received a similar invitation to join the order.

The open clash between the Federation and the order, nevertheless, was postponed until the autumn. The trade union leaders waited until a general convention of the Knights of Labor for a final word on their "peace" terms. The convention took place on October 9, 1886, at Richmond, Va., with 658 delegates representing 700,000 members. The majority was emphatically against unity with the trade unions, and only a minority fought for coöperation with them. The 75 delegates of the New York District Assembly 49, especially, were stubbornly opposed to unity. Finally, Powderly went over to their side.

J. R. Buchanan, who led the minority, describes the Richmond convention as follows:

"It was at Richmond that the seal of approval was placed upon the acts of those members who had been bending every energy since the Cleveland special session to bring on open warfare between the order and the trade unions. The contest between the exclusivists and the bi-organization representatives was fierce, and it never waned for one moment during the two weeks of the session. The bitterness of feeling engendered by the strife between these two elements

THE KNIGHTS AND THE FEDERATION 197

entered into every matter of any consequence which came before the body. . . . A resolution was adopted ordering all members of the Order who were also members of the Cigar Makers' International Union to withdraw from the latter organization; failure to comply with said order meaning forfeiture of membership in the Order of the Knights of Labor. The majority by which the resolution was adopted was not, comparatively, large, but it was enough; and the greatest labor organization up to that time known in this country received its mortal wound at Richmond . . ." (Buchanan: *The Story of a Labor Agitator,* pp. 313-316).

In view of the fact that the Knights had practically declared open war upon the trade unions, the latter united their forces still more closely and answered the challenge. On December 8, 1886, a conference of trade union leaders was held at Columbus, Ohio, which refused a seat to the delegate of the Window-Glass Workers' Association on the ground that "said organization is affiliated with the Knights of Labor, and is not a trade union within the meaning of the call for the convention." Nevertheless, the conference made another attempt to bring about an understanding between the Federation and order by electing a special committee to meet a similar committee of the Knights and discuss the matter all over again. The committee met on December 11, but nothing came of the discussion. The trade union committee demanded acceptance of the former proposition of the trade unions, and the committee of the Knights told the conference that it could not alter the decision of its own convention. It also refused to promise that the organizers of the order would not interfere with the strikes of the trade unionists or would not attempt to draw the members of the trade unions into the order. Then "the Federation in its turn unanimously declared war upon the Knights and announced the decision to carry hostilities into the enemy's territory."

"We condemn the acts of the Knights above recited," the declaration of the Federation says, "and call upon all workingmen to join the unions of their respective trades, and urge the formation of national and international unions and centralization of all under one head, the American Federation of Labor."

As has already been pointed out, at this Columbus convention the present American Federation of Labor was formed, uniting into one organization the Federation of Organized Trades and Labor Unions of the United States and Canada and many national unions which were not affiliated with the Federation. Samuel Gompers was elected president of the new organization. In his fight with the Knights of Labor Gompers spared neither time nor energy. To justify his policy he developed a peculiar "philosophy" of organization—he emphatically rejected the idea of organizing the workers into industrial unions embracing skilled as well as unskilled.

As far as his attitude toward the Knights of Labor was concerned, Gompers later declared: "It (the order) undertook to wipe out the lines of industry and make one whole organization of all classes of labor." But to Gompers, of course, such a thing as "one whole union of all classes of labor" was not only "unattainable" but "unnatural." He compared a labor movement on industrial lines to an army in which all units were abolished and all soldiers combined into one body. What would happen to such an army? "Chaos and confusion would reign," says Gompers, "if an order were given to it to advance. The greatest safety for such army corps, made up in such a fashion, would be in remaining stationary. An order to advance would be its own annihilation" (Gompers: *Labor and the Common Welfare,* pp. 12-13). So did Gompers seek to justify his narrow, sectarian policy.

Open and brutal war between the Federation and the Knights was now set in motion. From then on the feud was carried out by the leaders of the trade unions mercilessly and with the greatest energy. The order began to decline. Its leaders soon learned their mistake and attempted to correct it, but to no avail. At the Minneapolis convention of the Knights, in October, 1887, Powderly ruled that the decision instructing the members to withdraw from the International Cigar Makers' Union or forfeit their rights in the order was no longer in force, as it was against the constitution of the organization. It was thought that such a ruling would extinguish the fire. But it was too late. The trade union leaders would no longer listen to a plea for peace with the Knights. They saw that victory was on their side, and carried on the war until the "enemy" was entirely exterminated.

The greatly needed unity between the skilled and unskilled workers was not brought about at a time when such unity would have entirely changed the course of American labor history.

CHAPTER XXI

THE SOCIALISTS, TRADE UNIONS, AND POLITICAL ACTION, 1886-1900

THE Socialist Labor Party, which alone represented the revolutionary labor movement in this country, made considerable progress in the last 15 years of the nineteenth century. Its greatest success was among the foreign-born workers, especially the Germans. The sixth convention of the party was held in September, 1887, at Buffalo, N. Y., with 37 delegates representing 33 branches. But at that time the party already had about 70 branches. The New York section was instructed to elect the national executive committee and to recall it, if necessity arose.

Two important questions were left unsolved by the Buffalo convention which soon led the party to a split—first, independent political action in the parliamentary field, and second, the party's attitude toward the trade unions. The New York *Volkszeitung* and its followers maintained that the party was not ripe for independent political action and therefore they urged that more attention be paid to the trade union movement. On the other hand, the official party organs—*The Workingmen's Advocate* and *Der Sozialist*—"were enthusiastic advocates of independent socialist politics, and rather inclined to underrate the importance of socialist activity in the trade unions" (Hillquit: *History*, etc., p. 256).

The New York section of the party supported the position of the *Volkszeitung* and decided to remove the national secretary, W. L. Rosenberg, and the members of the executive committee. But the latter refused to give up their posts and organized their own faction, which after a few years disappeared. The *Volkszeitung* faction survived the struggle and remained as the Socialist Labor Party. The next convention was held in October, 1889, with 27 delegates present, representing 33 branches. Membership was continuously increasing. In 1896 the party had 200 branches and was active in 25 states. But the highest point of development was reached in 1899 when it had 350 branches, and was active in 30 states. During its early days the S. L. P. many times joined with other "workingmen's" parties in election campaigns. Later it took up independent political action. Its candidates for various offices in national elections received 25,666 votes in 1893, 30,120 in 1894, 34,869 in 1895, 55,550 in 1896, and 82,204 in 1898.

As to the party's attitude toward the trade union movement, Hillquit reports that:

"At almost every one of its conventions the Socialist Labor Party proclaimed its sympathy with the objects and methods of the labor unions, and called upon its members to join the organizations of their trade; in a number of instances the party sought direct representation in the central bodies of organized labor; its official organs supported the trade unions, and in many important strikes the socialists were found on the side of the strikers, aiding, counseling, and at times directing them in their battle. But notwithstanding these efforts, the influence of the Socialist Labor Party on the trade-union movement was for a long time rather insignificant. The socialists were as yet numerically too weak to permeate the much-ramified labor movement and to shape its course as they had hoped to do, and voices were at times raised within the party protesting against its activity in the unions as a waste of time" (*Ibid.*, p. 215).

The Socialist Labor Party, as such, had no clear and definite attitude toward the trade unions. Nevertheless, it never came out against them in those days. On the contrary, it often supported them, and individual sections and the majority of its members were active in the unions and gained great influence there. Especially were they successful in the city central bodies, such as New York, Rochester, Buffalo, Cleveland, and Cincinnati. In New York the socialists had ideological control of the powerful city central organization. The United German Trades, as well as the United Hebrew Trades, were fully controlled by them.

As far as the Knights of Labor were concerned, the socialists were always on friendly terms with them, and many locals of the order openly sympathized with the socialists and their ideals. Many of the leaders of the Socialist Labor Party were members of the order. And in the nineties when the order grew weak the socialists were determined to capture its leadership. They succeeded in getting control of the famous District Assembly 49 of New York. Throughout the order the socialists became so influential that their support of Sovereign's candidacy for the presidency defeated Powderly. An agreement was made with Sovereign that he would appoint Lucien Sanial, a socialist, as editor of the *Journal* of the Knights of Labor. But Sovereign did not live up to the agreement and the friendship between the Socialist Labor Party and the order became strained. Finally the convention of the Knights in December, 1895, at Washington, D. C., refused to seat Daniel De Leon, editor of *The People,* an official organ of the Socialist Labor Party, as a delegate from District Assembly 49. From then on, relations between the order and the S. L. P. were entirely severed.

Relations between the S. L. P. and the American Federation of Labor ended in the same way as those with the Knights of Labor.

As already stated, when the Federation of Organized Trades and Labor Unions of the United States and Canada was organized in 1881, Samuel Gompers was considered by the bourgeois press a supporter of the social-

THE SOCIALISTS AND POLITICAL ACTION

ists. He really did sympathize and work with the left wing of the trade unions. Even after he was elected president of the Federation he remained for some time friendly to the socialist movement.

Gompers at that time spoke even of the emancipation of the working class from wage slavery. In 1887 he said: "I believe with the most advanced thinkers as to ultimate ends, including the abolition of the wage-system." And even as late as 1896, speaking of the necessity of always bearing in mind the immediate interests of the wage-earners, he exclaimed: "Even if but to gain a milestone on the thorny road to emancipation" (Gompers: *Loc. cit.,* p. 5.)

But step by step Gompers became more conservative and his clash with the socialists became sharper. And Gompers' policy was also the policy of the American Federation of Labor. Nevertheless, the struggle with the socialists was not to be taken lightly, for by participating in the trade unions they had gained considerable influence and won many sympathizers.

Finally the controversy developed into an open struggle. At the Federation convention of 1890, in Detroit, Mich., the New York Central Labor Union demanded a charter from the Federation, and Gompers came out against granting it on the ground that the New York section of the Socialist Labor Party belonged to the New York Central Union and the latter was, therefore, not a "pure and simple" trade union. After a long and bitter discussion Gompers' position was carried by 1,699 votes against 525. This did not mean, however, that Gompers had now become an open enemy of the socialists. Not at all. He said that he was not opposed to the socialists, but that he did not want a political party to belong to the Federation. He still maintained that he was also for the final emancipation of the workers from wage slavery, but not with the help of a political party.

"I am willing to step aside if that will promote our cause, but I cannot and will not prove false to my convictions that the trade unions pure and simple are the natural organizations of the wage-workers to secure their present material and practical improvement and to achieve their final emancipation" (*Ibid.,* p. 3).

Even after the Detroit convention the socialists remained for some time in the trade unions and actively participated in their work. At every convention of the Federation they proposed resolutions with socialist tendencies. The life and death conflict between the socialists and Gompers' followers began only in 1895.

In that year, the same in which the socialists broke their connections with the Knights of Labor, they started open warfare against the Federation. They simply became "tired" of working in the mass organizations which were led by the conservatives, Gompers or Sovereign. It appeared to them that the socialist movement was going forward at entirely too slow a rate, that their influence in these mass organizations was not rising as fast as they wanted it to, and they grew desperate. Finally, they came to the conclusion that there was no hope of ever capturing these organizations for socialism. These organizations were firmly in the hands of the conservative leaders and the latter would never give up their leadership. These leaders were becoming bureaucrats; they had organized a machine in the trade unions which was willing to fight every progressive element to the bitter end. Only one road, therefore, seemed open to the socialists: to withdraw from the old trade unions and form new unions, which from the very beginning would be under the influence and leadership of the socialists and would remain forever as militant, revolutionary organizations.

This was the decision of the Socialist Labor Party membership and its leadership with De Leon at their head. Accordingly, the Socialist Trade and Labor Alliance was formed in 1895. Its object was two-fold: to help the S. L. P. to accomplish its goal, and to get rid of the conservative trade unions which "only stand in the way of the revolutionary movement." Now De Leon openly appealed to all organizations of the Federation and Knights of Labor and invited them to join the Alliance. Numerous unions responded to the appeal and withdrew from the Federation. Three months after its formation the Alliance had issued 200 charters, and units were organized in New York, New Jersey, Massachusetts, Rhode Island, Ohio, Pennsylvania, and other states. At the height of its development the Alliance had about 20,000 members. Its stronghold was New York City.

In spite of temporary success, the Socialist Trade and Labor Alliance never succeeded in attracting large masses of workers. Only the most advanced, the revolutionary section of the working class, joined its ranks, while the masses remained in the old trade unions under the leadership of Gompers and his colleagues. Within three years the Alliance reached its zenith and declined. At the Buffalo convention of 1898 only 114 local unions were represented and only 54 were actually paying dues. On the other hand, the Federation at this time had on its rolls about 300,000 members.

The leaders of the Federation now turned their heaviest guns against the socialists.

"Perhaps of all the enemies with whom the trade unions have to contend," Gompers wrote in the *American Federationist* in April, 1896, "there is none more dangerous, and often villainous, than he who under the mask of sympathy with the toilers struggling for justice sets forth a patent scheme and nostrum for the immediate and absolute remedy of all the ills to which the workers are heir."

And a few years later, in 1903, Gompers, when he was already soul and body for peaceful collaboration with the employers at any cost, declared:

"It has made, and will make, our work doubly difficult, because there are employers who have refused and do refuse to confer for the adjustment of

THE SOCIALISTS AND POLITICAL ACTION 203

difficulties and disputes when they are led to believe by declaration that property is in danger of confiscation."

And the socialists (at least some of them) did make such declarations while speaking about the expropriation of the bourgeoisie. Then turning directly to the socialists, he continued:

"I am not with your party because I want to be in line with the declaration that the trade union policy, the movement and the work, must be unhampered by your political nostrums."

Still further, directing his guns against the socialist ideal itself, he exclaims:

"I want to tell you socialists that I have studied your philosophy; read your works upon economics. . . . I have heard your orators and watched the work of your movement the world over. I have kept close watch upon your doctrines for 30 years. . . . And I want to say that I am entirely at variance with your philosophy. I declare it to you, I am not only at variance with your doctrines, but with your philosophy. Economically, you are unsound; socially, you are wrong; industrially you are an impossibility" (*Ibid.*, pp. 175-179).

We do not hear any more from Gompers about the "thorny road to emancipation!"

The erroneous attitude of the socialists of 1895 toward the trade unions was exceedingly costly to the revolutionary movement of the country. This was the beginning of the running away of the revolutionary workers from the organized masses and leaving them at the mercy of a handful of conservative, reactionary leaders of Gompers' type.

"Few men have made a greater impression upon the American labor movement," says William Z. Foster, "than Daniel De Leon. His principal accomplishment was to work out the intellectual premises of dual unionism so effectively as to force its adoption and continuance as the industrial program of the whole revolutionary movement for a generation. He was an able writer, an eloquent speaker, a clever reasoner, and a dominant personality generally. But despite his brilliance he was essentially a sophist and a utopian. He particularly lacked a grasp of the process of evolution. He made the fundamental mistake of considering the old trade unions as static, unchangeably conservative bodies, and in concluding that the necessary socialist unions had to be created as new organizations. He did not know that the labor movement is a growth, from conservatism to radicalism, and structurally from the craft to the industrial form. De Leon's industrial program of dual unionism was merely the typical utopian scheme of throwing aside the old, imperfect, evolving social organism and striving to set up in its stead the new, perfect institutions.

"In the past there had been dual unions organized in opposition to the old trade unions (witness for example the American Railway Union founded by Eugene V. Debs), but the S. T. and L. A. was the first of a general character and a revolutionary makeup. Its foundation clearly marked the embarkation of the radical movement upon its long-continued and disastrous program of dual unionism."

"But if the S. T. & L. A. failed as an organization," continues Foster, "the idea behind it, of revolutionary dual unionism, made steady headway. More and more the radical movement, from left to right, became convinced that the trade unions were hopeless, more and more it turned its attention to dual unionism. . . .

"Strangely enough, the longer the dual union policy was followed, the more logical it seemed, notwithstanding its failure to build any new unions of consequence. This was because of the fact that as the revolutionary elements continued their tactics of quitting the old unions the latter, suffering the loss of their best life's blood, withered and stagnated. More and more they became the prey of standpatters and reactionaries; less and less they presented an aspect calculated to appeal to revolutionaries. Dual unionism became almost a religion among rebels. No longer would they even tolerate discussion of the proposition of working within the old unions . . ." (W. Z. Foster: *The Bankruptcy of the American Labor Movement*, pp. 26-29).

The result was that the revolutionaries completely isolated themselves from the masses of the organized workers and became a sect, loudly chanting their principles, diligently guarding their revolutionary innocence and integrity, but hopeless, helpless, and without any influence among the masses.

On the other hand, the withdrawal of the revolutionary workers from the old trade unions brought great harm to the entire labor movement:

"Dual unionism is a malignant disease," says Foster, "that sickens and devitalizes the whole labor movement. The prime fault of it is that it wastes the efforts of those vigorous elements whose activities determine the fate of all working class organizations. It does this by withdrawing these rare and precious militants from the mass trade unions, where they serve as the very mainspring of vitality and progress, and by misdirecting their attention to the barren and hopeless work of building up impossible utopian industrial organizations. This drain of the best blood of the trade unions begins by enormously weakening these bodies and ends by making impotent every branch of the labor movement as well; for the welfare of all organized labor, political, industrial, coöperative, educational, depends upon the trade unions, the basic organizations of the working class, being in a flourishing condition. Dual unionism saps the strength of the trade unions, and when it does that it undermines the structure of the entire working class organization" (*Ibid.*, p. 30).

And this wrong industrial policy of the American revolutionary workers continued until after the World War when the American section of the Communist International was established and this policy was completely rejected.

Now let us consider briefly the attitude of the American Federation of Labor toward political-parliamentary action in general.

The forerunner of the present Federation, the Federation of the Organized Trades and Labor Unions of the United States and Canada, refused to give its support to any political party as such, through all of its existence from 1881 to 1886. Nor did the numerous so-called "workingmen's" parties of that period get any sympathy from the Federation, either. It urged its members to support in the elections "those who are real friends of labor," regardless of their political affiliation. Even more than that: "the legislative committee forbade any member from publicly advocating the claims of any of the political parties."

THE SOCIALISTS AND POLITICAL ACTION

Only once was a departure made from this "non-partisan" policy, in 1886, at the time of the formation of the present Federation. The exponents of independent political action obtained a majority in the convention and "urged a most generous support to the independent political movement of the workers."

"Time has arrived," the convention declared, "when working people should decide on the necessity of united action as citizens at the ballot box" (American Federation of Labor: *History*, etc., Vol. II, p. 317).

In 1889 the Federation again refused either to organize or to help organize an independent political party of the workers. And this "non-partisan" policy of the Federation was maintained not only during the period under discussion, that is, up to 1900, but ever since.

Two main arguments were advanced against participation of the Federation in independent parliamentary action. First, inasmuch as the workers were not well organized economically, they could not by any means organize politically; and second, participation by the trade unions in independent political-parliamentary action meant death to them.

"It is ridiculous to imagine," declared Gompers at the convention of 1894, "that the wage-workers can be slaves in employment and yet achieve control at the polls. There never yet existed coincident with each other, autocracy in the shop and democracy in political life. In truth, we have not yet achieved the initial step in the control of public affairs by even a formal recognition of our unions."

This argument means that the workers must first organize into powerful economic organizations and only then begin to dream of organizing a political party of their own.

In the same report to the convention Gompers advanced the second argument against political action in the following manner:

"The National Labor Union, the predecessor of the American Federation of Labor, entered the so-called independent political arena in 1872 and nominated its candidate for the presidency of the United States. It is equally true that the National Labor Union never held a convention after that event. The disorganized condition of labor, with its tales of misery, deprivation, and demoralization, from that year until the reorganization of the workers about 1880, must be too vivid in the minds of those who were trade unionists then and are trade unionists now to need recounting. In view of our own experience, as well as the experience of our British fellow-unionists, it would be wise to steer our ship of labor from that channel whose waters are strewn with shattered hopes and unions destroyed . . ." (*Ibid.*, pp. 318-319).

Gompers was not only absolutely opposed to the trade unions participating in independent political action, but he was also a master in defending his position, though his main weapon was demagogy. In 1896 he cleverly made a distinction between political action and party political action, also between political action and parliamentary action. He argued as follows:

"Beyond doubt few, if any, will contend that the workers should refuse to avail themselves of their political rights or fail to endeavor to secure such demands which they make by the exercise of their political power. The fact is, however, that our movement distinctly draws the line between political action in the interest of labor and party political action. This was more particularly emphasized at the last convention when it was declared as the settled policy of the American trade union movement that party political action of whatsoever kind shall have no place in the movement of the American Federation of Labor. . . .

"There is, too, an entirely erroneous impression regarding trade union activity and its influence. It is often imagined and asserted that political action exists exclusively at the ballot box. Nothing can be further from the fact than this. There is not an action which the unions can take, whether it be an increase of wages, an hour more leisure secured for the toilers, a factory rule modified, or even any other condition changed and improved, without it being at the same time a political act, having its political effect and its political influence" (Gompers: *Loc. cit.*, p. 126).

Ten years later, in 1906, Gompers still repeated the same argument:

"There are some men who can never understand political action unless there is a party. As a matter of fact, there is no worse party-ridden people in the whole world than are the people of the United States. It is nothing but party, party, your party and my party. It is the abomination of American politics. Men vote for their party regardless of what that party stands for. . . ."

Then follows a whole line of examples of what the Federation had accomplished on the political field without participating in any party political action. For instance:

"Trade unionists, by their political action, abolished slavery in Hawaii"; "secured the lien laws, which guarantee a man his wages when he has worked"; "the breaker boys, who work in the mines of Pennsylvania, were liberated through the miners' strike"; also: "Who secured the safety appliances in the mines, in factories and workshops? Who secured the blowers that are now used to carry off the dust from the polisher and the buffer in the machine shops? Do you remember our fight here years ago for the abolition of the tenement house work system?"

Therefore, the argument of 1894 that as long as the workers are not well organized economically they cannot dream of organizing politically, and also that participation of the trade unions in independent political action means death to the unions—this argument no longer served the purpose of Gompers and he entirely forgot it in 1896. And 10 years later he discovered an entirely new argument against independent political action of the workers, namely, that the workers can and do attain the same political ends, as well, and even better, without a political party of their own.

Gompers was absolutely correct when he pointed out in 1896 that the use of the ballot box is not the only political action. "Every class struggle

THE SOCIALISTS AND POLITICAL ACTION

is a political struggle," said Karl Marx. Every struggle of the workers, whether for higher wages, or shorter hours, or better conditions in the mills, mines, and factories, is a political struggle. Every victory of the workers is also a political victory. In view of the fact that the socialists in those days, as well as the socialists in our times, limited political action of the workers to the ballot box, Gompers' argument on this question was absolutely in place and correct.

But this argument of Gompers became absolutely wrong and detrimental to the labor movement and to the cause of the working class in general, when he employed it against a working-class independent political party, which is opposed to the bourgeois parties and is organized to challenge their political power and influence.

On the surface it appears from his various utterances that Gompers continued to be absolutely opposed to any and all political struggle. Such a conclusion is found to be utterly erroneous upon closer scrutiny of the facts. Gompers was opposed to and bitterly fought against a working class political party, and at the same time he supported and worked with both bourgeois parties. The American Federation of Labor never was a "non-partisan" organization" in the real sense of the word. It always was and still remains the tail of either the Republican or Democratic Party. In state and city elections it usually supports candidates of both capitalist parties. As far as logic is concerned, Gompers had very little use for it, as is the case with every demagogue. On one hand, he was in favor of forming the trade unions as independent organizations of the working class in the factories, mines and mills, while at the same time he was opposed to the organization of the workers outside of the factories, mills, and mines into a political party of their own, separate and distinct from the capitalist parties. In the factories the workers are marshalled in their own organization and fighting their enemies, while outside of the factories they are in the bourgeois party, making common cause with their enemies. On the other hand, Gompers did not understand or did not want to understand that a political party of the working class acts in other fields than at the ballot box. It acts as a leader of the working class, uniting all sections of that class under one banner. The organization of the working class is complete only when the workers are organized independently on both fields, on the economic as well as on the political, fighting their enemy as a class, with both fists. The socialists maintained that political action is limited to the ballot box, Gompers argued that a political party of the working class does not and cannot go further than the ballot box.

Gompers' political policy became the policy of the American Federation of Labor. It is organizational separation of the workers from the capitalist class in the factories, and unity of the workers with the capitalist class in political parliamentary action.

This policy is detrimental to the labor movement. It demoralizes and holds back the trade unions themselves. It does not allow the workers completely to separate themselves from the capitalist class. It does not allow the workers to stand once and for all against the capitalists, as one class against another.

CHAPTER XXII

STRIKES AND STRUGGLES FOR THE EIGHT-HOUR DAY, 1886-1900

CONSTITUTIONAL rights of the workers mean nothing as soon as they come into conflict with the interests of the bourgeoisie. The slogan of the ruling class is: "The end justifies the means."

As the class struggle developed and the workers began to organize more solidly, the bourgeoisie sought and found new means of fighting their class enemy, the workers. After the militant struggles of 1886 the injunction was invented.

The first labor injunction was issued in this country in 1888, in Massachusetts, against the strikers of the English Springhead Spinning Company. The court enjoined the strikers from "the act of displaying banners with devices as a means of threats and intimidation to prevent persons from entering into or continuing in the employment of the plaintiffs." If the workers failed to obey these restrictions, if they displayed forbidden devices or in any way threatened the scabs, they were to be arrested and brought before the same judge who issued the injunction to be punished for "contempt of court."

Punishment for violation of an injunction is usually imprisonment for a few months, or a fine, or both. The judge becomes a dictator in the real sense of the word, as far as the strikers are concerned. He has the power to take away from thousands of workers their constitutional rights of freedom of speech, press, and assembly, or the right even to walk along the street where the employer's property is located. The workers are confronted directly by the state, which uses all its powers to suppress them.

"When a strike, the embryo of insurrection against the existing system of class relationships, assumes proportions of a nature challenging in the least the system of capitalist exploitation and oppression," says Jay Lovestone, "the employers abrogate the civil law, the law governing the class relationships during the armistice in the class war. The injunction against workers in struggle with their employers is an act of military siege in the arena of class relationships. It robs the workers of the right to trial by the ordinary procedure. The judge becomes the military officer acting as the prosecutor, the jury, and the injured party. The menace to the capitalist interests is then so fundamental that the judge throws off his mask of impartiality, and poses as an open representative of the employer whose interests have been injured by the revolt of the workers against his right to exploit them unmercifully.

"The full force of the government is brought to bear on the workers. The revolt is crushed. Whatever advantages the workers may have had in the suddenness of their attack, whatever advantages they may have had from the first successes in the skirmish, from their solidarity, are nullified. The workingman's strike army is ordered disbanded, dispersed if necessary by the force of arms. Working class solidarity is declared a crime against the 'public.' The officers of the workers' army are branded as rebels; they are court-martialed by the military tribunal of one judge. The revolt against the exploiter is crushed. The strike is broken. The challenge to the authority of the profit system—the government—is disposed of swiftly and decisively. Profits are saved. The workingmen are beaten. This is a picture of the class war to-day in America. The rôle of the injunction is to break strikes by bringing up against the workers the heavy artillery of the capitalists—the undivided military, judiciary, and financial support of the government, in short, the full political power of the ruling class" (Jay Lovestone: *The Government—Strikebreaker*, pp. 218-219).

As the labor movement developed, the injunction was used more and more frequently as an instrument for breaking strikes. Indeed, in the twentieth century there has been no strike of major importance in this country in which the injunction has not been used against the workers.

According to *Bradstreet's*, in 1887 345,073 workers participated in strikes. The majority of these strikes ended in defeat. Only about 38 per cent of those involved won their demands. In 1888 about 211,000 workers took part in strikes and about 50 per cent of them won their demands.

One of the most important strikes was a victorious walkout of 60,000 steel workers in Pennsylvania and Ohio, conducted by the Amalgamated Association of Iron and Steel Workers, in 1888. At the end of 1887 the Knights of Labor struck against the Philadelphia and Reading Railroad Company, in whose mines 80,000 were employed. Those engineers and firemen who belonged to the Knights of Labor also joined the miners in the struggle. But the railroad brotherhoods supported the company and filled the places of the striking engineers and firemen with their members.

On February 27, 1888, the locomotive engineers' and the locomotive firemen's brotherhoods declared a strike against the Chicago, Burlington and Quincy Railroad Company. This was the opportunity for the Knights of Labor to be revenged on the brotherhoods, which only two months before had broken the strike of their brothers in the Knights. And the latter did really help the railroad companies to break the strike. In both instances the real victors were the employers. They crushed both strikes with the help of the workers themselves.

The eight-hour issue again arose to stir the working class. Shortly after the general strike of 1886 the employers had succeeded in taking away from the workers the fruits of their victories. Another struggle for shorter hours became necessary.

"In 1888 the combined forces and influences of the employing and speculative classes had so thoroughly swayed the unorganized working people into sub-

THE STRUGGLE FOR THE EIGHT-HOUR DAY

mission, that every meeting night of labor organizations the question of a reduction in wages had to be met. Employers, without consulting their employees, simply posted notices that reductions would take place and if they did not strike that was the end of it. Obnoxious rules were forced on the workers and they were compelled to sign ironclad contracts giving up their right to organize for self-protection. Labor was humiliated, browbeaten, and scourged. But the spirit of labor was not broken.

"It was in these dark days that the proclamation was sent over the world that the eight-hour day would be enforced May 1, 1890. From that moment a change took place. Hope was instilled into the minds and hearts of the workers to supplant despair. To the rallying cry of eight hours the working people again stood erect and staunch in their manhood. The tide had changed. This appeal was answered with enthusiasm" (American Federation of Labor: *History*, etc., Vol. I, p. 10).

Renewal of the struggle for the eight-hour day on May 1, 1890, was proclaimed by the American Federation of Labor at its convention in December, 1888:

"It is true, as many say," declared the convention, "the eight-hour movement in 1886 was not entirely successful. It is also true no movement that has for its object the improvement of conditions of a whole people ever could succeed in the first, aye, even in the second attempt. It is always a hard struggle to achieve any improvement, but the benefits we gained in 1886 and since then by reason of the eight-hour movement are sufficient to encourage us to make the venture again. We should not lose sight of the fact that as a result of the movement in 1886 a number of trades have reduced their hours from 10 and 12 to eight; others from 12 and 14 to 10 and nine, and many thousands of workmen who before that time worked 14 to 18 hours a day have had their hours reduced to 12" (*Ibid.*, pp. 215-216).

The eight-hour day was to be established through a general strike. As in 1886, all the workers in the United States, organized as well as unorganized, were to leave their jobs on May 1, 1890, and demand from the employers shorter hours of labor. The workers had seen enough of separate craft strikes being lost. Their experience of 1886 proved to them that only through a general strike could they achieve their great aim and gain for themselves the shorter work-day.

The convention instructed the executive council to distribute literature on the subject, pointing out the necessity for shorter hours, and calling upon all workers to join their forces for the struggle.

An intensive agitation was immediately started for the general strike. For the first time paid organizers were dispatched to various points to organize the labor forces. Everywhere in the industrial centers of the country mass meetings were held; everywhere the workers hailed the decision of the Federation with the greatest enthusiasm. The workers of Europe congratulated their American brothers on their noble efforts to lighten the burden of toiling humanity. The International Labor Congress in session in Paris in 1889, at which the Second International was formed, voted to hold simultaneous demonstrations in support of the eight-hour day throughout Europe on May 1, 1890. It is to this eight-hour movement, inaugurated in the United States and supported by the rejuvenated Socialist International, that the International Labor holiday of May First owes its origin.

Here again we have to emphasize the fact that the Knights of Labor refused to take part in the eight-hour movement. It is true that the order was already very badly demoralized. Nevertheless, it still had some influence among the masses and its refusal to join hands with the trade unions had its effect. Of course, this refusal of the order delivered a final blow to the order itself, and assured its final decline as a factor in the labor movement.

The masses of the workers, hundreds of thousands of the rank and file of the American Federation of Labor, met the proposal of a campaign for the eight-hour day with outstretched hands. Their leaders, however, from the start expressed doubt as to the success of the general strike and, later, fear of its consequences. They were afraid that they might not be able to control the forces which would be set in motion by the great stoppage. They spread rumors that the masses of the workers were not so enthusiastic about the eight-hour movement this time as they had been in 1886, although the agitation now stirred much larger numbers.

The expected happened. At the convention in 1889 the leaders of the Federation gave up the idea of the general strike. Instead, the convention empowered the executive council to select one union to declare a strike for the eight-hour day in its industry. After that union had won, another was to follow, and so on, until step by step the eight-hour day would be established in all industries. In order to assist the striking union financially, the convention levied an assessment of 2 cents a month on each member.

A wrangle started over these assessments. The decision of the convention required an amendment to the constitution. Some of the unions, such as the printers and clothing workers, objected to the assessments. Instead of unity, discord and demoralization riddled the ranks.

It was now clear to every one that this movement which had showed such great promise was destroyed. The trade union officials, led by Gompers, by renouncing the general strike brought division and discouragement into the ranks of the working class. They were not so naïve as not to know that separate, small strikes cannot defeat a powerful, united, armed ruling class; they were not so naïve as not to know that such an insane division of the army of workers thrown into the battle section by section, thus giving sufficient time to the employers to crush each section separately, could only bring defeat. Rejection of the general strike disheartened the masses. The great enthusiasm for the movement began to decline, and the closer it drew to May 1, 1890, the clearer it appeared that the dastardly action of the leaders of the Federation had divided and defeated the eight-hour movement before it was fairly launched.

The carpenters were selected as the union to declare the eight-hour strike on the date set, and the miners were to follow later. The Brotherhood of Carpenters at that time was probably the strongest union in the Federation, at least financially. Also, the carpenters are highly skilled workers, and therefore it is much easier for them to win a strike. According to secretary Patrick J. McGuire they won the eight-hour day in 137 cities, and gained a nine-hour day in most other places (Commons: *History*, etc., Vol. II, p. 477).

As far as the miners were concerned, it was agreed that it was too late to wage a strike the same year. The Federation convention of 1890 decided that the miners should go on strike for the eight-hour day on May 1, 1891. But the United Mine Workers was very much weakened in 1891, large sections of the miners were unorganized, and therefore on the eve of May 1 the miners declined to strike. Later Gompers himself admitted that a strike of the miners alone would have been easily beaten by the coal companies.

In 1891 the bakers asked the Federation for aid in their strike for the eight-hour day. But the convention left the question to the executive council, which in its turn decided that the time was inopportune for such a move and, therefore, refused to support the bakers. The 1892 convention of the Federation was satisfied with issuing instructions to the executive council to carry on *agitation* for the eight-hour day.

Thus the eight-hour movement of the period was dissipated by the trade union leadership. Gompers and his colleagues by this time were coming closer to the bourgeoisie and were showing more and more fear at the militancy of the rank and file.

The year 1892 saw another outbreak of sharp struggles. The hardest and most brutal fight fell upon the steel workers of the Carnegie Brothers Company, known in the history of the labor movement as the Homestead strike.

The Amalgamated Association of Iron and Steel Workers in 1891 had 24,068 members and was considered the strongest union in America. As far back as 1889 the steel magnates had been forced to deal with it and to sign a three-year contract. Before the expiration of the contract, on July 1, 1892, new negotiations were started. The employers demanded that the workers accept a reduction in wages. On May 30 they issued an ultimatum that the union must either sign a new agreement on or before June 29, or be no longer recognized. The union refused to yield, and on July 1 the workers at Homestead, Pa., were locked out. In 1892 Homestead had a population of about 12,000 composed almost exclusively of the steel workers and their families.

Even before breaking off negotiations Frick, the superintendent of the

Carnegie Steel Company, made an agreement with the Pinkerton secret service agency, which contracted to send 300 provocateurs and sluggers into Homestead. Frick ordered a wire fence three miles in length and 15 feet high to be erected around the factory. This act shows that the employers were prepared in advance for a bitter-end struggle.

From Homestead the strike spread to other steel centers. In Pittsburgh the workers of the Carnegie and other companies struck in sympathy with their brothers at Homestead. In Duquesne, Pa., the steel workers joined the union in July and went out with it.

Now the steel operators decided to put through their murderous scheme. At midnight of July 5 the Pinkerton men arrived by river and attempted to land at Homestead. All of them were armed with guns and revolvers. But the workers knew the plans of their enemies in advance, and were on guard day and night against a sudden attack. Learning of the arrival of the Pinkertons, thousands of men, armed as they could, went to the water front to prevent the gunmen from landing. The latter thought to frighten the workers by displaying their guns, but the strikers were ready to accept the challenge. The Pinkertons opened fire. A pitched battle ensued. When the fight was over at least half a dozen men on both sides were dead and a number seriously wounded. The gunmen were defeated and held in captivity until the evening of July 6, then driven out of town.

Failing to defeat the strike with the help of the Pinkertons, the employers now invited to their assistance the Pennsylvania state militia. The little town of Homestead looked like an army camp. After a few months of struggle and suffering the steel workers were driven to submission. Their militant resistance was crushed; the interests of the Carnegie Company were again secure. The successful methods of the Carnegie Company were immediately copied by other steel concerns, and the industry was swept clean of trade unionism for years to come. The steel workers were again left helpless slaves in the hands of the most powerful group of American employers.

The Homestead strike was probably the first time the workers came into conflict with a powerful modern corporation, which not only had enough money to hire gunmen and provocateurs, but also behind which the government stood with all its forces of suppression and oppression.

Another important labor battle took place on July 11 of the same year in the Coeur d'Alene mining district of Idaho. The organized miners were in revolt against continuous reductions in wages.

"After a bloody fight the miners seized the property and drove the strikebreakers out of the district. In the course of the battle a large quartz mill was destroyed by an explosion. The governor, his own forces being utterly inadequate, called upon the President, and on July 12 the federal troops were ordered to Coeur D'Alene, martial law was declared, and the strike came to an end" (Commons: *History*, etc., Vol. II, pp. 497-498).

THE STRUGGLE FOR THE EIGHT-HOUR DAY 215

The miners were once more defeated, with loss of life.

On August 13 the railroad switchmen of Buffalo went on strike for shorter hours and an increase in wages. There were only 400 of them, but they fought so well that they succeeded in preventing the railroad companies from replacing them with scabs. Then the state came to the assistance of the railroad magnates, and on August 18 the governor sent in several thousand state troops.

"The national officers of the switchmen's union asked for a conference with the national officers of the brotherhoods of engineers, firemen, conductors, and trainmen, to consider the proposition of a sympathetic strike. But it came to nothing, since Arthur, of the engineers, refused to appear, and the other organizations, though willing to aid the switchmen, could not decide to act without the engineers. On August 24, the strike was consequently called off" (*Ibid.*, p. 498).

About the same time the miners of Tennessee launched an attack against the coal companies, which were employing convicts. Prisoners were put to work at very low pay, while the miners walked around idle.

The miners, who were in the Knights of Labor, had long been preparing to put an end to this system. In August those at Tracy City overcame the companies' armed guards and set 300 prisoners free. On August 15 the same was done at Inman, while on August 17 the miners of Oliver Springs followed suit. On August 18 the men at Coal Creek set 1,500 prisoners free.

"During 1892 the militia was permanently stationed in the mining districts, and friction with the miners had time to arise. The operations which began with the liberation of the prisoners in Tracy City, on August 13, were followed by a serious war between the militia and the armed miners. In several instances entire train loads of militia were taken captive and disarmed, but the final victory was with the militia. The mines were retaken from the miners and the prisoners were put back to work" (*Ibid.*, p. 499).

There were two main reasons for the failure of these strikes: first, the determination of the employers to crush the rebellious workers with the help of the government, and second, division in the ranks of the workers. In every instance the strikes were conducted by separate craft unions. When the steel workers of Homestead and Pittsburgh were struggling with the armed forces of the employers and the state, the steel workers in other centers and the workers of other industries were indifferent to the struggle. When the miners of Coeur d'Alene were striking, the miners of other districts were indifferent. When the switchmen of Buffalo were begging for help, the other railroad unions turned their backs on them. Therefore, it was easy for the united forces of capitalism to drown the militant workers in blood for daring to challenge the rule of the bourgeoisie.

Discontent began to develop in the trade unions. There was an element which maintained that it was impossible for the workers to gain anything through trade unionism, and therefore suggested parliamentary as a substitute for industrial action. Of course, this conclusion was fundamentally wrong, as was proved by later experience. The trade unions, that is, the economic organizations of the workers, cannot be replaced by a political party.

Another element in the trade unions came to the correct conclusion that the craft unions had outgrown their usefulness, due to the fact that capital had been organized into corporations and trusts, and that therefore the workers must combine their craft organizations into industrial unions. As a result of the failure of the Coeur d'Alene miners in 1892, the Western Federation of Miners was formed in 1893 as an industrial union. Similar unsuccessful isolated struggles moved the United Mine Workers of America to take under its jurisdiction all workers inside and around the mines. When the Buffalo strike failed, Eugene V. Debs, secretary of the Locomotive Firemen's Railway Brotherhood, resigned from his position and began agitating for an industrial union of the railroad workers. In 1893 the American Railway Union was established under his leadership, aiming at one powerful organization of all railroad workers. The new union had a successful beginning and by 1894 there were 150,000 workers in its ranks, with 465 locals. The leaders of the railroad brotherhoods were opposed to this industrial union.

In 1893 there was an extensive industrial depression. Several million workers were thrown on the streets.

The crisis lasted until 1897. Previously, whenever a period of industrial depression came the trade unions disappeared. But the crisis of 1893 did not destroy the unions entirely. During the years 1893 to 1897 the trade unions did not grow—the American Federation of Labor maintained its membership at about 275,000—nevertheless, they maintained their existence. Therefore with this period the trade union movement became a stable factor in the class struggle of the country. As in the past, during the crisis the employers began a general offensive against wages, and thus with 1894 we witness a wave of defensive struggles on the part of the workers. During this one year about 750,000 workers took part in various strikes. The most important were the strike of the miners which started on June 21, and that of the workers of Pullman, Ill., which began on May 11.

The United Mine Workers of America at this time had only about 20,000 members, but when it declared a strike not less than 150,000 workers joined hands in the struggle against their common enemy. The miners demanded the scale of wages of May, 1893. The employers on their part declared another reduction. Therefore the strike for higher wages became a desperate struggle to resist the new cut. In July, after three months of effort, the miners went back to work defeated.

But the strike of the workers in the railroad shops at Pullman was even more impressive.

"The Pullman strike," Perlman says, "marks an era in the American labor movement because it was the only attempt ever made in America of a revolutionary strike on the continental European model. The strikers tried to throw against the associated railways and indeed against the entire existing social order the full force of a revolutionary labor solidarity embracing the entire American wage-earning class brought to the point of exasperation by unemployment, wage reductions, and misery . . ." (Perlman: *Loc. cit.,* pp. 136-137).

But, of course, the efforts of the revolutionary workers of Pullman were in vain, for the other unions did not respond to their appeal. By this time the unions were under the full control of the conservative leaders. They were indifferent to the militant struggle of their brothers at Pullman and allowed the bourgeoisie to crush them.

The Pullman strike began May 11, 1894. It grew out of a demand of certain employees in the shops of the Pullman Palace Car Company for restoration of the wages paid during the previous year. In March, 1894, the Pullman employees had voted to join the American Railway Union. On June 21 the American Railway Union decided to help them win their demands by refusing to handle Pullman cars after June 26, in case the Pullman Company did not concede the men's demands. As was expected the company absolutely refused to have anything to do with the strikers or the American Railway Union. The strike immediately spread through Chicago and vicinity. At the same time, the General Managers' Association, an organization in existence since 1886, declared a holy war against the strikers and the union. According to the report of the commission which was appointed by President Cleveland to investigate the situation,

"United States deputy marshals to the number of 3,600 were selected by and appointed at the request of the General Managers' Association and of its railroads. They were armed and paid by the railroads, and acted in the double capacity of railroad employees and United States officers while operating the railroads. They assumed and exercised unrestricted United States authority when so ordered by their employers, or whenever they regarded it as necessary" (*Debs: His Life, Writings, and Speeches,* p. 197).

These deputy marshals were composed of the lowest element of the Chicago population—thieves, thugs, highwaymen, and other criminals.

An era of disorder started. The deputy marshals began to provoke the strikers and to destroy railroad property in order to attach the guilt to the union and thus help to destroy it. On July 27 Eugene V. Debs and other officials of the union were arrested, indicted, and placed under $10,000 bail. The judge also issued an injunction forbidding them to take any part in the strike. On July 13 the union officials were brought before the United States Court for contempt of court on the score that they had violated the injunction and urged the railroad workers to go on with the strike. They were found guilty and sent to jail. President Cleveland, faithfully carrying out the instructions of the railroad companies, sent federal troops to Chicago. On July 13 the American Railway Union proposed peace on condition that the employers promise not to persecute those who took part in the strike. The General Managers' Association absolutely refused to deal with the union. It was clear as daylight that the companies were determined in advance to crush the militant organization of the workers—an endeavor in which they succeeded.

Debs, who was president of the American Railway Union during the strike, has the following to say of its course:

"The Pullman Company, backed by the combined railway corporations, represented by the General Managers' Association, resolved to crush the union. They not only failed, but the union paralyzed their traffic and defeated them all. Seeing that the union was triumphant they changed their tactics. They had the United States marshal of Illinois swear in an army of deputies, ostensibly to protect property, but in fact to incite tumult. In his official report to the council of Chicago the chief of police said that these 'deputies' consisted of thieves, thugs and ex-convicts, the worst element that had ever been turned loose on any city. As soon as the deputies began to operate, as directed by their leaders, and under cover of night, trouble began, and this is what the corporation wanted. Peace and order were fatal to them as turbulence and violence were fatal to the union. They understood this perfectly. Hence the deputies and disorder. Immediately these thugs began to perform the capitalist papers and Associated Press flashed broadcast the falsehood that the strikers were on the warpath and threatened to destroy every living thing. The falsehood caught on like magic. Far and wide the cry went: 'Down with the A. R. U.! Down with anarchy!' The tide turned. The triumphant union and defeated corporation changed places. With practically the whole population aroused against the A. R. U. every outrage upon it was not only possible, but perpetrated with mad zeal in the name of patriotism. The A. R. U. had no press, no way of getting its side before the people, and thousands of the very workers in whose behalf it was fighting and had staked everything, turned upon it and joined in the flood of angry denunciation that was launched upon it.

"Injunctions by the hundreds were issued and served by all the courts between the Ohio and the Pacific. A half dozen burly ruffians, by order of the federal authorities—precisely whom could never be learned—backed up a cart at the union headquarters, forced their way into the offices, sacked them, taking records, books, private papers and unopened letters, without warrant of any description, nailing up the headquarters and hauling the booty to the federal building.

"Thousands of falsehoods were coined and circulated by the capitalist press, shifting the blame of lawlessness and crime from the instigators to innocent men; the leaders were arrested without charges and jailed without trial, headquarters were broken up, a special grand jury was sworn in expressly to indict, a notorious capitalist union hater being made foreman, and a hundred other flagrant violations of the law and outrages upon justice were committed in the name of law to defeat justice and enthrone corporate rapacity.

"The venality of capitalist government never made so bold an exhibition of itself. It was scandalous beyond expression and shocking to the last degree. Every department of the federal government was freely placed at the service of the railroad corporations and Republican and Democratic officials vied with each other in cheerful servile obedience to their masters.

THE STRUGGLE FOR THE EIGHT-HOUR DAY

"When the government and its capitalist lackeys had completed their service as corporation scavengers, General Miles, the military satrap, like a vulture stuffed with carrion, pompously exclaimed at a plutocratic banquet in honor of his gallant services:

"'I have broken the backbone of this strike.'

"Such sublime heroism in such a holy cause, Grover Cleveland, Nelson Miles, *et al.*, will not be forgotten nor remain unrewarded" (*Debs: Loc. cit.*, pp. 111-114).

What did the other trade unions do at the time when the railroad companies and the capitalist state were crushing the American Railway Union with arms and falsehood? As far as the reactionary leaders of the brotherhoods were concerned, they were as much opposed to the A. R. U. as the railroad companies themselves, so there could be no question of their helping the strikers. On July 12 the officials of the A. R. U. called a conference of all national trade unions to consider ways and means of assisting the strikers. Twenty-five unions, members of the American Federation of Labor, sent delegates. In the name of the A. R. U., Debs appeared and urged the participants to call a general strike. But it was soon demonstrated that the trade union officials had in mind something entirely different from assisting the A. R. U. or the thousands of Pullman workers who were heroically fighting the combined forces of the railroad corporations and the bourgeois state. The conference decided that "it would be unwise and disastrous to the interests of labor to extend the strike any further than it had already gone," and urged the workers to go back to work, defeated. Such was the assistance the strikers received at the hands of the conservative trade union officials. Instead of financial and moral support they were scolded, discouraged, and told to submit to the enemy. This dastardly action was of tremendous help to the railroad companies. The Pullman strike of 1894 was crushed by the united front of railroad companies, the capitalist state, and the conservative national trade union officials.

The miners' general strike of 1897 also deserves to be mentioned. After all its failures and the prolonged industrial crisis, the United Mine Workers remained with only about 10,000 members. But in 1897 industry began to revive, and the price of coal rose. The mine owners were amassing huge profits, while the wages of the workers were low and great poverty existed among them. This was an auspicious occasion for the union to increase its influence and to widen its ranks by defending the most elementary interests of the miners. In spite of its numerical weakness, therefore, the union declared a general strike in the real sense of the word, for with the exception of West Virginia, the workers of all the coal fields joined with the United Mine Workers in the struggle for a larger piece of bread. The courts hurled injunctions against the strikers, forbidding them to hold meetings or to persuade those who were desirous of going back into the mines not to work. Many strikers were arrested and placed behind prison bars for violating these injunctions. Nevertheless, the workers were determined to fight to the bitter end.

"The general strike of 1897 ended in the central competitive field after a 12 weeks' struggle," Perlman says. "The settlement was an unqualified victory for the union. It conceded the miners a 20 per cent increase in wages, the establishment of the eight-hour day, the abolition of the company stores, semi-monthly payments, and a restoration of the system of fixing interstate wage rates in annual joint conferences with the operators, which meant official recognition of the United Mine Workers. The operators in West Virginia, however, refused to come in" (Perlman: *History*, etc., p. 169).

This was the first great victory for the miners, and from then on the union grew rapidly.

On October 12, 1898, the workers of the Chicago-Virden Coal Company went out. The company built a stockade around its property and put 60 gunmen in charge of it. The agents of the operators lured 150 workers into the stockade after assuring them that there was no labor trouble at hand. But trouble did follow. The gunmen opened fire on the strikers and killed 12 and wounded from 30 to 40. These mercenaries had committed so high-handed a crime that John R. Turner, then governor of Illinois, publicly denounced them. He said:

"I therefore, charge the owners and managers of this company as being lawbreakers and morally and criminally responsible for the bloodshed and disgrace to our state, and I further charge every man in their employ, as detective or guard in the stockade, or on the train, who participated in this fiendish outrage, as guilty of murder!" (Jay Lovestone, *Loc. cit.*, p. 132).

By the close of the nineteenth century only the most backward, the most ignorant sections of the proletariat could fail to see that bourgeois democracy is nothing but a dictatorship of the capitalist class.

CHAPTER XXIII

THE INDUSTRIAL "MIRACLES" OF THE TWENTIETH CENTURY

In none of the previous periods did American capitalism develop at such speed as during the first quarter of the twentieth century. Imperial America now ranges over the earth and has built its spheres of influence in every corner. Capitalist Europe has practically become a colony of the imperialism of the United States. American capital opened for itself the doors of backward Asia, and to-day the capitalists of this country are seriously threatening the interests of the imperialists of Great Britain. England, France, and Japan dare not take a step in Asia without the agreement of the Washington government, which with its armed forces faithfully guards the interests of the financial kings of Wall Street. South and Central America are under the economic and political hegemony of the United States imperialists.

One can hardly find a spot on the globe where no American capital is invested or where the industrial or agricultural products of America are not seen. The American navy has made its power felt on every ocean. Wherever the workers show resistance to their oppressors, either in Asia, Africa, or in the southern republics of the western continent, our battleships are dispatched to "protect the property and lives of our citizens."

It would be hard to find a bourgeois country throughout the world which is not indebted to the United States. And behind every dollar loaned to other countries stands the Washington government with its mighty army, navy, and other military forces.

The development of United States imperialism, which began its career with the Spanish-American War of 1898 by annexing or getting complete control over the Philippines, Porto Rico, Guam, Cuba and other islands in the Pacific, was effected almost entirely during the first quarter of the twentieth century, which also witnessed the imperialist World War.

Before the World War the United States was indebted to Europe to the amount of $5,000,000,000 in the form of railway and other stocks and securities. But the war transformed America from a debtor nation into a creditor nation. Now the war debts alone of Europe to the United States total $11,000,000,000. The same bourgeois countries of Europe borrowed several billion dollars from American capitalists after the war to reconstruct their shattered finances and industries and to crush the revolts of their workers. At the end of 1926 the American investments in foreign countries amounted to $13,000,000,000.

These imperialist "miracles" were made possible only by enormous industrial expansion at home. Only the surplus capital of the United States was transferred to the other countries.

RISE OF INDUSTRY IN THE UNITED STATES, 1900-1920

Year	Number of Establishments	Number of Workers	Amount of Capital (in thousands)	Value of Products (in thousands)
1900	207,514	4,712,763	$ 8,975,257	$11,406,927
1910	268,491	6,615,046	18,428,270	20,672,051
1915	275,791	7,036,337	22,790,980	24,246,435
1919	289,768	9,103,200	44,678,911	62,910,202
1923	196,309	10,282,306		60,550,998

During the two decades of this century the number of workers in our industries almost doubled, the invested capital increased five times, and the value of industrial products increased more than five times.

This industrial growth has expressed itself almost exclusively in the form of large-scale production. In place of many individual capitalists there arose great industrial corporations and trusts. Small-scale production was pushed further into the background and large capital began to play a still more dominant rôle. For example, as far back as 1914 the value of the products of individually owned enterprises, numbering 148,-436, amounted to $1,925,518,298, while the value of the products of corporation enterprises, numbering only 78,151 in the same year, reached $20,181,279,071, or 83 per cent of all industrial products. At the same time the individually owned enterprises employed only 707,658 workers, while the corporation-controlled factories had 5,649,646 wage workers.

There is no doubt that concentration and centralization of production from 1914 to 1925, especially during the World War, have become even greater. Indeed, to-day American industry is completely in the hands of a few powerful trusts or corporations. The steel industry is completely controlled by the steel trust, the sugar industry is in the hands of the sugar trust, the oil industry is in the clutches of the oil trust, the mines and railroads are controlled by a few corporations, the textile industry is almost completely trustified, and even the clothing industry is rapidly passing into the hands of a few large companies.

As a result of this development the workers have been brought together into large industrial armies. Gigantic factories have been established where hundreds and sometimes thousands of workers are employed. Under such conditions the class struggle naturally becomes sharper. The differences between the capitalist class and the working class become more clearly defined.

INDUSTRIAL "MIRACLES" OF TWENTIETH CENTURY

All these changes finally lead to the point where it becomes harder for the bourgeoisie to withstand the attacks of the working class; it needs greater and greater power to defend its class interests against strikes and revolts. This power expresses itself in the form of the bourgeois state. The power of the federal government has increased enormously. The governments of the various states have been pushed into the background and the federal government has become almost omnipotent. There has been a remarkable growth in the number of civil service employees. In 1884 there were 13,780 employees on the payroll of the national government; in 1912 there were 278,000; in 1916 they increased to 439,798; while in 1918, in the midst of the war, this number reached 917,760. After the war the number of government employees decreased considerably, yet in 1921 there still were 597,482 on the federal payroll. This strengthening of the national government is absolutely necessary for the protection of incorporated capital and for the maintenance of the proletarian army under the yoke of capitalism.

"In all the struggles between capital and labor," says John Pepper, "the federal government assumes the rôle of arbitrator. The force of the government exercised against the coal and railroad strikes of the summer of 1922, with its deep going and nation-wide interference, which is unparalleled in the history of the United States, is a tremendous and fearful sign of the growth of the centralized government power. The Daugherty injunction, the use of troops in 15 states, the brutal persecution of struggling workers in all of the 48 states was so blatant and clear, that the whole country could see and understand that the American government in its third crisis (that is during the World War), had grown into a mammoth monster of centralization similar to that of the old European governments" (John Pepper: *For a Labor Party*, p. 25).

The twentieth century furthermore has witnessed enormous increases in the military forces of the state. These are necessary, first of all, for the suppression of the labor movement at home and, secondly, for the defense of the imperialist interests of the United States in foreign lands. The United States standing army in 1924 numbered 132,953 men, and in the navy there were 95,453 men, making a total of 228,406. For the maintenance of the national government of the United States in 1925-1926 Congress appropriated $3,788,745,778. Of this sum $674,581,000, or 22 per cent of all the expenses of the national bourgeois state, was allotted to the army and navy. This does not include the cost of the various state militias, with a total of 185,273 men. And all of these armed forces are organized for the purpose of maintaining the rule of the capitalist class over the proletariat.

Population increased by 30,000,000 during the first 20 years of the twentieth century, from 75,994,575 in 1900 to 105,710,620 in 1920.

Never had immigration been so great as it was in the beginning of the present century. In the period of 14 years, from 1900 to 1914, over

13,000,000 immigrants landed on the shores of this country. When the imperialist World War started, immigration decreased heavily, but even at that, from 1914 to 1924 about 4,000,000 immigrants came in. And these millions of immigrants were almost exclusively workers. They came directly into our factories and mines. In all of the fundamental industries of the country the great majority of workers are foreign-born.

PROPORTION OF FOREIGN-BORN WORKERS TO NATIVE WORKERS IN THE BASIC MANUFACTURING INDUSTRIES

Industry	Percentage of Foreign-born Workers
Iron and steel	58
Bituminous coal	62
Slaughtering and meat packing	61
Woolen and worsted	62
Cotton goods	62
Clothing	69
Leather	67
Furniture	59
Oil refining	67

(Clarissa Ware: *The American Foreign-Born Workers*, p. 10)

The twentieth century also saw a great change in the American working class in the direction of uniformity and stabilization. This process was especially marked during the war on account of the decrease in immigration.

In the past there were many opportunities for a worker to escape from the proletariat into the ranks of the bourgeoisie. A small sum of money and a little "brains" were sufficient to secure a store or a small industrial enterprise. New immigrants came into the industry and filled the places of those who had gone into the upper class.

But with the beginning of the twentieth century a great shift has taken place in the conditions of industry. Big capital has become the dominant power. To become an employer in most industries now requires a large sum of money or credit. It is now very hard for a worker to get away from his class. The former process has been reversed. Instead of workingmen becoming small business men, small business men are going bankrupt and returning to the army of the workers. Hundreds of thousands of farmers are leaving their farms and joining the proletariat. Between 1920 and 1924 no fewer than 2,000,000 farmers went bankrupt and drifted to the industrial centers.

As in the last century American capitalism has not escaped industrial crises and panics. During the period of 25 years since the century opened the country has passed through three great and far-reaching economic depressions. The first one occurred in 1907-1908. It was conservatively estimated that about 5,000,000 workers were thrown out on the streets jobless. Every industrial city was overcrowded with homeless and unemployed. Destitution was widespread, and many cases of actual starvation were reported.

Then gradually the crisis receded and again "prosperity" dawned upon American capitalism. But this prosperity did not last long, for by 1913 another depression started. The collapse of industry was even greater, the army of employed was larger, and the suffering of the workers more intense than in 1907-1908. The World War cut short the depression of 1913, otherwise it might have lasted for a long time. Europe was set on fire, the murder of millions became the order of the day. The demand for clothing, food, machinery, ammunition, machine guns, leaped skyward. Once more our industries began to grind with maddening speed in order to supply Europe with all these necessaries of war. Orders were coming fast, overproduction disappeared, and by 1915 the army of the unemployed was almost completely demobilized. Our country was again experiencing unheard-of "prosperity."

Then the German submarines began to send our ships to the bottom of the Atlantic—ships which were filled with ammunition and supplies for delivery to England and France. The bourgeois press of our country began to clamor that our rights were being violated by those "damnable Germans!" These violations had to be stopped! We had to go to war! And so we went to war in 1917, for the simple reason that German submarines were threatening to cut short the profits which Wall Street magnates were making on the European massacre and to further extend American imperialist interests. Now jobs were to be had by everybody. Millions were sent to Europe to die for the profits of our capitalist class, others were put to the wheel to sweat.

Finally the "world was made safe for democracy" and the great war came to an end. American industry had to go back to peace-time production. Once more appeared signs of a coming storm. With the year 1920 depression and unemployment set in, and by 1921 they had reached their highest point. About 10,000,000 were thrown out of work.

CHAPTER XXIV

THE LABOR ORGANIZATIONS, 1900-1914

THE trade union movement had no great cause for rejoicing at the beginning of the twentieth century. The same barriers to progress, the same difficulties, the same opposition from the bourgeoisie continued as before. On the other hand, the trade union leaders became more and more conservative, their attitude toward the efforts of the workers to organize themselves and to fight against their class enemy became cooler and cooler. The capitalists were joining hands and rapidly perfecting their economic and political organizations. They were forming gigantic corporations and creating powerful trusts, advancing in all directions as never before, while our trade unions were dragging along listlessly. This can be seen from the record of their membership.

MEMBERSHIP OF THE A. F. OF L. AND OTHER UNIONS, 1900-1914

Year	A. F. of L.	Total Trade Union Membership
1900	675,000	865,000
1902	1,000,000	1,374,300
1903	1,450,000	1,912,900
1904	1,675,000	2,072,600
1906	1,425,000	1,906,300
1908	1,630,000	2,090,400
1910	1,550,000	2,138,000
1912	1,780,000	2,440,800
1914	2,000,000	2,674,000

It is true that the membership of the American Federation of Labor more than doubled during the 14-year period—from 675,000 in 1900 it advanced to 2,000,000 in 1914, while the membership of all trade unions advanced from 865,000 to 2,674,000. Nevertheless the fact remains that the trade unions did not advance at the same rate as the organized might of the bourgeoisie. Also, as in the past, the trade unions at the beginning of the present century were unable to make their influence felt among the masses of the unskilled workers, which are several times larger in number than those of the skilled. And the main reason for this sad situation has always been that the trade unions lack to a pitiful degree the desire and determination to advance into the masses of the unskilled. The American Federation of Labor has never failed at its annual conventions in declaring for the necessity of organizing the unorganized, but there never has been a sincere, nation-wide, energetic campaign to organize these masses. The trade unions have remained the monopoly of the skilled section of the working class, a fortress, to a very great extent, against any attempt of the unskilled upon the privileges of the skilled, insofar as these privileges still exist.

There has always been an element in the trade union movement which understood the inefficiency of the craft form of organization and how it had outgrown its usefulness in view of the great concentration and centralization of capital. Separate, narrow, independent craft unions were long ago unable to cope with the well-organized employing class. It is necessary to learn from the employers and organize along the same lines as they—along industrial lines. In one industry there should be only one powerful labor union, embracing all workers in that industry. At the present time, due to the form of organization of the A. F. of L., in every industry there are dozens of small, weak, independent craft unions, each having its own organization machinery, each with its own set of petty, conservative officials. If one craft declares a strike, other crafts often remain at work and thus assist the employers in crushing the rebels. Only industrial unions can eliminate this intolerable situation, unite the workers for successful struggle on the economic field, and furnish an effective basis for the political mass organization of labor.

But this new and effective form of trade union organization has been met with animosity and stern opposition by the American Federation of Labor or, rather, by its conservative leadership. The convention of 1903 emphatically and explicitly condemned those who advocate industrial unionism. It raised the same old bug-a-boo which was raised against independent political action of the working class, namely, that it would mean the death of the existing trade unions to attempt to reorganize them on a new, industrial basis.

"The attempt to force the trade unions into what has been termed industrial organization," the convention declared, "is perversive of the history of the labor movement, runs counter to the best conceptions of the toilers' interests now, and is sure to lead to the confusions which precede dissolution and disruption. It is time for our fellow-unionists entrusted with the grave responsibility to help stem the tide of expansion madness lest either by their indifference or encouragement their organizations will be drawn into the vortex that will engulf them to their possible dismemberment and destruction."

The convention expressly rejected the idea that industrial unions would strengthen the power of the workers and make their struggles with the employers more successful.

"The advocates of the so-called industrial system of labor organizations," the declaration continues, "urge that an effective strike can only be conducted when all workmen, regardless of trade, calling or occupation, are affected. That this is not borne out by the history of strikes in the whole labor movement is easily demonstrable. Though here and there such strikes have been temporarily successful, in the main they have been fraught with injury to all. The so-called industrial system of organization implies sympathetic strikes, and these time and experience have demonstrated that as a general proposition they should be discarded, while strikes of particular trades or callings have had the largest number of successes and the minimum of defeats."

Finally, *"splendid advantages have been obtained by the trade unions without the necessity of strikes or the interruption of industry"* (American Federation of Labor: *History*, etc., Vol. I, pp. 246-247).

But even this emphatic stand of the Federation against industrial unionism could not silence the demand for a change in the form of organization. The exponents of industrial unionism pointed, as an example, to the successful industrial unions of the miners and the brewery workers. In the Federation convention of 1912 the miners' delegation again proposed a resolution for industrial unionism, but it was once more rejected. The same process was repeated at the convention of 1914. Thus the Federation systematically and continuously fought the efforts to bring about a change in the form of union organization.

As far as parliamentary action is concerned, the Federation remained the tail of the bourgeois parties during this period as well as in the past. Gompers' policy of "reward your friends and punish your enemies" continued as the established policy of the Federation. But this detrimental policy met, as it always must, with failure after failure. "Labor friends" whom the Federation endorsed turned their backs upon the workers and their organizations as soon as they were elected. These failures were so open, so clear to everybody, that even the trade union officials could stand them no longer. In 1906 a conference was held, with 117 officials of the national trade unions present, to consider the grievances of the workers against the "friends of labor" in government offices and national and state legislatures. But, of course, they did not find it wise to get rid of that wrong policy of "rewarding friends and punishing enemies." On the contrary, they decided to appeal to the "hearts" of the legislators in Washington and drew up a "Bill of Labor's Grievances" to be presented to them. Only those who are absolutely bankrupt politically could stoop so low before the enemies of labor as did the trade union officials in this "bill of grievances."

"We present these grievances to your attention," pleaded the leaders of the trade union movement, "because we have long, patiently and in vain waited for redress. There is not any matter of which we had complained but for which we have in an honorable and lawful manner submitted remedies. The remedies for these grievances proposed by labor are in line with fundamental law, and with the progress and development made necessary by changed industrial conditions.

"Labor brings these, its grievances, to your attention because you are the representatives responsible for legislation and for failure of legislation. The toilers come to you as your fellow-citizens who, by reason of their position in life, have not only with all other citizens an equal interest in our country, but the further interest of being the burden-bearers, the wage-earners of America. As labor's representatives we ask you to redress these grievances, for it is in your power to do so. Labor now appeals to you, and we trust that it may not be in vain. But if perchance you may not heed us, we shall appeal to the conscience and the support of our fellow citizens."

Of course, Congress turned a deaf ear to this bill of grievances, and the trade union officials had to "appeal to the conscience and support of our fellow citizens." But their appeal amounted only to affirmation of the Federation stand in 1897 when it declared:

"Resolved, that the A. F. of L. most firmly and unequivocally favors the independent use of the ballot by the trade unionists and workmen, *united regardless of party*, that we may elect men from our own ranks to make new laws and administer them along the lines laid down in the legislative demands of the A. F. of L., and at the same time secure an impartial judiciary that will not govern us by arbitrary injunctions of the courts, nor act as the pliant tools of corporate wealth. That as our efforts are centered against all forms of industrial slavery and economic wrong, we must also direct our utmost energies to remove all forms of political servitude and *party slavery*, to the end that the working people may act as a unit at the polls at every election" (*Ibid.*, pp. 320-327).

And this meant in practice no more nor less than opposing the political party of the working class and supporting the "friends of labor" in the old capitalist parties. The trade union leaders either did not understand or did not want openly to declare to the workers that the congressmen, as well as the President, are representatives of the capitalist class; that therefore, they must support and defend the interests of that class; and that if the workers want to get any recognition from these officials they must be able to bring pressure to bear upon them through their own independent political action in the form of a political party of the workers, for the workers, and by the workers.

In the twentieth century the conservative trade union leaders openly joined hands with the bourgeoisie and began to propagate the idea of class collaboration. The embodiment of this coöperation between the trade union officials and the bourgeoisie is found in the National Civic Federation, organized by the capitalists for the spiritual enslavement of the organized workers. For a number of years August Belmont, a powerful capitalist, was president of this organization and Samuel Gompers was vice-president. In 1906 Gompers proudly declared, "I think I can without vanity claim to be one of the earliest members of the National Civic Federation. I had faith in it; I had faith in the idea," that is, that peaceful collaboration with the employers is beneficial to the workers, because "our best common interests are conserved by meeting [with the employers] in the conciliation board and our endeavors to bring about a common understanding upon contested points." And again in 1911 Gompers repeated that "by reason of our coming together much strife has been avoided, and many reconciliations established where the relations between employer and employee have been ruptured" (Gompers: *Loc. cit.*, pp. 36-37).

Therefore, as far as the trade union leaders were concerned, they united with the employers organizationally and spiritually, and if we still find strikes and struggles in this period it is not because the leadership wanted it, but in spite of the leadership.

The detrimental policy of dual unionism which was adopted and vigorously pursued during these years by the revolutionaries was of great assistance to the class collaboration plans of the conservative trade union officials. Dual unionism helped to minimize the opposition in the trade unions to class collaboration, because the opponents of class collaboration —the socialists and the revolutionary unionists—had left the old unions and organized themselves into revolutionary industrial unions of their own, leaving the organized masses completely in the hands of the class collaborationists. As has been pointed out, the first separation of the revolutionists from the organized masses took place in 1895 when the socialists under the leadership of De Leon organized the Socialist Trade and Labor Alliance. Though these efforts brought only failure and disappointment, nevertheless the revolutionists continued to harp on the policy of dual unionism and in 1905 they formed the Industrial Workers of the World.

Tired of the slow progress of the conservative trade unions, on February 3, 1905, a handful of revolutionary union leaders held a conference and issued a manifesto to the organized workers calling a convention on June 27, 1905, at Chicago, Ill., for the purpose of launching a new organization. On the appointed date 186 delegates met, and after 12 days of debate the Industrial Workers of the World was formed. The most important unions represented at the convention were the Western Federation of Miners with 27,000 members; the American Labor Union, 16,750; the United Metal Workers, 3,000; the United Brotherhood of Railway Employees, 2,087; and the Socialist Trade and Labor Alliance, 1,450. Among the outstanding figures present were Eugene V. Debs, Daniel De Leon, and William D. Haywood (Paul F. Brissenden: *History of the I. W. W.*, p. 74).

The principles of the new organization were stated in the preamble to the constitution as follows:

"The working class and the employing class have nothing in common. There can be no peace so long as hunger and want are found among millions of working people and the few, who make up the employing class, have all the good things of life.

"Between these two classes a struggle must go on until all the toilers come together on the political, as well as on the industrial field, and take and hold that which they produce by their labor through an economic organization of the working class, without affiliation with any political party.

THE LABOR ORGANIZATIONS

"The rapid gathering of wealth and the centering of the management of industries into fewer and fewer hands make the trade unions unable to compete with the ever-growing power of the employing class, because the trade unions foster a state of things which allows one set of workers to be pitted against another set of workers in the same industry, thereby helping defeat one another in wage wars. The trade unions aid the employing class to mislead the workers into the belief that the working class have interests in common with their employers.

"These sad conditions can be changed and the interests of the working class upheld only by an organization formed in such a way that all its members in any one industry, or in all industries, if necessary, cease work whenever a strike or lockout is on in any department thereof, thus making an injury to one an injury to all."

As the new organization was composed of a great variety of elements, (socialists, syndicalists, anarchists, trade unionists, and others), there very soon developed an internal struggle and a factional fight. The second convention was held in 1906 at Chicago, with 93 delegates representing 60,000 organized workers. There were two opposing camps at the convention and their fight ended in a split. The faction led by Vincent St. John represented the main body of the I. W. W., but the most important organization, the Western Federation of Miners, withdrew, thus greatly weakening the movement.

Soon another factional struggle developed, this time between the political and the industrial wings of the I. W. W. The organization itself was now on the decline, having only about 5,000 members in good standing. The fourth convention, in 1908, ended in another split and the formation of two rival I. W. W.'s, one with its center in Detroit, Mich., the other in Chicago, Ill. The Detroit faction disintegrated entirely and the Chicago faction remained as the I. W. W. It changed, however, the principles which had been adopted in 1905, by rejecting all mention of political action. The second paragraph of the preamble was changed to read as follows:

"Between these two classes a struggle must go on until the workers of the world organize as a class, take possession of the earth and the machinery of production, and abolish the wage system."

And two new paragraphs were added:

"Instead of the conservative motto, 'A fair day's wages for a fair day's work,' we must inscribe on our banner the revolutionary watchword, 'Abolition of the wage system!'

"It is the historical mission of the working class to do away with capitalism. The army of production must be organized, not only for the every-day struggle with capitalists, but also to carry on production when capitalism shall have been overthrown. By organizing industrially we are forming the structure of the new society within the shell of the old" (André Tridon: *The New Unionism*, pp. 97-99).

By this act the I. W. W. became a purely industrial organization, categorically rejecting even the idea of the necessity of a political party of the workers.

The structure of the organization is that workers of a particular industry in a particular city form a local industrial union; these local industrial unions of the same industry, in various cities, make up a national industrial union; the national industrial unions of allied industries form a department; finally, these departments and their constituent national industrial unions make up the national I. W. W.

Concerning the methods of the I. W. W., Vincent St. John states:

"As a revolutionary organization the Industrial Workers of the World aims to use any and all tactics that will get the results sought with the least expenditure of time and energy. . . .

"No terms made with an employer are final. All peace, so long as the wage system lasts, is but an armed truce. . . .

"The I. W. W. realizes that the day of successful long strikes is past. . . .

"The I. W. W. maintains that nothing will be conceded by the employers except that which we have the power to take and hold by the strength of our organization. Therefore we seek no agreements with the employers.

"Failing to force concessions from the employers by the strike, work is resumed and 'sabotage' is used to force the employers to concede the demands of the workers" (*Ibid.*, pp. 103-104).

Thus the Industrial Workers of the World adopted revolutionary tactics in their relations with the employers. They showed great militancy, great devotion to the cause of the working class, and led a few important strikes, attracting the attention of a large section of the working class. The capitalists immediately condemned the new organization and spared neither energy nor time in crushing it.

But in spite of its temporary important successes, the I. W. W. did not reach the goal set for it by its founders. It never succeeded in organizing great masses of workers. Even at its highest point it never had more than 60,000 members. During the same period the conservative, old-line trade unions were growing much faster than the revolutionary I. W. W. One doubtful success of the I. W. W. was that for a number of years it supplied a shelter for the revolutionary unionists and prevented them from performing their revolutionary duties in the conservative trade unions.

The Western Federation of Miners, for instance, was a most militant and promising organization. It carried on a number of aggressive struggles in behalf of the metal miners of the West, especially in Colorado, Idaho, and Montana. It also participated in the formation of the I. W. W. But when in 1907 the federation decided to withdraw from the I. W. W., these revolutionists refused to follow it and remained in the I. W. W., declaring open war upon the organization which they had created with their own hands. The result was that the miners' federation fell into the hands of conservative, reactionary leaders who led it into the American Federation where it almost entirely disintegrated (Foster: *Bankruptcy of the American Labor Movement*, pp. 35-36).

Directly opposite circumstances surrounded the formation of another union in this period, the Amalgamated Clothing Workers of America.

In the men's clothing industry existed the United Garment Workers of America, which was a trade union in name only, for in 1912 it had only about 5,000 members. Then, as now, it belonged to the A. F. of L.

In 1912 the New York members of the organization decided to strike against intolerable conditions in their industry. Though their ranks were numerically weak, at least 50,000 workers joined the strike. This fact proved beyond doubt that with only a very little effort these tens of thousands of distressed tailors could be organized into the union. But the leaders of the United Garment Workers of America paid no attention to this question. The workers stood solid in the strike and were firmly determined to fight until their demands were granted. But the president of the union without any previous consultation with the strikers accepted arbitration and told the workers to go back to work. Some did not want to obey this order, and remained out, but the strike was demoralized by this action of the leadership and broke up. Now the members became even more disgusted with their leaders, and the radical workers directly accused the president and the rest of the national officials of selling them out to the bosses. They determined to work hard within the union until the next convention and then oust the traitors from the leadership.

The convention assembled on October 14, 1914, at Nashville, Tenn. The credentials committee rejected the credentials of the majority of the delegates from large cities in order to prevent the convention from being captured by the radicals. But even among the delegates who were accepted were some who were opposed to the union's policies and leadership and demanded that the delegates rejected by the credentials committee be seated. The chairman refused to put their motion to a vote. The insurgent delegates thereupon left the convention and joined those who had been rejected, hired another hall and declared themselves the representatives of the United Garment Workers of America. It is true that the "rebels" did not comprise the majority of the delegates (they numbered 110 while those who stayed with the reactionary officials numbered 165), but they represented the large cities and the bulk of the membership.

The insurgents sent delegates to the following convention of the A. F. of L. and demanded that they be recognized as the representatives of the United Garment Workers. But Gompers closed the door on them and told them that the Federation would have nothing to do with "outlaws." Then the fight was carried into the courts over the name and property of the union. The court naturally decided in favor of the "regulars," and the "rebels" were left with empty hands. They held their second convention on December 9, 1914, formulated policies for the new organization, and named it the Amalgamated Clothing Workers of America. The Amalgamated Clothing Workers was to be a progressive industrial union. Its principles were thus set forth in the preamble to its constitution:

"The economic organization of labor has been called into existence by the capitalist system of production, under which the division between the ruling class and the ruled class is based upon the ownership of the means of production. The class owning those means is the one that is ruling, the class that possesses nothing but its labor power, which is always on the market as a commodity, is the one that is being ruled.

"A constant and unceasing struggle is being waged between these two classes.

"In this struggle the economic organization of labor, the union, is a natural weapon of offense and defense in the hand of the working class.

"But in order to be efficient, and effectively serve its purpose, the union must in its structure correspond to the prevailing system of the organization of industry."

And further:

"The working class must accept the principles of industrial unionism or it is doomed to impotence.

"The industrial and inter-industrial organization, built upon the solid rock of clear knowledge and class consciousness, will put the organized working class in actual control of the system of production, and the working class will then be ready to take possession of it" (Budish and Soule: *The New Unionism*, pp. 160-170).

The new organization took up energetically the campaign to organize the unorganized clothing workers and carried on a militant struggle against the chief abuses in the industry. As conditions were more than ripe for such a move the new union met with success. When the World War broke out and the situation was favorable for organizing, the Amalgamated Clothing Workers extended its influence throughout the men's clothing industry and by 1920 had enrolled nearly 200,000 members. At the same time the United Garment Workers, though favored by the A. F. of L., remained a small union with no influence in the clothing industry.

Nevertheless, the Amalgamated Clothing Workers cannot be considered a dual union. It "was not built by dual union methods." As Foster says:

"It developed out of the work of an organized minority within the old U. G. W. The traditional way of dual unionism and the very essence of its program, is for the handful of militants to devise ideal unions, set them up in competition with the old trade unions, and to engage with the latter in an open struggle for control of the industry, a process which almost always results in simply stripping the old unions of their militants and leaving those organizations in the hands of the reactionaries" (Foster: *Bankruptcy*, etc., pp. 52-53).

The militants in the United Garment Workers did not employ these tactics. They worked inside of the old union to win the majority of the rank and file. They succeeded, and captured the United Garment Workers, but with the help of Gompers and the bourgeois courts that name was taken away from them and they were forced to take a new name for their organization.

Politically the workers had no great successes in this period. As already pointed out, the Socialist Labor Party in 1895 had broken its contact with the trade unions and with the Knights of Labor and organized its own Socialist Trade and Labor Alliance, which only succeeded in isolating the socialists from the organized workers. The S. L. P. got further and further away from the masses. De Leon's leadership was unable to understand and properly weigh the new conditions. It did not even dream of changing its tactics in order to win the masses for the socialist movement. It was absolutely stubborn not only against the old trade unions, but also against its own members. Any one who dared criticize the leaders or propose new policies for party work was declared an enemy of the organization and driven out of it.

In spite of this intolerance, the number of those who were dissatisfied with the party leadership constantly increased. They demanded a change in party policy and tactics toward the trade unions. This opposition rallied around the German party paper, the New York *Volkszeitung*. The party convention of 1896 left it to the New York section to elect the new national executive committee. The election was held in 1899 and the opposition won. The new committee immediately decided to eliminate the old officials from the responsible positions. The latter refused to give up their posts. There resulted two organized factions, each calling itself the Socialist Labor Party.

The "insurgents" called a convention of all sections which rejected the old committee and the old party officials. The convention took place in Rochester, N. Y., with 59 delegates. The delegates were highly enthusiastic because their credentials showed that they represented the majority of the party. Their first and most important action was the rejection of the Socialist Trade and Labor Alliance and the adoption of a resolution expressing solidarity with the trade unions. Thus the Rochester convention completely changed the tactics of the party in its industrial work.

Another important step was taken by the delegates when they invited the Social Democratic Party, headed by Eugene V. Debs, to join them. This Social Democratic Party had been organized on June 7, 1898, at Chicago, at a convention of all socialist and semi-socialist groups remaining outside of the Socialist Labor Party. In 1900 it had about 5,000 members.

Unity committees were elected from both sides to carry on negotiations. After long deliberation it was agreed to call a unity convention on July 29, 1901, at Indianapolis. A total of 124 delegates represented 10,000 members, and succeeded in setting on foot the Socialist Party of the United States. The growth of the new party was rapid, and within three years the membership doubled. The second national convention of the Socialist Party was held in 1904 with 184 delegates present. By this time the party was much stronger, not only numerically but also in influence among the masses. The Socialist Party was now definitely for working within the old trade unions, and that helped it to make contact with the trade movement, especially in the needle trades. In the American Federation of Labor itself the influence of the socialists rapidly increased, and even began to threaten the conservative Gompers machine. At the Federation convention of November, 1902, at New Orleans, for example, the socialists proposed the following resolution:

"Resolved that this twenty-second annual convention of the American Federation of Labor advise the working people to organize their economic and political power to secure for labor the full equivalent of its toil and the overthrow of the wage system."

This resolution provoked a lengthy and heated debate, and was finally rejected only by a vote of 3,744 to 3,344. It shows to what degree socialist influence had spread in the ranks of organized labor in the short time since De Leon's policy of dual unionism was repudiated. In the presidential elections of 1904 the party's candidate, Eugene V. Debs, received 402,312 votes. The Socialist Labor Party, on the other hand, was by this time merely a small sect without influence or prestige.

Membership in the Socialist Party in 1909 was 50,000; in 1910, 58,011; in 1911, 84,716; in 1912, 118,045; in 1913, 95,957; in 1914, 93,579.

But as time went on the Socialist Party also developed a policy of getting out of the trade unions. In spite of the fact that at the time of the split from the Socialist Labor Party the Socialist Party had declared its sympathy with the old trade unions, in a short time a left wing developed inside the party which again began to advocate dual union tactics. As far as the right wing of the party was concerned, it stood for work within the old unions, but entirely for opportunistic purposes. It did not advocate making the trade unions a powerful instrument of the workers in their struggle with the employers, neither did it want to revolutionize the old unions and build them up. The right wing wanted the unions only for the purpose of securing their financial support and their votes during parliamentary elections. The trade unions were necessary to the leaders of the right wing of the party only to the extent to which they helped them in their political career.

This struggle between "lefts" and "rights" within the party led to a situation where the convention of 1912 expressed equal allegiance to both the new dual unionism and the old trade unions. In other words, the Socialist Party was to be neutral on the trade union question. The convention expressed itself in favor of industrial unionism, but did not state its policy for bringing about this unionism. It did not state whether it expected to effect the desired result through amalgamation of the old craft unions or through building up new unions opposed to the old ones. George D. Herron, one of the leaders, expressed its position as follows:

"Not by trying to commit socialism to trade unionism, or trade unionism to socialism, will the socialist end be accomplished. It is better to leave the trade unions to do their distinctive work, as the workers' defense against the encroachments of capitalism, as the economic development of the worker against the economic development of the capitalist, giving unqualified support and sympathy to the struggles of the organized worker to sustain himself in his economic sphere. But let the socialist also build up the character and harmony and strength of the socialist movement as a political force, that it shall command the respect and confidence of the worker, irrespective of his trade or his union obligations. It is urgent that we so keep in mind the difference between the two developments that neither shall cripple the other. The socialist movement, as a political development of the workers for their economic emancipation, is one thing; the trade union development, as an economic defense of the workers within the capitalist system, is another thing. Let us not interfere with the internal affairs of the trade unions, or seek to have them become distinctively political bodies in themselves, any more than we would seek to make a distinctive political body in itself a church, or a public school, or lawyer's office."

This position of the Socialist Party toward the trade unions was middle ground between the "rights" and the "lefts." That the exponents of dual unionism were influential in the S. P. at that time can easily be seen from the fact that the party's undisputed leader, Debs, was an enthusiastic supporter of the I. W. W. and of the policy of smashing not only the old trade unions, but all unions which were not based on the principle of the class struggle. In a speech on November 23, 1905, Debs declared:

"At the very threshold of this discussion I aver that the old form of trade unionism no longer meets the demands of the working class. I aver that the old trade union has not only fulfilled its mission and outlived its usefulness, but that it is now positively reactionary, and is maintained, not in the interest of the workers who support it, but in the interest of the capitalists who exploit the workers who support it.

"The United Mine Workers, in point of numbers a powerful labor organization, embraces a large majority of the coal miners of the country. Is this organization of any real benefit to the coal miners? . . .

"These miners are well organized. They have the numbers. They ought to have real economic power. But they lack it. And why? *For the simple reason that they are not organized upon the basis of the class struggle.* Their principle is not right; and it is for this reason that their organization has the hearty support of the coal operators of the country. . . ."

And further:

"Now if you are a workingman and if you believe that you have an economic interest in common with that of the capitalist who employs you, remain in the old trade union. That is where you belong. If that is your conviction we do not want you to join the Industrial Workers. You do not properly belong to us. You belong to the American Federation of Labor and its affiliated organizations. But, if you believe, as I believe, that the working class have economic interests of their own, separate and apart from and in conflict with the economic interests of the capitalist class, then you should, and sooner or later will have to, sever your relations with the old trade union and join the Industrial Workers, the only union organized upon the basis of the class struggle" (*Debs: Loc. cit.*, pp. 375-380).

As time passed, the position of the Socialist Party on the trade union movement degenerated more and more toward dual unionism. The result was that the socialist influence among the organized masses was weakened and the Socialist Party met the same fate as the Socialist Labor Party which had declared war against the old trade unions—complete isolation from the masses.

Another important step was taken by the Socialist Party in this period, which placed it on a purely opportunistic path and eliminated from its basis the principle of the class struggle, namely, *it rejected the use of force*. At its convention in May, 1912, at Indianapolis, at which 277 delegates were present and which was completely captured by the right wing, the following amendment to the constitution was adopted:

"Any member of the party who opposes political action or advocates crime, sabotage or *other methods of violence* as a weapon of the working class to aid in its emancipation shall be expelled from membership in the party. *Political action shall be construed to mean participation in elections for public office and practical legislative work along the lines of the Socialist Party platform*" (*Political Guide for the Worker,* Socialist Party Campaign Book, 1920, p. 46).

In other words, the Socialist Party rejected all revolutionary action. From that time on all of its work and all of its hope were centered on the ballot box. All of its political action has been limited to participation in election campaigns in order to get governmental jobs for its leaders.

CHAPTER XXV

Strikes and Labor Cases, 1900-1914

THE leaders of the trade union movement openly declared in the twentieth century that their highest aim was not to lead the workers in their struggles with the employers, but to do all in their power to avoid struggles. The officials of the American Federation of Labor and of the various national unions voiced the opinion that a strike was something bad, to be avoided at all costs, and they did their best to prevent strikes from taking place. "Beware of entrance to a quarrel!" became their slogan.

In his testimony before the Committee on Labor of the United States House of Representatives, on February 11, 1904, Gompers declared:

"And let me say, gentlemen, that the officers of an organization of labor who have served any considerable period of time as officers, having the responsibility that comes from defeat, seek by every means within their power to avert and avoid contests and conflicts. It is not true, the charge that is so often made against the labor leaders, so-called, of inciting strikes and contests and conflicts, in order, so our opponents put it, to earn our salaries.

"The men who are most successful in the movements of labor, in having the confidence and good will and respect of their fellow-workmen, are the men who have done most to avert and avoid strikes" (Gompers: *Loc. cit.*, p. 65).

In other words, Gompers maintained that a "wise" leader of the trade unions will use all means in his power to prevent strikes and conflicts from occurring.

Largely as a result of this policy, during this period we do not find such militant, far-reaching, and bitter strikes and uprisings of the workers as marked previous periods.

In September, 1900, the anthracite miners went out for an increase in wages. Though the union had only about 10,000 members, not less than 100,000 men in the anthracite fields joined the strike. On one hand, the workers showed great solidarity and determination to fight to the end. On the other, the presidential elections were coming, and therefore the astute politician Mark Hanna, McKinley's campaign manager, interfered and suggested to the mine owners and to the president of the miners' union, John Mitchell, that they get together and arrange a compromise. The owners agreed to give a 10 per cent raise in wages and also to meet a committee of miners to settle the dispute. The union accepted this settlement and the strike was ended. In April, 1901, the agreement was renewed for another year. But at the expiration of the agreement in 1902, the miners demanded shorter hours—nine instead of 10—and recognition of the union. The mine owners refused to grant these demands, and on May 9 another strike began.

This struggle was from the very beginning a general strike in the real sense of the word, for 150,000 anthracite miners left the mines. Assessments of $1 a week were levied on the bituminous coal miners to help their brothers, about $2,000,000 being collected in this way. Collections were also made among the workers of other industries. After five months it seemed that the strikers would win. But President Roosevelt came to the assistance of the mine owners by appointing a special Anthracite Coal Commission to investigate and settle the dispute. Both sides—the mine owners and union officials—submitted and the strike was called off. The miners were told by their leaders to keep their mouths shut and wait for word from the commission. Not less than six months had to elapse before the commission rendered its decision, according to which the miners received 10 per cent increase in wages, nine hours, and a right to place their own representatives at the scales; but recognition of the union was not granted. The commission also demanded that the union cover half the expense of maintaining the commission, which became a permanent institution to settle disputes. The rank and file were dissatisfied with the decision and demanded a new strike. Now the miners had to fight not only the employers and the government, but also their own leaders who demanded that the decision of the commission be accepted. Having the union machinery in their hands, the leaders forced the membership to accept the decision. During the strike a special convention of the United Mine Workers was held to consider the question of calling out the bituminous miners also. But the bituminous agreement had not yet expired. The union officials placed the agreement with the operators above the interests of the workers and succeeded in defeating the motion for a general coal strike.

In 1904 the mine owners declared a reduction in wages. The regular convention of the union took place on January 18-27, but the question of wages and of a strike against the reduction was left to a special convention which was to meet on March 5. The special convention also failed to take definite action and left it to the membership to decide by a referendum vote. This was a clever trick of John Mitchell, who saw that the majority of the convention was in favor of a strike and so worked to have the question left to the "will of the members themselves." The bourgeois press immediately declared that there would be no strike because the "operators say so." At the same time the officials of the union sweated day and night to convince the members that they should accept the reduction. With all strategic positions in their hands, and by threatening the members with real and unreal dangers involved in the strike,

STRIKES AND LABOR CASES 241

they succeeded in obtaining a majority vote for the acceptance of the reduction.

At once Eugene V. Debs in the *Social Democratic Herald* accused John Mitchell of selling himself and the membership to the mine owners. Mitchell, naturally, defended himself and tried to prove that the miners had not lost anything because even after the reduction their wages were still higher than they had been a few years before (Debs: *Loc. cit.,* pp. 157-179). This incident clearly revealed that the union leaders had a secret deal with the operators and had shamefully betrayed the interests of those whom they were elected to represent and defend. When John Mitchell died in 1919, he left $250,000 worth of property (Sylvia Kopald: *Rebellion in Labor Unions,* p. 39).

Probably the first activities of the Industrial Workers of the World which attracted the attention of the general public were in connection with the defense of Charles H. Moyer, William D. Haywood, and Pettibone, the leaders of the Western Federation of Miners, who were charged with murder. On February 17, 1906, the Idaho police captured these three men in Denver, Colo., and spirited them by train to Idaho, where they were charged with killing ex-Governor Steunenberg, who had been murdered on December 30, 1905. It was clear that the whole affair was a conspiracy of the mine owners and the government to get rid of these militant labor leaders. The I. W. W. immediately issued an appeal to the workers all over the country to come to their rescue. The case attracted great attention. In a short time over $11,000 was collected for defense purposes. The socialists also were very active in the efforts to save the three labor leaders. The bourgeois press loudly clamored for the lives of the victims. The trial finally came on May 9, 1907, and lasted for 84 days. The star and almost the sole witness against the accused was one Harry Orchard, who in the witness chair openly and coolly admitted having committed at least 20 murders, not counting other crimes of lesser magnitude (Brissenden: *Loc. cit.,* pp. 170-175). While in jail Orchard was shown great respect by the governor of the state and other high officials. It was said that he became very religious, and well-known clergymen testified to his "change" of character. Soon he became a hero in the eyes of the "respectable" citizens of the United States. The prosecution quickly passed from the activities of the accused to the activities of the Western Federation of Miners. But the testimony of the degenerate, Orchard, was easily refuted, and not a grain of doubt was left in the minds of the workers that the case was a "frame-up," a conspiracy of the capitalist class to destroy the Western Federation of Miners by first legally murdering its active leaders. Though the court was anxious to send the accused to the gallows, it feared the labor movement which, by this time, was convinced of the innocence of the men and demanded their exoneration. A verdict of not guilty was therefore rendered, and Moyer,

Haywood, and Pettibone went free. They were saved from the gallows by the militant section of the working class.

The I. W. W. strike at Goldfield, Nev., which started on November 27, 1907, also attracted wide attention. All bourgeois forces were united to crush the miners, who were being led by the I. W. W. and the Western Federation of Miners. The officialdom of the A. F. of L. also joined hands with the employers because it was afraid that the I. W. W. might absorb the membership of the Federation into its ranks. The governor of Nevada hastened to request the President of the United States to send federal troops into the strike area. Naturally, the President heeded the request. It was estimated that the employers spent not less than $100,000 to defeat the strike, but their efforts failed against the determination and solidarity of the miners (*Ibid.*, pp. 191-202).

The strike of the workers of the Pressed Steel Car Company, of McKees Rocks, Pa., led by the I. W. W., was also bitterly contested. About 6,000 were involved in the struggle, which lasted for two months.

But the most important strike led by the I. W. W. during this period was the textile strike of Lawrence, Mass., which started on March 11, 1912, against a reduction of wages. At the start about 14,000 workers came out, but by March 14 their number had increased to 23,000. When the strike began the Lawrence textile workers were very poorly organized. It was estimated that the I. W. W. did not have more than 1,000 members, while the membership of all other unions, composed of the highly skilled, was not larger than 2,500. But conditions were ripe, and the strike soon became general. The employers seized the opportunity to put an end to the I. W. W. in Lawrence once and for all. They had provocateurs plant 28 sticks of dynamite in three different places in the city and then "discovered" them before they exploded. The strikers, of course, were blamed for wanting to "blow up the city." But later a business man of Lawrence, who had no connection with the strikers, was arrested, tried, and "convicted of conspiracy to injure by the planting of dynamite." He was fined $500! (*Ibid.*, pp. 288-289). We can imagine what would have happened to a worker who had been caught at so criminal an act.

The solidarity of the strikers was so strong that neither provocation nor the brutality of the police and hired thugs could disrupt their front. Men, women, and children besieged the textile mills to prevent scabs from entering them, fought bravely with them and with the agents of the bourgeois government, and won. They won an increase in wages of from 5 to 20 per cent, and additional pay for overtime. Those who gained most were the unskilled workers, mostly women operatives.

As a result of the Lawrence strike the wages of the textile workers all over New England were increased. And most important was the fact that "this strike demonstrated that it was possible for the unskilled and unorganized workers (preponderantly immigrants of various nationalities) to carry on a successful struggle with their employers. It showed what a latent power there is in the great masses of semiskilled and unskilled workers" (*Ibid.*, p. 291).

Yet the leaders of the I. W. W. greatly overestimated the results of the strike. For instance, Vincent St. John, then secretary of the organization, exclaimed that the "victory in the Lawrence mills means the start that will only end with the downfall of the wage system." The general executive board recommended to the convention in September, 1912, the use of direct action, declaring that "militant direct action in the industries of the world is the weapon upon which they must rely and which they must learn to use" (*Ibid.*, p. 296).

After this successful strike the prestige of the I. W. W. greatly increased and the membership of the organization in Lawrence reached 14,000; it also established contacts with other textile centers of New England.

It did not take long for the employers to take back the fruits of this victory by dividing and intensifying the work. Whereas the workers had gained an increase in wages of from 5 to 20 per cent, the employers by various means compelled them to yield about 50 per cent more production.

Nevertheless the bourgeoisie viewed the strike with great anxiety and dread. They were afraid that the unskilled masses might rise all over the country and deal a mighty blow to their profits. For example, the *Survey*, in an editorial "After the Battle," on April 6, 1912, exclaimed:

"On all sides people are asking: Is this a new thing in the industrial world? . . . Are we to see another serious, perhaps successful, attempt to organize labor by whole industrial groups instead of by trades? Are we to expect that instead of playing the game respectably, or else frankly breaking out into lawless riot which we know well enough how to deal with, the laborers are to listen to a subtle anarchistic philosophy which challenges the fundamental idea of law and order, inculcating such strange doctrines as those of 'direct action,' 'sabotage,' 'syndicalism,' 'the general strike' and 'violence'? . . . We think that our whole current morality as to the sacredness of property and even of life is involved in it" (*Ibid.*, p. 295).

The movement which was thus developing under the I. W. W., with its militant strikes in the East and West, looked as if the Knights of Labor, which had led the unskilled workers in the eighties, had been resurrected.

"The trained eyes of the leaders of the American Federation of Labor," says Perlman, "espied in the Industrial Workers of the World a new rival which could best be met on its own ground by organizing within the Federation the very same elements to which it especially addressed itself. Accordingly at the convention of 1912, held in Rochester, the problem of organizing the unskilled occupied a place near the head of the list. The miners' national union picked up in earnest the gauntlet thrown down by the new revolutionary organization and succeeded in building up in the anthracite coal region a large organization of foreigners, which in point of fighting ability and permanence did not lag behind the organization in other districts where the percentage of foreigners was smaller" (Commons: *History*, etc., Vol. II, pp. 523-524).

With the exception of the miners' union which seriously took up the question of organizing the workers on an industrial basis in the coal industry, the Federation satisfied itself with a resolution on the necessity of organizing the unskilled workers, and did not initiate an organization campaign on a nation-wide scale.

This period also saw the workers once more in conflict with the courts.

The employees of the Bucks Stove and Range Company of St. Louis, Mo., who were members of the International Brotherhood of Foundry Employees, went on strike against the lengthening of working hours. The *American Federationist,* the official organ of the A. F. of L., published a notice in its pages that this company was unfair to labor. The employers brought charges against the *Federationist,* and on December 18, 1907, Judge Gould issued an injunction against the strikers and forbade the officials of the A. F. of L. to interfere with the affairs of the said company either by word of mouth or by print. The officials of the Federation refused to obey the injunction and Gompers, Mitchell, and Morrison were sentenced to six months to a year in jail for contempt of court.

Then followed the famous case of the Danbury hatters. When the hatters went on strike the employers got out an injunction against them, and later sued the union for damages which their business had sustained during the strike. The case reached the Supreme Court of the United States, which rendered a decision in 1908 according to which a union is responsible for damages sustained by the employers on account of a strike. This vicious decision was based on the Sherman anti-trust act which was adopted by Congress in 1890, according to which the trade unions are also considered trusts opposed to interstate commerce. The Federation replied with a campaign against the decision of the Supreme Court and also against the Sherman Act. In 1912 Congress adopted the Clayton Act which declares that "the labor of a human being is not a commodity," and that therefore the unions cannot be persecuted under the Sherman anti-trust act. This act of Congress was hailed by the officials of the American Federation of Labor as "Labor's Magna Carta" and a great victory for their "non-partisan" political action. But it did not take long to learn that this joy of the trade union leaders was without foundation, for even after the passage of the Clayton Act the persecution of the trade unions did not diminish in the least. Indeed, the bourgeois courts issued injunctions and imprisoned those who disobeyed them even more energetically than before. The ruling class always finds ways to persecute workers, law or no law, when they demand their rights.

The strike of the anthracite miners of 1912 also deserves attention. The agreement with the mine owners expired on April 1, and 150,000 miners went out. Once more the miners showed great class solidarity, for the union at that time had only about 29,000 members in all three districts, but the answer to the strike call was general, even unorganized miners joining the fight. The miners demanded a 20 per cent raise in wages, full recognition of the union, the "check-off" system, a yearly agreement, and establishment of a better method than the board of arbitration for the settlement of disputes. But even before the strike was in full swing, negotiations were started behind closed doors. The result was that the union officials signed an agreement which gave the miners a 10 per cent raise in wages and a change in the arbitration commission, but rejected the demand for recognition of the union, the check-off system, and, what was worse, the duration of the agreement was extended to four years. For four years the workers were to be tied to the employers under such conditions and for such wages as were stated in the agreement. Regardless of possible changes in living conditions during this long period, the miners could not strike for any increase in wages.

The rank and file of the union were bitter against this agreement, but the officials, with President White at their head, set to work to force it upon the members, and it was approved by a "referendum vote."

In the clothing industry, also, trade unionism began to extend its roots through militant and stormy strikes.

The International Ladies' Garment Workers' Union was organized on June 3, 1900. Although socialistic aims were incorporated in its constitution, nevertheless the union remained weak and in a precarious condition until 1907. A great change in the life of the organization occurred when in 1907,

"the reefermakers, led by refugees from the Russian Revolution of 1905, went out in mass and stayed on strike for nine weeks, showing such common determination and spirit that they won most of their demands and put courage into the rest of the workers in the needle trades. For the first time in years it seemed possible to win direct results through strong organization and fighting tactics. . . . In 1909 another surprising mass movement gave proof of the workers' heightened morale. The small local of waist and dressmakers in New York called a strike, expecting about 3,000 to respond. Instead 30,000 went out, including workers of all races, except a few native-born women. No such strike of women had before been known or thought possible. It aroused the public as never before to the sufferings of the needle workers . . ." (Budish and Soule: *Loc. cit.,* pp. 81-82).

The strike was a success, though not a complete one, and it greatly encouraged other workers of the needle trades to fight for betterment of their conditions. What was most important was that from this time on trade unionism had come to stay in the needle industry. On July 8, 1910, the members of the same union declared a general strike which involved 45,000 workers, men and women, demanding recognition of their union. The employers obtained an injunction against the strikers and attempted to break their resistance with scabs. But this action of their enemies only made the workers more determined. The police began to arrest the strikers in mass, but they could not break their courage. The struggle lasted for two and a half months and ended in victory for the workers, though again it was not complete. As a result a 50-hour week was established, wages were raised from 25 to 100 per cent, and a board of sanitary control was formed. Concerning recognition of the union, the employers promised that they would maintain such conditions in the factories as had been won by the union, pay such wages as were stated in the agreement, and in hiring new help would give preference to the unionists. On the other hand, the employers reserved for themselves the right to choose from the unionists those whom they desired (*Ibid.*, p. 117).

The first great strike in the men's clothing industry took place in October, 1910, in Chicago, when 40,000 workers demanded better working conditions, recognition of the union, a 48-hour week for cutters, and a 54-hour week for tailors. The officials of the United Garment Workers, who had a local with a few members, hoping that they would successfully fool the strikers, hastened to make a contract with the employers which recognized none of the workers' demands. That same day the strikers almost unanimously rejected the agreement by a general vote and decided to continue the fight. Starvation and bleak winter began to threaten thousands of families. Nevertheless the workers would not surrender. On a cold day in December, 20,000 strikers met in a park and decided to go on with the strike. The Chicago Federation of Labor came to their financial assistance; the workers of other cities also sent money and clothes. Yet the ruling class was once more victorious. "On February 3, this cold and hungry army, unable to hold out longer, capitulated without conditions and went back to work" (*Ibid.*, p. 123). Once more the workers of the men's clothing industry remained helpless, until the Amalgamated Clothing Workers of America was organized in 1914 and took up the fight to better their conditions.

In following the struggles of the needle workers it is necessary to remember that they are almost exclusively foreign-born—Jews, Poles, Italians, Lithuanians, and Russians. Until the World War all the unions in the needle industries except the United Garment Workers, which existed only on paper, were more radical or progressive than any other set of trade unions in the country. They were led by socialists or their sympathizers. In their constitutions they have the socialist aim, abolition of the capitalist system. Under militant leadership these unions rescued the needle workers from the most oppressive of industrial conditions. But after the war a change took place in their character and tactics.

CHAPTER XXVI

The Trade Unions and the World War

The World War started on August 4, 1914, in the midst of a great industrial depression in the United States. Orders soon began to pour in from Europe for American goods, mainly for ammunition. By the end of 1915 American industry had so improved that the army of unemployed had almost entirely disappeared. And as the war progressed, as more and more lives and property were destroyed, more ammunition, more machine guns, more uniforms were necessary for the armies. Thus in 1916 our industry was in full swing and long lines of our ships were carrying munitions and other necessaries of war to Europe. The capitalist class of the United States were not interested in the fact that their help to France, England, and Belgium would surely lead us into the war. Like so many hungry hounds, they were interested only in their increased profits. As far as the American workers were concerned, with the exception of the class-conscious minority, they were not greatly concerned as to where the ammunition was going or for what purpose it was being used. As long as they had a chance to work, what did they care about what the future had in store for them!

The revival of industry had an effect upon the trade unions, too, although not as suddenly as might have been expected. The prolonged crisis had greatly weakened them and it was rather hard for them immediately to begin an extensive campaign to organize the unorganized. Furthermore the leaders of the trade unions had no desire whatsoever to undertake such a difficult task. Hence it was only in the middle of the imperialist war, when the United States also was driven into the slaughter, that the ranks of the unions began to swell. The membership of the American Federation of Labor increased from slightly over 2,000,000 in 1914 to 3,045,000 in 1919. About 1,000,000 workers joined the unions without any effort on the part of the unions to get them in. There can be no doubt that if the American Federation of Labor officials had not betrayed the workers by promising the capitalist class and their government not to organize the workers during the war, the number of trade unionists would have increased by many more millions. Those who under the pressure of the rising cost of living came and practically begged admission were taken into the Federation, but the latter did not move a finger to organize the masses of the unskilled workers.

248 HISTORY OF THE AMERICAN WORKING CLASS

With the exception of the I. W. W., which was most bitterly persecuted for its opposition to the war, the membership of the independent trade unions such as the Amalgamated Clothing Workers and the railroad brotherhoods also increased.

The attitude of the trade union leaders toward the war changed with times and conditions. Before and at the beginning of the World War, in 1914, they were strongly for peace. But when the German submarines began to threaten the profits of our capitalists, these leaders suddenly became the greatest chauvinists and the most faithful agents of the imperialist bourgeoisie.

Ten years before the war, in 1904, Samuel Gompers, president of the American Federation of Labor, said:

"True to the highest and best conception of human life the trade union movement, from its first inception, has been opposed to war. It recognized that though others may fall, the brunt of war is borne by the working people; not only upon the battlefield itself, but the burdens thereafter which war entails. We cannot be indifferent to, restrain our feeling of horror, nor withhold our sympathies from, the slaughtered thousands of human beings, even in the Far East, regardless of the country toward which our predilections lie" (*Official Report of American Federation of Labor Convention,* San Francisco, November, 1904).

Ten years later, one month after the World War had begun, Gompers continued to sing the same pacifist tune:

"The war that was declared bears most heavily upon the workers of Europe —they make the rank and file of the armies; they endure the greatest hardships both at home and on the battlefield. If they live they will go home to find that they must begin all over again. The work of years will have been swept away. Savings, trade organizations, trade benefits, economic power— all will have vanished as the flowers of the fields.

"Twentieth century nations must adopt as a principle of government that peace is a basis of all civilization. . . . Peace is the fundamental necessity for all government and progress—industrial, intellectual, social, and humanitarian. Without peace all these are as nothing. One of the main purposes of government then must be the maintenance of international peace" (Samuel Gompers: *Labor and the War,* pp. 13-38).

On January 16, 1916, speaking before the National Civic Federation, Gompers rejected his own pacifism, and spoke about a war for "idealism." He said:

"My belief that war was no longer possible was based upon what I desired rather than upon realities because I felt so keenly the brutality, the destruction, and the waste of war. It seemed to me that war and conditions of war cut through the veneer of civilization and disclosed the brute in man. . . . The pacifists and those who hold to policies of non-resistance have failed as I had failed to understand and to evaluate that quality in the human race which makes men willing to risk their all for an ideal. Men worthy of the name will fight even for a 'scrap of paper' when that paper represents ideals of human justice and freedom. The man who would not fight for such a scrap

THE TRADE UNIONS AND THE WORLD WAR

of paper is a poor craven who dares not assert his rights against the opposition and the demands of others. . . . Resistance to injustice and tyranny and low ideals is inseparable from a virile fighting quality that has given purpose and force to ennobling causes in all nations" (*Address at the annual meeting of the National Civic Federation,* January 18, 1916).

Nevertheless, as late as May 26, 1916, speaking before the League to Enforce Peace, at Washington, D. C., Gompers continued to say that labor was against war. He declared:

"No class has more to lose and less to gain in war than the workers. No class renders such sacrificial service during war and bears such staggering burdens after war as does labor. In war, labor sees the results of years of struggle for wider justice swept away. In one mad moment the clock of industrial progress may be turned back for a generation. War diverts the mind of people from constructive work of humanity and democratizing the relations of men. Recognizing this, working men the world over have avowed their allegiance to the cause of peace and have sworn undying opposition to the force that makes for war" (Gompers: *Labor and the War,* p. 69).

But on October 13, 1916, as we were getting nearer to the war, Gompers openly worshiped even those who were fighting for the czars and kaisers. He stated:

"I am free to say that in our international relations I was an ultra-pacifist until the breaking out of this war. I was willing to go the limit to stop war or prevent war. But when I found that the people responded to their colors, whether for kaiser, czar, president, or king, I made up my mind that I have been living in a fool's paradise, and that after all it is necessary for men to be prepared to defend themselves" (*Address before the Wilson Eight-Hour League,* October 13, 1916).

At the beginning of the war the American bourgeoisie also spoke for peace. President Wilson also spoke against this country's joining the war during all of 1915 and 1916. He said that "we are too proud to fight." But as soon as the profits of Wall Street were endangered by the German submarines, Wilson changed his song and demanded a war against Germany. Therefore, the "ideals" for both Wilson and Gompers were supplied by the interests of the bourgeoisie who were making unheard-of profits out of the slaughter in Europe.

The affiliation of the leaders of the A. F. of L. with the National Civic Federation, and their friendly relations with the largest capitalists in the country, brought results. It appears that these leaders felt the pulse of the master class very well on the eve of the approaching storm and did their best to fulfill the wishes and desires of their masters. Gompers went so far as secretly to conspire with the ruling class to drag this country into the World War. At the end of 1916 when the government and the bourgeoisie assured the people of the United States that we were "too proud to fight," Gompers knew that they were covertly preparing for war. He not only knew, but even helped the militarists in their preparation. He agreed with their plans in every detail, and later admitted that he had accepted the position on the advisory commission to the Council of National Defense before it was even organized. "I received notification of my appointment in October (1916)," he admitted. "The Council of National Defense held its first meeting in December" (Samuel Gompers: *Seventy Years of Life and Labor*, Vol. II, p. 352).

On that commission, Gompers himself stated, he worked hand in hand with the manufacturers and bankers. He said:

"I invited to assist me on the War Committee on Labor a group of representatives of organized labor, prominent employers, important financiers, publicists, and technicians."

Among others there were John D. Rockefeller, Jr., V. Everit Macy, and Theodore Roosevelt, Jr. (*Ibid.*, p. 302).

At the beginning of 1917 an intensive agitation was started for war. The bourgeoisie raised the slogan: "German militarism must be crushed! It has insulted our honor and interfered with our rights on the seas!" The same slogan was taken up by the trade union leaders. They also talked about war and prepared for it.

On March 12, 1917, Gompers called a conference of "representative officials of all national organizations, both those affiliated with the A. F. of L. and those not affiliated, to consider the position which American labor should take toward the war situation." At the conference, in addition to the members of the executive council of the A. F. of L., were 148 officials of 79 affiliated organizations, five unaffiliated organizations, and five departments of the A. F. of L. And this congregation of trade union bureaucrats declared "in the holy name of Labor, Justice, Freedom, and Humanity":

"A world war is on. The time has not yet come when war has been abolished.

"Whether we approve it or not, we must recognize that war is a situation with which we must reckon. The present European war, involving as it does the majority of civilized nations and affecting the industry and commerce of the whole world, threatens at any moment to draw all countries, including our own, into the conflict. . . .

"The present war discloses the struggle between the institutions of democracy and those of autocracy. . . .

"We, the officers of the national and international trade unions of America in national conference assembled in the capital of our nation, *hereby pledge ourselves in peace or in war, in stress or in storm, to stand unreservedly by the standard of liberty and the safety and preservation of the institutions and ideals of our republic.* In this solemn hour of our nation's life, it is our earnest hope that our republic may be safeguarded in its unswerving desire for peace; that our people may be spared the horrors and the burdens of war; that they may have opportunity to cultivate and develop the arts of peace, human brotherhood, and a higher civilization.

"But, despite all our endeavors and hopes, should our country be drawn into the maelstrom of the European conflict, we, with these ideals of liberty and justice herein declared, as the indispensable basis for national policies, *offer our service to our country in every field of activity to defend, safeguard, and preserve the republic of the United States of America against its enemies whosoever they may be, and we call upon our fellow workers and fellow citizens in the holy name of Labor, Justice, Freedom, and Humanity to devotedly and patriotically give like service"* (American Federation of Labor: *History*, etc., pp. 65-68).

Instead of voicing a mighty protest against an attempt to drag the country "into the maelstrom of the European conflict," instead of threatening the financial kings and ammunition manufacturers of Wall Street with the mighty fist of organized labor, instead of raising the slogan "Hands off Europe," these trade union leaders "in this solemn hour of our nation's life," even before war had been declared, in advance pledged the loyalty of organized labor to war and militarism. There cannot be a grain of doubt that they knew perfectly well that this country was being dragged into the war by the capitalists whose interests were endangered by cutting down the exportation of munitions to Europe. But they not only approved of these steps, but also covered this approval with the mask of "justice, freedom, and humanity."

The trade union bureaucrats and the leaders of the social-democrats of Europe had no justification for calling upon the European workers to defend their "fatherlands." Still less justification was there for the American trade union leaders to call upon the American workers to defend the interests of Wall Street. History has never seen a more flagrant, a more shameless betrayal of the working class than that performed by Gompers and his colleagues during the World War.

There can also be no doubt that this pledge of the trade union leaders to support the war in the event of the country's being dragged into it, greatly strengthened and encouraged the militarists.

On April 2, 1917, President Wilson appeared before Congress and demanded a declaration of war against Germany. On April 6 war was officially declared.

The executive council of the American Federation of Labor at its session in February, 1918, officially declared that *"this war is an honorable war."* Gompers exclaimed:

"This is a war against war, that is what this war is. It is a crusade, a war of the enraged civilian populations defending their menaced liberties and democracies. It is not a capitalist war. . . . If ever there was a war in which the vital interests and the rights of the masses of the people of our democratic countries were involved, this is the war" (*Address before the London, England, Trades Council,* September 22, 1918).

The American Alliance for Labor and Democracy, a creation of the trade union bureaucracy to poison the minds of the workers during the war, proclaimed:

"We recognize in this great struggle at arms a war that is essentially *labor's war*—a war of the useful people of the world against the agents and institutions of tyranny and oppression and we are resolved to remain with this struggle to its victorious conclusion."

Except for the Industrial Workers of the World, the American Federation of Labor and all larger independent unions as well were made part of the war machinery. And to crown their loyalty to the ruling class, the leaders of the A. F. of L. made an agreement with the government promising not to conduct strikes during the war. More than that: they even promised to help the government and the employers to suppress those who dared to strike. And what was most treacherous to the working class was the pledge of the leaders not to organize unorganized workers during the war (A. M. Bing: *War-Time Strikes and Their Adjustment*, pp. 171-173). Thus the leaders bound the trade unions hand and foot and turned them over to the capitalist government.

On the other hand, the capitalist government also made some "concessions" to lure the workers and to fasten them more securely to the wheel of war. Thus it recognized "for the first time in the history of the United States the right of the workers to organize into trade unions and bargain with their employers through their own representatives" (*Report of the Secretary of the National War Labor Board*, 1919, p. 523). The government organized the War Labor Board composed of representatives of the government, trade unions, and employers, and empowered it to settle all labor disputes.

The government and the labor leaders recognized the necessity to them of peace in industry during the war. This peace was arrived at entirely at the expense of the workers; for as far as the employers were concerned all the promises of the government in favor of the workers remained promises only. On the other hand, the labor leaders solemnly carried out their pledges to the capitalist government. In cases where the workers, unable to endure their oppressive conditions any longer, revolted and declared a strike, they were attacked and crushed by the united efforts of the employers, government, and labor leaders. How effectively strikes were suppressed during the war is shown by the records. In 1917 there were 4,324 strikes, while during 1918 there were only 1,515. With the exception of the machinists' strike in Bridgeport, Conn., one looks in vain for a large mass strike during the war.

It is necessary to emphasize once more that the organized workers were made part of the war machinery by the trade union officials, not only those affiliated with the A. F. of L., but also all the other large national organizations. Even the leaders of the Amalgamated Clothing Workers of America, under whose guidance the union had demonstrated such militancy in the past, dealt with the war agencies of the government and when in 1918 a strike of the tailors occurred, it was "submitted to the arbitration of an 'advisory board,'" a government agency (Budish and Soule: *The New Unionism*, p. 152).

After promising to be loyal to the employers and their government during the war, the labor leaders accepted all the measures of the government with hardly a word of opposition. They even approved wholeheartedly the compulsory military service law which was passed by Congress when it was certain that there would not be a sufficient number of volunteers to go to Europe to fight for the interests of the Wall Street profiteers.

There were opponents of war, of course, mainly from the ranks of the I. W. W. and the socialists. A reign of terror was instituted against those who dared speak their minds. On June 17, 1917, Congress passed the so-called "espionage act" which on May 18, 1918, was amended and further strengthened. Though it was alleged that that law was directed only against German spies, its main object was to strangle the revolutionary workers who were fighting for the rights of their class. The rights of freedom of speech, press, and assembly were entirely forgotten, all constitutional guarantees were taken away from those who objected to the war; those who dared open their mouths against the slaughter found themselves in prison, or lost their lives at the hands of the terrorists, the "100-per-cen ers." The conservative trade union leaders who crowned themselves with "justice, freedom, and humanity" did not raise a voice against this reign of terror. On the contrary, they fully approved of the persecution of the revolutionists and in many instances actually helped the bourgeoisie in their repressive work. Gompers declared that "a man who is a traitor to his country is on a par with the scab in his trade." Those who opposed the interests of Wall Street were declared "traitors to their country" and therefore "scabs in their trades." Thus political persecution was effectively combined with the economic persecution of the revolutionary workers. They were made "men without a country" and without a job.

The Industrial Workers of the World tried to oppose the war, although, of course, they were unable to stem the tide. Their devotion to the cause of the working class knew no limits; many of them did not flinch at losing their lives. The capitalist government let loose its agents upon the I. W. W. to destroy it root and branch. The employers of the western states, where the influence of the I. W. W. was greatest, breathed much easier, and seized their opportunity to destroy this small group of revolutionary unionists.

By 1917 the I. W. W. had attained its highest development numerically. By trades, the membership was composed of 30,000 lumber workers, 40,000 metal miners, 24,000 agricultural workers, 15,000 building trades workers, and about 10,000 in other occupations.

On June 1, 1917, the I. W. W. lumber workers of the Northwest started a strike. The government at once dispatched federal troops to put down the uprising. The troops arrived at Cle Elum, Wash., hunted down all those who were on picket duty, took them to Ellensburg, and interned them for several months without any charges being preferred against them. But in spite of this terror the strike went on and by July 15 there were no fewer than 50,000 lumber workers out fighting for the eight-hour day and better conditions in the camps.

On June 12, 1917, 14,000 miners at Butte, Mont., went out. Later 24,000 miners of Arizona followed them. On July 10 the "Patriotic League" of Jerome, Ariz., armed itself, attacked the strikers under cover of night, and took them in freight cars to Prescott. There they kept them in captivity for three weeks.

At 5 o'clock in the morning of July 12, 2,000 thugs and business men, officials of the companies, armed themselves and began a general attack upon the miners at Bisbee. No fewer than 1,200 strikers and their sympathizers were dragged out of their beds half-naked; they were carried to Lowell, forced into freight cars, and hauled to Columbus where they were taken over by troops and interned in a concentration camp for three months. One miner was killed.

On August 1, 1917, hired murderers kidnaped Frank Little, a member of the general executive board of the I. W. W., at Butte, Mont., dragged him out of town, and hanged him to a railroad trestle.

And so through the whole war the members of the I. W. W. were brutally persecuted and terrorized. Offices of the union were ransacked and destroyed. On November 13, 1917, 47 delegates assembled for a convention were arrested and imprisoned. Many of them were kept in jail until December, 1918, and only then released under heavy bail. Not less than 1,000 members of the I. W. W. at one time or another were behind prison bars. Some were released, others sentenced to long terms in prison, still others deported (*American Labor Year Book,* 1919-1920, pp. 191-193).

An especially notorious plot of the ruling class was its attempt to send Mooney and Billings to the gallows. On July 22, 1916, during the preparedness demonstration in San Francisco, a bomb exploded killing nine persons and wounding 40. The crime was the work either of a provocative agent or an idiot, in all probability the former. The government and the employers of the Pacific coast knew very well that their real enemies—the revolutionary workers—did not commit the outrage. Nevertheless, they immediately hunted down and arrested four leaders of the radical labor movement—Thomas Mooney, Mrs. Rena Mooney, Warren Billings, and Israel Weinberg—charging them with murder.

Witnesses were freely hired, corrupted, and brought in to testify against the accused. The testimony of 60 men and women clearly proving the innocence of the victims had slight effect upon the packed jury and the court. The trial ended on February 9, 1917. Billings was sentenced to life imprisonment and Thomas Mooney to death. Although the chief witness for the government, a certain Oxman, admitted perjury, all appeals for a new trial were without result and December 13, 1918, was the date set for Mooney's execution.

The labor movement of the world was convinced of Mooney's innocence and determined to save his life. Great mass meetings and demonstrations were held throughout the United States and in the industrial centers of South America and Europe. The workers and peasants of Soviet Russia demanded freedom or a new trial for Mooney and Billings. Finally, the workers of this country threatened the government with a general strike. Only then, on November 28, 1918, did the governor of California commute the death sentence to life imprisonment. But the workers were not satisfied, and the International Workers' Defense called a National Labor Congress on the Mooney Case, for January 14-17, 1919. With 1,000 labor union delegates present, the congress decided to call a general strike on July 4, if before that time Mooney was not released or granted a new trial. The leaders of the American Federation of Labor were opposed to the general strike and therefore it did not assume the expected proportions. Nevertheless, nearly 1,000,000 workers joined the four-day protest.

The innocence of Mooney and Billings has been proved beyond doubt. Nevertheless, they are all still behind the bars.

CHAPTER XXVII

American Socialists and the World War

The workers throughout the world impatiently awaited the answer of the European socialists to the World War. For decades they had been the leaders of the workers in the struggles against the capitalist class. At their national and international congresses they repeatedly declared that they were opposed to war, that in case of danger of an imperialist war in Europe they would work unceasingly to destroy this danger and save humanity from the horrors of an armed conflict. The workers of Germany, France, Belgium, Austria, England, where Social-Democratic parties were strong, trusted the socialists and were ready to go through fire with them. The Social-Democratic Party of Germany, especially, had great influence among the masses, and was the leader of the international social-democracy.

What disappointment swept the ranks of the workers when they heard that the social-democrats of each country had exclaimed, together with their own bourgeoisie: "Down with the class struggle! Our fatherland is in danger! Long live our fatherland!" Only the Bolshevik Party of Russia, the Socialist Party of Italy, and small groups of revolutionary socialists elsewhere remained true to their mission, to the cause of the working class, and opposed the imperialist war, declaring war upon war.

What was the attitude of the Socialist Party of the United States? It condemned the war in strongest terms. The executive committee of the party, on August 12, 1914, eight days after the war started, issued a manifesto declaring:

"The Socialist Party of the United States hereby extends its sympathy to the workers of Europe in their hour of trial, when they have been plunged into bloody and senseless conflict by ambition-crazed monarchs, designing politicians, and scheming capitalists.

"We bid them to consider that the workers of the various nations involved have no quarrel with each other, and that the evils from which they suffer—poverty, want, unemployment, oppression—are inflicted upon them not by the workers of some other country, but by the ruling class of their own country.

"The Socialist Party of the United States, in conformity with the declarations of the International Socialist movement, hereby reiterates its opposition to this and all other wars, waged upon any pretext whatsoever. . . .

"The Socialist Party of the United States hereby expresses condemnation of the ruling classes of Europe. . . .

"The Socialist Party of the United States hereby calls upon all foreign-born workingmen residing in this country . . . to hold joint mass-meetings for the purpose of emphasizing the fraternity and solidarity of all working people irrespective of color, creed, race or nationality. . . .

"The Socialist Party of the United States hereby pledges its loyal support to the Socialist Parties of Europe in any measure they might think it necessary to undertake to advance the cause of peace and of good will among men.

"The Socialist Party of the United States hereby calls upon the national administration to prove the genuineness of its policy of peace by opening immediate negotiations for mediation and extending every effort to bring about the speedy termination of the disastrous conflict."

On August 14, 1916, the executive committee of the party issued another manifesto in which it raised the slogan "Starve the war and feed America," by demanding from the government:

"The seizure of all plants and industries responsible for the increase in prices and their operation by the government for the benefit of the people." And "we also demand that the exportation of money and of munitions of war to European nations be prohibited. . . . We call upon the people everywhere to hold mass-meetings and to send resolutions to the President and Congress demanding immediate and decisive action."

In the middle of September, 1914, the committee sent a cable to the party officials and members of the International Socialist Bureau from the warring countries, urging the Socialist parties to work for peace. The cable said:

"In the present crisis, before any nation is completely crushed, socialist representatives should exert every influence on their respective governments to have the warring countries accept mediation by the United States. This can be done without loss of prestige. Conference should be held at The Hague or Washington. Have cabled Socialist parties of 10 nations this action. Wire reply."

On September 19, 1914, the committee appealed to the Socialist parties of Europe to meet in an international congress and discuss the question of peace. In this appeal it said:

"The Socialists of the United States of America offer their deepest sympathy and their brotherly hand to the European workers now in the midst of a world war.

"We do not presume to pass judgment upon the conduct of our brother parties in Europe. We realize that they are victims of the present vicious industrial, political, and military systems and that they did the best they could under the circumstances.

"We appeal to you in the name of socialism, and acting in agreement with your own proclamations, we ask you to help us to stop this mass murder. . . .

"At the International Congress in Stuttgart a resolution was adopted by which the international socialist movement pledged itself not only to make every effort to avert the outbreak of war, but also, should war break out, to strive with all our might to bring the war to a speedy termination.

"The socialists of the war-stricken European countries have worked faithfully and heroically in the spirit of the first part of this resolution. . . .

"The socialists of the world must now proceed at once to the realization of the second clause of the resolution—'to work for the speedy termination of the war.'"

In all of these manifestoes the leaders of the Socialist Party, though bitterly condemning war, failed miserably on two very important questions, either consciously or unconsciously. First, even after learning of the treacherous rôle of the Second International and its leading parties in putting themselves completely at the disposal of the bourgeoisie, they did not recognize and point out this treachery to the masses; worse, they exonerated the traitors before the workers of the world by declaring that the "socialists worked faithfully and heroically in the spirit of the first part of" the Stuttgart resolution which pledged the socialists to make every effort to stay the hand of the militarists. Second, they satisfied themselves with expressing sympathy for the European workers, and did not call upon them to declare war against war, war against their own bourgeoisie and their treacherous leaders. Instead of urging the workers of the world to fight for peace by waging a merciless struggle against their own bourgeoisie, they repeatedly asked them to accept the mediation of the capitalist government of the United States—of the ruling class of this country, which was fattening upon the slaughter of the European workers. Instead of organizing a nation-wide campaign for an embargo upon ammunition and other war supplies, they first called upon the foreign-born workers to hold mass-meetings and express their solidarity with their brothers in Europe, and then appealed to "the people everywhere" to send resolutions to the President and Congress demanding that these representatives of the capitalist class force the home capitalists to renounce their enormous war profits.

In 1915 the German submarines sank the British ship *Lusitania,* carrying several Americans to watery graves. The militarists of this country seized on the incident to start open propaganda for war with Germany. The executive committee of the Socialist Party held its meeting in May and issued an appeal "To the People of the United States." After condemning the militarist agitation, the appeal concluded:

"We call particularly upon the workers of America to oppose war and all agitation for war by the exercise of all the power in their command. . . .

"Let us proclaim in tones of unmistakable determination: 'Not a worker's arm shall be lifted for the slaying of a fellow-worker of another country, nor turned for the production of mankilling implements or war supplies! Down with war! Forward to international peace and the world-wide solidarity of all workers!'"

At the same meeting the committee adopted a "peace program" in which it demanded peace without "indemnities and annexations," establishment of "the international federation of the world," "universal disarmament, as soon as possible," and the like. The committee also proposed to the membership of the party to adopt by referendum vote a new section in the constitution, as follows:

"Any member of the Socialist Party, elected to an office, who shall in any way vote to appropriate money for military or naval purposes, or war, shall be expelled from the party."

This amendment was adopted by a vote of 11,041 to 782.

In 1916 the German submarines increased their activity, and the danger of war loomed larger. The Socialist Party committee again issued a manifesto, reaffirming "its unalterable position against war," condemning secret diplomacy, again reiterating the charge that "business interests of this country, bankers, the Wall Street gang, and especially the munition manufacturers" were those who "are exerting their influence through every conceivable channel to the end that this country be plunged into the bloody maelstrom." "Knowing these facts," the manifesto declared, "we call upon all workers and those opposed to war to hold mass meetings and voice their protest in unmistakable terms, denouncing the attempt to stampede the people of the United States into a war that they do not want. We call upon the people to demand that this country keep its hands out of the European madhouse."

In the presidential campaign of 1916 the Democratic slogan for Wilson was: "He kept us out of war." The Socialist Party nominated candidates and adopted a platform devoted entirely to the war question. It again repeated its "steadfast adherence to the principles of international brotherhood, world peace, and industrial democracy," condemned the agitation for preparedness, expressed opposition to militarism and war, demanded that the power be taken from the President "to lead the nation into a position which leaves no escape from war," and called for a referendum of the entire nation before war could be declared.

Early in 1917 the Socialist Party again invited the socialists of Europe to meet in an international congress for the purpose of reviving "the Socialist International on the basis of a concerted working class movement for an immediate, just, and lasting peace."

The war clouds continued to gather on the American horizon. On February 2, 1917, the emergency committee of the Socialist Party met and "in behalf of the great multitude of socialists in the United States" and "in order to preserve peace in our country" sent a letter to the President demanding an embargo upon the exportation of food and war supplies to Europe. The letter ended with the following peculiar and ridiculous prayer: "Follow the example of your illustrious predecessor, Thomas Jefferson, Mr. President, and have a complete embargo placed on all shipments. It will end the war."

A few days more, and diplomatic relations with Germany were severed. The storm was about to break. The executive committee of the Socialist

Party hastened to issue another manifesto to the American workers, once more condemning the militarists, and ending with the appeal:

"Workers of America, awake!
"The hour is grave, the danger is imminent, silence would be fatal.
"Gather in masses and demonstrations!
"Let your voice of vehement and determined protest resound from one end of the country to the other.
"Send telegrams or letters to President Wilson, to the United States Senators and Congressmen. . . .
"Down with war!
"Down with the inhuman social system that breeds wars!
"Long live peace!
"Long live international solidarity of the workers of all nations!"

On March 30, 1917, Congress met. It was as clear as day that President Wilson would demand war on Germany. The Socialist Party emergency committee sent another letter to Wilson, saying, "we earnestly urge you to oppose declaring war against Germany or declaring that a state of war exists," and "we also urge that if the question of declaring war is to be voted upon at all, it shall be put to a referendum vote of the adult citizens of the United States, both men and women."

But in spite of all the begging and praying, in spite of all purely pacifist letters, manifestoes, and resolutions, on April 6 the Washington government declared war upon Germany, as dictated by the munition manufacturers and the financial kings of Wall Street.

What do these quotations from the official documents of the Socialist Party show?

First of all, they show that the socialist leaders of this country childishly and ridiculously placed almost their entire hope in the agent of the ruling class, President Wilson, believing that he would or could save the country from the World War. Secondly, the socialists said a great deal about war, played a lot with phrases, but did very little to fight the war danger. They thought that to save the working class from war it would suffice to write a few lofty resolutions of protest and hold a few mass meetings. There is not a single instance of the Socialist Party's initiating special united front anti-war committees and trying to involve the labor movement of the country in an active campaign. We do not find that the socialists ever appealed to the trade unions and other labor organizations to join hands with them to fight the purposes of Wall Street. Not only should they have appealed to the labor organizations for a fight against the bourgeoisie, but they should also have carried on an intensive campaign in these organizations to unite them for the struggle. It is important to emphasize this failure of the socialists, especially in view of the fact that they had quite an influence at that time in the unions. They were the leaders, for example, of the unions in the needle trades. What did these socialist leaders of the trade unions do? Did the party

AMERICAN SOCIALISTS AND THE WORLD WAR 261

committee see to it or did it decide that these trade unions together with the party should begin an active campaign against the war? Nothing of the kind.

At the end of 1916 it was clear that this country was being pushed into the European conflagration. The socialists knew this as well as anybody. But the Socialist Party did not exploit the presidential election for the mobilization of the masses against the war. Its main campaign argument was: "Vote for our candidates and we will save you."

In November, 1916, the annual convention of the American Federation of Labor met at Baltimore, Md., with a number of socialists present. Did the Socialist Party or the socialist delegates at the convention raise the slogan "Fight the war, fight the dogs of Wall Street"? No. Instead of proposing a resolution condemning the ruling class and their government in their efforts to drag the country into war, and demanding united efforts on the part of the organized workers against the threatened danger, the socialists demanded from the convention "cheap food." And in order to get this "cheap food" they introduced a resolution for nationalization of the food industries and for placing an embargo upon the exportation of food products to Europe. A great wave of joy swept over the leaders of the Socialist Party when the Federation convention appointed a committee to investigate their proposal for reduction of the cost of living.

On this point the Socialist Party, as a revolutionary party of the proletariat, failed miserably. It did not perform its revolutionary duty. It declaimed about the war, protested against it, painted it in the most horrible colors, but did not organize the working masses to fight it.

When war was officially declared, the executive committee of the party called a special convention for April 7-14, 1917, at St. Louis, Mo., to consider the situation. Two hundred delegates were present. The convention was strongly against the war. Two resolutions were proposed on the question. The majority resolution received 140 votes and the minority resolution only 50 votes. Later both were submitted to the membership for a referendum vote, and the great majority of the members voted for the majority resolution. It declared:

"The Socialist Party of the United States in the present grave crisis solemnly reaffirms its allegiance to the principle of internationalism and working class solidarity the world over, and proclaims its unalterable opposition to the war just declared by the government of the United States.

"The Socialist Party of the United States is unalterably opposed to the system of exploitation and class rule which is upheld and strengthened by military power and sham national patriotism. We, therefore, call upon the workers of all countries to refuse support to their governments in their wars. The wars of the contending national groups of capitalists are not the concern of the workers. The only struggle which would justify the workers in taking up arms is the great struggle of the working class of the world to free itself from economic exploitation and political oppression, and we particularly warn the workers against the snare and delusion of so-called defensive warfare. As against the false doctrine of national patriotism we uphold the ideal of international working-class solidarity. In support of capitalism, we will not willingly give a single life or a single dollar; in support of the struggle of the workers for freedom we pledge our all.

"The working class of the United States has no quarrel with the working class of Germany or of any other country. The people of the United States have no quarrel with the people of Germany or any other country. . . .

"We brand the declaration of war by our government as a crime against the people of the United States and against the nations of the world.

"In all modern history there has been no war more unjustifiable than the war in which we are about to engage.

"In harmony with these principles, the Socialist Party emphatically rejects the proposal that in time of war the workers should suspend their struggle for better conditions. On the contrary, the acute situation created by war calls for an even more vigorous prosecution of the class struggle. . . ."

Then followed the practical steps which the socialists proposed in their fight against the war. They were to wage a "continuous, active, and public opposition to the war, through demonstrations, mass petitions, and all other means within our power." They would maintain an "unyielding opposition to all proposed legislation for military and industrial conscription," they would oppose with all their strength "any attempt to raise money for payment of war expenses," they would carry on "consistent propaganda against military training and militaristic teaching in the public schools."

The minority resolution of the St. Louis convention, which was rejected by the membership, with the greatest contempt, declared:

"Congress has declared that a state of war exists between this nation and Germany. War between the two nations is a fact.

"We opposed the entrance of this republic into the war, but we failed. The political and economic organizations of the working class were not strong enough to do more than protest.

"Having failed to prevent war by our agitation, we can only recognize it as a fact and try to force upon the government, through pressure of public opinion, a constructive program."

In other words, the minority proposed to the Socialist Party the acceptance of the war as a fact and the cessation of all opposition to it. Such a course would really have meant supporting the war and assisting the militarists to prosecute it.

During the membership vote on the St. Louis resolutions, the emergency committee of the party issued another declaration in which the leaders presented two demands to the government: a referendum vote of the people on the federal conscription act, and a clear statement from the government as to the aims of the war and the terms upon which peace would be made. It also called "upon the people of this country" to hold mass meetings on "the Fourth of July," to protest against the actions of the government:

"The Fourth of July is the most American of American holidays. Most of the others are imported. But this day is supposed to mark the beginning of American liberty. On this day the Declaration of Independence was signed; on this day the Liberty Bell first rang out the joyous message. . . . We, therefore, call upon the people of this country to make this Fourth of July mark the beginning of a new spirit of independence. Our forefathers in 1776 cast off the bonds of political slavery on this day; let us gather to repudiate the fetters of military slavery that have been forced on us in 1917."

Not a word about the workers and their organizations. They are substituted by the "people." Their class interests are not mentioned. The appeal was put entirely on a patriotic basis, when the crying necessity was to carry on a campaign amongst the masses of the workers in order to arouse them against those who had dragged the country into war. The decision of the St. Louis convention was, therefore, violated. The convention had pledged the socialists to oppose the war and conscription with all means at their command, while the manifesto of the leaders demanded that the capitalist government submit these questions to a referendum vote of the "people." Secondly, the convention declared and emphasized the fact that "our entrance into the European war was instigated by the predatory capitalists in the United States who boast of the enormous profit of $7,000,000,000 from the manufacture and sale of munitions and war supplies and from the exportation of American food stuffs and other necessaries. They are also deeply interested in the continuance of war and the success of the allied powers through their huge loans to the governments of the allied powers and through their commercial ties. It is the same interests which strive for imperialistic domination of the western hemisphere."

But even before the membership of the party had voted upon this declaration and statement of the aims of the capitalist war, the leaders of the party "forgot" these aims and asked the government, the ruling class, to state them to the people of the United States once more. They said:

"Some say we are fighting for democracy, others say that it is to protect Morgan's loans to the allies. Some say we are at war because of the invasion of Belgium, others say it is because of what is going to happen to the world's trade routes and markets. So the American people demand a clear cut, definite statement from President Wilson and his Department of State as to what agreements have been made with the allied governments. Above all, we who did not want to enter this war want to know the terms on which it will be brought to a close."

This is more than sabotage of the resolution of the St. Louis convention. It is open betrayal.

The rank and file of the Socialist Party and some of its leaders accepted the declaration of the St. Louis convention in all sincerity and fought against the war as best they could. They went into the meetings and organizations of the workers and made their protests. Many of them suffered at the hands of bourgeois terrorists. Others were arrested and clapped into prison. The socialist newspapers which raised their voices against the war were prosecuted and suppressed.

But there were also some leaders who maintained the position of the minority of the St. Louis convention and soon became open supporters of the imperialist war, such as Russell, Spargo, Walling, and Stokes. They left the party. Others remained in the party and helped the government put through a "constructive program"—these were the socialist leaders of the trade unions. They did not say a word against the war. On the contrary, they helped the government make the organized workers a part of the war machine.

CHAPTER XXVIII

After the World War, 1918-1920

The armistice was declared on November 11, 1918. The end of the slaughter was greeted by the working class with the greatest joy.

An industrial crisis was expected in the United States as soon as the war was over and the manufacture of munitions stopped. But the crisis did not arrive until 1921.

Three important factors delayed the panic. First, the storehouses of the country were emptied during the war and they had to be filled again; second, it took more than a year to demobilize the 5,000,000 men drafted into the army, and during this time they had to be fed and clothed; and, third, Europe was completely bankrupt economically and needed American products to rehabilitate itself. It is true that it could not pay for these products, but our capitalists supplied them on credit and the government of the United States pledged that this country would stand behind every dollar loaned to Europe by the American financiers and manufacturers. After the war America became the supporter of almost all the European capitalist countries which were prostrated by the conflict. Our bourgeoisie feared that the workers of Europe, after they were through fighting for the capitalists and imperialists, might turn against their real and only enemy—their own ruling class, as the workers and peasants of Russia had done. Hence, our Hoovers and Wilsons, those clever agents of Wall Street, were busy sending food and clothes to the starving and freezing people of Hungary, Austria, Germany, France, and Italy, to keep them from revolution.

But when the army was finally demobilized, when Europe was completely engulfed in the pockets of Wall Street, and when the storehouses were overflowing with goods, the inevitable crash came.

The profits of the capitalists, the wages of the workers, and the cost of living also reached their highest points after the armistice, at the end of 1919 and in the beginning of 1920.

According to government estimates, taking the workers of all industries, the annual average wage amounted, in 1918, to over $1,078 or $20.73 a week; in 1920, in the period of the greatest prosperity, average wages reached $1,367 a year, or $26.30 a week; in 1921, when the industrial depression started. the average weekly wage went down to $20.

Without comparing these wages with the cost of living we cannot learn the real economic situation of the working class after the war. Between 1913 and 1919 wages had increased 55 per cent, but during the same time the cost of living had increased 104 per cent. Thus after the war, during the height of prosperity, the workers of this country earned less than in 1913. The annual earnings of an average working class family at the end of 1919 and the beginning of 1920 was $1,367. According to the United States Bureau of Labor Statistics, the same family needed an income of $2,262.47 a year, or $43.51 a week, to make a decent living. Therefore, in 1919 the average American working class family could not boast of a decent living, since it had a yearly shortage of about $900.

But although the wages of the workers did not keep pace with the rising cost of living, the profits of the ruling class during the war increased threefold. For example, all corporations having an annual net income of $1,000,000 or more, in 1913 made $438,000,000 net profit, or 8 per cent on the invested capital, while in 1917 the profits of the same corporations reached the total of $1,234,000,000, or 24 per cent on the invested capital. All the corporations of the country put together made about $4,000,000,000 profit every year during the World War. The number of millionaires also increased tremendously. In 1914 there were 7,508 of them; in 1915, 10,671; in 1916, 17,085; in 1917, 19,103 (*American Labor Year Book, 1919-1920*, p. 273).

Now it is clear why the ruling class of this country called the latest war "a war for democracy." It is also easier to see how hypocritical really were Samuel Gompers and other labor leaders who said that this war "is not a capitalist war."

The war was over and the "brotherhood" between workers and employers which had been established by the labor leaders and the government suddenly broke down. It broke down against the will and the desire of the trade union bureaucrats.

The cost of living was increasing enormously, wages were not rising at the same rate, and as soon as the workers found that the war restrictions were beginning to be lifted, they began to stir and demand their most elementary rights. Having won in Europe the "war for democracy," they now began to demand something for themselves at home, in the factories and workshops.

The American Federation of Labor convention at Atlantic City, N. J., on June 7-24, 1919, adopted a so-called "reconstruction program" which, according to the leaders, was "not only the most complete, and the most constructive proposal yet made in this country for the reconstruction period," but which "constitutes practically the only program in existence having to do with the period of rebuilding the national life on a peace basis." The main points of this program are as follows:

"Democracy in Industry—It is essential that the workers everywhere should insist upon their right to organize into trade unions, and that effective legislation should be enacted which would make it a criminal offense for any employer to interfere with or hamper the exercise of this right or to interfere with the legitimate activities of trade unions.

"Unemployment—Unemployment is due to underconsumption. Underconsumption is caused by low or insufficient wages. Just wages will prevent industrial stagnation and lessen periodical unemployment. . . . Just wages will create a market at home which will far surpass any market that may exist elsewhere and will lessen unemployment.

"Wages—There must be no reduction in wages; in many instances wages must be increased.

"Hours of Labor—The day's working time should be limited to not more than eight hours. . . . The week's working time should be limited to not more than five and one-half days.

"Women as Wage-Earners—Women should receive the same pay as men for equal work performed.

"Child Labor—It must be one of the chief functions of the nation through effective legislation to put an immediate end to the exploitation of children under 16 years of age.

"Public Employees—Public employees must not be denied the right of organization.

"Coöperation—Trade unions secure fair wages. Coöperation protects the wage-earner from the profiteer. Participation in these coöperative agencies must of necessity prepare the mass of the people to participate more effectively in the solution of the industrial, commerical, social, and political problems which continually arise.

"The People's Final Voice in Legislation—Adequate steps must be taken which will provide that in the event of a Supreme Court declaring an act of Congress or of a state legislature unconstitutional and the people acting directly or through Congress or a state legislature should reënact the measure, it shall then become the law without being subject to annulment by any courts.

"Political Policy—The disastrous experience of organized labor in America with political parties of its own amply justifies the A. F. of L's non-partisan political policy.

"Government Ownership—Public and semi-public utilities should be owned, operated, or regulated by the government in the interests of the public.

"Federal and State Regulation of Corporations—Legislation is required which will so limit, define, and regulate the powers, privileges, and activities of corporations that their methods can not become detrimental to the welfare of the people.

"Freedom of Expression and Association—We insist that all restrictions of freedom of speech, press, public assembly, association and travel be completely removed, individuals and groups being responsible for their utterances.

"Workmen's Compensation—Workmen's compensation laws should be amended to provide more adequately for those incapacitated by industrial accidents or occupational diseases.

"Immigration—We urge that immigration into the United States should be prohibited for a period of at least two years after peace has been declared.

"Taxation—There should be provided a progressive increase in taxes upon incomes, inheritances, and upon land values.

"Education—Education must not stifle thought and inquiry, but must awaken the mind concerning the application of natural laws and to a conception of independence and progress. Education must not be for a few but for all our

people. The right of the teachers to organize and affiliate with the movement of the organized workers must be recognized.

"*Housing*—The government should inaugurate a plan to build model homes and establish a system of credits whereby the workers may borrow money at a low rate of interest and under favorable terms to build their own houses.

"*Militarism*—The trade union movement is unalterably and emphatically opposed to 'militarism' or a large standing army.

"*Soldiers and Sailors*—Soldiers and sailors, those who entered the service in the nation's defense, are entitled to the generous reward of a grateful republic."

Such was the reconstruction program of the trade union leaders, which contains nothing more than a lot of general declarations and abstract demands. It is hard to believe that the authors of this program themselves seriously thought it would get any attention from "a grateful republic," that is, from the ruling class. It remained a dead letter. In the meantime, the government and capitalists were rapidly preparing to show the workers what the Wall Street "grateful republic" had in store for them.

In February, 1919, the railroad shopmen demanded a raise in wages because the cost of living had increased greatly since 1918 while their pay had remained stationary. But the government immediately jumped into the situation. President Wilson, who had forbidden the workers to demand higher wages during the war, now declared that they had no right to ask any increase in wages because the government was busy "lowering the cost of living." Here and there the workers went on strike over the heads of their leaders, who agreed with the government's policy in every detail, but their struggle could not be successful because it was not general. Moreover, it had to be conducted against the united forces of the government, railroad companies, and trade union bureaucrats. The latter signed an agreement with the government and employers not to tolerate such nonsense as demands for higher wages during the reconstruction period. This was the first great post-war lesson to the workers of the United States.

Then came the steel strike—an epoch-making struggle which furnished the labor movement with many vital lessons.

The steel workers had waged many other bitter struggles with their employers in the past, but all of these struggles sink into insignificance compared with the gigantic fight of 1919. They had challenged the power of "the strongest capitalist aggregation in the world" (Perlman: *Loc. cit.*, p. 248). The steel trust, or the United States Steel Corporation, was formed in 1901 and every time the steel workers attempted to improve their conditions they were crushed mercilessly. The trust raised the open-shop flag high over the steel industry and kept it there effectively.

Before the formation of the steel trust in 1901 there was in existence the Amalgamated Association of Iron, Steel, and Tin Workers which had about 24,000 almost exclusively skilled workers. At the same time hundreds of thousands of unskilled steel slaves had no organization of any kind. Even the organization of the skilled was almost completely exterminated in 1909, or at least undermined to such an extent that it was of no practical value. The trust now had a free hand to exploit and oppress its slaves to the utmost. The result was that at the beginning of the World War the wages of the steel workers were a little lower than before the strike of 1892. During the war the employers amassed enormous profits while the conditions of the workers were atrocious.

The war brought in its train a great opportunity for the workers to organize, for the government and the ruling class could not afford to have a general stoppage in such an important industry as steel. But the steel workers could not accomplish this task without outside assistance. It was the manifest duty of the trade union movement, especially of the American Federation of Labor, to start an immediate campaign to organize the steel slaves. There can be no doubt that such a campaign would have been crowned with success. But did the leaders of the A. F. of L. seize this opportunity? Did they perform their most elementary duty to the working class? Of course not. They signed an agreement with the government in which they promised not to organize workers into trade unions during the war period. This included the steel workers.

On April 7, 1918, William Z. Foster proposed a resolution to the Chicago Federation of Labor calling for a conference of all national and international unions connected in any way with the steel industry, during the next convention of the A. F. of L. on June 10-20. The resolution was adopted by the Chicago Federation of Labor as well as by the A. F. of L. But instead of holding the conference immediately, during the convention, with the delegates of those national and international unions, the calling of the conference was left to Gompers, who hesitated and delayed for several weeks. The meeting finally took place on August 1; thus the Federation wasted over a month of valuable time.

The conference decided to proceed with the work and formed the National Committee for Organizing Iron and Steel Workers, composed of one delegate from each of 24 international unions interested in the steel industry. Gompers accepted the position of chairman of the committee, and William Z. Foster, who later became the leader of the campaign and of the strike, was elected secretary-treasurer. The unions which united their forces against the steel trust comprised about 2,000,000 members. Now the question arose as to what should be the form of the steel workers' organization. The success of the undertaking required that they be organized into a single powerful industrial union. But the various craft unions stood in the way of such an organization, each seeking to get a group of workers for itself. Therefore, it was decided to organize the steel workers into 24 different unions, all of them working hand in hand during the campaign. Later the campaign and the strike proved that this method was a source of weakness. Nevertheless, the agreement of these

24 unions to work on a united front was a great step forward and looked promising.

"The conference had removed the barriers in the way of the campaign. But when it came to providing the large sum of money and the numerous crews of organizers that were immediately and imperatively needed to insure success, it failed dismally. The internationals assessed themselves only $100 apiece; they furnished only a corporal's guard of organizers to go ahead with the work; and future reënforcements looked remote" (Foster: *The Great Steel Strike and Its Lessons*, p. 25).

It is clear, therefore, from the very beginning that the international unions which participated in the national committee did not take the organizing campaign seriously. They acted as if they had joined in the undertaking against their will. Unnecessary delays, failure to supply the necessary funds and organizers, and, on account of these shortcomings, limiting the campaign to one district, the Chicago district—all this meant only a waste of valuable time and giving the steel trust a chance to prepare for the challenge.

But in spite of all delays and difficulties the national committee started the campaign to organize the steel slaves by the beginning of September, 1918. The workers welcomed the organizers with outstretched hands and joined the unions by thousands. The employers sought to hold them back by increasing their wages a few cents. But the scheme did not work this time, and the success of the campaign was astonishing to all who were involved in it. On the eve of the strike there were 250,000 trade unionists in the steel industry (*Ibid.*, p. 65).

In the midst of this important campaign some of the union leaders wanted to wreck everything and betray the workers into the hands of the steel trust. On May 15, 1919, the officials of the Amalgamated Association of Iron, Steel, and Tin Workers wrote a letter to Judge Gary, chairman of the United States Steel Corporation, telling him that "there is a serious disturbing element in the industrial world at the present time, a great spirit of unrest has spread over our common country," and that "it is the patriotic duty of all good citizens to use their every effort to stem the tide of unrest." They requested Gary to meet the representatives of the Amalgamated Association in order to "promote and insure that harmony and coöperation that should at all times exist between employer and employee." But Gary did not see any necessity for dealing with these petty traitors, and slammed the door in their faces by declaring that "we do not confer, negotiate with, or combat labor unions as such," and that "we stand for the open shop."

After receiving such a rebuke from the steel trust there was nothing left for the officials of the Amalgamated Association but to remain in the national committee.

Another serious attempt against the success of the campaign was made by Samuel Gompers himself. First of all, in the midst of the campaign he tendered his resignation as chairman of the national committee. This action on his part was very important, for it meant that the American Federation of Labor as such removed itself from the campaign and the responsibility attached to it. Secondly, when it was decided to call out the steel workers on October 1, Gompers, disagreeing with this action of the committee and remaining faithful to his agreement with President Wilson not to organize workers during the war, refused even to take part in the committee's deliberations. Thus he shamelessly deserted half a million workers in their most critical hour.

The steel magnates began to persecute the workers who joined the unions. Thousands of them were discharged, and demanded protection from their organizations. Those who were thrown out of work, as well as those who still remained in the mills, demanded an opportunity to fight their masters. Their clamors could not be ignored by the national committee. The time had come when the leaders had either to lead the masses into the struggle or remain generals without an army.

On May 25, 1919, the national committee called a conference of the representatives of the organized steel workers; 583 were present. The delegates demanded action, for the persecution was so great, so many workers had been sacked, that something had to be done or everything would be wrecked. The conference instructed the national committee to open negotiations with the employers, demanding increases in wages, shorter hours, better working conditions, and recognition of the unions.

In accordance with these instructions, the national committee elected a special committee, with Gompers at its head, to negotiate with the steel trust. On June 20, 1919, Gompers addressed a letter to Gary, very politely telling him that the workers did not want much, only an amelioration of their conditions and "by American understanding, not by revolutionary methods or the inauguration of a cataclysm," also, that "we believe in the effort of employer and employees to sit down around a table" (*Ibid.*, pp. 74-75). This letter was entirely ignored by the chairman of the steel trust. At the same time the persecution increased, and the workers continued to clamor for action. The situation became tense. Gompers, as already stated, resigned from the national committee. John Fitzpatrick, president of the Chicago Federation of Labor, was appointed in his place.

On July 20, 1919, a further conference was called of all 24 unions. It decided to submit the question of a strike to a referendum vote of the membership. It also adopted the following demands to be submitted to the employers:

"1. Right of collective bargaining; 2. Reinstatement of all men discharged for union activities with pay for lost time; 3. Eight-hour day; 4. One day's rest in seven; 5. Abolition of 24-hour shift; 6. Increase in wages sufficient to guarantee American standard of living; 7. Standard scale of wages in all trades and classifications of workers; 8. Double rates of pay for all overtime after eight hours, holiday and Sunday work; 9. Check-off system of collecting union dues and assessments; 10. Principles of seniority to apply in the maintenance, reduction, and increase of working forces; 11. Abolition of company unions; 12. Abolition of physical examination of applicants for employment" (*Ibid.*, p. 77).

The referendum was overwhelming. Not less than 98 per cent of the vote was for a strike. In many steel centers the vote was unanimous.

The national committee once more tried to open negotiations with the steel companies, and on August 26 another letter was addressed to Judge Gary begging him for a conference. To this letter Gary replied that "our corporation and subsidiaries decline to discuss business with them [the unions]," and that "the corporation and subsidiaries are opposed to the 'closed shop'" and "they stand for the 'open shop.'"

Then the national committee reported to the executive council of the American Federation of Labor, which approved its acts and decided to ask President Wilson to mediate between the organized steel workers and Gary. Gompers went to the White House and presented the situation to the President, telling him that all the men were asking for was a conference with the employers to present their grievances. Wilson promised to see Gary and try to induce him to agree to a conference with the men. "In order to give him [President Wilson] a chance to work, the unions withheld the setting of the strike date."

"A week passed," Foster recites, "with no word from the President. Conditions in the steel industry were frightful. The companies, realizing the importance of striking the first blow, were discharging men by the thousands. The unions could wait no longer. They had to move or be annihilated" (*Ibid.*, pp. 84-85).

The labor leaders found themselves between the devil and the deep sea. They were mortally afraid to lead the army into the fight, but they realized that if they refused, they would lose their entire following.

On September 4 the negotiations committee with Gompers at its head again turned to President Wilson and opened their hearts to him.

"The executive committee, relying upon the case as presented to you last week and your earnest declaration to endeavor to bring about a conference for the honorable and peaceful adjustment of the matters in controversy, *have thus far been enabled to prevail upon the men not to engage in a general strike. We cannot now affirm how much longer we will be able to exert that influence.*"

When the national committee met on September 9, a telegram was received from Wilson's secretary, Tumulty, telling them that the President had not succeeded in arranging the promised conference with Judge Gary. Some of the members of the committee were still not satisfied with this rebuff by the President and sent him another telegram, again repeating that "it will be impossible to hold our men much longer from defending themselves by striking unless some genuine relief is vouchsafed them," and they again begged him to act. But the President, being a faithful agent of the steel trust, did not act. Again Wilson's secretary replied that it was impossible to arrange a conference.

There was no other alternative for the national committee than to declare a strike. Gompers warned the committee of the grave dangers. But what could the committee do in the circumstances, when the workers had almost unanimously voted for a strike and when no help was coming from the President in whom the labor leaders had placed their last hope? It was, therefore, decided to call out the men on September 22.

"Then came a bolt from the blue," Foster says. "Next morning the newspapers carried a telegram from Secretary Tumulty to President Gompers requesting that the strike be held off until after the Industrial Conference, beginning October 6th. The committeemen could hardly believe their eyes, because the telegram that they received from Mr. Tumulty had said absolutely nothing about postponing the strike."

Nevertheless, it was true, President Wilson did communicate with Gompers and demanded that the strike be postponed. Finally Gompers transmitted that telegram to the national committee, adding on his part: "You are aware of the reason which prevented my participating further, the past few days, in the conference with the representatives of the various national and international unions involved in this question." He also suggested that the committee "endeavor to conform to the wish expressed by the President" (*Ibid.*, pp. 87-89).

This last meant that Gompers knew in advance the attitude of the government toward the strike but had kept it a secret not only from the workers but also from the national committee.

Woodrow Wilson had a definite purpose in mind when he condemned the strike in advance. He knew that this action would be of tremendous help to the steel trust, for if the workers now went on strike the bourgeois press would shout: "These foreigners would not even yield to the advice of the President of the land!" Finally even Gompers told them not to strike, but "these bolsheviki would not listen!"

The national committee began to waver. But the demand of the steel workers for action became greater and greater.

"Immediately after the story got abroad that the strike might be postponed, they met in their unions and notified the national committee that they were going to strike on September 22, regardless of anything that body might do short of getting them definite concessions and protection. Many long weary months they had waited patiently, under the urgings of the organizers, for a chance to redress their grievances. And now when they had built their organization; taken their strike vote; received their strike call and were ready to deliver a blow at their oppressors, the opportunity of a generation was at hand, and they were not going to see it lost. They would not postpone indefinitely, and in all likelihood break up altogether, the movement they had suffered so much to build, in the vague hope that the Industrial Conference, which they had no guarantee would even consider their case, and which was dominated by their arch enemies, Gary and Rockefeller, would in some distant day do something for them. . . . Under such circumstances the workers could not consent to the withholding of the strike. Practically all the steel districts in the country solemnly warned the national committee that they would strike on September 22, in spite of any postponement that was not based on positive assurances that justice would be done. *The control of the situation was in the hands of the rank and file"* (*Ibid.*, pp. 91-92).

Finally the national committee decided to go along with the workers. But once more it knelt before President Wilson and begged for mercy, saying that it could not control the situation any longer.

The national committee had aroused forces which it no longer could hold in check.

On September 22, 1919, 365,000 workers left the mills and declared war upon their enemy—the steel trust.

The employers were well prepared to meet the workers. In every steel center martial law existed. The workers were forbidden in many places to walk in groups even on the sidewalks. In many instances armed gunmen of the steel trust attacked innocent women and children and beat them. They entered the homes of workers, robbed and clubbed the inmates. In Hammond, Ind., five workers were shot down from behind, and many more were wounded.

The bourgeois press raised the cry that the strike was nothing less than an attempt of the bolsheviks on the very life of the "grateful" republic. Priests and ministers of the church joined the chorus against the strikers. Some of them openly urged their faithful parishioners to shoot down the strikers on the slightest provocation (See *Full Text of the Sermon* preached by Rev. P. Moyneaux, pastor of St. Brendan's Church, Braddock, Pa., on Sunday, September 21, 1919).

Probably never before in the history of the class struggle in this country was there such extensive mobilization of scabs. "Probably half the strike-breaking agencies in the country were engaged in recruiting them," says Foster. It was estimated that not less than 40,000 Negroes were brought in by the steel companies. Of course, these Negro workers were victims of the system which makes it possible for the exploiters to use the workers of one race to defeat the workers of another race. It was a great lesson, especially to the organized labor movement. It showed that the trade unions can no longer neglect this very important section of the workers. They, too, must be brought into the ranks of the organized workers, or the struggles of the latter cannot succeed.

Even more disastrous was the treachery of the Amalgamated Association of Iron, Steel, and Tin Workers, the most important union in the steel industry. The Amalgamated Association was composed of highly skilled workers, and "had agreements covering the skilled steel making trades, but when the laborers struck, these skilled men had to quit also. The break in the Youngstown district came when the Amalgamated Association virtually forced the laborers back to work in these shops in order to get them in operation . . ." (Foster: *Ibid.*, p. 176).

The association took the same action in other districts also. "In Cleveland the charters were taken from local unions that refused to abide by the agreement." The other trades affiliated with the national committee protested against the enforcement of the clause. They declared that this agreement of the association with the employers was void

"because it violated trade union principles and fundamental human rights. . . . But all arguments were in vain; the Amalgamated Association officials were as adamant. They held their agreements with the employers to be sacred and to rank above any covenants they had entered into with the coöperating trades. They would enforce them to the letter. . . . Being a federated body, the national committee had to bow to this decision and stand by helpless, while its effects worked havoc with the strike" (*Ibid.*, pp. 173-175).

The leaders of the Amalgamated Association were arch traitors to the cause of the working class. "Their action was treason," Foster says, "not only to the steel workers but to the whole labor movement."

The most important reason for the failure of the steel strike of 1919 was the lack of support on the part of the organized workers of the United States. Even the leaders of the 24 international unions which composed the national committee had no confidence in the workers and in the success of the campaign to organize them; they delayed, wavered, ran from Judge Gary to President Wilson and begged for mercy when strong, determined, energetic action was necessary. If these 24 international unions, embracing over 2,000,000 organized workers, had wholeheartedly supported the struggling steel men, the organization campaign and the strike itself would have taken an entirely different turn and success would have been almost certain.

As far as the American Federation of Labor is concerned, it did very little in this gigantic struggle. Gompers, its president, had secret dealings with Wilson, and deserted the movement at a critical time. During the strike the Federation never massed all of its forces behind the workers.

Neither did the railroad brotherhoods lift a finger to help them. The latter looked with confidence to their well-organized brothers on the railroads for a helping hand, but in vain. With no qualms of conscience the brotherhoods manned the trains which brought scabs into the steel districts from all over the country.

The mining industry is very closely connected with steel. The same steel trust controls many coal corporations. It was the duty of the United Mine Workers of America, who at that time had the situation in the mining fields well in hand, to come to the assistance of the steel workers. But they did not. The leaders of the United Mine Workers even refused to fight the mine-owners who attacked their own members, so great was their desire to avoid a combined struggle of the miners with the steel workers against the ruling class and its government.

On October 31, 1919, the agreement with the coal barons expired and the next day not less than 500,000 miners went on strike. Great joy swept the ranks of the steel workers because a combined struggle of the men in these two basic industries would surely defeat the ruling class. The latter saw this clearly, and used all its tricks to get the miners back to work. The leaders of the miners' union assisted the ruling class in these efforts. They had lived on very peaceful terms with the capitalist government during the war, helping the latter to send 60,000 miners to France to be killed in the name of the almighty dollar, and now they would do nothing to disturb these peaceful relations. The government, on the other hand, was determined to get the miners back into the mines even at the point of a gun. On October 24, 1919, President Wilson declared:

"From whatever angle the subject may be viewed, it is apparent that such a strike in such circumstances would be the most far-reaching plan ever presented in this country to limit the facilities of production and distribution of all the necessities of life. A strike under these circumstances is not only unjustifiable; it is unlawful."

And Attorney-General Palmer, on October 29, as the miners' strike became inevitable, violently condemned it in the following terms:

"The facts present a situation which challenges the supremacy of the law, and every resource of the government will be brought to bear to prevent the national disaster which would inevitably result from the cessation of the mining operation" (Jay Lovestone: *Loc. cit.,* pp. 13-14).

Congress immediately passed a resolution giving the administration full power to deal with the situation and "vindicate the majesty and power of the government."

On November 8 the Department of Justice procured for the coal operators an injunction restraining the union officials from aiding the strike in any way by "messages of encouragement or exhortation," and from using the union funds for strike benefits (*Ibid.,* p. 15).

Three days later, on November 11, the leaders of the United Mine Workers called off the strike. John L. Lewis declared: "We are Americans. We cannot fight our Government." Ellis Searles, editor of the *United Mine Workers Journal,* added: "The United Mine Workers will not fight the Government. It is their Government just as it is the Government of every other citizen. It is their Government just as it is the Government of the coal operators." The New York *Times,* commenting upon the surrender of the miners' leaders to the government, observed in its editorial of November 12, 1919: "That is Americanism, it is a conclusion stated in an American way."

The miners were ordered to go back to their tasks without further ceremony. Now the ruling class breathed more easily, for its object had been attained. It could once more turn all its guns against the steel workers, who were left alone on the battlefield. The reactionary miners' officials saved the situation for the ruling class of the United States. Their surrender was a death blow to the steel strike and a disaster to the whole labor movement.

A few unions did come to the assistance of the steel strikers morally and financially. In fact, their assistance was more generous than that of the unions directly connected with the industry. The International Fur Workers' Union, for example, contributed $20,000; the International Ladies' Garment Workers' Union donated $60,000; and the Amalgamated Clothing Workers, which does not belong to the A. F. of L., gave $100,000. The total collection amounted to $418,141.

The defeat of the steel strike of 1919 was a body blow to the entire labor movement of America. If this strike had been won, to-day there would be about 400,000 trade union steel workers; their success would have encouraged the masses of unskilled hands in other heavy industries to follow their lead; the offensive of the ruling class would have been defeated then and there. Well did the ruling class understand this fact, and therefore it used all of its power to crush the strike. Only the trade union bureaucrats failed or did not want to understand it, and thus allowed the ruling class to destroy this most promising and far-reaching of movements.

On the other hand, the steel strike furnished a very valuable lesson to the class-conscious section of the American workers. First of all it demonstrated clearly that the ruling class will use any and all means to smash any movement tending to introduce trade unions into the heavy and basic industries. Second, it convincingly disproved the contention that it is impossible to organize or to lead into a fight the great masses of unskilled workers, the majority of whom are foreign-born, and that therefore these masses will forever remain a servile tool in the hands of the industrial masters to reduce wages and make conditions worse for the American-born workers.

"But if the Americans and skilled workers generally proved indifferent union men in the steel campaign," Foster says, "the foreign unskilled workers covered themselves with glory. Throughout the whole affair they showed an understanding, discipline, courage, and tenacity of purpose that compared favorably with that shown in any organized effort ever put forth by workingmen on this continent. Beyond question they displayed trade-union qualities of the very highest type. Their solidarity was unbreakable; their fighting spirit invincible. They nobly struggled onward in the face of difficulties that would try the stoutest hearts. They proved themselves altogether worthy of the best American labor traditions" (*Ibid.*, pp. 200-202).

The strike of the men's clothing workers of New York for a 44-hour week was also one of the most important strikes of the period. During the war the Amalgamated Clothing Workers became a strong organization embracing almost all of the workers in the men's clothing industry. On the day the armistice was declared, November 11, 1918, the New York employers declared a lockout, aiming to destroy the then militant union. The workers, on their part, declared a strike and demanded a 44-hour week. The strike affected 60,000 organized clothing workers and lasted for three months, ending with a victory for the union.

"The victory in the New York strike was followed by victories in Rochester, Baltimore, Boston, Philadelphia, and other cities where the 44-hour week was granted by the employers to avoid general strikes" (*American Labor Year Book*, 1921-22, pp. 166-168).

In January, 1919, the harbor workers of New York City, 17,000 strong, went out for the eight-hour day. The strike was so successful that for five days not a ship moved. Immediately the employers and the government began maneuvering to destroy the strike. The National War Labor Board asked the workers to go back, promising them a peaceful settlement of the dispute. The workers were inveigled into accepting the board's proposition. But the decision of the board was a complete victory for the employers. "This so enraged the harbor workers that on March 4 they went on strike a second time." The strike lasted for six weeks, the workers displaying perfect solidarity,

"until an official of the International Longshoremen's Association by his influence over the Tidewater Boatmen's Union and the Lighter Captain's Union induced this group of strikers to settle with the employers and then had the Railroad Administration demand that these men be permitted to work with the scabs that had been recruited for a number of tugs. Faced by division in the ranks and dissension created by this international official, the strikers were ordered back to work by the affiliation leaders, and the case of the workers on the vessels of the private boat owners was referred to a committee from the unions and the owners created at the suggestion of Mayor Hylan" (*Ibid.*, p. 169).

Thus where the government and the employers failed to break the solidarity of the workers, the labor officials succeeded.

The Seattle, Wash., general strike of 1919 was another struggle of momentous significance. On January 21, 32,000 shipyard workers quit to force a revision of the wage scale set by the Macy Wage Adjustment Board. The strikers immediately appealed to the Seattle Central Labor Council for assistance. The latter submitted the question of a general strike to a referendum vote of its affiliated unions. The organized workers of the city displayed wonderful class solidarity, for both conservative and radical trade unions voted to come to the aid of the shipyard workers. One hundred and ten unions voted to join the walkout.

The general strike started on February 6. It was probably the first effective general strike in the United States. Not only factories, but all the city institutions were suddenly closed. The employers and their hired press exclaimed that this was the beginning of a revolution in America and that the instigators of this "calamity" were none other than the "Russian Bolsheviki!" Mayor Ole Hanson issued an ultimatum that if the strike were not called off by 8 o'clock on the morning of February 8 the city would be placed under martial law and armed force would be used. But the act of this petty politician only enraged the workers the more, and on February 8 the strike was as solid as at any time previous to the issuance of the mayor's ultimatum. Hanson dared not enforce his threat. All this time the city's life was completely in the hands of the workers. An unarmed labor guard patroled the streets; order prevailed everywhere.

The strike ended on February 11. It disintegrated from within. Some of the conservative unions deserted the struggle, claiming that it had accomplished its object as a demonstration of working-class solidarity and sympathy with the shipyard hands, and told their members to go back to work. Other unions insisted that the general fight be continued until the demands of the shipyard workers were conceded. The general strike was ended and the shipyard workers were left alone to struggle with their employers and the government. Their fate was naturally sealed. After a month's struggle they submitted, completely defeated. Their demands for increased wages were not granted; worse yet, the employers refused to recognize their union (*Ibid.*, pp. 170-171).

On February 3, 1919, the textile workers of Lawrence, Mass., started a strike which lasted until May 20. As soon as the war was over the textile barons began a campaign for a general reduction of wages. The workers revolted against these cuts. Though they were almost entirely unorganized, for the United Textile Workers had in their ranks only a few hundred, the walkout was highly effective. About 32,000 joined the strike, and every mill in the city was closed. For the first few weeks the ranks of the workers were absolutely solid. Later "about 10,000 English-speaking workers, mostly French-Canadians and Irish-Americans, rapidly drifted back to the mills." But from 15,000 to 20,000 workers stuck together doggedly through the 16 long weeks of the strike. As usual in such bitter fights,

"the strikers, the general strike committee, and the leaders who came to their help, suffered every form of vilification and persecution—newspaper hostility, citizens' committees, police brutality, denial of open air meetings even on private property, paid spies in the strike committee and among the people, attempts to frame up the leaders, and finally the use of lynch law by masked vigilantes upon two of the strike leaders."

But even this reign of terror could not break the strike, and on May 20 the employers submitted, granting a 15 per cent raise in wages and a 48-hour week. The Lawrence victory was also a victory for the textile workers of other New England cities. For the time being it stemmed the employers' offensive against wages.

CHAPTER XXIX

THE BEGINNING OF THE COMMUNIST MOVEMENT

ALL these war and post-war events could not occur without affecting in one way or another the working class of America, especially its class-conscious section.

Take, for instance, the great treachery of the European socialists of the Second International, in joining hands with the bourgeoisie and helping the latter to turn the workers into cannon-fodder. What was the attitude of the American socialists towards this treachery? There was a controversy in the Socialist Party on this vital question. We have already shown by official documents that in no instance did the leaders of the party openly and clearly condemn the position of the Second International; in no instance did they call upon the rank and file of the German, British, French, or Belgian Social-Democratic parties to rise against their traitors. The American socialist leaders' slogan was: "We do not presume to pass judgment upon the conduct of our brother parties in Europe." Some openly tried to exonerate the socialist traitors of Germany; others could not see why the French socialists should be condemned for "defending their fatherland" against "German militarism." But at the same time the conviction was ripening among the members of the Socialist Party that their European "brothers" (the socialist leaders) had committed an unpardonable crime against the working class.

The great Russian Revolution was another matter in which the socialists of the world failed—in which they again betrayed working class interests. For the first time in the history of the human race, on November 7, 1917, 150,000,000 workers and peasants delivered a death blow to the rule of their czars and capitalists and established the dictatorship of the proletariat in the form of "soviets" or workers' and peasants' councils. Immediately the whole bourgeois world rose as one against Soviet Russia —the first working class republic in the world. It attempted to smash the new system and bring back the czars to their throne and the capitalists to their counting houses, by means of blockade, lies, provocation, and armed force. The Russian menshevik-socialists and the social-revolutionaries joined hands with the counter-revolutionists and the whole capitalist world in a war against the revolution, against the Soviet government and against the communists (bolsheviks).

In those trying days active help from the workers of the world was needed. Sympathy and well-polished phrases could not repel the machine

BEGINNING OF THE COMMUNIST MOVEMENT

guns of the counter-revolutionary and foreign armies. A fight against the ruling classes was the only real assistance possible to the Russian Revolution.

On the other hand, the Russian Revolution echoed through Germany, Austria-Hungary, and other central European countries. The workers of these countries started to think and to rise against their masters. A general strike spread over Germany and Austria, the German army began to disintegrate. The end of the World War was brought about not by American, French, and British armies, but by the Russian Revolution which undermined the armies of the Central Powers.

On November 11, 1918, the cannon ceased roaring. The soldiers who were still alive went back home, to be met at their gates by starvation. The bourgeoisie found itself in a critical situation; it began to waver in the face of the rising working class. It really looked as if the world revolution was going to engulf all the capitalist countries and put an end to the system of exploitation, wars, and pestilence. Early in 1917 the czar of Russia was overthrown; in the fall of the same year an end was put to bourgeois rule in Russia; at the end of the following year the German kaiser was overthrown and the Hapsburg dynasty in Austria-Hungary went to pieces; the soldiers of England and France refused to shoot down the Russian workers and peasants in Siberia and Murmansk.

What was the attitude of the Social-Democracy in these critical hours? Did it come to the assistance of the Russian Revolution? Did it call upon the workers of the capitalist countries to rise and overthrow their masters and put an end to the capitalist system?

On the contrary, when the workers of Germany revolted and made efforts to establish their own rule, the Social-Democratic Party of Germany joined hands with the ruling class and assisted it in defeating the German Revolution. The great communist leaders of Germany, Karl Liebknecht and Rosa Luxemburg, together with tens of thousands of their comrades, died at the hands of the Social-Democrats and capitalists, now united. In Hungary the social-democrats helped the bourgeoisie to overthrow the Soviet government and institute the white terror.

How could the revolutionary workers of the world be expected to look calmly upon these traitorous deeds of the social-democrats? Through the initiative of the Russian Bolshevik Party, which by this time called itself the Russian Communist Party, and the Spartacus group of Germany, an international congress of the revolutionary workers was summoned for March 2-6, 1919, in Moscow, the capital of the first working-class republic.

"We, communists, representatives of the revolutionary proletariat of the different countries of Europe, America, and Asia, assembled in Moscow," declared the manifesto of the congress to the working class, "feel and consider ourselves followers and fulfillers of the program proclaimed 70 years ago (This refers to the *Communist Manifesto* of Marx and Engels, issued in 1848). It is our task now to sum up the practical revolutionary experience of the working class, to cleanse the movement of its admixtures of opportunism and social patriotism, and to unite the forces of all the true revolutionary proletarian parties in order to further and hasten the complete victory of the communist revolution."

The manifesto ended with the following burning appeal to the toiling masses:

"Proletarians of all countries: In the war against imperialistic barbarity, against monarchy, against the privileged classes, the bourgeois state and bourgeois property, against all forms and varieties of social and national oppression—unite!"
"Under the standard of the workmen's councils, under the banner of the Third International, in the revolutionary struggle for power and the dictatorship of the proletariat, proletarians of all countries, unite!"

The congress rejected the idea of the social-democrats of "peacefully and gradually introducing socialism by electing socialists in governmental offices of the capitalist state," and adopted revolutionary tactics for the overthrow of capitalist rule. Its crowning work was the establishment of the Communist International.

The call of the Communist International resounded through all parts of the world. Everywhere the revolutionary proletariat received it enthusiastically, broke off their relations with the social-democrats, and organized themselves into communist parties or groups. In some countries the majority of the members of the Socialist Party went over to the Communist International. No middle road was left. One had either to follow the social-democrats and the bourgeoisie, or side with the communists and the proletarian revolution.

What was the position of the right wing leadership of the American Socialist Party? It refused to condemn the treachery of the Second International, and supported the Russian Revolution only with words. It refused to join whole-heartedly in the formation of the Communist International, and continued to talk about resurrection and rehabilitation of the Second International. Those members and leaders who supported the Communist International and demanded a change in the party program in view of the great changes brought about by the war and by the workers' revolutionary movement in Europe, were accused of aping the Russians and of importing Russian methods to America. In January, 1919, the national executive committee of the party decided to send delegates to the Berne Congress which was being held in order to revive the Second International.

Change in party tactics and program was out of the question as far as the chief spokesmen of the party were concerned. "A gradual development into socialism" remained the cornerstone of their philosophy. They continued to maintain that the working class can and will accomplish its complete emancipation from capitalism through parliamentary elections alone, through replacing republican and democratic officials by socialist representatives. Their last word to the workers remained: "A vote for socialism is the only vote that will count in the long run" (Socialist Party: *A Political Guide for the Workers*, 1920, p. 27).

The Socialist Party would have nothing to do with the proletarian revolution, or the dictatorship of the proletariat.

"The Socialist Party strives by means of political methods, including the action of its representatives in the legislatures and other public offices," reads its platform, "to force the enactment of such measures as will immediately benefit the workers, raise their standard of life, increase their power, and stiffen their resistance to capitalist aggression. Its purpose is to secure a majority in Congress and in every state legislature, to win the principal executive and judicial offices, to become the dominant and controlling party, and when in power to transfer to the ownership by the people of industries, beginning with those of a public character, such as banking, insurance, mining, transportation, and communication, as well as the trustified industries, and extending the process to all other industries susceptible of collective ownership as rapidly as their physical conditions will permit" (*Ibid.*, pp. 34-35).

This meant that neither the war, nor the post-war revolutionary movement of the European workers, had taught the right wing leaders of the Socialist Party anything. They droned the same old song, that Socialist Party representatives, elected into governmental positions, step by step, peacefully and gradually, would remove the capitalist system from the face of the earth. The Socialist Party remained only a parliamentary vote-catching machine.

The majority of the members of the S. P., especially those of the foreign language federations, and some of the leaders, began to struggle against the opportunism of the right wing chiefs such as Berger and Hillquit. Beginning with 1918 there appeared a powerful, well organized left wing in the Socialist Party, having as its object the capture of the party for revolutionary socialism. The official party organs, excepting those of the federations, were closed to the revolutionary socialists or left wing. They therefore issued in pamphlet form *The Manifesto and Program of the Left Wing of the Socialist Party* and distributed it widely among the members. In their manifesto the left wing pointed out the enormous changes that had taken place during and after the war, the causes that had led to the great slaughter, and the treachery and downfall of the social-democracy of Europe. They held that conditions made it imperative for the Socialist Party to change its program and tactics. They pointed out that even in America the working class was beginning to awaken from the effects of the war and "a series of labor struggles is bound to follow —indeed, is beginning now."

"Shall the Socialist Party," the left wing manifesto asks, "continue to feed the workers with social reform legislation at this critical period? Shall it approach the whole question from the standpoint of votes and the election of representatives to the legislatures?"

The revolutionaries demanded that

"on the basis of the class struggle, then, the Socialist Party of America must reorganize itself, must prepare to come to grips with the master class during the difficult period of capitalist readjustment now going on. This it can do only by teaching the working class the truth about present-day conditions; it must preach revolutionary trade unionism; and urge all the workers to organize into industrial unions, the only form of labor organization which can cope with the power of great modern aggregations of capital. It must carry on its political campaigns, not merely as a means of electing officials to political office, as in the past, but as a year-round educational campaign to arouse the workers to class-conscious economic and political action, and to keep alive the burning ideal of revolution in the hearts of the people."

The Manifesto of the Left Wing further stated that the proletariat cannot capture the bourgeois state and use it for the benefit of the working class. The proletariat must overthrow and destroy this state and organize its own state power, the dictatorship of the proletariat. It also demanded that the Socialist Party sever all relations with the social patriots and centrists who were attempting to revive the Second International, and that it participate instead in the organization of the new, the Communist International.

The left wing became a great power in the Socialist Party and seriously threatened the right wing leadership. In national elections to various party posts the left wing candidates received an overwhelming majority. For international delegate, for instance, John Reed of the left wing received 17,235 votes, while Victor Berger received only 4,871; for international secretary, Kate Richards O'Hare, supported by the left wing, polled 13,262 votes, while Morris Hillquit got only 4,775 votes; out of 15 seats on the national executive committee 12 were captured by the left wing. From 75 to 80 per cent of the membership was thus with the revolutionary element.

The right wing leaders of the party, however, despite their crushing defeat in the elections, would not relinquish their leadership. They were determined to "rule or ruin." They repudiated the results of the election, proclaiming themselves the masters of the party, and issued a call for an emergency national convention on August 30. But they were quite sure that in the convention they would receive the same overwhelming defeat as in the elections. They therefore decided on another step to assure themselves of a majority. They suspended the Russian, Ukrainian, Polish, Hungarian, South Slavic, Lettish, and Lithuanian federations and the party organization of the state of Michigan; a little later the same was done with the organizations of Massachusetts and Ohio; not less than 60,000 members found themselves outside the party.

On June 21, 1919, 94 delegates of the left wing met in national conference in New York City to consider the party situation and the next steps in the fight for the party leadership and new policies. A difference of opinion was disclosed as to whether a Communist Party should be organized immediately, or whether the struggle should be continued within the Socialist Party until the emergency convention which was scheduled to take place within two months. The proposal to organize a new party immediately was defeated by a vote of 55 to 38. The majority decided to participate in the Socialist Party emergency convention and fight there for a communist program. On the other hand, the minority of the left wing conference, representing mostly the foreign language federations and the state organization of Michigan, was determined to have nothing to do with the Socialist Party convention and to make immediate efforts for the formation of a Communist Party. It issued a call for a convention to be held on September 1 to organize such a party.

When the Socialist Party emergency convention met in Chicago on August 30, the right wing leaders had the situation well in hand. They unseated the left wing delegates and when the latter refused to leave the hall the police were called to remove them. These expelled delegates met the next day and organized the Communist Labor Party. The following day, September 1, the convention called by the majority of the left wing assembled and launched the Communist Party of America.

Attempts were made to merge these two communist factions into a single party, but in vain. Those who had come for the purpose of organizing a Communist Party demanded that the members expelled from the socialist convention pass through the credentials committee as individuals and not as a group. The latter refused to concede this demand. Unity was therefore not accomplished, and two communist parties were formed at about the same time—the Communist Labor Party and the Communist Party.

The Communist Party of America, on the day of its foundation, September 1, 1919, adopted the following program:

First Program of the Communist Party of America.

"The Communist Party is the conscious expression of the class struggle of the workers against capitalism. Its aim is to direct this struggle to the conquest of political power, the overthrow of capitalism, and the destruction of the bourgeois state.

"The Communist Party prepares itself for the revolution in the measure that it develops a program of immediate action, expressing the mass struggles of the proletariat. These struggles must be inspired with revolutionary spirit and purposes.

"The Communist Party is fundamentally a party of action. It brings to the workers a consciousness of their oppression, of the impossibility of improving their conditions under capitalism. The Communist Party directs the workers' struggles against capitalism, developing fuller forms and purposes in this struggle, culminating in the mass action of the revolution.

"The Communist Party maintains that the class struggle is essentially a political struggle; that is, a struggle to conquer the power of the state.

"The Communist Party shall keep in the foreground its consistent appeal for proletarian revolution, the overthrow of capitalism, and the establishment of a dictatorship of the proletariat. As the opposition of the bourgeoisie is broken, as it is expropriated and gradually absorbed in the working groups, the proletarian dictatorship disappears, until finally the state dies and there are no more class distinctions.

"Participation in parliamentary campaigns, which in the general struggle of the proletariat is of secondary importance, is for the purpose of revolutionary propaganda only.

"The Communist Party shall make the great industrial struggles of the working class its major campaigns, in order to develop an understanding of the strike in relation to the overthrow of capitalism.

"The Communist Party shall participate in mass strikes, not only to achieve the immediate purposes of the strike, but to develop the revolutionary implications of the mass strike."

On the trade union question the program declared:

"The Communist Party must engage actively in the struggle to revolutionize the trade unions. As against the unionism of the American Federation of Labor, the Communist Party propagandizes industrial unionism and industrial union organization, emphasizing their revolutionary implications. Industrial unionism is not simply a means for the everyday struggle against capitalism; its ultimate purpose is revolutionary, implying the necessity of ending the capitalist parliamentary state. Industrial unionism is a factor in the final mass action for the conquest of power, as it will constitute the basis for the industrial administration of the Communist Commonwealth.

"The Communist Party recognizes that the A. F. of L. is reactionary and a bulwark of capitalism.

"Councils of workers shall be organized in the shops as circumstances allow, for the purpose of carrying on the industrial union struggle in the old unions, uniting and mobilizing the militant elements; these councils to be unified in a central council wherever possible.

"It shall be a major task of the Communist Party to agitate for the construction of a general industrial union organization, embracing the I. W. W., W. I. I. U., independent and secession unions, militant unions of the A. F. of L., and the unorganized workers, on the basis of the revolutionary class struggle."

The program also declared:

"The Communist Party will wage the struggle against militarism as a phase of the class struggle to hasten the downfall of capitalism.

"The struggle against imperialism, necessarily an international struggle, is the basis of proletarian revolutionary action in this epoch.

"There must be close unity with the Communist International for common action against imperialism.

"The Communist Party emphasizes the common character of the struggle of the workers of all nations, making necessary the solidarity of the workers of the world."

At the same time the Communist Labor Party adopted a program as follows:

Platform and Program of the Communist Labor Party

"The Communist Labor Party of America declares itself in full harmony with the revolutionary working class parties of all countries and stands by the principles laid down by the Third International formed at Moscow.

"The Communist Labor Party proposes the organization of the workers as a class for the overthrow of capitalist rule and the conquest of political power by the workers. The workers organized as the ruling class, shall, through their government, make and enforce the laws; they shall own and control land, factories, mills, mines, transportation systems, and financial institutions. All power to the workers!

"The Communist Labor Party has as its ultimate aim: The overthrow of the present system of production, in which the working class is mercilessly exploited, and the creation of an industrial republic wherein the machinery of production shall be socialized so as to guarantee to the workers the full social value of their toil.

"Communist Labor Party platforms, being based on the class struggle, and recognizing that this is the historic period of the Social Revolution, can contain only one demand: The establishment of the dictatorship of the proletariat."

And on the trade union question:

"We favor organized party activity in coöperation with class-conscious industrial unions, in order to unify industrial and political class-conscious propaganda and action. Locals and branches shall organize shop branches, to conduct communist propaganda and organization in the shops and factories, and to encourage the workers to organize in one big union.

"The party shall propagandize industrial unionism and industrial union organization, pointing out their revolutionary nature and possibilities.

"The party shall make the great industrial battles its major campaigns, to show the value of the strike as a political weapon."

The Communist Labor Party decided to participate in parliamentary elections and to

"maintain strict control over all members elected to public office—not only the local organizations, but the national executive committee."

"In order that the party shall be a centralized organization capable of united action, no autonomous groups or federations independent of the will of the entire party shall be permitted."

We see that in their first programs and platforms the Communist parties were for industrial unionism and for building new revolutionary unions. They were for abandoning the reformist trade unions of the American Federation of Labor. But this position was completely changed in a short time. In their second programs they rejected the I. W. W. policies and the idea of building new unions as dual unionism, and declared themselves in favor of working within the reformist unions for propaganda purposes. For instance, the Communist Party in its second program, adopted in July, 1920, declared:

"The Communist Party rejects the idea, as advocated by the I. W. W., of 'smashing the A. F. of L.' in order to reconstruct the trade unions. . . .

"The Communist Party recognizes trade and industrial unions as a field for the propagation of communism to the masses. Our task is to inculcate and crystallize communist understanding among the masses, over the heads of the union bureaucracy. . . . Just as we enter the bourgeois parliaments for our revolutionary propaganda, so must the Communist Party enter the most reactionary unions for communist propaganda and agitation" (*The Communist*, August 1, 1920).

The Communist Labor Party, which by this time had united with a split-off section of the Communist Party and changed its name to United Communist Party, changed its position on this question at about the same time, for in its second program it declared:

"The United Communist Party confirms the present necessity of militant workers remaining with the large mass of organized workers regardless of the declared reactionary aims of these unions, and, by determined and coördinated strength, turning those unions to a revolutionary course. The United Communist Party, section of the Communist International, is the instrument for that coördination of revolutionary work within the unions" (*The Communist*, No. 13).

At once the American bourgeoisie scented danger in the communist movement, and determined to strangle it at its very inception by declaring both the parties illegal and starting a general offensive against them. Great reaction, by far surpassing in severity the reaction during the war, swept the country at the end of 1919 and in the beginning of 1920. The blow was directed primarily against the communists and their organizations. This was a strategic move of the ruling class. It was preparing for an offensive against the general labor movement. It realized the importance of smashing the most advanced, the most class-conscious revolutionary section of that movement first. Under the instructions and guidance of Mitchell Palmer, attorney-general, intense persecution was carried on not only against the leaders of the Communist parties, but against the rank and file as well. Members were arrested and jailed by thousands. During the hearings before the Senate Judiciary Committee, Mitchell Palmer made the following report on the persecution of radicals:

"1. Number of warrants for alien anarchists issued from July, 1919, to January 1st, 1921 6,328
"2. Number of alien anarchist warrants served same period........ 4,138
"3. Number of alien anarchist warrants cancelled.................... 2,919
"4. Number of alien anarchists ordered deported................... 1,119
"5. Number of alien anarchists deported........................... 505"

Another item of testimony by Palmer before the Committee on the Civil Appropriations Bill for 1921 is as follows:

"In the latter part of January, 1920, our field reports indicate that 52 per cent of our work in the country was in connection with the so-called radical movement."

On this occasion he said that 6,396 warrants had been issued, that the salaries of Department of Justice men had been raised to $8 a day, and that over 40 per cent of the yearly budget of the department had been spent in investigation of radicals (John Pepper: *Underground Radicalism*, pp. 16-17).

Such a sudden and concerted attack by the government could not help but create confusion and temporary demoralization in the Communist ranks, especially since the movement was so young. The weaker members of the parties were frightened away. Only the most class-conscious, the bravest, and the most convinced revolutionary men and women remained faithful to the cause. These mass persecutions forced the Communist Parties to organize underground in order to escape annihilation. Those who maintain that the communist movement went underground in order to appear picturesque or adventurous are either unaware of the facts or are not interested in the truth. The underground reorganization was a bitter necessity. It was indispensable to protect the nucleus of the movement which had narrowly escaped destruction. The communists publicly declared that they were reorganizing not in order to hide their faces or aims from the masses, but to continue the struggle. As far back as 1922 in their Labor Day manifesto they declared:

"The communists are not a sinister, secret band of conspirators. Our aim, liberation of the workers, the abolition of wage slavery, working class control of industry, and state power, can only be achieved if the great masses of the workers stand with us.

"Workers' rule is only possible when the millions of workers support the communist program. It is an essential feature of the communist program to convince the majority of the workers of the truth of the ideas of communism.

"We do not have a single point in our whole program which we wish to conceal from the millions of workers. In the first communist program ever issued, the founders of scientific communism, Marx and Engels, long ago declared: 'The communists disdain to conceal their aims.'

"We have nothing to conceal from the workers. We once more appeal to the workers to look upon the persecution of the communists as a matter concerning all workers as well.

"The communists are to-day outlawed because the capitalists are planning to outlaw the whole working class . . ." (Pepper: *Loc. cit.,* p. 18).

But the change to an underground existence had a great effect upon the young and as yet weak communist movement. Even before the change its contact with the masses of the workers had not been very broad. Now it was almost entirely isolated from these masses and, of necessity, became a movement of narrow sectarian character, with a revolutionary program, but with very little revolutionary influence among the workers. Both parties recognized the necessity of carrying on open work also, but they lacked the proper organizational means for such activity.

The trade unions and other mass labor organizations were entirely indifferent to the persecutions of the communists, while their reactionary leaders supported the government.

Under the guidance of the Communist International, to which both

Communist Parties had pledged their undivided allegiance, and forced by the conditions of the movement, unity between the two parties was accomplished in May, 1921. The unity convention accepted the name of Communist Party of America for the united party, and the latter's program was adopted as a basis for the new program. The united Communist Party not only renounced the policy of smashing the old conservative trade unions and proclaimed the necessity of working within them in order to carry on communist propaganda and agitation; it also stated that it was its revolutionary duty to save these unions from the destruction into which they were being led by the incorrect policy of the conservative leadership, and to reconstruct them on a new basis by amalgamating them into industrial unions. The communists also declared that they would no longer be satisfied with the mere propagation among the masses of their final aims, such as the overthrow of bourgeois rule, and the establishment of the dictatorship of the proletariat in the form of soviets, but that they would also actively participate in the every-day struggle and would fight in the front ranks against the ruling class for the daily needs of the workers.

On the question of communist work within the trade unions the program of the united Communist Party declared:

"The Communist Party condemns the policy of the revolutionary elements leaving the existing unions. These elements must remain with the large masses of organized workers. The Communists must take an active and leading part in the everyday struggles of the unions. They must carry on a merciless and uncompromising struggle against the social-patriotic and reactionary leaders, criticize them and expose them and drive them out of power. The Communist Party will develop from its ranks the most determined fighters in the labor movement, who through courage, sacrifice, and class-consciousness, will inspire the masses with a spirit of determined struggle and win them over for the proletarian revolution. Only in this way can the disintegration of the unions be prevented, the reactionary leaders ousted from control, the bureaucratic machinery destroyed and replaced by the apparatus of shop delegates, and the trade unions broadened in scope and gradually developed into industrial unions.

"Bearing in mind the necessity of the closest contact of the communists with those workers who have not yet reached a revolutionary understanding, and the intensity of the struggle which requires the closest unity and solidarity of the workers on the economic field, the communists shall not foster artificial division in the labor movement, nor deliberately bring it about. On the contrary, they must use all measures, short of giving up the revolutionary task in the unions, not hesitating to employ strategy, to avoid giving reactionary leaders the pretext to expel them . . ." (*The Communist,* July, 1921).

This new policy meant that the Communists were determined to rid the trade unions of their reactionary leadership and turn them into the organs of class struggle.

The Communist forces were still very weak, even after the unity of both parties. For instance, at the unity convention it was reported that the united party had no more than 12,000 members. This shows that only a very small percentage of the revolutionary socialists who had either left the Socialist Party or had been expelled from it and joined the communist movement had passed through the fire of reaction of 1919-1920 and remained faithful to their ideals.

After its separation from the left wing in 1919, and after the whole party apparatus had passed completely and securely into the hands of the right wing leaders, the Socialist Party rapidly declined, not only in intellectual vigor, but in membership. Before the split, in 1919, the party could boast of 104,822 members, but by 1922 only about 11,000 were left.

MEMBERSHIP OF THE SOCIALIST PARTY FROM THE BEGINNING OF THE WORLD WAR (*American Labor Year Book*, 1923-1924, p. 125)

Year	Members	Year	Members
1914	93,579	1919	104,822
1915	79,374	1920	26,766
1916	83,284	1921	13,484
1917	80,379	1922	11,019
1918	82,344	1923	12,000

At the emergency convention of August 30, 1919, the Socialist Party still declared its desire to unite with the Communist International by admitting the parties of the latter into a "reconstituted Socialist International" composed only of those parties "which declare their strict adherence by word and deed to the principles of the class struggle." It still paraded as a revolutionary organization and played with revolutionary phrases. For instance, in its manifesto, which was adopted after expelling the left wing with the help of the police, among other things, it declared:

"Even in the United States the symptoms of a rebellious spirit in the ranks of the working masses are rapidly multiplying. The widespread and extensive strikes for better labor conditions, the demand of the two million railway workers to control their industry, the sporadic formation of labor parties apparently, though not fundamentally, in opposition to the political parties of the possessing class, are promising indications of a definite tendency on the part of American labor to break away from its reactionary and futile leadership and to join in the great emancipating movement of the more advanced revolutionary workers of the world.

"Recognizing this crucial situation at home and abroad, the Socialist Party of the United States at its first national convention after the war, squarely takes its position with the uncompromising section of the international socialist movement. We unreservedly reject the policy of those Socialists who supported their belligerent capitalist governments on the plea of 'national defense,' and who entered into demoralizing compacts for so-called civil peace with the exploiters of labor during the war and continued a political alliance with them after the war. We, the organized socialists of America, pledge our support to the revolutionary workers of Russia in the maintenance of their Soviet Government, to the radical socialists of Germany, Austria and Hungary in their efforts to establish working-class rule in their countries, and those socialist organizations in England, France, Italy and other countries, who during the war, as after the war, have remained true to the principles of uncompromising international socialism.

"To win the American workers from their ineffective and demoralizing leadership, to educate them to an enlightened understanding of their own class interests, and to train and assist them to organize politically and industrially on class lines in order to effect their emancipation—that is the supreme task confronting the Socialist Party of America."

The manifesto finally concluded: "Long live the international socialist revolution, the only hope of the suffering world!" (*Ibid.*, pp. 413-414). But by 1923 the Socialist Party declared open war on the Communist International, swept aside and forgot entirely its revolutionary phrases of 1919 and in the trade union movement became a tool in the hands of the "reactionary and futile leadership" in its crusade against the communists and other revolutionary workers.

CHAPTER XXX

Period of Militant Labor Struggles, 1921-1927

By crushing the steel strike of 1919-1920 the steel trust opened the way for a general capitalist offensive against the workers. Not without reason did the whole ruling class stand so generously behind the steel trust in its fight.

The National Association of Manufacturers and other employers' organizations raised the cry: "Down with trade unions! Long live the American plan for our factories and industries! Long live the open shop!" This cry was seized by the bourgeois press and spread from coast to coast. Everywhere the employers welcomed it. Eradication of union conditions in the shops and factories, reduction of wages, and destruction of the unions themselves, became a basis for the united front of the ruling class against organized labor, as a reward to the workers for their services in the World War.

Only the workers could not grasp the importance of a united front against their arrogant class enemy. They allowed the capitalists to crush the strikes in the meat-packing and the steel industries. They saw the United Mine Workers go down on their knees before the government and the mine owners, and remained silent. They allowed themselves to be divided and defeated section by section. The employers took advantage of this weakness, and openly and secretly organized their grand offensive which reached its culminating point in 1922.

The conditions were most favorable for the employers' offensive. Firstly, the employers had enriched themselves enormously during and immediately after the war, and did not lack funds for fighting organized labor. Secondly, never before in the history of the United States was the government so completely in the hands of big business, trusts, and corporations, as after the war. Thirdly, by the end of 1920 the army recruited for the war was demobilized and millions of soldiers came back to the factories looking for their old jobs. Then, too, the foreign markets were not clamoring so frantically for our goods, and American exports were being substantially reduced; from $10,170,000,000 worth of exports in 1920-1921 they fell to $6,379,000,000 in 1921-1922. By 1921 a great wave of unemployment swept the country; millions of wage-earners found themselves on the streets. This was the employers' opportunity to reduce the wages of those who were still at work, and to deliver a great blow to the trade unions which during the war had gained strength but now, led by conservative leaders and pursuing the old, craft, opportunistic policy, were helpless in the face of the great industrial depression.

The reduction of wages was general all over the country and in most places reached enormous proportions. In 1921 the New York State Industrial Commission investigated wages in 1,648 establishments and found that they were 20 per cent lower than in 1920. The Wisconsin State Industrial Commission investigated the wages of the workers of 211 concerns, or one third of all the workers in the state, and found that they were 45 per cent lower than in 1920 (Jay Lovestone: *Loc. cit.*, p. 33). Similar cuts had taken place in other parts of the country. In some places the reduction was even greater than in New York and Wisconsin, reaching from 50 to 75 per cent.

But an entirely different situation prevailed as far as the profits of the capitalists were concerned. Although business had decreased, still by reducing wages, the employers had managed to maintain the same high level of returns. If anything, profits had even increased. The profits of the American Telephone and Telegraph Company, for instance, in 1920 amounted to $51,821,215 while in 1921 they reached $54,002,703. The net profits of the American Woolen Company amounted to $4,626,855 in 1920, but in 1921 they increased to $6,006,648. The Atchison, Topeka, and Santa Fe Railroad Company increased its profits from $37,380,590 in 1920 to $41,268,307 in 1921.

The working class found itself in dire straits. Wages were not advancing at the same rate as the cost of living, but there was even imminent danger of their being reduced. The proletarian battle-line had been broken by the bourgeoisie in the defeat of the steel workers and in forcing the communist movement underground.

In 1920 the miners of West Virginia began a struggle to organize into the United Mine Workers. They were met by strong opposition from the mine owners and the government. There were a few open clashes in which many miners lost their lives. The bloody fights in the vicinity of Matewan and Tug River and in Logan and McDowell counties will remain in the history of the labor movement of America as the best proof of how far the bourgeoisie is prepared to go in its struggle against the workers. Martial law was proclaimed in every coal district of West Virginia. All the forces of oppression were concentrated in the state to smash the miners' efforts to organize into a union. Thousands of miners' families were evicted from their homes.

Losing hope of assistance from any source, the railroad switchmen and maintenance-of-way men went on strike, without permission of their leaders, nay, against the will of these leaders. The latter immediately declared the strike illegal and joined hands with the employers to crush it. The Railroad Labor Board, a governmental institution, also branded the strike as illegal, further declaring that it would have nothing to do with an "insurgents' organization." Under such conditions, when the employers, the government, and the labor leaders joined hands against them, the defeat of the workers was assured from the very beginning.

All these events showed that the ruling class was insatiable. Drunk with its early victories it was marching forward bent on destroying every vestige of labor organization. With the dawn of 1922 an era of great industrial storms began.

"Never before had the country witnessed such bitter class conflicts," says Lovestone. "Textile workers, soft stone cutters, granite cutters, miners, and railwaymen were the vanguard of the heroic army of resistance to the employers' wage-cutting and union smashing offensive. Never before in our industrial history have there been such large numbers on strike and never before have the workers remained out for such long periods. Outwardly, these and the many other strikes appear only as disputes over wages or hours of labor. Fundamentally, the strikes of 1922 were far more significant. They were a revolt against the powerful campaign waged by the captains of finance and industry to uproot every vestige of working class organization. The strikers fought these battles primarily to uphold these organizations which they had built up through years of painful struggle" (Lovestone: *Loc. cit.*, p. 12).

The industrial depression, and the detrimental policy of Gompers and the American Federation of Labor of "sitting around the table with the employers and talking things over" had weakened the labor unions and their resistance to the attacks of the ruling class. On the eve of the great capitalist offensive the decline in union membership was tragic. The International Seamen's Union from 115,000 members in 1920 was reduced to 50,000 by 1921. The American Federation of Labor lost 700,000 members. The Brotherhood of Maintenance-of-Way Men lost 125,000 members (*Ibid.*, p. 35).

On the other hand, the employers were steadily organizing their assault. The National Association of Manufacturers and the United States Chamber of Commerce acted as open organizations, while the National Open Shop Association carried on its work secretly. The latter attended to the corruption of the press, church, pulpit, and politicians, and to the supplying of scabs, spies, and gunmen to the manufacturers. Facts have been disclosed which prove that these employers' organizations in their fight against the unions maintained close contact with the United States army and the American Legion. Wherever strikes took place, wherever fights occurred, these forces of "law and order," the soldiers and the legionaires, were used to protect the scabs and the masters' property.

In this offensive the capitalists did not hide their aims and desires. They declared openly that they intended to wipe the unions out of American industry. The United States Chamber of Commerce adopted the following resolution by a vote of 1,676 against four:

"The right of open shop operation, that is the right of the employer and employee to enter into and to determine the conditions of employment relations with each other, *is an essential part of the individual right of contract possessed by each of the parties"* (*Ibid.,* p. 17).

William H. Barr, president of the National Founders' Association, declared on October 15, 1919:

"A change has been brought about by the determination of men to free themselves from the unsound and unnatural control so imposed upon them. To-day, that determination is manifest in the open-shop movement. Its progress is a matter of economy to those who began it; of consolation to those engaged in industry; and a stimulant to the patriotism of every one. A partial, but careful survey of irresistible activities in behalf of the open-shop shows that 540 organizations in 247 cities of 44 states are engaged in promoting this American principle in employment relations. A total of 23 national industrial associations are included in these agencies. In addition, 1,665 local chambers of commerce are also pledged to the principle of the open-shop."

Later, on January 16, 1921, J. Philip Bird, general manager of the National Association of Manufacturers, stated:

"More than 500 organizations in 250 cities have now endorsed the open-shop plan and prominent manufacturers declare they could not stem the tide if they wished" (*Ibid.,* p. 18).

Judge Gary, chairman of the United States Steel Corporation which had smashed the strike of 1919-1920 with blood and fire, had the following to say on the open-shop at a meeting of the stockholders of the corporation on April 18, 1921:

"I believe they [the labor unions] may have been justified in the long past, for I think the workmen were not always treated justly; that because of their lack of experience or otherwise they were unable to protect themselves; and therefore needed the assistance of outsiders in order to secure their rights.

"But whatever may have been the conditions of employment in the long past, and whatever may have been the results of unionism, concerning which there is at least much uncertainty, there is, at present, in the opinion of the large majority of both employers and employees, no necessity for labor unions; and that no benefit nor advantage through them will accrue to any one except the union leaders.

"But still our opinion is that the existence and conduct of labor unions, in this country at least, are inimical to the best interests of the employees, the employers, and the general public" (*Ibid.,* p. 20).

On November 23, 1920, the American Employers' Open-Shop Association sent a communication to the employers of various cities, inviting them to join the association and promising:

"1. Should you be threatened with a labor controversy or strike, you can immediately get in touch with us and we will handle that situation for you.

"2. Should you want *an undercover man on the inside* among your employees, we will also furnish you such a man, and you will receive daily reports on what is going on.

"3. In the event of trouble, we will replace any man that may strike against you.

"4. We establish welfare clubs in your plant from which you derive a lot of benefit; and all manufacturers are alive to this issue."

In another circular the Open-Shop Association asks that its work be kept a great secret:

"This work must be clothed with the utmost secrecy, as we have found that publicity usually defeats our purposes. For this reason you can feel sure that we will treat the matter in strict confidence" (*Ibid.*, pp. 21-23).

And so on. The forces of the ruling class were well organized and trained for the attack.

On May 1, 1921, the International Typographical Union declared a strike which lasted a year and which cost $10,000,000. The result was not a complete victory for the union, nevertheless it did to a certain degree stem the employers' attempt to destroy union conditions.

On May 5, 1921, the workers of the packing industry went out to protect their union and to defeat a reduction of wages. In order to show the public their "fairness" to their men the owners of the packing industry organized "company unions" under the control of the bosses and allowed them to vote on the question of whether the workers would agree to a reduction in wages or not. Naturally, the unions controlled by the bosses did decide in favor of the reduction of 8½ cents an hour. This time the government's conciliation board decided not to approve the reduction, and demanded that both sides submit the question to arbitration. The workers quickly accepted this demand of the government, but the latter would not move a finger to compel the employers as well to submit to arbitration. On the contrary, it clubbed and arrested the workers who had accepted its decision! The strike was long and bitter. It was lost—crushed by the united forces of the employers and the government.

In August, 1921, the New England textile employers reduced wages by 20 per cent. Having no organization, the workers had to give in. Only six months later, in January, 1922, another reduction was declared, this time of 22½ per cent. This was too much! A strike began on January 22, 1922, in the Pawtucket Valley and spread like wildfire to the other textile districts of New England, embracing Maine, New Hampshire, Vermont, Rhode Island, and Massachusetts. Not less than 100,000 workers in the cotton mills joined in the fight against the wage reduction and the attempt to lengthen the working hours from 48 to 54 weekly.

Even before the reductions took place the wages of the workers were miserable, and when they were cut by 42½ per cent there was little left of them. According to the figures of the American Cotton Manufacturers' Association itself, the following were the weekly wage scales in the North and South in June, 1921:

Grade of Worker	North	South
Skilled male	$21.78	$16.65
Unskilled male	18.08	10.99
Composite	18.71	13.99
Women	15.61	11.65

The average weekly wage of the common laborer in the North was $15, semi-skilled and skilled labor, $17 to $18. It can be readily seen that in view of the high cost of living these wages were far from sufficient to enable the workers to make both ends meet.

The employers were well prepared to meet the revolt. They had organized in advance and armed a great force of scabs and mercenaries from the slums of the large cities. The government, as usual, lined up with the employers.

"With their enormous wealth they [the employers] controlled the state institutions," says W. E. Vinyarn, "and quickly the militia was thrown into the strike areas with instructions to shoot to kill. Private armies were also recruited, and the mills became small fortresses, with machine guns on the roofs, and thugs and gunmen at every turn. Police were armed with shotguns. All this array of millions and of guns was pitted against the soup-kitchens and solidarity of the striking cotton workers. The guns killed several of the strikers, but solidarity kept the mills closed" (*Labor Herald,* April, 1922, pp. 9-10).

The courts issued vicious injunctions taking from the strikers the right not only to picket the mills but even to sit on their own porches when the scabs were passing by on their way to or from work. In some places the strikers were even prohibited from looking through their windows at the scabs or in the direction of the mills.

Nevertheless, despite this terror, despite the lack of organization, the workers' spirit forced a compromise. The employers retracted their last reduction, first at Lawrence, Mass., then in other cities. The strike ended on September 1, 1922, after more than seven bitter months.

It is true that in some cities the strikers were completely defeated and went back to work for reduced wages; but in most places they won concessions and made the first successful stand against the capitalist offensive.

During the strike there were not less than a dozen small unions in the industry, each with its own program and machinery of petty officials. The leaders of each of these unions wanted to head the strike and to drive the other leaders into the background. Inevitably, a fight ensued between the United Textile Workers, the One Big Union, the Amalgamated Textile Workers of America, the Federation of the Textile Workers, and others. Instead of a united fight against the employers the leaders of these unions were fighting among themselves like cats in a bag and criminally dividing the workers.

On April 1, 1922, 600,000 miners left the pits in protest against the attempt of the coal barons to reduce wages. Probably never before had the miners responded with such unanimity to the call to quit work. The United Mine Workers had about 500,000 members, and about 100,000 unorganized miners of West Virginia and Western Pennsylvania joined in the struggle.

PERIOD OF MILITANT LABOR STRUGGLES 299

In 1920, upon the advice of the government, a two year contract had been signed between the union and the mine owners which was to end on April 1, 1922. But in that contract it was stated that before April 1 the union and the employers should come together and try to renew the contract. As the date drew near the union invited the owners to negotiate, but the latter refused and declared a wage reduction of from 25 to 35 per cent. This was the signal for a general strike.

The employers and the government were anxious to get the miners into a fight. First of all, there were millions of men out of work who could be used to break the strike. Secondly, there was a great surplus of coal on which the owners wished to keep up the price. All factors in the situation were considered, and the owners decided to pay no attention to the agreement of 1920 but refused to deal with the union. The bourgeois government, which attacks the workers ruthlessly if they even dream of violating a contract, now openly declared:

"The government's position has long been known to be that sooner or later there would have to be a show-down in the mine fields. *Its attitude is that if a strike must be, it must be, and the sooner the issue is disposed of, the better*" (Lovestone: *Loc. cit.*, p. 76).

When it was apparent that the coal strike was inevitable, Governor Sproul of Pennsylvania called a conference of all the sheriffs of the state and instructed them "to suppress revolts before they start." On April 1, 1922, the New York *Times* reported that the

"Police authority has been vested in the constabulary and the state is taking no chances of being caught unprepared. Scattered through the anthracite belt are squads of the state police who are prepared for any emergency. They are equipped with riot clubs and well trained horses, and pistols and machine guns are at their command. These squads will coöperate with the sheriffs of the different counties, and there has been fair warning that any disturbance of the peace will be strenuously dealt with. There are numbers of deputy sheriffs in readiness for any call."

On the same day reports appeared that guns and munitions were being shifted in great quantity from the southern part of Ohio to the national guard which had promised to help the owners crush the strike. In West Virginia constables were being drilled for strike duty many weeks in advance, and a federal judge issued an injunction against the United Mine Workers making it practically illegal to strike in the state. On June 16, it was reported from Brownsville, Pa., that 1,200 mounted police had attacked 8,000 miners on parade and many of the latter were wounded.

Governor Sproul of Pennsylvania sent 1,100 soldiers into the bituminous fields of western Pennsylvania to guard the army of men that was to flock back to the mines, but the army did not flock.

This was the response of the government to the miners whose leaders had declared in 1919: *"We cannot fight our government."*

In the face of this attempt of mine owners and government to reduce wages, the miners presented their demands, the most important of which were a 20 per cent raise in wages and a single agreement for both bituminous and anthracite fields. This last demand was fundamental, for through separate agreements for anthracite and bituminous fields, terminating at different periods, the workers are divided, making impossible a general strike without which victory for them is unattainable.

The same forces that had been used against the steel workers in 1919-1920 were now employed against the miners. In every city and town affected by the strike practical martial law was proclaimed, a naked and brutal dictatorship of the capitalists was inaugurated. Men, women and children of the strikers were attacked, terrorized, and beaten.

The mine owners attempted to fill the mines with strike-breakers; this resulted in open clashes. The most important of these occurred near Herrin, Ill. Between the towns of Marion and Herrin there is a strip-mine operated by the Southern Illinois Coal Company. The company attempted to open the mine with strikebreakers and gunmen brought from the slums of Chicago and thus break the front of the miners. On June 10, professional scabs were armed and taken into the mine, and others were left to guard the workings from attack by the miners. On June 21st a group of unarmed strikers were approaching the mine to persuade the strikebreakers and operators to abandon work as it might lead to a serious situation. But as they neared the mine, the superintendent and his hired gunmen opened fire and two unionists were killed.

Early next morning hundreds of miners from all corners of the county marched on the mine to even scores with the murderers of the two miners. The mine was surrounded. The guards again began to shoot, but now the situation was different for the miners were prepared for all eventualities. When the battle was over, 19 of the gunmen were dead, others were beaten and hustled from the vicinity. The coroner's jury rendered the following verdict:

"We, the jury, find that the deaths were due to the acts, direct and indirect, of the officials of the Southern Illinois Coal Company. We recommend that investigation be conducted for the purpose of fixing the blame upon the individuals responsible."

"Revenge!" cried the capitalists all over the country. The bourgeois press began a savage campaign against the workers, and clamored for merciless retribution. The Illinois Chamber of Commerce collected $100,000 from its members for the campaign. Two hundred and fourteen strikers were arrested and indicted for murder. President Harding officially congratulated the chamber of commerce in a telegram on August 22 to "My Dear Mr. Hamlin," its spokesman, saying:

"I note with genuine interest the activities of your association to see that justice is done in Williamson County. . . . It is a gratifying thing to know

PERIOD OF MILITANT LABOR STRUGGLES 301

that there is a determination that justice shall be done. . . . There is of course a conscience in Illinois which will not tolerate such a disgraceful thing. It will be very pleasing to me and reassuring to the whole country to know that this conscience is finding expression" (*Ibid.*, pp. 121-122).

But the miners of Illinois were not dismayed by this hue and cry of the bourgeoisie. They had been attacked with guns and they had defended themselves with the same weapons. The enemies of labor could not find a jury to convict their intended victims. The employers' guilt was too clear to hide.

President Harding wanted to break the strike with government troops, but failed. On July 18, Harding appealed to 28 state governors requesting them to urge the mine owners to open their mines with such men as were willing to work, promising them full protection. The operators rejoiced at this generosity and were sure they would this time put an end to the United Mine Workers' Union. Governor Sproul sent 1,100 soldiers, Governor McCray of Indiana sent 1,000, and the governors of other states did the same in their efforts to live up to Harding's appeal. But the miners declared, "You cannot dig coal with bayonets." The union leaders who in 1919 had declared "we won't fight our government" did not again dare to raise the white flag in 1922. Six hundred thousand miners were now determined to fight to the bitter end. The strike remained effective 100 per cent.

Months passed and no end of the strike was in sight. Thousands of miners' families began to feel the pinch of starvation. The wonderful militant spirit of the strikers began to wane. Now came the time for John L. Lewis, president of the United Mine Workers, to play his treacherous rôle. Instead of encouraging the miners to continue the fight, instead of calling the pump men out on strike and thus forcing the owners either to risk the destruction of their property or concede the demands of their workers, Lewis got in touch with the government which was trying to break the strike with machine guns, and began to talk about the troubles of the coal industry, about its "over-development." Finally, on August 15, he proposed a separate agreement with the bituminous coal owners. The latter accepted Lewis's proposal and signed an agreement terminating on March 31, 1923.

The anthracite miners were now left to fight the operators alone. On September 3 Lewis invited the anthracite owners to a conference, promising that the union would not insist on its demand for higher wages or a single agreement for both fields. The anthracite coal barons were willing to sign an agreement ending on August 31, 1923, five months after the bituminous agreement.

In this long and bitter struggle the miners won only to the extent of not submitting to a reduction in wages. On the other hand, thanks to the treachery of their leaders, they lost the struggle against separate agreements, terminating at two different periods. This meant continued division of the miners' army. It was a great victory for the coal barons, for, after defeating one section of the miners, they could concentrate all their forces against the other.

Another treachery of the miners' leaders was their desertion of the men in West Virginia and western Pennsylvania. About 100,000 unorganized miners of these two states had joined hands with their union brothers in the strike. They hoped that they would be taken into the United Mine Workers and have their conditions improved. This solidarity of the miners of West Virginia and western Pennsylvania was the factor which tipped the scales in favor of the union. They should not have been left alone to continue a hopeless fight. But the union leaders "forgot" these men entirely when they made the agreement with the bituminous coal operators. The unorganized miners continued the fight heroically; but after a few months their sufferings became unbearable. Finally, in order to put the finishing touch to his treachery, Lewis told the miners of Somerset and Fayette counties, Pennsylvania, to go back to work immediately if they did not wish the support of the union to be entirely cut off. The men submitted.

This desertion of the West Virginia and western Pennsylvania miners severely affected not only these men, but the entire United Mine Workers. These miners are still unorganized. Victory in the strike would have drawn them into the organization and introduced unionism into those fields, which have always been effectively used against the organized miners. Responsibility for any danger to the union which arises from the existence of about 200,000 miners outside of the fold must fall upon the national leaders of the miners' union.

It is almost impossible to describe the hardships of these deserted miners. The New York Municipal Investigating Committee has the following to say on this question:

"Finally, these men, already harassed and unable to earn a wage to live, as distinct from a living wage, left their work when their existing insufficient incomes were slashed and a hope for improved conditions for themselves and their babies was flatly denied them.

"Scores of these miners, poverty-stricken and unable to go through the coming winter unless help was given them, poured out such tales of suffering and mistreatment as would melt any heart except that in the stony bosom of a coal baron. We have seen in the tents, in the hencoops, and in the stables where the miners and their families sought shelter after having been summarily evicted and driven from their homes by the coal and iron police, hungry babies and women whose feet were bare and bleeding and whose limbs were thinly clad. . . .

"No Egyptian pharaoh, rearing for his glory a towering monument, ever drove men harder than these miners were driven. No czar was ever more autocratic than these predatory interests of big business" (Lovestone: *Loc. cit.*, p. 74).

PERIOD OF MILITANT LABOR STRUGGLES 303

The third strike of great importance in this period was the railway shopmen's strike of 1922, in which about 500,000 men were involved.

During the war the railroads had been put under government control in order to furnish efficient transportation of war necessaries. At the close of hostilities the railroads were again turned over to private control, and a Railroad Labor Board, composed of representatives of the companies, the trade unions, and the "public" was set up for the purpose of maintaining peace between the workers and their employers. In war time, when the capitalists needed uninterrupted transportation, concessions were made to the railway employees, Congress passed the basic eight-hour law, wages were raised, the workers were allowed to organize into trade unions, and an agreement was made establishing uniform conditions on all railroads throughout the country. As in all other industries, as soon as the war stopped the railroad companies began to take back all concessions and to destroy the unions.

On March 19, 1921, the companies demanded from the Railroad Labor Board the right to reduce wages. The board agreed, and wages were reduced, on the average 12 per cent. This gave the companies about $400,000,000 extra annual profit. On April 14, 1921, the board abrogated the national agreement, thus taking away from the workers the conditions of employment which they had won by a long struggle. Then followed reductions in wages one after another. The resulting yearly loss to the workers in wages alone was:

Shop crafts	$371,817,996
Maintenance-of-way employees	315,803,835
Clerks and freight handlers	146,699,147
Signalmen	10,373,168
Stationary firemen and oilers	2,145,235
Other railway employees	96,352,490
Total loss wage	$943,191,871

These cuts affected mainly the lower strata, the unskilled and semi-skilled workers. The skilled crafts, such as engineers, firemen, conductors, and switchmen, suffered much less. This difference in treatment by the railroad companies and the government was clever tactics; it was a conscious plan to divide the workers. If the same reductions had been made throughout, the result would have been a general railroad strike, which neither the companies nor the government desired. They well understood the value of the policy, "Divide and rule."

Finally, on July 1, 1922, 400,000 railway shopmen joined ranks against their enemies. The strike was declared by the following six crafts: The International Brotherhood of Blacksmiths; International Alliance of Amalgamated Sheet Metal Workers; International Brotherhood of Boilermakers, Iron Ship Builders and Helpers of America; Brotherhood of Railway Carmen of America; International Association of Machinists; and International Brotherhood of Electrical Workers. These last six unions constituted the Federated Shop Crafts in the Railway Employees' Department of the American Federation of Labor. Within a few days these workers were joined by thousands of clerks and maintenance-of-way men, plumbers, freight handlers, molders, common laborers, and truckers, bringing the number of workers involved close to the 500,000 mark.

In addition to the usual array of troops and professional strikebreakers, university and college students were recruited by the thousand for strikebreaking duties. The railroad companies again showed their ability to use the "democratic" government for the protection of their interests. When on June 27 the American Federation of Labor informed the Association of Railway Executives that unless something was done immediately the strike was inevitable, De Witt Cuyler, president of the association, immediately replied:

"You demand that we accept your decision and reject that of the Labor Board. . . . To submit now to your demands . . . would be to recognize your power and authority as greater than that of the government. . . . If you strike it will be against an order of a governmental tribunal—it will be a strike against the government of the United States."

On July 10, 1922, the New York *World* in big headlines printed the following:

"Anticipating disorder when the railroad shops of the country open to-day for return of such strikers as may wish to save their seniority and pension rights and for new employees, the authorities of five states have mobilized their national guard. The sixth, Illinois, with 300 men already on strike duty in Clinton, is practically in a state of mobilization, with militiamen in camps or on waiting order at many points. The five states mobilizing are California, Indiana, Missouri, Mississippi, and Kansas."

And on July 11 we were informed that:

"In many of those places where outbreaks or rioting were feared the *shops opened under protection of national guardsmen's guns*. In other places United States marshals were on hand to preserve the peace and protect life and company property, and, so far as the record shows, in each place the authority of the troops or marshals was respected.

"Attorney-General Daugherty, after a conference with President Harding, announced he had authorized the appointment of deputy marshals at various points in the West and Southwest and would continue to do so 'whenever justified and required.'

" 'Law and order,' read the Attorney-General's statement, 'must be preserved, life and property protected. Transportation of the mails must not be interfered with and interstate commerce must not be interrupted. The President has been fully advised and has the situation fully in hand.' "

As soon as the strike began the chairman of the Railroad Labor Board announced that those who had struck were no longer railroad employees. Later the majority of the board adopted a resolution urging the railroad companies to open their shops with scabs and to organize in place of the existing unions new ones, composed only of the scabs and the "desirable" railroad workers. On July 11 President Harding issued a proclamation instructing the authorities to maintain the movement of trains and approving the recruiting of strikebreakers. Thus the government took upon itself the responsibility of defeating the strike. In almost every important railroad center what amounted to martial law was declared. Without counting the government's expenses, the railroad companies alone spent ten of millions of dollars in breaking the strike. Evans Clark of the Labor Bureau computed that:

"The normal expense of guarding railroad property is about $1,000,000 a month which goes in wages to private policemen. In July Class I roads spent $6,000,000 in wages to special officers. In August they spent $7,500,000 and in September $5,700,000. The average for the three months was 540 per cent more than the normal amount . . ." (*Nation*, December 27, 1922, p. 715).

On August 1 Attorney-General Daugherty secured an injunction for the companies.

"The strikers were forbidden to call those who robbed them of their jobs 'strikebreakers.' The order not only completely shut up the workers and prevented the leaders from issuing any orders by word of mouth or pen to the workers, but it also completely tied up all union funds."

Elsewhere Daugherty declared:

"So long and to the extent that I can speak for the government of the United States, I will use the power of the government within my control to prevent the labor unions of the country from destroying the open shop. . . .

"There comes a time in the history of all nations when the people must be advised whether they have a government or not.

"No union or combination of unions can, under the law, dictate to the American union. When the unions claim the right to dictate to the government and to dominate the American people and deprive the . . . people of the necessities of life, then the government will destroy the unions, for the government of the United States is supreme and must endure."

Daugherty's words were true: The capitalist state came out of the struggle victorious, the strike was crushed, and the shopmen's unions were almost entirely exterminated. On September 13, 1922, an agreement was reached by which the reduction of wages was accepted, the strikebreakers kept their places, and the shopmen lost their seniority rights. The workers therefore lost everything. But even this vicious agreement was signed by only a few companies. About half of the strikers went back to work, and about 200,000 of them remained to continue the struggle. Some later found employment in other industries, others went back to work for the same companies without any agreement, helpless in the hands of their employers. The strike was officially declared off on February 1, 1925, though it had been crushed long before.

The familiar reasons for the failure of the strike were all present. First of all, there was the determination of the government and the railroad companies to break the strike and destroy the shopmen's unions regardless of cost. Second, the workers lacked organizational unity, being divided into seven or more organizations. Third, the American Federation of Labor refused full support to the strike. From every corner of the country came hundreds of resolutions from its affiliated unions, demanding a general strike for the protection of the railroad workers, but the leaders of the Federation absolutely refused to yield to this wholesale demand of the masses and thus allowed the railroad companies a free hand. The fourth, and probably most important reason, was the treachery of the leaders of the other railroad brotherhoods. The Brotherhood of Maintenance-of-Way Employees decided by referendum vote to strike, but when the designated hour arrived, E. F. Grable, grand president of the brotherhood, refused to issue the call. He even went further: On July 2, 1922, a correspondent of the New York *World* reported:

"Last night he was busy in Detroit ordering the men who had quit to return to work and instructing the heads of other system unions not to permit their men to quit. 'We have promised the Railroad Labor Board that we would not quit now,' he said, 'and every promise we made will be kept.'"

It is true that the membership of the Maintenance-of-Way Employees revolted against their traitorous chief, and Grable was thrown out of his position at the next convention. But the damage had been done.

The leaders of the other railroad brotherhoods not affiliated with the American Federation of Labor, namely, the engineers, conductors, firemen, and trainmen, played the same rôle as Grable, by openly helping to crush the shopmen's strike. They not only refused to call out their men, but when the latter had quit their posts in many places, and refused to risk their lives for the sake of the companies, these leaders peremptorily ordered the members of their brotherhoods back to work or face being ousted from the organization. In other places the members of the brotherhoods refused to work when they saw that they were constantly confronted by armed soldiers, cossacks, and strikebreakers, but again they were told by their leaders to go back to work or suffer expulsion from the union. This dastardly action of the leaders of the brotherhoods was greatly appreciated by the capitalists. For instance, the *Wall Street Journal* on October 17 declared:

"It is no paradox to say that their inability to stand shoulder to shoulder throughout the strike was the most fortunate thing that could have happened, first for the country at large and eventually for the investors in railroads."

PERIOD OF MILITANT LABOR STRUGGLES

Craft unionism divided the workers of the railroads and played directly into the hands of the ruling class.

"In the struggle only seven of the 16 railway unions struck," Lovestone says. "When compared with the solidarity of the capitalists the collapse of craft unionism is appalling. Against this divided front of the workers the capitalists on the railways presented a mighty compactness of organization unrivaled by the employers in any other industry" (*Ibid.*, p. 179).

The loss of this great strike made concerted action of the railroad workers impossible for a long time to come. The shopmen's unions were almost entirely wiped out, and in their places company unions were formed, which now seriously threaten all labor organizations on the railroads.

Besides these gigantic, bitter struggles of the textile workers, miners, and railway shopmen, many other important battles were fought by labor in this period. On November 14, 1921, the International Ladies' Garment Workers' Union declared a general strike in New York City which involved 55,000 workers and lasted for nine weeks. It ended with a victory for the workers.

On June 15, 1922, 10,000 workers in the children's clothing industry of New York went on strike under the leadership of the Amalgamated Clothing Workers of America. The struggle lasted a month and the workers won. Forty thousand members of the same Amalgamated union in the men's clothing industry in New York City went out on June 21, 1922, to compel the employers to maintain union conditions in the shops. After two weeks' fighting the employers submitted.

The Industrial Workers of the World, during this capitalist offensive, were living through a great crisis, probably the greatest in their existence. Persecution of I. W. W. members had not stopped since the war. Many of the most active were in jail all over the country. Nevertheless, the greatest defeat of the I. W. W. came from within. These persecutions began to react on the leaders of the movement, until the convention of 1920 rejected any use of force in the struggle with the ruling class. Among other things, the convention declared that the I. W. W. "does not now, and never has believed in or advocated either destruction or violence as a means of accomplishing industrial reform," firstly, because this reform can never be accomplished by such means; secondly, industrial history has "taught us" that as soon as the strikers employ force and unlawful means, the government immediately turns its forces against them and the strike is crushed; thirdly, these tactics destroy the tendency for constructive work to which the organization is dedicated. This declaration was an indication of ideological bankruptcy and a surrender to opportunism. Instead of fighting the ruling class, the Industrial Workers of the World accepted as their main object "constructive work" in the capitalist system, or "forming the structure of the new society within the shell of the old."

It is true that the period of 1920-1923 witnessed the greatest and most bitter industrial conflicts; it is also true that the masses of workers demonstrated greater endurance and solidarity than ever before; and, finally, it is true that the great offensive of the ruling class was to a certain degree checked. Nevertheless, taking the situation as a whole, the workers of this country received a terrific blow from the bourgeoisie. Wages were mercilessly reduced; almost everywhere union conditions won only after many years of hard struggles were wiped out; and worst of all, in many industries the trade unions were almost entirely destroyed, while in others they were so weakened that they were left helpless to protect the most elementary interests of their members. This is clearly shown by the loss of union membership. The American Federation of Labor had 4,078,740 members in 1920, and by the end of 1923 there were only 2,926,468. The same is true concerning the independent unions. For example, the Amalgamated Clothing Workers of America was reduced from about 200,000 members to a little over 100,000.

The strike of the Passaic textile workers in 1926 was the outstanding event in the labor movement of this period. It attracted the attention of the entire country and became an expression of the revolt of unorganized and greatly exploited workers. For the first time in the history of this country a strike was conducted on a large scale under communist leadership.

Passaic, N. J., is a typical textile town. The owners of the textile factories are also owners of most of the town and its institutions. The pay of the textile workers is meager, their life is a tale of privation. Before the strike 22 per cent of the workers received wages between $10 and $15 per week, 33 per cent received between $15 and $20 per week, 23 per cent received between $20 and $25 per week, the remainder receiving either less than $10 or over $25 per week. The low wages have forced hundreds of mothers with large families and their little children into the factories.

On October 5, 1925, the mill-owners made a 10 per cent cut in the wages of the workers. This wage slash meant an end to the patience of the workers. The communists were in the meantime carrying on the work of organization and agitation among the textile operators. A United Front Committee was formed in the Botany mill. By January, 1926, 1,000 workers joined the union. On January 25, a committee went to the owners of the mill to present the demand of the workers for the return of their former wages. The answer was the discharge from work of the members of the committee. Immediately the workers of the Botany mill, about 6,000 strong, went on strike. Before the week was over, about 3,000 workers of the Garfield mill and the Passaic Spinning

Co. joined the Botany strikers. A few days later other factories went on strike until the numbers reached about 16,000 and the entire textile industry of Passaic was at a standstill.

Now the workers, under the leadership of the United Front Committee, no longer talked about the return of slashed wages but they presented their own demands which were: (1) A 10 per cent increase over the old wage scale; (2) return of money taken from the wage cut; (3) time and a half for overtime; (4) a forty-hour week; (5) decent sanitary conditions; (6) no discrimination against union workers; and (7) recognition of the union.

Mass demonstrations and mass picketing were organized on a scale never heard of before in the labor movement. Men, women and children marched by thousands along the streets and before the factories with the song of class solidarity on their lips. The brutality of the police knew no bounds. Firemen and gas bombs were used freely to smash the picket lines. Under the name of the "Citizens' Committee" an army of thugs and terrorists was mobilized to help the employers smash the strike. But no amount of terrorism would frighten the strikers under the militant communist leadership.

A relief campaign was organized on a large scale and successfully conducted. An appeal for financial assistance to the Passaic strikers reached practically every nook and corner of the country. The response was tremendous. Donations of money, clothing, food and all sorts of necessities began to pour in. Several kitchens were organized which fed thousands of workers' children daily.

The aim of the United Front Committee was to organize the unorganized, to join the main stream of the American labor movement, that is, to affiliate with the American Federation of Labor through the United Textile Workers, to fight for the amalgamation of all existing organizations in the textile industry, and to win the demands of the workers. The slogan was: "The united front of the workers against the united front of the bosses."

The strikers immediately expressed their desire to join the American Federation of Labor. In their letter to the Executive Council of the Federation they declared:

"The step taken by the last convention of the American Federation of Labor in directing the Executive Council to take energetic steps to organize the textile workers throughout the country is most significant and important. In appreciation of this, we call upon the Executive Council of the American Federation of Labor, in line with this decision to use its experience, prestige and power to establish the unity of all existing labor organizations in the textile industry in a campaign to end wage cuts and organize the industry. The United Front Committee of Textile Workers of Passaic pledges its wholehearted support to any move towards that end which will be initiated by the Executive Council. We pledge ourselves that if such a move is made, we will do everything in our power to achieve such unity through the American Federation of Labor. Never before in the history of the textile industry were conditions so ripe for the organization of the workers.

"We most sincerely and earnestly hope that the Executive Council will consider this proposal in the spirit in which it is made.

"The United Front Committee of Textile Workers is not a dual organization. It does not desire to set up an organization distinct and apart from the American Federation of Labor. We will be the first to hail enthusiastically any proposal that the American Federation of Labor will make to establish unity in order to combat the intolerable conditions that are forced upon the workers and to organize the industry."

In answer to this appeal of the strikers a statement appeared in the daily press made by the Executive Council of the Federation, then in session in Cincinnati, in which, among other slanderous attacks upon the strikers, the officials declared:

"Facts disclose that the so-called 'United Front Committee' which organized and is carrying on a strike in Passaic, N. J., has no relationship to the American Federation of Labor. The leaders of the United Front Committee are prominently identified with the communistic movement in the United States. It is reasonable to conclude, because of their relationship to the Communist Party, that they are interested in advancing the cause of communism. . . .

"The membership of organized labor should not contribute funds to be used for the purpose of advancing the cause of a dual organization or to pay the salaries of Communist leaders who are seeking the destruction of the American Federation of Labor and the substitution of a communistic organization in its stead."

This was a vicious attack upon the strike. It was a weapon in the hands of the bosses to smash the strike and the latter exploited it to the greatest extent. They declared that they would have nothing to do with the organization which has been condemned by the American Federation of Labor as a dual organization and whose aim it is to overthrow the government. In their answer to the statement of the Executive Council the strikers repudiated the charges and once more expressed their willingness to join the Federation. They pointed out that the "committee was elected by the committee conducting this strike to meet with a committee of the United Textile Workers to enter into arrangements for complete affiliation. These negotiations were blocked by the action of Mr. McMahon, President of the United Textile Workers, who declared that until the strike was ended, no action could be taken along these lines."

Great mass pressure was brought against the leaders of the American Federation of Labor who attacked the strikers, at the same time that they were waging a desperate fight against the mill owners. Finally, these leaders began to change their attitude and expressed their willingness to accept the textile workers into the Federation, provided Albert Weisbord, a communist and the leader of the strike, be eliminated from the strike leadership. Because the communists had no other desire than to win the strike and bring the textile workers into the main stream of the American labor movement and would not do anything to give a pretext to the leaders of the Federation to sabotage the strike, Weisbord voluntarily withdrew from the strike leadership, leaving in his place trained and faithful leaders to continue his work.

After this pretext was taken away from the Federation leaders, there was nothing else left for them to do, but to accept the Passaic workers into the United Textile Workers, which is affiliated with the Federation, and thus Local 1603 of the U. T. W. of A. was born. Now, being part of the main body of the labor movement, the workers plunged themselves into the struggle with renewed energy and enthusiasm.

The mill owners who expressed their readiness before to settle the strike with the conservative United Textile Workers, now that the workers were part of the U. T. W. (and the latter proposed to open up negotiations), declared, "as far as we are concerned the strike is over," and that they would not deal with the strikers. They started a new offensive against the workers. Twenty-one strikers were arrested and charged with bombing a strikebreaker's home. The third degree was used to force confessions from the arrested workers and they were held incommunicado. Then their bail was set up, amounting to about $400,-000. Some of them are still waiting for trial.

After a few more weeks of bitter struggle, on December 13, 1926, 321 days after the strike began, the Botany mill owners capitulated to the union and settled on the following terms:

(1) Right of workers to organize in a legitimate organization; (2) if a grievance should arise, the right of collective bargaining; (3) closed shop not demanded; (4) if any other demand made, not agreed on by both parties, the workers to continue working and the question to be arbitrated between these parties: Mill—Workers—Third Party; (5) help taken back without discrimination; (6) no outside help employed after date of settlement until strikers reemployed.

The other companies fell in line and made similar settlements with their workers.

This settlement was not a hundred per cent victory for the workers; nevertheless, it was a victory.

The Passaic strike teaches us many important lessons. It shows that it is possible to organize the unorganized workers despite the bitterest resistance of the employers and the government; it shows that the workers under militant leadership are willing to go through the greatest suffering and make the greatest sacrifices in the fight against their employers and that the only effective way to fight them is to organize a united front of the workers against the united front of the bosses. In this strike we saw communist leadership in action. Those who followed closely the Passaic strike and were interested in its favorable outcome had nothing but praise and admiration for this leadership. It fought bravely, always in the front ranks of the battle. It unloosed latent forces of the workers and organized them for action, effectively overcoming every difficulty, defeating the most brutal and naked police terrorism and out-maneuvering the enemy at every point of the struggle. It rallied the greatest mass support to a local strike on a scale unknown before in this country.

The Sacco and Vanzetti case overshadowed all other events of the last few years in America and reëchoed throughout the world. The two Italian workers were put to death in the electric chair in Boston, on August 23, 1927.

Nicola Sacco was born in 1891 in Terremoggiore, Italy. He came to America in 1908, where he spent most of his time as a worker in the shoe factories. Bartolomeo Vanzetti was born in 1888 in Villa Falletto, Italy. In 1908 he came to America and worked at various trades.

Both Sacco and Vanzetti soon became agitators and organizers. They belonged to that section of the working class which feels the burden of the capitalist system and fights against it. They were schooled in actual struggles of the workers. As Vanzetti put it: "I learned that class-consciousness was not a phrase invented by propagandists, but was real, vital force, and that those who felt its significance were no longer beasts of burden but human beings" (Eugene Lyons: *Life and Death of Sacco and Vanzetti*).

In New England we find two major industries—the shoe industry and the textile industry. In both of them hundreds of thousands of workers are oppressed and exploited. They are unorganized. They are forced to work—when there is work—long hours for small pay. Both of these industries are continually threatened with crises and unemployment. The textile industry of New England is on the decline. It feels very keenly the competition with textile factories in the South.

The discontent among the shoe and textile workers of New England is very great. From time to time they revolt and fight militantly. Some of the bitterest class battles were fought by the textile workers of Massachusetts.

Sacco and Vanzetti were agitators and organizers of the workers and therefore were dangerous to the employers. They took active part in every struggle of the workers to better their conditions.

In the "red" hysteria of 1919-1920 Sacco and Vanzetti together with thousands of foreign-born workers were arrested as "dangerous to the peace and prosperity of the United States" or as "alien anarchists." As active and influential militants they were chosen by the open shop bosses of New England to pay the penalty with their lives so that other workers may be taught to abstain from forming militant organizations. It was

PERIOD OF MILITANT LABOR STRUGGLES

not quite convenient to kill them as radicals. Therefore, they were framed up and convicted as criminal murderers.*

An agitation to save Sacco and Vanzetti swept the country and the entire world as the day of their doom was drawing nearer. Almost in every city of the country Sacco-Vanzetti committees were organized, mainly under the leadership of communists and left wing trade unionists. In New York City the Sacco-Vanzetti Emergency Committee represented 400,000 organized workers.

There was only one power that could have saved Sacco and Vanzetti —the power of the organized workers of America. But the great masses of the workers led by the conservative leaders failed to come to the rescue of the two victims. Probably never before was the united front of the workers needed more than during that historical event. The communists pointed out from the very beginning that only a powerful mass movement could stay the hand of the executioners and set free the two innocent workers. Again and again they called upon the organized workers to marshal their forces behind Sacco and Vanzetti. But their influence was not sufficiently strong to arouse the great masses.

As far as Sacco and Vanzetti were concerned, not even for a moment through the whole fight did they have any hope or confidence in the government or the courts. Too well did they know their enemy to have any faith in it. Time and again they declared that their entire hope was in the hands of the working class.

There were three factors working against the united front of the working class during the entire fight in behalf of Sacco and Vanzetti: they were the Boston Sacco-Vanzetti Committee, the leaders of the American Federation of Labor and the Socialist Party. The leaders of the Boston Sacco-Vanzetti Committee devoted almost all of their attention to the legal fights in the courts and did not make a serious attempt to mobilize the great masses behind the struggle. On the contrary, they discouraged the mass protests of the workers. Some of them made bitter attacks against the Communists, who did everything in their power to rally the masses on behalf of Sacco and Vanzetti. They became open tools of the socialists in their fight against the militant workers, when a unity of the workers was essential.

The leaders of the American Federation of Labor refused to have anything to do with the general strike to save Sacco and Vanzetti. It is true that the Federation at its Detroit Convention adopted a resolution asking for a new trial for Sacco and Vanzetti, but this resolution remained only a scrap of paper.

The Socialist Party repeatedly rejected appeals from the Workers

* For a complete treatment of this famous case read, Eugene Lyons: *Life and Death of Sacco and Vanzetti,* and Felix Frankfurter: *The Case of Sacco and Vanzetti.*

(Communist) Party to make a joint fight for the lives of Sacco and Vanzetti. Together with the leaders of the conservative unions, they openly came out against the general strike called for August 22nd, the eve of the execution of Sacco and Vanzetti.

Therefore, the general strike did not materialize to such an extent as it would have, if the entire organized labor movement had participated in it. Instead of thousands of workers, millions of them would have joined in a mighty protest against the capitalist executioners. A powerful general strike would have snatched Sacco and Vanzetti out of the electric chair.

Sacco and Vanzetti faced their death bravely. Till their very last breath they challenged the power of their enemies. In their last message to the workers, dated August 21, 1927, they declared: "Only two of us will die—our ideal, you, our comrades will live by millions. We have won. We are not vanquished. Just treasure our sufferings, our sorrows, our mistakes, our defeat, our passion, for future battles for the great emancipation. We embrace you all and bid you our extreme good-bye. Now and ever, long life to you all. Long live liberty."

Sacco and Vanzetti died for the future victory of the working class.

CHAPTER XXXI

The Political Movement of the Working Class Since 1921

The Communist Party of America replaced the Socialist Party of the United States as the vanguard of the working class. Like the Social-Democracy of the world, the Socialist Party became a purely opportunist, reformist party, having as its aim not the overthrow of the capitalist system, but its improvement. Socialism became a happy dream of the obscure future about which we should talk only on Sundays and holidays, and at which humanity would arrive not through fights and struggles, not through a proletarian revolution, but by the peaceful road of brotherly love, by compelling the capitalist system gradually to retreat, step by step, before the reformist acts of the bourgeois parliament, which would be forced through by socialist representatives.

In its work the Socialist Party became the most bitter opponent of the communist movement and an instrument in the hands of the trade union officialdom in its fight against the communists. As far as their attitude toward the revolutionary movement in America is concerned, there is no difference between William Green, president of the American Federation of Labor, and Morris Hillquit, undisputed leader of the Socialist Party.

On October 20, 1926, the death of Eugene V. Debs, chairman of the party and its standard bearer in five national elections, removed the last sincere militant fighter from the leadership of the Socialist Party. In order to see how far the party has gone into the camp of the bourgeoisie, it is sufficient to point out its complete surrender to the bureaucracy of the American Federation of Labor, its stand on the League of Nations at its last convention held May 1-3, 1926, at which Hillquit led the debate for advocating the entrance of the United States into the alliance of the imperialist powers which is sponsoring the offensive against the Soviet Union and the oppression of the colonial peoples of Asia and Africa, and its open and shameful stand against the general strike on August 22, 1927, to save the lives of Sacco and Vanzetti.

The leadership of the revolutionary movement of America passed into the hands of the communists.

But as we have already pointed out, the communists were forced by the reaction in 1920 to organize underground. This condition made it difficult for the communist movement to function among the workers.

The Communist Party attempted to establish a legal press and a legal organization embracing communist and sympathizing workers, but the process was extremely hard and slow. Then the reaction began to recede somewhat, and with it the mass persecution of communists. The opportunity was afforded to organize on a broader basis and the communists took advantage of it to end their forced isolation. The executive committee of the Communist Party in conjunction with other organizations and groups which represented further desertions from the Socialist Party issued a call for a convention "to organize the Workers' Party of America." The convention was held on December 23-26, 1921, in New York City. The new party which now embraced all communist and revolutionary socialist elements, which had hitherto been separated by minor tactical differences, was launched and a program adopted. The program declared that

"The struggle of the workers even for the most elementary necessities of life is met with ruthless persecution and tends to become a fight for political power—a revolutionary struggle.

"The Workers' Party will base its policies on the international nature of this struggle. It will strive to make the American labor movement an integral part of the revolutionary movement of the workers of the world. The Workers' Party will expose the Second International which is continually splitting the ranks of labor and betraying the working masses to the enemy. . . ."

The Workers' Party emphatically condemned American imperialism and pledged itself to struggle against it. As far as Soviet Russia was concerned, the program declared that the Workers' Party looks upon it for leadership in the struggle against world imperialism.

With regard to the labor movement, the program stated that

"there has been up to the present no political organization that could lead and unify the workers against capitalism. With the Workers' Party such an organization makes its appearance in American life.

"The Workers' Party will centralize and direct the struggle of the laboring masses against the powerfully centralized opposition of their exploiters. It will courageously defend the workers, and wage an aggressive struggle for the abolition of capitalism."

The Workers' Party will endeavor "to consolidate the existing labor organizations and develop them into organs of militant struggle against capitalism, permeate the trade unions with truly revolutionary elements, mercilessly expose the reactionary labor bureaucrats and strive to replace them with revolutionary leaders." It will "participate actively in the election campaigns and the general political life of the country." It will "lead in the fight for immediate needs of the workers, broaden and deepen their demands, and develop out of their everyday struggle a force for the abolition of capitalism." It will "work for the establishment of a Workers' Republic."

"The Workers' Party stands for the principle of one union in each field. Dual unionism must be done away with. The revolutionary workers must remain within the mass organizations of the backward workers. The custom of seceding from the mass organizations to form smaller unions on the ground that the mass union is reactionary, must be abandoned. Attempts of the officialdom to expel revolutionary individuals or groups must be resisted by every possible means. The policy shall be consolidation, not division."

In August, 1922, the underground Communist Party held a convention at Bridgman, Mich., which was raided by government agents and over 30 delegates were arrested. On June 7, 1923, a conference of the party decided definitely to dissolve the underground organization and give the Workers' Party of America the right, when conditions warranted, to declare itself openly as the American section of the Communist International. From that time on the Workers' Party became the only communist party in America and the only American section of the Communist International.

The second convention of the Workers' Party was held at the end of December, 1922, in New York City, and adopted a new communist program.

"The Workers' Party will enter into every struggle involving the interests of the exploited class," the new program declares, "and through its slogans and programs of action will endeavor to develop the mass power of the workers. It will seek to unite ever greater numbers of workers in a common struggle so that each struggle will come to be, not a struggle of a small group of workers against a section of the capitalist class, but a struggle of the working class against the capitalist class."

The attitude of the Workers' Party toward the present government of the United States is as follows:

"The capitalist state, that is, the existing government, municipal, state, and national, is the organized power of the capitalist class for suppression of the exploited and oppressed workers. . . . The workers cannot wage a successful struggle against capitalist exploitation and oppression, while the government remains in control of the capitalists. The Workers' Party therefore declares that the class struggle is a political struggle, a struggle for the governmental power."

The Workers' Party declared openly that the American proletariat will not be able to emancipate itself from capitalist exploitation by parliamentary action alone:

"The Workers' Party will not foster the illusion, as is done by the yellow socialists and reformists, that the workers can achieve their emancipation from the oppression and exploitation of capitalism through the election of a majority of the members of the legislative bodies of the capitalist government and the executive officials of that government, and by using the existing government to establish the new social order. . . . The much talked of 'American democracy' is a fraud. Such formal democracy as is written into the constitution and the laws of the country is camouflage to hide the real character of the dictatorship of the capitalists."

In spite of this fact, the Workers' Party will participate in parliamentary campaigns, for it

"realizes the importance of election campaigns in developing the political consciousness of the working class."

"The Workers' Party favors the formation of a labor party—a working class political party, independent of, and opposed to all capitalist political parties. It will make every effort to hasten the formation of such a party and to effect admittance to it as an autonomous section."

On the other hand, the new program emphasizes the fact that

"a real labor party cannot be formed without the labor unions, and organizations of exploited farmers, tenant farmers, and farm laborers must be included. The Workers' Party will direct its propaganda and educational work to the end of arousing a mass sentiment of the labor party in the labor unions to secure the formation of such a party."

The attitude of the communists toward the old, conservative trade unions is also clearly stated:

"The division of the organized workers into craft unions is one of the greatest obstacles to the progress of the workers in this country against capitalism.

"In addition to the weakness of the craft form of organization the labor unions suffer from a fundamental error of policy. In place of waging a class struggle to free themselves from the grip of the capitalists they have pursued the policy of attempting to come to an agreement with the capitalists on the basis of 'a fair day's pay for a fair day's work.'

"The labor unions must be revolutionized; they must be won for the class struggle against capitalism; they must be inspired with a new solidarity and united to fight a common battle. The existing craft unions must be amalgamated and powerful industrial unions created in each industry. The reactionary official bureaucracy of the unions must be supplanted by the shop delegates' system.

"The Workers' Party declares one of its chief immediate tasks to be to inspire in the labor unions a revolutionary purpose and to unite them in a mass movement of uncompromising struggle against capitalism. It will use all the resources at its command to educate the organized workers to an understanding of the necessity of amalgamation of the craft unions into industrial unions.

"This end cannot be achieved if the revolutionary workers leave the existing unions to form feeble dual organizations. The work of transforming the labor unions must be carried on inside of the existing unions. The members of the Workers' Party will carry on their work within the existing unions to awaken the spirit of the class struggle and to bring about a reconstruction of the organization form so as to make of the unions powerful organized centers of the workers' struggle against capitalism."

The program further declares that

"the struggle of the farm laborers is the same in which the industrial workers are engaged. . . . The Workers' Party will seek to organize the farm laborers into unions of agricultural workers and to unite them with their brothers in the industrial centers for the common struggle against capitalism."

The party also claims that

"the interests of the working farmers, tenant farmers, and farm laborers are linked together with those of the exploited industrial workers and it is the aim of the Workers' Party to arouse them to a consciousness of this and to unite them with the industrial workers in a common struggle against their common exploiter. . . .

"The Workers' Party will support the Negroes in their struggle for liberation and will help them in their fight for economic, political, and educational equality. . . . It will endeavor to destroy altogether the barrier of race prejudice that has been used to keep apart the black and white workers and to weld them into a solid union for the struggle against the capitalists who exploit and oppress them."

The Workers' Party will propagate among the workers the necessity of of the soviet form of government.

"The experience of the workers in the struggle against capitalists has proved that the workers cannot take over the ready-made machinery of the capitalist government and use this to build a communist society. . . . The Workers' Party will carry on propaganda to bring to the workers an understanding of the necessity of supplanting the existing capitalist government with a soviet government."

And this soviet government will be a dictatorship of the proletariat.

"The existing capitalist government is a dictatorship of the capitalists. The soviet government of the workers will . . . be a dictatorship of the workers. The government expressing the will of the 30,000,000 workers will openly use its power in the interests of the workers and against the capitalists."

On international relations the second convention declared:

"The Workers' Party declares its sympathy with the principles of the Communist International and enters the struggle against American capitalism, the most powerful of the national groups, under the inspiration of the leadership of the Communist International."

The fourth convention of the Workers' Party, which was held on August 21-29, 1925, at Chicago, Ill., changed the name to the Workers' (Communist) Party of America and declared the party the American section of the Communist International.

After the presidential elections of 1924 two different points of view had appeared in the central executive committee of the party over the question of a labor party and other so-called "middle of the road organizations." The majority of the committee declared in its theses on policy:

"We approach this problem [of a labor party] from the point of view of whether the labor party slogan can now be used as a means of mobilizing masses of workers for immediate class political action, and we say that neither for the present nor for the immediate future can the labor party slogan be employed successfully for this purpose."

Referring to those who stood for immediate use of the labor party slogan the majority says:

"This non-communist conception of the rôle of our party manifests itself particularly in the tendency to resort to all kinds of new political organizations as substitutes for the Workers' Party whenever an opportunity presents itself to appeal to large masses of workers on concrete issues of everyday life."

And further:

"Therefore, every attempt by the Workers' Party to set up middle-of-the-way political bodies to take the place of the Workers' Party in the eyes of the masses is in direct violation of communist principles and if carried to any length will spell liquidation of the Workers' (Communist) Party."

On the other hand, the minority of the central executive committee stated their position on the labor party as follows:

"The first task of the Workers' Party is to become a mass Communist Party of workers. It can fulfill this task only by most actively participating in the establishment of a labor party. . . .

"The slogan 'For a farmer-labor party' supplies the propagandistic basis for the development of political consciousness of the masses.

"The slogan 'For a class farmer-labor party' remains the most effective agitational weapon we have for drawing the workers close to our party and building the Workers' Party."

Heated discussions ensued in the party press and party units on the theses of the majority and minority. Final decision of the question was left to the Communist International. On the question of continuing the labor party slogan the International approved the position of the minority, declaring that

"The minority of the central executive committee of the Workers' Party was right in having confidence in the vitality and future of the labor party movement."

The convention unanimously declared war upon the opportunistic tendencies of the so-called "Lore group" and officially expelled Lore from the party. Speaking of this fourth convention of the party, after analyzing the party's development from the third to the fourth convention, Ruthenberg, general secretary of the party, made the following summary:

"The fourth national convention marked the close of the period of struggle to prevent our party again degenerating into a propaganda society. It also marked the beginning of a new period in the history of the party—the period of the bolshevization of the party.

"This outcome of the national convention is a guarantee to the party that the struggle against sectarian errors has been finally won and that our party will, with the support of the Communist International, go forward to new achievements in developing itself as a mass Communist Party.

"The resolutions adopted by the fourth national convention lay the foundation for such a development of the party. In these resolutions . . . there is not a scintilla of sectarianism.

"The labor party campaign must again become a major activity of the party. It is not only to be a propaganda campaign, but the party must again stir into life and movement the working masses in the direction of actual organization of the labor party. . . .

"Closely connected with the labor party campaign is the work in the trade unions. . . . It will be one of the first tasks of the party to bring into the trade unions its whole membership and to mobilize it for action there. The trade unions are the greatest organized mass of workers in this country and offer the

POLITICAL MOVEMENT OF THE WORKING CLASS

greatest possibility for communist propaganda. Our work in the trade unions, under the slogans of the labor party, amalgamation, trade union unity, will create a solid foundation of party influence among the masses.

"In relation to the trade union work, the convention resolutions emphasize the part that organization of the unorganized will play in establishing communist influence among the organized workers. Our party must take up the task and make at least a beginning in the organization of the unorganized.

"The program for the struggle against imperialism, for work among the farmers, work among the Negro workers, and work among women, all outline concretely the tasks of the party in special fields which have not previously received sufficient attention.

"The resolution of the national convention for the liquidation of Loreism, which means a fight against all right wing opportunist tendencies in our party, represents another phase of the task of bolshevization."

Another important decision of the fourth convention was on the reorganization of the party on the basis of shop nuclei. The territorial branch form of organization is the form of the Socialist Party and does not correspond to the aims and principles of the Communist Party, which seeks to win the proletarian masses for the proletarian revolution. The communists must be organized in those places where the workers make their living, where they are exploited, and where they carry on the everyday struggle with their exploiters, and that place is in the factories, mills, and mines. Only through such a form of organization can they establish close contact with the masses and their immediate struggles. The fourth convention instructed the incoming central executive committee to take concrete steps to reorganize the party on this basis.

The formation of the Communists of America into a legal party, correct policy and intensive work in the trade unions and other mass organizations of labor, and sincere application of the slogan "To the masses," strengthened the communist influence among the workers and for the first time gave them a real and strong contact. In the beginning of 1924 the Workers' Party began to publish a communist daily in the English language, *The Daily Worker;* it also controls or publishes several dailies in other languages, such as Jewish, Ukrainian, Finnish, and Lithuanian.

The Workers' Party also participated in the presidential elections of 1924. Through the campaign, though in a very limited way because of its youth, it effectively spread revolutionary agitation and propaganda.

The fifth convention of the Workers (Communist) Party was held in New York August 31-September 5, 1927, with fifty delegates representing every part of the country from the Atlantic to the Pacific. Two outstanding features marked this convention: first, the consolidation and unification of the party's ranks and, second, the further extension of communist influence among the masses of the workers. It was recorded at the convention that in spite of very difficult objective and subjective conditions the party had made a substantial progress within the two-year period since the fourth convention. The report of the central executive committee, as well as the reports of the delegates from different parts of the country, pointed out the fact that the party has overcome the isolation in the trade unions as well as on the political field, in which it had found itself after the disruption of the labor party movement by the La Follette campaign, the trade union leadership and the Socialist Party during the presidential elections of 1924. This was accomplished through intensive mass work in which the communists were engaged during the last two years. In the agitation for a labor party, in the campaign for the protection of foreign-born workers, in the struggle against the danger of a new war, against the ravages of American imperialism in China and Nicaragua, against the injunctions in labor disputes, in the fight to save Sacco and Vanzetti, etc., as well as in the bitter struggles of the Passaic textile workers and of the New York needle trade workers, the communists were found in the forefront.

The fifth convention showed that the party had advanced very greatly politically and ideologically from the way it dealt with the problems confronting the party and the entire labor movement. Here were delegates from the bituminous coal fields of Western Pennsylvania and Illinois, miners themselves, directly from the battlefront. Here were also miners, delegates, from the anthracite coal regions of Pennsylvania, seriously discussing the situation in the coal industry and the crisis in the United Mine Workers of America. A delegate from Youngstown, Ohio, from the heart of the steel industry, painted a picture of the life of the steel workers and pointed out that only the communists and the left wing of the labor movement can and will organize the steel workers. Or still another one from Ford's factory in Detroit told the convention of the experience of the communists working at Ford's in distributing among the automobile workers 20,000 copies of *The Ford Worker,* which is published by the Ford party nucleus every second week. A delegate from the Pacific coast showed how the party has been carrying work among the sailors and longshoremen as well as among the lumber workers of the state of Washington. Then the leaders of the Passaic strike, followed by those active in the struggles in the needles trades, related their experiences, mistakes and accomplishments in the most bitter fights with the employers and the government forces.

The convention elected a central executive committee of thirty-eight members which is to hold its plenums at least once every three months. The central committee elected a political bureau of eleven members which leads the party between the meetings of the committee.

For the first time a convention of the American Communist Party was held without its staunch and most devoted leader, Charles E. Ruthenberg, who died on March 2, 1927. He was among the few leaders of the Socialist Party who raised his voice and fought militantly against the World War and who led in the founding of the communist movement in this country in 1919. At his death Ruthenberg was executive secretary of the Workers' (Communist) Party.

Working hand in hand with the Workers' Party there was the Young Workers' League, a communist youth organization and section of the Young Communist International. It was formed by revolutionists who split off from the Young People's Socialist League and by new communist youth groups. Its aim is to organize the young workers and to educate them to an understanding of their class interests in the capitalist system in order that they may join the fight with their older brothers and sisters for the emancipation of the working class. The Young Workers' League has also been reorganized on the shop nuclei basis.

The bitter strikes of the post-war period, in which the bourgeois state openly appeared as the protector of vested interests and as a strikebreaking agency of the employers, profoundly affected the political consciousness of the masses. The organized workers saw with their own eyes how the armed forces of the state were employed to crush strikes, and how the courts issued injunctions against the strikers in order to demoralize them and make their resistance ineffective. The government passes from one bourgeois party to another, from Republicans to Democrats, but as far as the workers are concerned, their position remains unchanged. Both parties are capitalist parties and both alike faithfully defend the interests of the bankers and manufacturers. Hence large sections of the organized workers began to think of the futility of expecting anything from the old capitalist parties. The so-called "non-partisan" policy of the American Federation of Labor, the policy of begging and praying for concessions from the enemies of labor, brought nothing to the workers. After a few decades of this policy the government of the United States appeared in the rôle of strikebreaker in 1919 and 1922 more openly and more ferociously than ever before.

Moreover, after the war the prices of agricultural products dropped to such an extent that millions of farmers were unable to cover the expense of raising their crops. No help was in sight. The railroad companies and the grain speculators control the farmers' fate. The same financial magnates, the same owners of factories and railroads who exploit the workers in the cities, sweat the poor farmers on the land. During the period 1920-1924, not less than 2,000,000 farmers went bankrupt, left their farms, and migrated to the cities. Millions of others were on the verge of bankruptcy. Therefore, in certain sections of the rural population, the idea also developed that nothing is to be expected from the old capitalist parties. If anything is to be done to relieve the farmers' circumstances, it must come through their own efforts. Large elements in the trade unions declared that the time had come when the workers must get off the old party wagon and undertake separate, independent, political action. On the other hand, the conservative trade union leaders, headed by

Gompers, were so closely affiliated with the old parties that they would not hear of any plan that proposed leaving the capitalists out, and were therefore emphatically opposed to a party of labor alone. Nevertheless, they were forced by the rank and file to make certain concessions.

The officials of the 16 railroad brotherhoods called a conference on February 20-21, 1922, at Chicago, Ill., to discuss the question of "progressive political action." There were 124 delegates present, mostly from the trade unions. There were also delegates from the Socialist Party, and from the Farmer-Labor Party which had its center in Chicago and which during the presidential elections of 1920 had polled 265,000 votes. The aim of the conference was, not to organize an independent political party of the workers, but to select the "progressive" and "better" candidates on the tickets of the old capitalist parties and help them to be elected. This was no more nor less than a continuation of the same Gompers "non-partisan" policy and a conscious sabotage of the demand of the labor union members for separation from the capitalist parties. The conference elected an executive committee of 15 members and instructed it to call another conference some time in December of 1922 for the purpose of discussing and considering the next step in uniting and mobilizing the forces of the farm and city workers for "political action."

At the same time the Workers' Party of America and the Trade Union Educational League had already successfully raised the slogan, "For a labor party." The Socialist Party was also on record for the formation of an independent party of labor. The Amalgamated Clothing Workers of America, the International Ladies' Garment Workers' Union, the United Mine Workers, the Chicago Federation of Labor, and many other large unions had expressed themselves in favor of an independent party. Therefore, large masses of the workers were waiting for the next meeting of the Conference for Progressive Political Action with great interest. The communists also decided to participate and to raise there the slogan, "For a labor party."

The second conference met on December 11-12, 1922, at Cleveland, Ohio. There were delegates from many large trade unions, representing about 2,000,000 organized workers, and from a few farmers' organizations with a membership of about 1,000,000.

The reactionary leaders arranged the votes in the conference in such a way that the local unions which sent delegates had practically no vote at all. Therefore the officials of the national and international unions were complete masters of the meeting. A strong protest on the part of the representatives of the rank and file members of the unions had no effect upon the bureaucrats. Besides, the conference refused to seat as delegates the representatives of the Workers' Party of America and the Young Workers' League, though this refusal did not pass without a fight. The credentials committee delayed the report on the communist representatives as long as possible, rendering it only after repeated demands. By that time the reactionaries had their machinery all prepared to defeat the seating of the communists. A few delegates took the floor and defended the latter, but they were in a minority. The bureaucrats were afraid of the communists for the reason that the latter had raised the slogan "For a labor party" and if they were admitted would ably defend it on the floor of the convention. The question of a labor party was also left until the last session of the conference, and was defeated by a vote of 64 to 52. Thus the conference remained what it had been from its very inception: a tool of the old capitalist parties, with the help of which the union bureaucrats and the Socialist Party effectively undermined for the time being the movement for independent political action on the part of organized labor.

The exponents of a labor party in the conference—the representatives of the Chicago Federation of Labor, the Amalgamated Clothing Workers, and the Farmer-Labor Party—showed a lack of courage and conviction in defending their point of view. They submitted to the right wing of the conference without a serious fight and they thereby also betrayed the labor party movement. As far as the Socialist Party was concerned, it miserably surrendered to the trade union bureaucrats also on the political field. The socialists themselves admitted that "The socialist caucus before the conference convened decided that it was impossible to secure the adoption of a socialist program or even the organization of an independent labor party at this conference" (*Socialist World*, December, 1922).

They therefore worked hand in hand with the reactionaries to defeat the proposal for a labor party.

The trade union bureaucracy, for the time being, had their way, and the Conference rejected the formation of a labor party.

Immediately after the Cleveland Conference for Progressive Political Action the Farmer-Labor Party withdrew from the movement, condemned those who were carrying on Gompers' non-partisan policy behind a mask, and issued a call for a national convention to take place on July 3, 1923, in Chicago, to which it invited all labor and farmer economic and political organizations, including the Workers' Party. The latter enthusiastically received the call as a new effort toward a labor party, and pledged itself to spare neither time nor energy to make the convention a success. The Socialist Party emphatically rejected the invitation, first because the communists would be present, and second, because they had pledged their loyalty to the Conference for Progressive Political Action.

Now the Communists started an intensive campaign for the Chicago convention, raising the question of a labor party at the meetings of trade unions and other labor organizations. The Trade Union Educational League sent a resolution on a labor party to about 35,000 local unions to be voted upon. Sentiment for independent political action of the workers ran high everywhere.

But the enemies of the working class were not asleep. They beheld a serious effort to detach the masses from the old capitalist parties, and started intensive operations to undermine the movement. Three elements united against it: the capitalists, the socialists, and the trade union officials. Their press and their spokesmen circulated groundless charges against the Chicago convention. The officials of the national unions not only condemned the gathering, but even threatened local, city, and state organizations with expulsion if they dared to participate. Gompers hastened to threaten the leaders of the Chicago Federation of Labor, who at that time were also the leaders of the Farmer-Labor Party—John Fitzpatrick, Edward Nockels, and Robert Buck—for their action in inviting the communists to the convention and violating his "non-partisan" policy. The latter began to waver, and practically doomed the campaign for the Chicago meeting.

Despite all these attacks and threats the convention met on July 3, with about 600 delegates representing several hundred thousand organized workers. But there were no representatives from any large national union. It was a convention of the representatives of city central labor bodies, of local unions, the Workers' Party, other labor organizations, the Farmer-Labor Party, and about half a dozen various state farmer-labor parties. It was apparent from the very beginning of the convention that the great majority was in favor of the formation of a labor party or farmer-labor party.

What happened just prior to the meeting was told by Ruthenberg as follows:

"A sub-committee of the central executive committee of the Workers' Party was sent to Chicago two weeks before the July 3rd conference for the purpose of carrying on official negotiations with the Farmer-Labor Party in regard to the working program for the July 3rd conference. This committee met with a committee of the Farmer-Labor Party. In the conference it was agreed by the representatives of the Farmer-Labor Party that if the representation at the July 3rd convention was sufficient (and it was considered that if there were a half-million workers represented that would be a sufficient number) a federated farmer-labor party should be formed. . . ."

But immediately after the opening of the meeting it was apparent that the national leaders of the Farmer-Labor Party had surrendered to the pressure of the American Federation of Labor and were ready to wreck the very convention which they themselves had called together. When the committee on organization reported proposing to organize a new party, Fitzpatrick took the floor and in the name of his party declared that he and his colleagues would have nothing to do with the new party, and invited the organizations represented at the convention, with the exception of the Workers' Party and other political groups, to join the old Farmer-Labor Party under his leadership. This was a breach of the agreement with the Workers' Party and contrary to the call for the convention. The great majority of the delegates were shocked by the behavior of the leaders of the Farmer-Labor Party, and by a vote of 500 to 40 decided to proceed with the work of forming a new party. The result was that the Federated Farmer-Labor Party was organized with a simple program of immediate demands for the workers and farmers, such as an eight-hour day, nationalization of industry, minimum wages, abolition of child labor, five-year moratorium on debts for the farmers, and abolition of landlordism.

Now more than ever before the enemies of independent political action waged a campaign against the Federated Farmer-Labor Party. In this campaign they were joined by the leaders of the Chicago Federation of Labor, who declared that the new party was a communist organization and a bolshevik enterprise to start a "revolution" in America! These tactics of the bourgeoisie and the trade union officialdom worked excellently in repulsing from the movement those who were not class-conscious. Only about 100,000 affiliated with the newly formed Federated Farmer-Labor Party, mainly the communists and their sympathizers. On the other hand, the communists who were now the leaders of the movement, did not carry on an intensive campaign for affiliations with the Federated Party in the fear that such a campaign might split the local and state labor parties which were then in process of formation.

In such circumstances the development of the Federated Farmer-Labor Party was hindered and the movement at first so promising began to disintegrate. In spite of this failure, the exponents of a labor party did not lose courage. The communists again raised the slogan "For a labor party" in all working-class organizations, and sought support from the masses. Suddenly a new hope dawned: The Farmer-Labor Party of Minnesota, which was a mass party and had representatives in the United States Senate as well as in the state legislature, decided to call an all-inclusive national convention on June 17, 1924, at St. Paul to consider the coming presidential elections and the formation of a national farmer-labor party. The labor party movement suddenly received a new impetus and new enthusiasm. A vigorous campaign was started for the St. Paul convention. Again the Workers' Party, as well as the Federated Farmer-Labor Party, spared neither time nor pains to make the convention a success. On the other hand, the enemies of independent political action once more lost no time in condemning the movement. This offensive again came from the same sources: capitalists, socialists, and trade union officials.

At the same time the Conference for Progressive Political Action once more appeared on the scene. Its national committee had decided to summon a convention on July 4, at Cleveland, to discuss the coming presidential campaign. A move was initiated to support Senator La Follette for President. La Follette in turn whole-heartedly approved the C. P. P. A., and violently condemned the St. Paul convention. The left wing of the St. Paul convention, led by the communists, did not expect anything better from La Follette as a representative of the petty bourgeoisie, and his attack did not in the least discourage them or change their attitude toward the convention. But the right wing of the convention, composed of farmers from the western states and the Minnesota Farmer-Labor Party, began to doubt the success of the convention and to lean toward the La Follette candidacy.

The St. Paul convention met on June 17, but the representation was not up to the expectations of its enthusiastic supporters. It was apparent that the united attack by the bourgeoisie, trade union officials, socialists, and La Follette had seriously crippled the movement. Nevertheless there was no lack of enthusiasm in the convention itself. Three important questions were to be decided: first, the relation to the C. P. P. A. convention which was to take place only a few days later; second, the attitude toward the candidacy of La Follette; and third, the formation of a labor party.

The majority of the convention was under the influence of the communists and their sympathizers, and gave the following answer to these three questions: The national committee chosen at the convention should participate in the Cleveland meeting and propose to the C. P. P. A. a united front during the elections; La Follette's candidacy should be supported only on condition that he run on the Farmer-Labor Party ticket and submit to the control of the national committee of the St. Paul convention; the national committee was instructed to work unceasingly for the establishment of a labor party based on the trade unions, but also including all of the political parties and groups of the workers and poorer farmers.

The C. P. P. A. refused to seat the representatives of the St. Paul convention, emphatically rejected the united front proposition for the elections, and with the greatest enthusiasm decided to support La Follette's candidacy on his own conditions and platform. Later even the executive council of the American Federation of Labor endorsed La Follette, declaring that this action in no way meant support for or approval of the movement for a labor party. The same was done by the independent unions such as the Amalgamated Clothing Workers. The Socialist Party also got on the La Follette band wagon and renounced its independence as a political party in behalf of a candidate who was absolutely opposed to the labor party movement. Almost all of the farmer-labor parties of the western states, including the Farmer-Labor Party of Minnesota, which had participated in the St. Paul convention, lined up with the La Follette movement.

Of the movement initiated at St. Paul, there were only the Workers' Party and its close sympathizers left. The central executive committee of the party therefore decided to withdraw its support from the St. Paul Farmer-Labor candidates and set up its own ticket with a communist platform. Later the national committee of the St. Paul convention withdrew its nominees and by a majority came out in support of the candidates of the Workers' Party.

La Follette received about 4,822,000 votes—far from the number necessary to elect. Great disappointment swept the ranks of his followers, who were convinced that they would surely ride into the White House on this progressive-republican horse. The American Federation of Labor immediately announced its withdrawal from the Conference for Progressive Political Action, and the railroad brotherhoods, the backbone of the movement, came out openly against any new party. With La Follette there remained only a handful of liberals, petty bourgeois politicians, and socialists. The latter clung till the very last.

In 1927 there was a revival of the labor party movement. The Farmer-Labor Party of Minnesota, which had been wrecked almost entirely by the La Follette movement during and immediately after the elections of 1924, reorganized its forces and became a real political factor in that state. The communists, who had been expelled and defeated two years ago, again participated. There were also signs of revival of the farmer-labor party movement in North and South Dakota, Washington, Pennsylvania, Connecticut and Massachusetts. It proved to be only temporary and short-lived. There was no labor party ticket in the presidential elections of 1928. Various state labor parties allied themselves with the old political parties, for the most part with the Democratic Party as the "lesser evil." In the atmosphere of the "great prosperity," Herbert Hoover was swept into office by the popular vote of 21,392,190 as against 15,016,443 votes cast for Alfred Smith, candidate of the Democratic Party. The Socialist Party, with Norman Thomas as its candidate, received about 250,000 votes as compared with 919,800 votes in 1920, the previous national election in which it ran its own candidates. The Communist Party was credited with 50,000 votes, as compared with 33,000 votes in 1924, the first presidential election in which it participated, and it was on the ballot in 32 states.

The nominating convention of the Socialist Party, held April 13-17, 1928, and the election platform adopted by it showed the complete bankruptcy of the Socialist Party leadership. It was convinced that Hoover's prosperity was to be everlasting. The new era of socialism was to be ushered in by a peaceful, evolutionary growth and, therefore, the workers and capitalists were to forget their differences. Under the leadership of Morris Hillquit, the right-wing leader of the party (who died on October 7, 1933), the convention decided to delete the words "class struggle" from the application for membership, thus giving official sanction to admission into the party of people from all classes and of widely divergent views, a policy which had been practiced for some time. The petty-bourgeois parliamentary character of the party was shown further by the decision to hold conventions only in the presidential years and by the invitation "to labor, fraternal and other sympathetic organizations to join the Socialist Party in a body . . ." (*The American Labor Year Book*, 1929, p. 152). In its election platform, the party gave its support to the League of Nations, favoring the entry of the United States under conditions "which will . . . promote the peace of the world." (*Ibid.*, p. 152).

The Communist Party reaffirmed its revolutionary position in an election program which it named "The Platform of the Class Struggle," adopted at the National Nominating Convention held on May 25-27, 1928, in New York. The Convention was attended by 296 regular and 150 fraternal delegates from 39 states. Far from being taken in by the "prosperity" of capitalism, the Party was already raising the question of economic crisis. The platform pointed out that "there is unemployment not only at times of crises; it is there at all times. Unemployment on a mass scale is a 'normal' phenomenon of this glorious capitalist society." Accordingly the Party raised the demands for unemployment insurance at the expense of the employers and the state; for the immediate enactment of a federal law providing for a general 40-hour, 5-day working week; for immediate relief; for a public works program with trade union wages for the workers and for the abolition of all vagrancy laws. In addition, the Party raised the demand for a federal social insurance law.

The Platform declared for the "abrogation of government by injunction," the "prohibition of the use of guards, gunmen, deputy sheriffs, militia or federal troops in labor struggles," and "unrestricted right to organize, to strike, and to picket, free speech, free press and free assemblage for the working class." Internationalism held a prominent place in the Platform, which raised the slogan of "not a man, not a gun, not a cent for the imperialist army and navy," and demanded "complete and immediate independence for all American colonies and semi-colonies." The defense of the Soviet Union was pledged and recognition by the United States government demanded.

The stock market crash in the autumn of 1929 was the first major break in the front of prosperity and reflected a deep-going economic crisis which was soon to break out in full force. Viewed as a part of the general post-war crisis of capitalism, the crisis in the United States marked a definite end to the upward swing of American capitalist economy and the beginning of a downward trend of which the economic crisis was the first major phase. Under these conditions the communists no longer raised the slogan for a labor party. In fact, with conditions ripe for the development of a mass revolutionary movement, this slogan could easily become an instrument of the ruling class to be used in diverting the workers away from the revolutionary path. The slight resurgence of labor party propaganda in 1933 appeared more openly as an instrument of the bourgeoisie to keep the workers from the communist movement. The capitalist class, wrote Earl Browder, General Secretary of the Communist Party, has to create a new weapon to "replace the discredited parties and leaders. . . . They must give new forms to the old capitalist policies, they must cover them up with new phrases about a 'new way,' even a 'revolutionary way'." Therefore, "the farmer-labor party, or labor party, or new party, or radical party, or people's party, will be brought forward for this purpose." Now the attitude of the Communist Party is: "Not the 'farmer-labor party' and the 'restoration' of capitalism with fascism, but the Communist Party and the revolutionary overthrow of capitalism . . ." ("What About This Labor Party Talk?" *Daily Worker,* September 9, 1933).

During the upsurge in the labor movement in 1933, "left" reformists led by A. J. Muste proposed to dress the defunct Conference for Progressive Labor Action with a new name, the American Workers Party. By the use of radical slogans they hoped to halt the radicalized workers midway on their road to the Communist Party and turn them against it. Browder's analysis of the rôle of such a party in the present period applies with full force to the Muste group.

The new policy regarding the labor party was part of a general reorientation under changed conditions. The years 1928-1929 witnessed a complete internal change in the Communist Party. During this period factionalism was wiped out with the aid of the Communist International and the Party was ready to tackle seriously the problem of building a mass revolutionary movement. The struggle against factionalism proved to be a political struggle against opportunism both of the "right" and "left" varieties. On October 27, 1928, the opportunists of the "left," a small group led by James P. Cannon, a member of the Political Bureau of the Party, were expelled from the Party as "counter-revolutionary Trotskyists." Internationally this group adhered to the program of Leon Trotsky and his followers in the Communist Party of the Soviet Union, who denied the possibility of building socialism in the Soviet Union and rejected the Leninist conception of alliance between the workers and the small and middle farmers in the struggle for socialism under the proletarian dictatorship. This group was further characterized, both in the Soviet Union and on the international field, by an approach to various problems which on the surface seemed "more revolutionary" but which was in essence opportunist. Trotsky and his followers were engaged in organizing active opposition to the Soviet Government and supplying capitalist apologists with ammunition for their anti-Soviet campaign. The further development of this group made even more apparent its anti-Soviet and anti-Communist character. In 1933 the followers of Trotsky started agitation for the establishment of a "new international" in conjunction with "left-wing" socialist groups as opposed to the Communist International and its parties. They do not deny that their program calls for the formation of a secret opposition party in the Soviet Union having as its objective the overthrow of the Communist Party which is at the head of the dictatorship of the proletariat. They are, therefore, a counter-revolutionary group despite their "left" phrases. In the United States as well as abroad they are devoid of any mass following.

The expulsion of the Cannon group was followed by an intensive inner struggle against right opportunism, which pervaded the leadership. Jay Lovestone and others in the leadership of the Party designated the Hooverian period as the "Victorian Age" of American capitalism, a comparison which predicted for the United States a long period of further progressive development similar to that which faced England during the reign of Queen Victoria in the last half of the nineteenth century. According to them, therefore, the United States was exempt from the decay that was plunging all capitalist countries into an unprecedented crisis. In 1927 this group was formulating "a program for the period of prosperity," (see *The Communist,* July-August, 1927); in 1928, when there were already undeniable signs of a developing crisis in a number of industries, these were termed temporary and were taken to "indicate even greater growth for American imperialism"; in 1929, after the Wall Street crash, Lovestone characterized the Wall Street crash as a "panic" which did not come as a result of the decline of American capitalist economy but "as the result of the very strength of American capitalist economy."

With such an outlook the Party was left almost totally unprepared for the unprecedented economic crisis which had already been clearly foreseen by the Communist International two years before the Wall Street crash. This "exceptionalism" in the diagnosis of American conditions, led also to exceptionalism in the application of Communist policy and to the formulation of policies and tactics detrimental to the development of a mass revolutionary movement. The inability of the Party to rid itself of factionalism and opportunism, as was exemplified by its Sixth Convention in 1929 which was turned into a defense of the opportunist line of the Lovestone faction, led to the intervention of the Communist International. An Open Letter addressed by the International to the party members, calling upon them to rid the Party of factionalism and right opportunism, was adopted on May 14, 1929. The majority faction leaders, with few exceptions, opposed the letter and launched an open struggle against it after its adoption. They were expelled from the Party as renegades. The membership almost unanimously supported this action.

An enlarged meeting of the Central Committee in October, 1929, attended by about 100 leading functionaries, endorsed the expulsion of the Lovestone group, and characterized this action as marking "the liquidation of the old factional situation and the basic unification of the Party, with the restoration of normal relations with our World Party, the Communist International" (Earl Browder, "The October Plenum of the Central Committee, C. P. U. S. A.," *The Communist*, November, 1929).

Under the title of "The Communist Party of the U. S. A. (Opposition)," the Lovestone group continued an isolated existence, traveling further and further to the right and openly fighting the Communist Party in all its activities. In the trade union field it has thrown its support to the bureaucracy of the American Federation of Labor in the struggle against the industrial unions of the Trade Union Unity League. On all fronts it has taken up the fight against communism.

With the expulsion of the right opportunists in 1929, the Communist Party consolidated its ranks and was now better prepared to face the tremendous tasks and responsibilities called forth by the new national and international situation.

CHAPTER XXXII

THE REVOLUTIONARY TRADE UNION MOVEMENT

IN the post-war period the leadership of the reformist trade unions frankly and openly continued the policy of class collaboration. The defeat of the great strikes of 1919-1922 was utilized by the reformist labor leaders to divert the workers from strike struggles. It is true that these leaders were always opposed to the policy of class struggle, during the World War even surrendering the right of the workers to strike, but never before was class collaboration pursued in such a systematic and intensive way as after the war.

The Forty-Third Convention of the American Federation of Labor held November 17-25, 1924, at El Paso, Texas, announced "industrial democracy" as its objective. Lest this term be misconstrued, Gompers took special pains to deny any revolutionary implications and defined the "new philosophy" as follows:

"The trade unions are not inclined toward the Marxian theory of government. On the contrary, they are manifesting a constantly growing interest and participation in the institutions dependent upon private and coöperative initiative, and personal and group adventure."

Matthew Woll, Gompers' faithful lieutenant, flatly told the world: "Industrial democracy cannot come through the workers alone; we need the help of the employers." In other words, the employers with the collaboration of the trade unions are to establish a paradise for the workers! Such is the philosophy of "industrial democracy" as advocated by the trade union class-collaborationists.

On December 13, 1924, Samuel Gompers died and the presidency of the American Federation of Labor fell to William Green, former secretary-treasurer of the United Mine Workers. Those who thought that Green would choose a different road from Gompers were sadly mistaken. The new president was met by the "respectable" citizens of the National Civic Federation with outstretched hands. His inauguration was participated in by C. R. Frederickson, president of the National Association of Manufacturers, and many other financial and industrial magnates. Greeting Green in his new position, one of these magnates declared:

"Mr. Green is representative of all people.... He is not radical. He labors for the good of all people. We can feel safe in his hands."

After his first meeting with the executive council of the Federation, Green delivered a speech at Miami, Fla., on February 12, 1925, to about

2,000 capitalists. Next morning the newspapers summarized his address as follows:

"William Green, president of the American Federation of Labor, last night pledged 5,000,000 members as supporters of the constitution of the United States, condemned imported labor theories, and pleaded for a stronger coöperation between employees and employers. The address made by the chief executive of all labor organizations set at rest any doubt about his attitude on matters of importance to labor, and dispelled the rumor that he was inclined to be radical in theories."

The same evening Green delivered another talk, this time to the Advertising Club, in which he declared:

"There seems to be an understanding of peace and unity between labor and capital in Miami. Labor and capital cannot hate each other if they understand each other. Misunderstanding is the cause of strife. Understanding means concord."

Then Edward Henning of the United States Department of Labor rose and in the name of the government passionately exclaimed:

"Thank God that when the reins fell from the palsied hands of Samuel Gompers, they fell into the virile hands of William Green."

The fostering of class collaboration, the open shop movement, and the war against communism go hand in hand. All three ideas come from the same source: the capitalist class. The reactionary trade union leaders are only bourgeois agents in the ranks of the workers, some of them conscious, others not. The result, of course, is the same in both cases: service to the capitalist class, treachery to the workers. Witness the *Minnesota Banker* of December, 1920, which said:

"There is no question as to the economic value of the open shop. But, at the same time, those who are pushing it must be most careful in their methods. The open shop movement is a powder magazine. A carelessly thrown match might start a nation-wide conflagration. The closed shop is zealously fought for by the radical wing of labor organization. The open shop can be the most readily brought about by the elimination of this element as a power in organized labor.

"The conservative labor man is one to whom sound argument and sound horse sense appeal. . . . This is the ideal thing to do and it can be done in many parts of the country. In others, where the radical element is too strongly entrenched, there is, of course, but one final thing to do, and that is to beat them by force. They must be locked out and licked until the conservatives see the light and realize that the rights of capital must be considered. This harsher method, however, should not be employed until all other plans have failed."

To crush the revolutionary element in the labor movement and to unite with and use the conservative element for their own advantage—such was the policy of the ruling class after the World War. It knew that the conservative trade union leaders could be the most effective tools in the war against the proletariat. And the bourgeoisie was not mistaken.

The forms of class collaboration vary at different times, developing to higher stages, from the "Baltimore and Ohio plan," through "Labor Banks" and "Labor Insurance Companies" to "NRA," in which the reformist trade unions become part of the bourgeois state machinery. The so-called "Baltimore and Ohio plan" was first accepted by the machinists' union and applied on the Baltimore and Ohio Railroad. The plan is defined as an agreement whereby the union purchases recognition from railroad management by supplying efficiency engineers, who, with the authority of the union behind them, speed up production, eliminate waste, reduce the cost of production, and eliminate "undesirable workers and union working rules that hamper efficiency in profit-making" (Earl Browder: *Class Struggle vs. Class Collaboration,* pp. 10-11).

The B. & O. plan was endorsed by the Portland convention of the A. F. of L. in 1925. It was whole-heartedly approved and supported by William Green and other leaders of the Federation, and is looked upon with great favor by the trade union officialdom as a whole.

Proof of how the B. & O. plan affects the unions is supplied by the same International Association of Machinists. In 1920 this union had 330,800 members in good standing, but in 1924 only 77,000 of them paid their membership dues! These figures speak louder than any words of condemnation.

The so-called "labor banks" are another form of class collaboration. The first "labor bank" was established by the Brotherhood of Locomotive Engineers in 1920, in Cleveland, Ohio. Then "labor banks" began to spring up one after another like toadstools after a rain. At one time there were over 30 "labor banks" with a capital of about $200,000,000. According to the labor misleaders, the rôle of these banks was to be tremendous.

The *Advance,* official organ of the Amalgamated Clothing Workers, maintained that the "labor banks" will become instruments in the workers' struggles. The labor movement "is coming to realize," it informed us, "that it holds in its own hands materials with which to create weapons as powerful as those used by capital. It is coming to know the value of credit and the power of banking institutions" (*Advance,* May 1, 1925). Sidney Hillman, president of the Amalgamated, in his speech at the Philadelphia convention of 1924, speaking about the "labor banks" and other business institutions of the union, proclaimed the following principle:

"We have accomplished something that was at first received with indifference and with a smile—we have gone into the banking business, and we propose, with your coöperation, to go farther, not only in the banking field, but in the general field of coöperation. After all, it is there that the hope of labor lies. After all, it is there that we not only get more power, but we also get a greater sense of the responsibility that is essential to the use of power. . . ."

THE REVOLUTIONARY TRADE UNION MOVEMENT 337

The "labor banks," it seems, are to replace the trade unions in bringing on a peaceful, evolutionary growth to "industrial democracy."

But the crisis either wiped out most of these banks, or transferred them directly into the hands of the capitalists' banking interests. To-day there are but few left.

The third main form of class collaboration is expressed in various insurance schemes. In studying the early history of the trade unions we find that many of them, especially those of skilled workers, had their origin in benefit and insurance societies. Especially is this true of the railroad brotherhoods. But as the class struggle became sharper, protection of wages became a greater necessity, the insurance phase of the brotherhoods receded into the background, and these organizations became more like real labor unions. But when after the war the capitalist offensive weakened the unions and the membership began to decline, instead of rejuvenating the brotherhoods through militant struggles with the employers, the leaders turned the wheel backward and threw into greater prominence the insurance phase of the organizations in order to prevent a general exodus of the members. It was an attempt to cause the unions to revert to their former state and therefore to destroy them as far as the fight with the employers for higher wages and better working conditions was concerned.

The second and the most dangerous phase of these "labor insurance" schemes accepted by the trade unions lies in the fact that they were considered and planned as pure and simple capitalist undertakings. Like the banks, the insurance companies were formed on account of the safety of the investment, and because the business was supposed to be most profitable. The El Paso convention of the A. F. of L. whole-heartedly approved this conception of "labor insurance." The leaders of the Federation investigated and found that insurance profits reach from 20 to 100 per cent.

Repudiation of the class struggle and collaboration with the bourgeoisie go hand in hand with the suppression of the militant spirit of the trade unions. It is self-evident that strikes and struggles are not much to the liking of the labor bureaucrats. If they still led strikes from time to time, it is only because the rank and file of the unions forced them to do so by threatening to leave them entirely. They did not want to remain without members, for they have a mission to perform: to "mix oil and water," to "wipe out the class struggle," to rivet the working class to the ruling class, and by so doing to lengthen as much as possible the existence of the present system.

In his speech at the Philadelphia convention, President Hillman of the "socialist" Amalgamated declared:

"We have our problems, and fortunately it is not necessary to apply the weapon of a strike for the solution of many of them. We have passed in our industry from the days of the jungle into an era of civilized ways of dealing with employers."

From the policy of deprecating strikes the labor leaders proceeded to break strikes whenever they occurred against their will. Examples of the strike-breaking rôle of the trade union bureaucrats are entirely too numerous to even try to enumerate.

Probably in no other country is the corruption of the labor leaders so shameful and so open as in the United States. It will suffice to mention only a few outstanding cases. John Mitchell amassed enormous wealth as president of the United Mine Workers. Frank Farrington of the Illinois miners was secretly an agent of the Peabody Coal Company, and when exposed openly became its paid official. The Brindell case in the building trades disclosed a corruption involving millions of dollars. The leaders of the New Jersey State Federation of Labor themselves admitted at the convention held in Camden, N. J., in 1927, that they accepted over $100,000 from the open shop manufacturers and employers. (For a detailed account of corruption of the leadership of the trade unions, see William Z. Foster: *Misleaders of Labor, 1927*.)

Corruption or bribery has an economic as well as a political basis and is not due solely to bad individuals in the labor movement. What is this basis? It is the surplus profits of American capitalism which has created the "aristocracy of labor." Out of enormous profits made by American imperialism through its gigantic investments and loans abroad, the capitalist class was able to throw some crumbs to the workers of skilled and strategical trades in industry. The employers have also been able to bribe the labor leaders in one form or another and utilize them for breaking labor struggles.

Yankee imperialism has loyal allies and supporters in the leaders of the American Federation of Labor. They openly support every war program of the United States, and oppose every move undertaken by the workers to assist the struggles of the colonial peoples against the oppression of the Wall Street imperialists. The Greens and Wolls have been the bitterest opponents of the recognition of the Soviet Union by the United States.

The effects of this class collaboration policy upon the trade unions were such that the membership of the American Federation of Labor fell from over four million in 1920 to 2,532,261 in 1932.

The communists led the fight within the labor movement against class collaboration and for a policy of class struggle. In 1920 the communists had rejected the idea of deserting the reformist trade unions in the American Federation of Labor and instead raised the perspective of working within these unions and of changing them into revolutionary instruments of the workers in the struggle for communism. They went further

THE REVOLUTIONARY TRADE UNION MOVEMENT 339

and repudiated not only the organization of new unions in industries where a more or less powerful union already existed but also the creation of new militant unions in the totally unorganized industries. This change of tactics coincided with the growth and seeming stabilization of the reformist trade unions. By 1920 the membership of the American Federation of Labor had reached the high point of 4,078,740, although only in the coal industry of all the basic industries of the country could it be said that the majority of the workers were organized.

The Second World Congress of the Communist International held in 1920, stated its position on this question as follows:

"The communists must join such [reformist] unions in all countries, in order to make of them efficient and conscious organs of the struggle for the abolition of capitalism and the establishment of communism. They must initiate the forming of trade unions where these do not exist. Any voluntary withdrawal from the economic movement, every artificial attempt to organize special unions, without being compelled thereto by exceptional acts of violence on the part of the trade union bureaucracy . . . represents a great danger to the communist movement. It threatens to isolate the most advanced, the most conscious workers from the masses, which are on the road to communism, it threatens to hand over these masses to the opportunist leaders, playing into the hands of the bourgeoisie. . . ." (*Theses and Statutes of the Communist International*, p. 52).

This policy was reaffirmed by the first Congress of the Red International of Labor Unions, held in Moscow in June, 1921. It declared that for the American revolutionary workers "the question of creating revolutionary cells and groups inside the American Federation of Labor and the independent unions is of vital importance. There is no other way by which one could gain the working mass in America, than to lead a systematic struggle within the unions" (*Resolutions and Decisions of the R. I. L. U. First World Congress*, p. 31).

With the entire emphasis based upon working within the old unions, the Trade Union Educational League, which was organized in 1920 by militant trade unionists, began towards the end of 1921 to make rapid gains in some of the trade unions. In its program, issued in February, 1922, the T. U. E. L. declared that it was not a trade union but "an informal grouping of the progressive and revolutionary elements throughout the entire trade union movement." It was to operate "within and in support of the trade unions, and by no means in opposition or in competition with them." Its aim was "to develop the trade unions from their present antiquated and stagnant condition into modern, powerful labor organizations, capable of waging successful warfare against capitalism." The theories, tactics, structure and leadership of the reformist unions were to be entirely revamped and the "demoralizing nonsense about harmonizing the interests of capital and labor," to be replaced by "the inspiring goal of the abolition of capitalism and the establishment of a workers' republic . . ." (*The Labor Herald,* March, 1922, pp. 6-7).

The first national conference of the League was held on August 26-27, 1922, in Chicago, with 45 delegates present from industrial centers of the United States and Canada. Just a few days before, 32 communists had been arrested at a Party convention in Bridgeman, Mich., and knowing that communists were the leading elements in the League, police raided its conference and arrested a few delegates. The conference, however, continued its work. It was decided to fight tooth and nail against any attempt on the part of the trade union bureaucracy to expel the revolutionary trade unionists. The "non-partisan" political policy of the American Federation of Labor was condemned and the conference pledged to carry on an intensive campaign for independent working-class political action. The League was to be an organization broad enough to embrace all progressive forces in the trade union movement.

One of the main slogans of the T. U. E. L. was amalgamation of the craft unions. This slogan was immediately echoed all over the country and everywhere found a great army of followers. The bitter struggles of the workers in 1922 had demonstrated the uselessness of craft unions and the slogan of amalgamation became the most important question on the agenda of the trade unions at meetings, conferences and conventions. It was, of course, bitterly opposed by the reactionary leaders. Yet no fewer than 16 state federations of labor endorsed amalgamation, and by 1923 the T. U. E. L. was an important factor in the American trade union movement.

The adoption of a resolution in favor of amalgamation by the Chicago Federation of Labor on March 19, 1923, was the signal for a campaign of slander and vituperation against the communists and the revolutionary unionists. At a meeting of trade union officials held at Hotel Morrison in Chicago on April 11 Gompers launched the campaign against the "reds." The T. U. E. L., he declared, "is an organization which attempts to dictate the policies of the trade unions." John L. Lewis, president of the United Mine Workers, and Ellis Searles, editor of the official organ of that union, bought a series of articles from a spy, and published them in various papers under their own names as the result of their own investigation of communist activities in America. These articles were but the invention of a fantastic, befuddled mind for the purpose of discrediting the communists. Later Chester M. Wright, head of the publicity department of the A. F. of L., also "investigated" communist activities, and fabricated a series of articles which he had printed in the name of the Federation. In both instances an attempt was made to show that the communists of this country, first of all, are out to capture and destroy the American Federation of Labor and all other "respectable" labor unions; that they then intend to get rid of the "democratic" government of America; and last but not least, that they will finally put an end to all the "civilized" institutions of the country.

The T. U. E. L., however, continued to grow in influence. On December 19, 1923, about 400 delegates unofficially representing all the 16 organizations of railroad workers held a conference in Chicago for the purpose of organizing the left wing in their industry. During June of the same year a conference of progressive miners was held in Pittsburgh where 200 delegates were present from 12 districts of the United Mine Workers.

The second conference of the T. U. E. L. took place September 1-2, 1923, in Chicago, with 103 delegates present from 90 cities in the United States and Canada. The organization had made great strides forward since its first conference. In almost every important industrial center and in almost every trade union, groups of militants had been formed and were carrying on work. The program of the League had been widely distributed among the craft unions. This continued advance led to an adoption of a policy of terrorism and persecution against the left-wing elements by the trade union bureaucrats.

The new campaign was started in the International Ladies' Garment Workers' Union, led by socialists who by this time fully rivaled Gompers in their bitter attacks on the revolutionary movement. In February, 1923, several of the most militant workers in Chicago were thrown out of the union for membership in the T. U. E. L. At the national convention of the union held on May 5-17, 1924, 16 communists and their sympathizers who had been elected as delegates despite the bitter campaign waged against them, were branded as "enemies" of the union by the socialist officials and thrown out of the convention. The socialist leaders of the International Fur Workers' Union went so far as to hire thugs to fight the militants at union meetings. In the Amalgamated Clothing Workers the Hillman administration joined forces with the socialists in a campaign of terror and persecution against the left-wingers, despite Hillman's show of impartiality and his pleas for unity at the 1924 convention. By 1925 the persecution of militants in the union was at its highest point. In New York not only were individual militants thrown out of the union, but entire Local 5 was suspended and reorganized. Other unions followed suit.

The left wing in the New York needle trades, however, continued to gain strength. By the end of 1925, three of the largest locals of the International Ladies' Garment Workers' Union, Locals 1, 9 and 22, having 30,000 members and making up 60% of the New York Joint Board of the Union, elected militants as their officials. All the 77 elected officials were expelled by the reactionary national leadership of the union. But the rank and file stood by their elected officials and after a campaign lasting three months the reactionaries were forced to stop persecution of militants. All those who had been expelled or suspended were reinstated with full membership rights. The struggle, however, flared up again a few months later in open warfare.

On July 1, 1926, the cloak and dressmakers of New York declared a general strike against the attempt of the employers to destroy the union conditions in the shops. The workers also demanded a raise in wages and a 40-hour week. While the leadership of the strike was mainly in the hands of the communists and the progressives, Morris Sigman, spokesman for the reactionary national leaders and president of the union, was also on the general strike committee. Although he declared that the national union leaders would support the strike, his actions disclosed that they had secret dealings with the employers to thwart the strike and thus discredit the left-wing leadership of the New York union. At the most critical period in the strike the Sigman machine bolted the strike committee, came out openly against the strike and invited the employers to negotiate a strike settlement with them over the heads of the left-wing leadership. The leaders of the A. F. of L. came to Sigman's aid, the New York locals were expelled from the union and a war of extermination declared against the entire left wing.

A similar situation developed in the Fur Workers' Union. On February 15, 1926, the fur workers of New York, under the leadership of the left wing, went on strike and for the first time in the history of the American labor movement a 40-hour week was won by the workers. This gave prestige to the left wing in the entire labor movement. Scenting great danger to themselves, the international officials of the union and the bureaucracy of the A. F. of L. launched a campaign to discredit the leadership of the strike. The Executive Council of the Federation appointed a special committee to investigate the conduct of the strike and charged that the leaders of the Fur Workers Joint Board of New York expended thousands of dollars in bribing the police, although the police had acted most brutally against the strikers. Although the charge was flimsy, one pretext was as good as another and the New York Joint Board of the furriers was expelled from the union. The left wing of the I. L. G. W. U. and of the furriers organized a joint committee for struggle against the reactionaries and the employers. The militants again captured the New York organization of the International Furriers Union and led a long but successful strike.

The militants continued to register strength in the other unions as well. The progressive candidates in the United Mine Workers polled 66,000 votes in the elections of 1926, on their enemies' own count. In the Machinists' elections the progressives polled 18,000 votes, in the Carpenters', 10,000.

As indicated by the elections the militants were strong in the United Mine Workers. On April 1, 1927, the bituminous coal miners, 190,000 strong, went on strike to force the coal companies to extend the Jacksonville agreement. The leaders of the union betrayed the miners by abandoning this demand in July, 1928, and ordering the districts to make individual settlements with each company. The militants fought this betrayal through the "Save the Union Committees." They attempted to reinvigorate the strike and continue it over the heads of the labor fakers. Despite the heroic efforts of the militants, aided by the Ohio-Pennsylvania Miners Relief Committee, the men were finally forced back to work in defeat. In October, 1927, 6,000 Colorado miners had struck under the leadership of the Industrial Workers of the World, and it looked for a time as if the I. W. W. would regain its former militancy. The strike was marked by the brutality of the government. A number of workers were killed and many wounded when machine guns were used against them. The strike was crushed and the I. W. W. disappeared from the field.

The left wing also played a leading rôle in the textile strike of 1928 in New Bedford. On April 9, 1928, the workers received a 10% wage-cut. Seven days later 25,000 workers went on strike. There were two forces in the field, the reformist American Federation of Textile Operatives and the left-wing Textile Mill Committee. The latter gained the leadership over the mass of strikers and extended the strike to Fall River, Mass. The New York experience was repeated. In the midst of the strike the American Federation of Textile Operatives joined the United Textile Workers of America, an A. F. of L. affiliate. The reactionary leadership accepted a five per cent cut in wages and called off the strike.

Experiences such as these led the communists to a careful reëxamination of their policies in the trade union field. It was found that the policy enunciated in 1920-1921, while it was basically correct, had been applied only in one of its aspects, with the result that all the efforts had been concentrated in the existing reformist unions. No efforts had been made to organize the unorganized independently of the reactionary trade union bureaucracy which ignored them completely. Nor had the communists taken the inititative in organizing new unions where none existed, as had been pointed out by the resolution of the Second World Congress of the Communist International. New unions of any kind or under any conditions were branded as "dual unions" having a disruptive influence on the labor movement as a whole. While the communists correctly condemned any action which would lead to a desertion of the masses of workers in the reformist trade unions, their application of this policy led in practice to a desertion of the vast majority of the workers who were totally unorganized and outside the pale of the existing trade union movement. Furthermore, the greatest body of unorganized workers were concentrated in the basic industries and were therefore the most decisive section of the workers to be won for communism. The communists clung to the hope that the old unions would be forced to carry through the task of organizing the unorganized in the basic industries. They failed to see that the trade union bureauracy would be forced to organize the unorganized only to the extent that the communists would become a powerful independent factor in organizing these masses, while at the same time continuing their struggle in the old unions.

The campaign of terror and expulsion of the militants in the old unions, the continued narrowing down of the reformist unions and the experiences of the struggle led the communists to gradually change their position in regard to trade union work. "It would be a grave error to make a fetish of unity with the old unions at all costs and to act upon the principle of confining our activities to them entirely," declared a resolution passed at an enlarged meeting of the Central Committee, in February, 1928. Because of the narrowing base of the A. F. of L. and the employers' offensive, the resolution continued, the communists must proceed "promptly, resolutely and aggressively to the formation of new unions." These unions, however, were to be connected up "to the main mass of the labor movement providing that such affiliation is made in such a way as to safeguard and promote left-wing policy and leadership."

The resolution passed at the May, 1928, enlarged meeting of the Central Committee, placed still stronger emphasis upon the importance of the new unions. It noted a "decline of the traditional craft unionism and beginnings of a new unionism among the great masses of unorganized" and called upon the Party to take the lead in building new unions among the unorganized masses. At the same time, however, the work in the old unions was to be continued, although the major attention of the Party was to be directed to building new unions among the masses of unorganized, who "under the pressure of wage-cuts, speed-up, unemployment, etc.," were beginning "to acquire new militant moods." The resolution warned against any tendency to neglect and desert the old unions, which was to be "counteracted by clearly stating the necessity of communists working within the A. F. of L. unions and laying down programs for this work" ("Resolution on Trade Union Work," *The Communist,* July, 1928).

This change in orientation led to the formation of revolutionary industrial unions. The Trade Union Educational League was reorganized into the Trade Union Unity League at a convention held in Cleveland, September 1, 1929, which was attended by 690 delegates representing 70,000 organized workers, some of them already representing new industrial unions, and others opposition groups in the reformist unions. The declaration of policy of the T. U. U. L. states:

"The Trade Union Unity League aggressively furthers the organization of new revolutionary industrial unions in industries where there are no unions and in industries where the existing unions are corrupt and impotent. The

THE REVOLUTIONARY TRADE UNION MOVEMENT

organization of the masses into new unions stands in the very center of the T. U. U. L. program. But this does not imply a policy of petty splits and individual withdrawals of the militant workers from the old trade unions where these have a mass character. . . . On the contrary, the T. U. U. L. organizes the left wing in those old unions and fights for their revolutionization."

The program of the T. U. U. L. is based upon the principle of the class struggle. It declared for a strenuous fight against all kinds of discrimination against Negro and foreign-born workers, for the organization of the unorganized and of all workers under the single banner of militant industrial trade unionism.

The first new industrial unions were organized in those industries where the T. U. E. L. and the communists had been most successful in work within the old unions, and where they had participated in the struggles of the workers. Thus the first to be organized towards the end of 1928 were the National Miners Union, with its main base in the bituminous coal fields of Pennsylvania and Ohio; the Needle Trades Workers' Industrial Union, with its main following in the needle trades of New York; and the National Textile Workers' Union, on the basis of the Textile Mill Committee of the New Bedford strike and support in the silk industry of New Jersey. Even before the first conference of the T. U. U. L. the latter union led a major strike in the South.

On April 2, 1929, the workers of the Manville-Jenckes mill in Gastonia, N. C., struck, under the leadership of the new National Textile Workers' Union against a wage-cut and dismissals of union members. The strike soon spread into the surrounding villages. Five companies of the National Guard were called out to crush it. On April 18, masked thugs attacked the strike headquarters and destroyed the relief store. The strike committee informed the governor of the state of the terror and warned him that the workers would protect themselves with arms if necessary. On June 7, the tent colony housing the strikers evicted from the corporation mill village, was fired upon by police. The workers defended themselves and in the struggle the chief of police, O. F. Aderholt, was killed. The strike leaders were immediately arrested and charged with first-degree murder. The charge was changed to second-degree murder when the prosecution was faced with a storm of mass protest from all parts of the country, and a jury could not be found to convict. Five strike leaders were sentenced to serve from 17 to 20 years of hard labor; two strikers from 12 to 15 years; and another, from 5 to 7 years. On April 14, thugs fired into a truck of strikers returning from a picnic, killing Ella May Wiggins, mother of five children and a tireless strike leader. The strike was crushed and the union was forced underground.

The strike was the most important and outstanding of a number which occurred in the South during 1929. On March 12, 1929, 4,000 rayon workers of Elizabethton, Tenn., went on strike. Here the United Textile

Workers of America assumed leadership of the strike only to betray it by making an agreement behind the backs of the workers which left matters practically as they were before the strike. On April 15, inspired by the militant strike in Gastonia, the rayon workers again walked out but were defeated by the widespread terror set loose by the employers and the local government.

The struggle in Gastonia undoubtedly influenced other strikes which occurred during that year. Textile workers of Marion, N. C., walked out against a wage-cut on July 11, 1929, under the leadership of the United Textile Workers. On October 2 sheriffs and deputies fired point-blank into a picket line of unarmed workers, killing six. This strike was also crushed. The street-car workers of New Orleans waged a militant strike in July, but were defeated by a reign of terror which took the toll of one worker killed and many wounded. The Gastonia strike, while it was lost and did not result in the establishment of the National Textile Workers' Union in the South, was significant in its militant attempt to reach the great masses of unorganized textile workers in the South, in raising sharply the program of solidarity and unity between white and Negro workers in the homeland of lynch terror, and in its influence upon the subsequent struggles of the southern workers. It proved to be the opening wedge into a hitherto unorganized territory for militant industrial trade unionism and communism.

Other unions which were organized and affiliated to the T. U. U. L., in addition to those already mentioned, were the Auto Workers Industrial Union, Marine Workers Industrial Union, Steel and Metal Workers Industrial Union, Food and Packinghouse Industrial Union, and the Shoe and Leather Workers Industrial Union. Although a number of the leading strikes during the crisis years were led by these unions and the T. U. U. L. at the end of 1933 could report a total membership in its unions and affiliated trade union groups of over 100,000, its growth was looked upon as being far from satisfactory. In the work of the communists there had been apparent a marked tendency to abandoning the work in the reformist unions. In face of the increased terror against militants in 1930-1933, it seemed to many that the easiest way out of the situation was to shrink in practice from the work in the old unions, at the same time not in the least abandoning the theory of the necessity of such work. The Central Committee of the Party repeatedly pointed out the danger of this tendency. The activities of the revolutionary unions and the work of the opposition groups in the old unions had to be properly coördinated and the work in the reformist unions undertaken with greater energy. Trade union unity was to be obtained on the basis of militant industrial unionism.

"Our approach to the problem of unity is the united front," writes William Z. Foster. "The united front must be built from the bottom and established in the struggle. In order to build the united front we must actually fight for it. . . . We must go to the workers, not wait for them to come to us. . . ." The militants in the reformist unions should fight for "the principle of 'one industry, one union'" and they are to base their unity movement, Foster continues, "at the bottom, in the shops, in the local unions, in the furtherance of the daily struggle. Wherever the left-wing is in control, or wherever it would strengthen the forces of the left-wing, we should not hesitate to organize the unorganized. But in any event we can only bring members into the corrupt A. F. of L. on the basis that they have a fighting chance, under left-wing leadership, to defend their interests. . . ." ("Some Elementary Phases of the Work in the Reformist Trade Unions," *The Communist*, June, 1932).

The upsurge of the workers in 1933, the influx of workers into A. F. of L. unions, and the formation of new independent unions placed sharply before the communists the necessity of intensifying their work within the reformist unions. The demagogic promises of Roosevelt's "New Deal" (see the next chapter) were taken seriously by many workers. The announcement by the President that the Industrial Codes under the National Industrial Recovery Act would guarantee the right to organize and to bargain collectively resulted, contrary to the expectations of the ruling class, in a great strike wave. The old trade unions were rejuvenated by large numbers of new members. Although the A. F. of L. claimed a million and a half new members at its 1933 Convention, a more realistic estimate places the number of new members in bona fide A. F. of L. unions at about 500,000. About 100,000 joined the revolutionary unions of the T. U. U. L. during this period and an equal number joined the independent unions. Alarmed at this growth in the trade unions, the employers and the government revived the company union system on a gigantic scale. The *Daily Worker* (December 22, 1933) estimated that by the end of 1933 several million workers had been forced into company unions.

Due to the influx of hitherto unorganized workers into the old trade unions, the character of some of them underwent a basic change. New blood was infusing a new militancy in organizations that were about ready for the scrap heap. In addition, it is especially noteworthy that the greatest growth took place among the workers in important industries, such as coal, textile, steel and food. The recruiting of large masses of workers in the A. F. of L. was facilitated by the left maneuvers of the officialdom on the question of wages and the shorter work-week, its leadership of strikes, although treacherous, and such organizational measures as lowering the initiation fees. The resolution of the Political Bureau of the Communist Party (December, 1933) pointed out that the policy of the bourgeoisie was "to transform the A. F of L. into a mass organization, which will be capable of disorganizing the struggles of the workers."

The same resolution also cites the "unwillingness or fear" of the workers to enter the revolutionary trade unions of the T. U. U. L. as well as the "weak and sectarian work" of these unions as reasons for their comparatively slow growth. Special emphasis is placed upon "the organization of opposition work within the mass unions," active participation in A. F. of L. union meetings, and systematic work within these unions "to fight from within for elected officials in the locals and for winning over these locals, to develop the initiative of the membership" by raising questions such as trade union democracy, the fight against the racketeers, etc. The demand is to be raised within the unions that strikes be carried through and that strike committees be elected at general meetings of all striking workers. At the same time, however, the resolution states that this does not mean the abandonment of the new industrial unions of the T. U. U. L. but, on the contrary, an intensification of work in that field to transform them into the center for militant industrial unionism.

The "Program of Action," adopted at a conference of communists active among the miners on December 16, 1933, in Pittsburgh, Pa., emphasized the building of a revolutionary opposition within the United Mine Workers. It stated:

"The policy of the Party has been throughout the building of the National Miners Union among the unorganized and the building of militant opposition within the U. M. W. of A. and the other miners' organizations. This policy undergoes a change only to the extent that the situation has changed. Thus, for example, while heretofore the mass of the miners of the Western Pennsylvania, Ohio and West Virginia fields were unorganized since 1928 and the N. M. U. had its main base there, at present the overwhelming majority of the miners in these fields are organized within the U. M. W. of A. The policy of the communists must therefore in the present conditions be to build the opposition movement within these unions, to assist the miners in carrying on the struggle against the operators, to expose the U. M. W. of A. bureaucrats, and fight for the election of militant miners to every post in the local unions, sub-district and district organization" (*Daily Worker*, December 23, 1933).

Similar steps were taken in the textile, marine and other industries to launch an energetic campaign for the organization of a militant opposition in the old unions.

Another important tendency to be noted during this period is the formation of independent unions, affiliated neither to the A. F. of L. nor the T. U. U. L. Some of them were formed as the result of the revolt of the workers against the A. F. of L. bureaucracy, such as the Progressive Miners of America (Illinois) and the United Anthracite Miners of Pennsylvania. The communists pointed out that leaders like Maloney and Capellini of the U. A. M. P., playing upon the opposition to the old bureaucracy, were also betraying these unions by negotiations behind the backs of the miners with the employers and the NRA. The communists set themselves the task of working within these independent unions with the purpose of winning the workers for militant struggle.

Independent unions were also formed in the textile, metal and shoe industries as a result of the struggle for higher wages and better working conditions under the NRA. These workers would have nothing to do with the A. F. of L. nor were they ready to join the Trade Union Unity League. The policy of the communists has been to encourage the organization of such unions and attempt to win their affiliation to the T. U. U. L. During the general strike of the silk workers in Paterson, N. J., in 1933, the National Textile Workers Union, affiliated to the T. U. U. L., proposed to the Associated Silk Workers and the United Textile Workers that one industrial union based on the class struggle be formed for the textile industry. The T. U. U. L. union was willing to merge itself into such an industrial union which would be independent of the A. F. of L. The reformist unions rejected the proposal.

A similar movement, however, was successful in the shoe industry, where the Shoe and Leather Workers Industrial Union, affiliated to the T. U. U. L., federated with a number of independent unions to form the United Shoe and Leather Workers Union with an initial total membership of 70,000. The amalgamation convention, held in Boston on December 11, 1933, defeated a motion to affiliate the new industrial union with the A. F. of L.

The movement for one union in the automobile industry was launched at a United Front Shop Conference in Detroit on December 17, 1933, called by the Auto Workers Union. Two hundred and twenty-five delegates were present, elected by workers of the Ford and General Motors shops, from the A. F. of L. auto locals and from the Mechanics Educational Society of America, an independent union. A similar movement has also been initiated in the furniture industry.

In the face of the employers' offensive and the more open alliance of the A. F. of L. leaders with the government and the employers, the slogan of unity in action and organization, on the basis of militant industrial unionism, will resound in all industries and among all workers with increased force.

CHAPTER XXXIII

The Crisis, 1929-1933

In the fall of 1933 the world economic crisis was in its fifth year. Every capitalist country in the world had been prostrated. Only the Soviet Union remained untouched by the great cataclysm. On the contrary, precisely in the period of the "great depression" did the Union of Socialist Soviet Republics make tremendous strides forward in the building of a socialist system of society.

The economic crisis is unprecedented in its severity, duration and universality. The present crisis differs fundamentally from the previous periodic crises of capitalism. It occurs on the basis of the general postwar crisis of capitalism. The temporary stabilization of the years 1923-1929 has given rise to a profound and acute crisis which is pregnant with new wars and revolutions. Secondly, the present crisis differs from previous ones in the sense that it is absolutely general, involving every nook and corner of the capitalist world, extending even to the most backward colonies and semi-colonies. Thirdly, the crisis occurs in the period of the existence of the Soviet Union which has withdrawn one-sixth of the earth's surface from the world system of capitalist economy. Fourthly, it takes place at a time when the whole world, with the exception of the territory of the Soviet Union, is completely divided among and exploited by the imperialist powers, especially the United States, England, France, Japan and Italy. This has the effect of intensifying the struggle of the colonial peoples for independence and of sharpening the antagonism between the powers to the point of war. Fifthly, the crisis takes place in the period of the existence of the Communist International with its 55 sections throughout the world devoted to the organization of the workers and peasants for the overthrow of capitalism.

At a time when bourgeois politicians and economists were hailing a new permanent era of prosperity, while the socialists were preaching the gospel of peaceful development from capitalism to socialism, the communists were able to foresee the coming catastrophe. As early as 1927, in his address before the Fifteenth Congress of the Communist Party of the Soviet Union, Joseph Stalin declared that "partial stabilization is giving rise to an intense crisis of capitalism, the maturing crisis is destroying stabilization." The Sixth World Congress of the Communist International, held in 1928, pointed out that under cover of seeming well-being internal and international antagonisms were being intensified and predicted that "the present stabilization period is growing into the period of *gigantic cataclysms.*" In a manifesto to the toilers of the world the International called upon them to prepare to meet the world-wide crisis. When Hoover was promising to banish poverty from the United States, the Communist International in an address to the American Communists in May, 1929, said:

> "With a distinctness unprecedented in history, American capitalism is exhibiting now the effects of the inexorable laws of capitalist development, the laws of decline and downfall of capitalist society. The general crisis of capitalism is growing more rapidly than it may seem at first glance. The crisis will also shake the foundations of the power of American imperialism."

It was in the United States where the post-war development of technique and productive capacity was most marked, that the economic crisis assumed its sharpest forms. The stock market crash in the fall of 1929 was a by-product of the economic crisis which had been developing for some time and itself tended to aggravate the crisis. Even during the height of post-war prosperity it was evident that the markets were remaining fixed, while production was increasing by leaps and bounds. Much of the new machinery was remaining idle. In 1927, for instance, steel ingot production was only 76% of capacity; automobile production in 1929, a record year, amounted to less than five and one-half million cars although the industry had a capacity of more than nine million. In the cotton textile industry nearly two and one-half million spindles were idle while millions of others operated only a few weeks or months.

At the same time a large permanent army of unemployed was being created. Speed-up and rationalization enabled a smaller number of workers to produce 40% more goods in 1929 than in 1919 and the output per worker rose 53.5% from 1919 to 1927. According to the highly conservative estimates published in *Recent Economic Changes in the United States,* the number of jobless between 1922 and 1927 never fell below one and one-half million. In 1928 the number of unemployed was estimated at four million by the Labor Bureau, Inc.

During the entire period of prosperity agriculture was suffering from a chronic crisis. Increased production of farm commodities brought about by technical improvements and expansion was confronted with a stagnant market in the country and a shrinking market abroad. In addition, farmers were suffering from a growing burden of indebtedness, incurred when farm products were selling at high prices. There was also a continually widening gulf between the prices which farmers received for their products and the monopoly prices which they paid for the goods they bought.

During the 1922-1929 period production rose to record heights. But the number of permanent unemployed, the decline in farm income and the rapid intensification of the contradiction between increased production and a restricted market made it evident that a severe crisis was in the making. In addition, wages were also dropping. From 1923 to 1929 factory production increased 18% but factory wage payments declined 3%.

The decline in industrial production began several months before the stock market crash. It was already evident in August and began to assume large proportions towards the end of the year. The stock market crash robbed millions of petty-bourgeois speculators and better paid workers of their savings and resulted in an enormous reduction in purchasing power. After April, 1930, the decline in production began to take on a catastrophic pace. By the time Hoover left office in March, 1933, industrial production fell by 51% as compared with July, 1929. This catastrophic drop brought the industrial output of the country down to the lowest levels since 1911, and, when measured in relation to population, down to the levels of the 19th century. Seventeen million workers were unemployed; agriculture was bankrupt; the entire banking system of the country was closed down.

When the decline in production is studied by industries the severity of the crisis is even more striking. Between July, 1929, and March, 1933, for instance, cement production dropped 65%, iron and steel 86% and lumber 78%. The production of steel ingots in 1932 had dropped 88% as compared with 1929, and pig iron production by 81%. In March, 1933, there were only 38 furnaces in blast as compared with 218 in June, 1929. The automobile industry in 1932 produced 1,426,000 vehicles as compared with 5,358,000 in 1929; construction contracts had dropped by 78%; bituminous coal production by almost half; lumber production was the lowest in 60 years.

Accompanying this drastic drop in production was an enormous growth in the number of unemployed and partly employed workers. According to the Federal Reserve Board, factory employment declined by 46% between June, 1929, and March, 1933. The Labor Research Association, in a careful estimate, found nearly 17,000,000 unemployed in November, 1932. According to the estimate of the Alexander Hamilton Institute, there were more than 17,000,000 jobless in March, 1933, distributed as follows:

Manufacturing	5,846,000	Railroads	803,000
Agriculture	1,253,000	Coal mining	282,000
Trade	2,951,000	Miscellaneous	3,713,000
Building	2,186,000		

In addition to these unemployed workers, there were millions employed only part time. Drastic wage-cuts and part-time employment had cut the average annual wages by almost half. In March, 1933, the Alexander Hamilton Institute, on the basis of current wage payments, estimated the average annual per capita income of those employed at $640 as compared with $1,157 in 1929. Secretary of Labor Perkins was forced to admit, on the basis of Bureau of Labor statistics, that "for every $10 paid out in weekly wages in 1926 by the plants surveyed only $4.31 was paid out in June, 1933."

It is erroneous to think that a rise in production would simultaneously and in the same degree reduce the army of unemployed. By the introduction of new and better machinery and especially through speed-up the employer is able to raise production to an enormous extent without at the same time employing more workers. It will suffice to point to steel production. In May, 1933, there was an increase in ingot production of 105% over the monthly average for the first quarter of 1933, while at the same time total wage earners employed increased only by 3.7%; average actual hourly earnings increased only 2.6%; total man-hours worked increased 40.8%; average weekly earnings, due to the greater number of hours worked, increased 25.2%. While tons produced per man-hour in May increased 43.2% over the monthly average for the first quarter of the year, wages per ton produced *decreased* by 32.8%.

This fact suffices to show that even should industrial production approach pre-crisis levels, which is highly doubtful, there will be an enormous army of permanent unemployed, reaching ten or more millions of workers who have been displaced permanently by rationalization in the process of production.

The development of the economic crisis sharply aggravated the chronic crisis in agriculture. While the prices for goods which the farmer bought remained relatively stable, the prices of farm products fell more than 60%. Farm income and farm land values dropped sharply. Millions of farmers were impoverished and bankrupt; while hundreds of thousands of others were actually foreclosed and driven off their lands. From July, 1929, to February, 1933, wholesale wheat prices dropped from $1.30 per bushel to $.48; corn from $1.00 per bushel to $.23; hogs from $11.20 per 100 pounds to $3.41; cotton from 19 cents to 6 cents a pound. According to the Department of Agriculture the gross farm income dropped by over 50% between 1929 and 1932. The value of farm property, including land and machinery, declined by $14,000,000,000 in two years, between 1930 and 1932. According to Bernhard Ostrolenk, agricultural economist, more than 30% of all mortgaged farms were worth less than their mortgages in 1932.

Most farmers during the crisis were unable to meet production costs, much less meet usurious debt charges and pay exorbitant taxes, and were therefore under the continual threat of bankruptcy and eviction. By 1932 forty out of every thousand farms were foreclosed for mortgages or taxes. The New York *Herald Tribune* estimates that there were 258,000 forced sales in 1932. Undoubtedly the number would have been much higher had it not been for the militant resistance put up by the farmers during the summer and autumn months.

The deepening of the crisis in industry and agriculture inevitably undermined the position of the banks. Although during the first stages of the crisis there were no major bank crashes, there was an enormous wave of small bank failures. The first to begin to fail in large numbers were the rural banks. In 1930, 1,345 banks, with aggregate deposits of $863,715,000, closed their doors. Among these was the Bank of the United States, in New York City, which crashed in December, wiping out the savings of hundreds of thousands of small depositors. This ushered in a whole series of fairly large urban bank failures. In 1931 bank failures reached the record peak of 2,298, with deposits totaling $1,681,510,000. The money and credit crisis which broke out in Europe in the summer of 1931 and Britain's abandonment of the gold standard in September, 1931, had immediate repercussions in the United States. During the last quarter of 1931, the panic had reached such a stage that banks were failing at the rate of 350 a month. Despite the effort of the Hoover administration to bolster up the banks through the Reconstruction Finance Corporation which was organized to advance funds, 1,453 banks failed in 1932 with deposits totaling $730,000,000. But the basic condition of the banks continued to grow more and more precarious due to the deepening of the crisis. Towards the end of January, 1933, deposits in closed banks averaged more than $1,300,000 for each bank, indicating that very large institutions were being affected. In February, 1933, a run occurred on the largest banks in Detroit, and in order to prevent their collapse, the governor of Michigan declared a state-wide banking holiday. Runs on the banks followed throughout the country and the financial panic was in full swing. Bank holidays were declared in one state after another and by March 4 the entire banking system of the country had shut down.

The devastating and comprehensive character of the crisis is also shown by the reduction in exports. From 1929 to 1932 physical volume of exports dropped by 48% in the United States, and in dollars by 69%. Except in the Far East, American exports had fallen in 1932 not only below the World War export figures but also below the yearly average of 1910-1914.

Needless to say, the whole burden of the crisis had been placed upon the shoulders of the working masses. Never before in American history had there been so sudden and so drastic a reduction of the standard of living for the broad masses of the population. Figures of production, unemployment and wage decreases do not give the entire story. Despite the fact that wholesale prices had dropped considerably, the retail prices which the workers had to pay had fallen very little, which amounted in reality to an additional wage-cut. Furthermore, the rationalization carried out during the crisis and the reduction in wages had a devastating effect upon the income of the working class. The temporary increase in production in the months from April to July, 1933, as a result of the "boom" stimulated by inflation, demonstrated what the workers were to expect even if there were to be a temporary recovery from the economic crisis. While production was increasing at an extraordinary rate, factory employment and payrolls rose comparatively little. From July, 1932, to July, 1933, the Federal Reserve Board index for factory production rose from 55 to 94. During the same period, the index for factory employment rose from 58.3 to 70.1, and the index for factory payrolls from 39.6 to 49.9. But even this comparatively small rise in factory wage payments was offset to a considerable extent by the rapid rise in retail prices and in the cost of living brought on by inflation. As for unemployment, even the bourgeois economist, Stuart Chase, after allowing for all possible benefits arising from an upturn, estimated that the number of unemployed in 1934 would be 12,200,000. Even this estimate, he admits, may be too low.

While the crisis in the capitalist world was sinking to lower and lower levels, impoverishing and degrading huge sections of the population, the Soviet Union was demonstrating the superiority of socialist economy. It was precisely in the years of the worst economic crisis that the capitalist world had ever experienced, that tremendous advances were made in the building of socialism. At the beginning of 1933 when the capitalist world was entering upon the deepest phase of the crisis, the first Five-Year Plan had laid the socialist foundations in the economy of the Soviet Union. In 1928, when the first Plan was inaugurated, the Soviet Union had just about reconstructed its industry and agriculture to the level of pre-war Russia. It was a level that was backward as compared with the capitalist countries. Between 1928-1933 a predominantly agricultural country had been changed into a predominantly industrial country, not on the basis of private ownership, but on the basis of the collective ownership by the workers and peasants of the means of production and the land.

A few key figures will suffice to demonstrate the tremendous achievements of the first Soviet state. The national income, measured in constant prices of 1926-1927, had increased by 67% from 1928 to 1932. While in the United States industrial production had decreased by over 50%, in the Soviet Union it rose by 118.5% from 1928 to 1932. If we take the key industries we find how thoroughgoing this increase was. During the same period, the production of pig iron increased by 83%, of coal by 79%, of oil by 80% and in machine building by 291%. The capacity of electric stations in 1932 increased by 144% as compared with 1928, and electric current production increased by 162% for the same period. By the end of 1932 the Soviet Union was first in the world in the production of tractors and agricultural machinery, first in Europe in the production of engineering machinery and pig iron, first in Europe and second in the world in the production of oil, third in the world in the production of electrical energy and fourth in the production of coal and chemicals.

The bumper 1933 harvest, one of the largest on record, marked the decisive success of the Soviet farm program. The first Five-Year Plan had contemplated the collectivization of six million peasant holdings, with a cultivated area of 52,000,000 acres. Actually, by the end of 1932, the Plan was overfulfilled two and one-half times—14,700,000 peasant households, or 61.5% of the total, had entered the collective farms and had sown 226,000,000 acres. The tremendous transformation that had taken place can better be understood if the following figures are taken: in 1928, 97.3% of the total sown area had been cultivated by individual peasants; in 1932 the individual peasants accounted for only 22% of the total sown area. By the end of the first Five-Year Plan, large-scale mechanized collective farming had become the dominant form of land cultivation in the Soviet Union.

In the United States at least 17,000,000 workers were unemployed during the height of the crisis. In the Soviet Union, between 1928 and 1933, unemployment had not only been totally eliminated, but the number of wage-earners increased from 11,559,000 to 22,804,300 or nearly doubled. During the same period the national payroll was quadrupled. Individual wages, therefore, had risen 100%!

The first Plan marked an all-round improvement in the living conditions of the masses, despite the great difficulties which they endured in making the building of Socialism possible. The achievements of a social and cultural character were just as stupendous as the advances in industry and agriculture which made the former possible. The general 7-hour workday (six hours in hazardous occupations) was established. The Soviet system of social insurance, with its provisions for sickness, old age, accidents, child-birth, vacations, etc., has no equal in any other part of the world. Universal compulsory education was established and illiteracy practically wiped out. In a country where cultural institutions had been closed to workers, there was created a vast system of technical schools, colleges, clubs, libraries, museums, theaters, movies, radio, sports, cultural circles, sanatoriums, etc.—created especially for the benefit of the workers. The system of health protection and care of children is far in advance of similar systems anywhere. Book and newspaper publishing has been developed to a greater extent than in any capitalist country. New forms and methods of labor have been created which establish the leading rôle of the worker and release his creative energy—such as, socialist competition, shock-brigades, counter-planning, business-accounting brigades, workers' inventions. Every opportunity for self-improvement is placed at the disposal of the worker, every inducement is given him to become more adept in his trade, to receive a higher education, or to become a technician. Nearly 3,000,000 highly qualified workers, including engineers, chemists and other technicians, were trained during the first Plan.

The future is even more promising, despite the ever-growing danger of imperialist attack against the Soviet Union. When the First Plan had been announced it was met by universal ridicule in capitalist circles. Its success, however, caused the announcement of the details of the Second Five-Year Plan on December 31, 1933, to be met with universal respect despite the stupendous advances it envisioned. There was no doubt that these would be achieved. The new Plan provided for an increase in the total production of the country from two and one-half to three times above the level of 1932, and nine times above the level of 1913. For industry it provided a total annual output by the end of 1937 of 103,000,000,000 rubles as compared with 43,000,000,000 in 1932, of which more than half was to be in goods of popular consumption. The first Plan had provided the basic industries necessary for the manufacture of the means of production; the second Plan placed more emphasis upon providing necessities for the population. Real wages are to more than double, the general consumption of goods is to increase threefold, retail prices are to be reduced thirty to forty per cent. When the Second Five-Year Plan is completed not only will illiteracy and semi-illiteracy have disappeared but there will be functioning a system of general compulsory polytechnical education in seven-year schools. Health funds will be tremendously increased and hundreds of new cultural and recreational centers opened.

The chief political tasks of the new Plan, as defined by the conference of the Communist Party of the U. S. S. R. held at the end of 1932, are: "the final liquidation of the capitalist elements and of the classes in general; fully to destroy the causes which give rise to class distinction and exploitation; to overcome the survivals of capitalism in the economy and in the consciousness of people; to transform the whole working population of the country into conscious, active builders of a classless, socialist society."

When the crisis broke out in the United States the workers were totally unprepared to meet the onslaught of the employers and the government. Lacking a powerful militant labor movement, misled by the American Federation of Labor officialdom, the first devastating inroads of the crisis were met by more or less passivity on the part of organized labor. In addition, in the face of the first sudden mass dismissals, the workers were cautious in undertaking economic struggles on their own account. Since the widespread strikes of 1919-1922, there had been a marked decrease in labor struggles coinciding with the period of "prosperity." In 1919, the number of workers involved in strikes were 4,160,300, and in 1922 the number was 1,612,500. By 1927 the number of strikers had decreased to 349,400 and in 1929, the banner year of "prosperity," there were 903 strikes in which 230,000 workers participated. In 1930, the first year of the crisis, the number of strikes had fallen to 618 in which 156,000 workers took part.

The attitude of the leadership of the American Federation of Labor was in large measure responsible for the passivity of the workers in the face of the crisis. Despite the increased unemployment and the falling off of production in certain industries during the years 1927-1929 the reformist unions continued to act upon the advice given by the Executive Council at the convention of the A. F. of L. in 1927: "Formerly labor has allowed spectacular incidents of strife to overshadow the more important events of constructive development and service. The Federation has taken the initiative in reversing this attitude. . . ."

At the very beginning of the crisis the trade union bureaucracy pledged coöperation with the employers. At the White House Conference of employers, the government and the leaders of the American Federation of Labor and the railroad brotherhoods, convened by President Hoover on November 11, 1929, they pledged not to seek wage advances or to strike during the economic crisis. In return for a vague promise from a group of open-shop industrialists that wages would not be reduced during the period, the labor officials promised according to the statement given out by Hoover, that "no movements beyond those already in negotiation should be initiated for increase of wages and that every coöperation should be given by labor to industry in the solution of its problems."

The trade union bureaucracy not only fulfilled its pledge but did everything in its power to prevent strikes when undertaken independently by the workers and to help crush them or betray them when they occurred. On their part, the employers and the government completely overlooked their part of the "bargain" and wages were cut on every hand. Although there were few strikes during the first crisis years, they were very bitterly fought and the oppressive measures used to crush them were more severe than in the past. The strike wave in the South continued into 1930. The largest strike occurred at Danville, Va., where textile workers engaged in a bitter struggle against a 10% wage-cut. Smaller strikes occurred at Bessemer City, N. C., and Elizabethton, Tenn., in the same year. In all of them the officials of the United Textile Workers and of the American Federation of Labor, who had announced a "Southern organization campaign," contributed to the defeat of the strikes by secret negotiations.

The outstanding struggles of the early crisis years occurred in the coal fields. On May 28, 1931, 40,000 miners in the bituminous coal fields of western Pennsylvania and eastern Ohio walked out under the leadership of the National Miners Union. The strike was militantly fought against sharpened company and government terror. The strike was crushed with the aid of the United Mine Workers officials who, with the help of Governor Pinchot of Pennsylvania, signed an agreement with the Pittsburgh Terminal Coal Company. The full force of government repression and coal corporation terror was brought to bear upon the miners of the Harlan, Ky., fields when they struck under the leadership of the National Miners Union at the beginning of 1931. The United Mine Workers and the I. W. W. appeared on the scene to split the ranks of the strikers. Hundreds of thugs were imported by the coal operators and deputized. On May 5 open warfare raged when an army of thugs opened fire upon a group of miners. In the battle one striker and three thugs were killed. This was the signal for even greater terror. Forty-four miners were arrested, charged with murder and some of them convicted to life imprisonment. Harry Simms, a youth organizer of the National Miners Union, was waylaid and murdered in cold blood by company thugs. The strike was defeated and the union driven underground.

The struggles of the unemployed overshadowed all other events in the labor movement during this period. The absence of any kind of social insurance, totally inadequate relief for the unemployed brought almost immediate privation and even starvation to workers as soon as they lost their jobs or exhausted meager savings. Almost from the time the first effects of the crisis began to make themselves felt in the form of mass dismissals the unemployed entered upon a struggle to save themselves from starvation. The Communist Party was the organizer and leader of this movement.

As we have seen in the previous chapter, as early as the beginning of 1928 the Communist Party had already formulated demands for the unemployed, which included unemployment insurance at the expense of the government and the employers, the 44-hour 5-day week, public works and immediate relief. Its proposal for a federal unemployment insurance bill demanded that the amount of compensation should be full wages, not exceeding $30 per week, for the entire period of unemployment. The unemployment fund to be established was to be provided equally by the employers and the government and its administration was to be in the hands of federal, State and city unemployment insurance commissions composed of representatives of trade unions, organizations of the unemployed and factory, mill and mine committees.

At the same time, the Party was already calling for the formation of unemployed councils and urging the unions to take the initiative in organizing the unemployed. It is historically significant, that almost two years before the crisis broke out, the communists formulated demands for the jobless and indicated the form of organization for them.

The gigantic unemployed demonstration on March 6, 1930, called and led by the Communist Party, the Unemployed Councils and the Trade Union Unity League, forced the government and the bourgeoisie generally to take open cognizance of the mass unemployment and undertake some relief activities. It was estimated that at least one and a quarter million workers participated in these demonstrations throughout the country, under the central slogan of "Work or Wages!" About 100,000 took part in the demonstrations in New York and Detroit; 50,000 on the Boston Common and in Chicago; 40,000 in Milwaukee; 30,000 in Philadelphia; about 20,000 in Pittsburgh, Cleveland and Youngstown, Ohio. Smaller demonstrations occurred in practically every industrial center.

As if pre-arranged, a nation-wide attack upon these demonstrations took place. Grover Whalen, police commissioner of New York, mobilized practically the whole police force armed with tear gas, riot guns and machine guns. As the demonstrators began to fall into line to march from Union Square to the City Hall in order to place their demands before the Mayor, a ferocious attack by police on horseback and on foot was let loose against the workers. Horses rode roughshod over defenseless men, women and children, clubs and billies rained down on the heads of the workers. At least a hundred workers had to be treated in hospitals. In the meantime, the members of the committee elected by the demonstrators to present their demands at the City Hall were arrested on the City Hall steps before they even had an opportunity to make their mission known. William Z. Foster, Israel Amter, Robert Minor, Joseph Lester and Harry Raymond were charged with "inciting to riot" and sentenced to six months in the workhouse. Appeal was denied and they served their terms. Equally brutal attacks occurred in other cities, including Milwaukee which boasted the socialist mayor, Hoan.

Despite this attempt to still the demands of the unemployed by open repression, these demonstrations achieved their major purpose. The federal government could no longer ignore the question of unemployment and the demands for relief brought so sharply to its attention. On the following day, President Hoover, Secretary of Commerce Lamont, Secretary of Labor Davis and Assistant Secretary of Commerce Klein met to consider unemployment. The only immediate result was a statement issued by Hoover reassuring the bourgeoisie and declaring everything to be normal. Nevertheless, the demonstrations forced local and state governments to undertake some relief activities and Washington to at least begin its first serious consideration of the problem.

The mood of the workers as revealed at the mass turnout in the demonstrations continued to express itself in the organization of the unemployed. On March 29, 1930, a National Preliminary Conference on Unemployment, called by the Trade Union Unity League, opened in New York, with 215 delegates from the industrial unions, the left-wing opposition groups in the reformist unions, some locals of the A. F. of L. and unemployed councils. The program adopted by the conference called for the organization of unemployed councils in all industrial cities, for the formation of joint committees of action composed of members of the councils and union locals. City committees or city councils of the unemployed were to be organized on which the unions were to have representation and which were to initiate and lead local struggles. From the beginning, the aim was to coördinate the struggles of the unemployed with those of the employed workers who were suffering severe wage-cuts, speed-up and a general attack upon their conditions as a result of the crisis. Struggles were to be waged on the basis of a broad united front including the members of the A. F. of L. locals and other unemployed organizations under the leadership of socialists or reformists. Besides the general demand for social insurance, demands for immediate relief adapted to the local situation were to be raised. No discrimination against Negroes or foreign-born workers in the administration of relief and complete equality for these workers in the organizations was a cardinal principle.

As unemployment grew by leaps and bounds during the years 1931-1932, the activities of the unemployed increased and many councils were organized on the basis of struggles for immediate relief, against evictions, for adequate housing facilities for the homeless unemployed, etc. The amount of relief that city and state governments and private charitable institutions were forced to disburse rose in direct proportion to the activity of the workers themselves. Hundreds of demonstrations were held on a neighborhood as well as state-wide scale. City, county and state hunger marches took place throughout the country. Rarely did a state legislature in the industrial areas convene during these years without being confronted either by a mass hunger march or a committee elected by the unemployed to present their demands.

Police brutality and repressive measures by the state marked all these struggles and increased in intensity as the crisis continued to deepen. We cannot here enumerate the thousands of such instances. But the cold-blooded massacre of unemployed workers by police and thugs of the Ford Plant in Dearborn, Mich., on Monday, March 7, 1932, overshadows all other local struggles of the period and deserves more detailed attention. It is of special importance for it is an outstanding example of the participation of both employed and unemployed workers in the struggle against starvation.

When Ford announced in 1929 that he would hire 30,000 additional men, thousands of workers from all over the country rushed to Detroit to find that no hiring was taking place. The thousands of men who waited in line all day and night in zero weather were dispersed by fire hose. When the same thing happened in 1930, 10,000 workers stormed the factory at Dearborn, near Detroit, and smashed the hiring office. When Ford dismissed thousands of workers at one stroke in the summer of 1931, they rebelled, smashing machinery and fighting off the company service men (thugs). Machine guns were set up in the plant and the workers threatened with death if they did not surrender. Dismissals continued and an increasing number of auto workers were facing starvation. In Detroit, where most of the Ford workers lived, the liberal administration of Mayor Frank Murphy (at present governor-general of the Philippines) was steadily reducing the relief rations. The Auto Workers Union and the Detroit Unemployed Councils called for a hunger march upon the Ford factory in Dearborn to demand jobs, relief and the abolition of the service department. On March 7, the coldest day of the year, 5,000 men, women and young workers marched upon Dearborn, which is a company town controlled by Ford. They were met at the city limits by a tear gas barrage let loose by the Dearborn police, but succeeded in pushing the police back for nearly two miles. At the plant the marchers were met by pistol and machine-gun fire, while Edsel Ford, Mayor Clyde Ford of Dearborn and ex-governor Fred Green calmly looked on. Four marchers were killed: Joe York, 19, Joe Russell, 16, both leaders of the Young Communist League; Coleman Leny, 25, and Joe de Blasio, 27. Twenty-two others collapsed under the withering fire and many others suffered club and gun wounds. Following the massacre a reign of terror set in. The wounded were put under arrest and chained to hospital cots; offices of the Trade Union Unity League, Auto Workers' Union, Unemployed Councils and Communist Party were raided. Communist leaders, including William Z. Foster, presidential candidate, were threatened with life imprisonment. "But within twenty-four hours of the massacre," says Robert Cruden, who gives an eye-witness account of the events in his *The End of the Ford Myth*, "it was plain to even the dullest capitalists in Detroit, that they dared not further antagonize the working class." Ford and his local government puppets had to back down and charges were dismissed against the arrested workers. On Friday, March 12, the four victims of the Ford massacre were buried. At least 40,0000 marched to the cemetery, which is located within view of the Ford plant, and swore "to avenge the four murdered workers." A monument, funds for which were donated by workers all over the country, marks the grave of Ford's victims.

Another outstanding local struggle took place in Chicago in October, 1932, when a united front movement forced the administration to rescind a 50% relief cut against 160,000 family men. The struggle was initiated by the Unemployed Councils of Chicago. The response was so great that the socialist-controlled Workers Committee on Unemployment and other unemployed organizations under reformist leadership were forced to participate in the united front. When it was evident that the struggle would assume mass proportions and threaten their control, the socialists decided to withdraw their organizations from the united front and disrupt it. But when they proposed withdrawal at a conference of their organizations the membership turned it down by a vote of 74 to 18. The

United Front Conference against the relief cut was attended by 700 delegates from 350 organizations. The movement was so militant that the workers not only defeated the cut, but also gained the right to demonstrate on the streets, which had been denied them.

The winter of 1931 saw the first hunger march upon Washington since the so-called Coxey armies converged upon the nation's capital in 1894. Organized by the Unemployed Councils, the Trade Union Unity League and the Communist Party, about 1,500 delegates of the unemployed poured into Washington on December 6 to present their demands to the 72nd Congress at its opening session. They found the city an armed camp. On their arrival, however, the federal government was forced to provide food and shelter for the marchers. On the following day, between rows of armed police, they marched to the Capitol. Tens of thousands of spectators were separated from the marchers by a fence. Machine guns looked down upon them from the Capitol steps. The committee elected to present demands before Congress, was forcibly prevented from entering the Capitol. Amidst shouts of "We demand unemployment insurance! We demand Relief! We Demand Bread!" the marchers turned to the White House to place their demands before the President. Here their committee was also refused admission. For the first time the "International" was sung and played on the Capitol grounds. Turned down by the federal government, the marchers adopted a draft of a bill for unemployment insurance and for immediate relief at the expense of the employers and the state, and called upon workers throughout the country to support their demands.

When Congress convened in December, 1932, they were faced with a second National Hunger March, organized by the Unemployed Councils, and composed of 3,000 marchers representing 250,000 organized unemployed and employed workers. Local preparations for the march had included struggles for relief and against evictions as well as numerous local and state hunger marches and demonstrations. In Chicago, St. Louis, Cleveland, New York and Philadelphia the city administrations had been forced to give relief or appropriate additional funds for this purpose. There was a marked improvement in the preparations over the previous year and as a result the march branched from every important industrial section in the country, including workers of all the major industries, Negroes, women and youth, and delegates from opposition groups in a number of A. F. of L. locals. As the National Hunger March gathered impetus, the newspapers were filled with predictions of an upturn in the crisis and open threats against the marchers, inspired by official circles in Washington. Obstacles and inconveniences of all kinds were placed in the way of the marchers. As the Eastern Column approached Wilmington, Del., it was halted by city police and officials who warned the workers against entering the city. The trucks, however, pushed on and the marchers were provided with quarters by the workers of the city. A fierce attack was launched by the police upon one group of delegates, mostly women, housed in an old church. But despite these obstacles and with the aid of the workers in the cities the columns pushed through and arrived in Washington intact. The marchers, however, were not permitted to hold their conference in the city of Washington. On a secluded highway near the city, roped off and surrounded by heavily armed police and detectives, their conference was held and their demands formulated. In spite of every effort to prevent them, the delegates marched through the streets of Washington and presented their demands to Congress. They demanded $50 cash winter relief for each unemployed worker plus $10 for each dependent, in addition to local and state relief.

Although the strength of the movement had not yet reached the point of forcing the passage of a federal social insurance bill, the National Hunger Marches made unemployment the leading national issue and demonstrated that the unemployed would put up a stubborn struggle for adequate relief. Furthermore, they prepared the way for the unification of the more or less isolated struggles of the unemployed into a national movement and placed the communist-led organizations in a position of national leadership. Last but not least, the hunger marches were a sharp rebuke to the skeptics and opportunists who maintain that the workers of America will never be roused to a serious struggle against the "democratic" government.

The first National Hunger March inspired the Bonus March of the World War veterans to Washington. Four hundred ex-servicemen, who participated in the first hunger march, held a conference in Washington where they decided to start a fight for the immediate payment of the bonus promised them by the government after the World War. The Ways and Means Committee of Congress turned down this demand when it was placed before them in April, 1932, by a delegation of the Workers' Ex-Servicemen's League. Thereupon the League called for a mass march of veterans to meet in Washington on June 7, 1932. The question of the bonus agitated the veterans throughout the country and the movement for the march developed rapidly and spontaneously. The leaders of the American Legion and the Veterans of Foreign Wars refused to permit their members to vote on the question and did everything in their power to stop the march. The veterans gathered in large contingents in all parts of the country and seized trains to transport them. The federal government used every possible device to stop the march but to no avail.

Official Washington was aghast and terror-stricken when 20,000 ragged veterans poured into the city bearing signs: "Heroes of 1917—Bums of

1932" and "We Fought for Democracy—What Did We Get?" The veterans represented a cross-section of the unemployed workers and petty-bourgeois masses of the nation. In its ranks there were unemployed workers, discharged white-collar workers, bankrupt farmers, ruined small businessmen, many of them still having strong illusions about the democracy for which they had fought, but all of them insistent upon obtaining immediate payment of the bonus.

President Hoover branded them as scums, criminals and reds! But when it became apparent that the veterans would not budge from their encampment in Camp Anacostia, on the outskirts of Washington, and from the semi-demolished buildings which served as their quarters in the city, government agents and traitors of the veterans were manipulated into the leadership of the Bonus Army. These included Walter W. Waters, a former factory manager of Oregon; H. B. Foulkrod, a stool-pigeon of the Burns Detective Agency; and Doak E. Carter, ex-detective of the Pennsylvania Railroad. These scoundrels attempted to crush the revolt of the veterans from within and instituted a reign of terror against the communists and other militant veterans in the army. Congress flatly turned down the demands of the veterans.

Five days after Congress adjourned, the District of Columbia Commissioners issued the order for evacuation. The veterans declared that they would not budge. Waters had to admit: "These men are no longer under my control!" On the morning of July 28, the police attacked the veterans within the city limits, the contingents under the leadership of the Workers' Ex-Servicemen's League. William Hushka, a Lithuanian worker from Chicago and a member of the League, and Eric Carlson were shot to death by the police. The veterans, however, repulsed the first police attack. Then Hoover called out the army to drive the former soldiers from the city and Camp Anacostia. Infantry, cavalry and machine-gun squads, in battle array, swept down upon the encamped veterans. Before a barrage of tear gas and at the point of bayonets the veterans were driven from their camp, fighting every foot of ground and giving battle with whatever missiles were at hand. The camp was burned to the ground. The charred remains of Camp Anacostia was the reply of the federal government to the demand for the payment of the bonus.

While recognizing the diverse elements of the Bonus March and the confused character of its program, the Communist Party appreciated its objective revolutionary character and gave it encouragement and support. The attitude of the socialist leaders hardly differed in any essential respects from that of Hoover. They branded the veterans as a selfish group seeking special privileges and did all in their power to defeat its purposes.

It was not until 1932 that the American Federation of Labor finally gave lip-service to the demand for unemployment insurance, the most pressing and immediate demand of the American working class. At the Boston Convention in 1930 the A. F. of L. bureaucracy rejected an unemployment insurance resolution with the ridiculous question: "Is it not true that unemployment schemes of the sort advocated in the resolutions before this Convention will tend to prevent the workers from joining in the movement to increase wages and improve working conditions because of fears that they might thus sacrifice their eligibility to unemployment insurance?"

At the Vancouver Convention in 1931 the proposition was again rejected on the ground that it would "amount to a virtual surrender on the part of the workers in the battles they are now waging in many industries for recognition of their right to organize" and that it is "calculated to give the employers increased power of control over the workers." These hypocritical evasions, however, could not suffice for long. Under pressure from its membership, the Executive Council of the Federation formulated a compulsory insurance plan on July 22, 1932. This proved to be merely a paper resolution, indicating, however, the strength of the movement for social insurance in the ranks of the A. F. of L. membership.

This movement was given organized expression at a conference, held on January 27, 1932, composed of rank-and-file delegates of A. F. of L. unions. The purpose of the conference was to unite all those in the Federation willing to organize and fight for unemployment insurance. The bill adopted by this conference provided for immediate unemployment insurance at full wages (on the basis of the yearly average) at the expense of the employers and the government, the insurance fund to be controlled and administered by committees elected by the workers. The conference set up the American Federation of Labor Committee for Unemployment Insurance to coördinate the work in the A. F. of L. unions and mobilize additional support for the Bill.

A national conference of the adherents of the Committee for Unemployment Insurance was held in Washington in 1933, simultaneously with the annual A. F. of L. Convention. Resolutions passed by the conference, one of which demanded that no A. F. of L. official participate in the NRA and another calling for unemployment insurance, were submitted to the A. F. of L. Convention by a delegate of the Cleaners and Dyers Union of Philadelphia. The resolutions were buried in committee by the A. F. of L. leaders and were completely suppressed. A speech by a delegate from Chicago, exposing racketeering in the unions, was expunged from the records.

The demand for social insurance, raised so sharply and pushed to the fore by the communists, is one of the most pressing and vital needs of the American working class. As we have already shown, even an industrial upturn in this country to the highest possible level, will leave a permanent army of jobless of over 12,000,000. This does not include the mass additions to it which will come from the impoverishment of other layers of the population, such as the farmers and the petty-bourgeoisie. This becomes more evident from day to day and the demand for social insurance promises to be one of the main rallying centers for the coming struggles of the American workers.

The years of deepening crisis also engulfed other layers of the population besides the proletariat in an open struggle for existence. The mass struggles of the farmers for relief, against foreclosures and burden of debt as well as the bitter struggles of the Negro people for bread, land and liberty, brought sharply home to all advanced workers the revolutionary potentialities of these allies in a decisive struggle against capitalism. The revolt on the countryside achieved a higher degree of militancy than had been reached even in the days of the populist movement of the 'eighties and 'nineties. The movement, led principally by the middle farmers but participated in by wide sections of the farm population, took the form of mass resistance to evictions and foreclosures, the mass boycott of the market and the use of picket lines to prevent the marketing of farm produce until the prices were raised, marches on county seats, etc. Here it must suffice to point out that the most important revolutionary aspect of the movement was the growing influence of the United Farmers League and the Committees of Action of the National Farmers Conference. For these organizations, as opposed to the reformist and demagogic Farmers' Holiday Association, the Farmers' Union, etc., were laying the groundwork for the unity of the poor and middle farmers with the proletariat.

The National Farmers' Conference held its second national meeting on November 15-18, 1933, in Chicago, with 702 delegates attending. Of these, 619 represented farmers' organizations in all parts of the country, including local groups of the Farmers' Holiday Association, the Grangers and the United Farmers League. Eighty-three fraternal delegates represented workers' organizations and other non-farmer groups. The Call to Action issued by the Conference stressed the demands for cash relief, cancellation of debts such as mortgages, interest, etc.; exemption of ruined and impoverished farmers from taxes and reduction of taxes for middle farmers; against foreclosures and evictions. It was pointed out that the Conference, as shown by the class composition of the delegates, had based its activities almost entirely upon the demands of the middle farmer while paying little attention to the small farmer and poor tenant. In the future the main emphasis was to be placed upon these strata of the farm population.

The Agricultural Workers Industrial Union, affiliated to the Trade

Union Unity League, led numerous strikes on the vegetable farms of California in 1932-1933, winning many of them.

The revolutionary wing of the farm movement stubbornly opposed every effort on the part of the federal régime and the reformist farm leaders to strengthen the bulwark of reaction on the countryside by obtaining certain benefits for the bigger farmers at the expense of the city proletariat and the poor farmers. Fascism obtains an important part of its mass support from the more well-to-do farmers either by promising them or actually granting them certain concessions. The struggle against fascism in this country demands that the workers form a fighting alliance with the poorer strata of the farm population in the struggle against impoverishment.

Just as the problems aroused by the crisis caused the communists to begin their first serious work among the farmers, the same period saw marked advances in gaining the support of large sections of the Negro people. Neither the Socialist Party in its entire history nor the organized labor movement had made any lasting or serious attempts to break down the race prejudice which had seeped into the ranks of the workers. When, therefore, the communists in the years 1928-1930 clarified their own position in regard to the Negro question and proceeded to wage a relentless struggle against white chauvinism and for equal rights for Negroes they opened the doors of the revolutionary movement to a whole new section of the population. Increased participation of Negroes, who suffered most of all from the crisis, in all phases of the labor movement was immediately apparent. In the organization and work of the new industrial unions, in the unemployed movement, in the activities of the International Labor Defense, Negroes played an active and leading rôle. The growth of the Communist Party in the South, especially in the Black Belt regions and in the heavy industrial area of Birmingham, bore eloquent testimony to the fact that the communists were in earnest in their struggle for Negro liberation. By the end of 1933, the Share-Croppers Union of Talapoosa County, Ala., and vicinity, which had engaged in two major struggles with the landowners in 1931 and 1933 and withstood the terror loosed against it, could report over 5,000 members. The communists were active in many other important sections of the deep South, sections which had hitherto been untouched by the revolutionary movement. The movement initiated and led by the communists in defense of the nine Negro boys framed on a charge of rape has become known throughout the world as the Scottsboro Case and has aroused larger and larger sections of the white working class, as well as of the Negro people, to the struggle for Negro liberation. It had a profound effect upon the Negro workers who had hitherto learned to distrust the labor movement due to the chauvinistic practices of the labor bureaucracy and the advice of their own nationalist leaders. A new period had been inaugurated in the relations between white and black labor in the United States.

In their program on the Negro question the communists have for the first time applied the full principles of internationalism and the experiences of the world-wide movement of the oppressed nations and colonial peoples for independence. The fundamental theoretical basis of this program is the characterization of the Negro people as an oppressed nation, which has been most assiduously retarded in its economic and social development by Yankee imperialism. As a result, every section of the Negro people suffers from discrimination and every form of degradation imposed by an oppressing nation. The economic basis for this oppression rests in the semi-feudal exploitation of the Negroes in the Southern Black Belt, where they form the majority of the population. Although millions of Negroes have migrated out of the Black Belt, especially since the World War, the whole social atmosphere of ostracism and persecution built over a long historical period in the South, still clings to them. The only way, therefore, the Negroes in all parts of the country can be assured of full and lasting equality, is by winning the right of self-determination in the Black Belt of the South. The struggle for this right, the communists point out, is bound up closely with the revolutionary struggle for the overthrow of the plantation and tenant system in the South and the establishment of state unity in that territory where the Negroes have historically formed the majority of the population and where they constitute the majority to-day. In the present period of imperialism this movement for land, equality and freedom constitutes a powerful revolutionary ally of the proletarian movement and can be led successfully only by the proletariat, white and black. The migration of large numbers of Negroes into non-Southern industrial areas as well as the industrialization of the South has increased the number of Negro workers and made possible the solidarity of white and black workers on the basis of a common struggle, thus strengthening the decisive class in the struggle for Negro liberation. This is the program adapted also by the League of Struggle for Negro Rights, which was reorganized in 1930 from the American Negro Labor Congress.

The presidential election of 1932 occurred when the whole machinery of production was approaching a stage verging on total collapse. Such a sane bourgeois professor as Irving Fisher of Yale University warned that "our very national existence is at stake" and that "halfway, traditional and timid measures will no longer do." His panacea was the speedy raising of the price level, and unless this was done, he said, "this country will soon be over the precipice with bloodshed and revolution" (*New York Times,* April 23, 1933). The campaign speeches of Franklin D. Roosevelt, Democratic candidate for president, reflected the ferment pervading the entire population, although it must be said that the slightly hysterical Yale professor had overstated the situation. Nevertheless, the state of affairs was extremely serious and the demagogy of Mr. Roosevelt inaugurated a new era in the policy of the ruling class. The god of the new gospel was the "forgotten man." On October 6, Roosevelt declared that he needs "a greater assurance of security. Old age, sickness and unemployment insurance are the minimum requirements in these days." On October 12, Roosevelt was "utterly unwilling that economy should be practiced at the expense of the starving people." And on October 20 he promised that "if starvation and need on the part of any of our citizens make necessary the appropriation of additional funds which would keep the budget off balance, I shall not hesitate to tell the American people the full truth and recommend to them the expenditure of this additional amount."

It was with the use of such demagogy on the principal issue facing the American masses that Roosevelt was swept into office by a vote of 22,521,525 as against 15,957,537 votes cast for Hoover. Despite pre-election predictions that the socialist vote would reach into the millions, Norman Thomas received 884,781 votes, or two per cent of the total vote cast, as compared with the high mark of 919,799 votes for Eugene Debs in 1920, which constituted over three per cent of the total vote. William Z. Foster, communist candidate for president, whose running mate was James W. Ford, the Negro leader, was credited with 102,991 votes, double the communist vote of 1928.

When Roosevelt stepped into office on March 4, 1933, the crisis had reached its lowest depths. Roosevelt's "New Deal," crystallized in the National Industrial Reconstruction Act, was adopted by Congress. The vast apparatus of propaganda at the disposal of the bourgeoisie was mobilized in its support in a campaign equaled only by the jingoism of the World War days.

Briefly, the NRA, as the policy of the new administration came to be termed, was a colossal effort to halt the economic collapse at the expense of the toiling masses. The Communist Party immediately called upon the workers to struggle against it. The measures undertaken under the NRA have the effect of intensifying all the contradictions of imperialism. The industrial codes are really aimed at squeezing out the small producer in industry, the smallest producers in agriculture and small business men. They accelerate the process of concentration in industry and banking into the hands of even fewer big capitalists. Big business and government is being openly merged and government appears frankly, to use Marx's phrase, not only as the executive committee of the bourgoisie as a whole, but specifically of the monopoly capitalists. Through federal and local mediation boards set up under the NRA every attempt was made to crush strikes. The leadership of the American Federation of Labor and other reformist unions was incorporated more than ever before into the government apparatus. In its unemployment policy and by its inflationary measures the "New Deal" aims to distribute poverty more evenly among the mass of the population, stabilizing the standard of living of the toiling masses at as low a level as is humanly possible.

With these measures the American bourgeoisie is adopting the extraordinary economic methods of fascism, while still retaining the front of democratic government. The open and avowed dictatorial repression and excesses of the Nazis and of fascism in Italy are still undeveloped because the ruling class in the United States is as yet not threatened by a powerful revolutionary movement. Nevertheless, the economic and to a certain extent the governmental apparatus of fascism is being developed at a tremendous rate under the Roosevelt administration.

With a demagogy more refined than that of Hitler, Roosevelt has only been able to enforce his policies by promises of various kinds to the masses. Thus, the NRA (Section 7) provides that the "employees shall have the right to organize and bargain collectively through representatives of their own choosing." But hardly were the new codes for industry formulated when it became apparent that this clause had only been inserted for campaign reasons. The code for the soft coal industry, approved and signed by the leaders of the A. F. of L. and the United Mine Workers, is characteristic of the strike-breaking character of the codes as a whole. It states specifically that "the management of the mine, the direction of the working force, and the right to hire and discharge are vested exclusively in the operator, and the United Mine Workers of America shall not abridge these rights." Strikes are virtually outlawed. The code states that in case of any disagreement there shall be no suspension of work but all differences must be turned over to the arbitration board. If the board fails to arrive at a decision the question is to be decided by an umpire whose decision is final and binding upon the workers.

The trade union bureaucracy has made much noise over the minimum wage and maximum hours of labor provisions of the codes. Section 7 of the NRA declares "that employers shall comply with the maximum hours of labor, minimum rates of pay, and other conditions of employment, approved or prescribed by the president." But in practice, because of the complete power of the employers and the presence of a large army of unemployed, the minimum wage has become the maximum wage. The employers have used every trick at their command to bring this about, such as firing old workers and hiring new ones at the minimum rate. Secondly, the minimum wage is a starvation wage. The textile code, for instance, provides a minimum wage of $12 in the South and

$13 in the North. Inflation has wiped out the benefits of those few cases where the minimum wage actually constituted a wage increase.

Even before the NRA was passed there was already noticeable a marked increase in strikes. The NRA became law on July 16, when textile strikes were in progress in all the New England states, in the South, in New Jersey, Pennsylvania and New York. The textile code was therefore the first to be passed in an effort to smash these strikes. The first code did not go into effect until August and a blanket code covering all industries not until September, although by that time strikes were increasing. In August and September alone over 400,000 workers went on strike. In Pennsylvania, from 70,000 to 100,000 miners struck three times, over the heads of the trade union officials, in order to force recognition of the United Mine Workers Union. The first major series of steel strikes since 1919-1920 took place under the leadership of the Steel and Metal Workers Industrial Union. Probably for the first time on so large a scale the steel and coal strikers coördinated their activities and stuck solidly together.

The NRA has very definitely undertaken preparations for the next imperialist war. The world-wide crisis has intensified the rivalries between the imperialist powers and war looms as never before. The public works program of Roosevelt provides for the expenditure of $3,300,000,000, mainly for war preparations. The program includes 32 new battleships and new equipment for the army and navy. Both Japan and England are no less active in equipping themselves for war. The fascist government of Germany is the chief instigator of war in Europe.

Days of intensive struggles for the workers are approaching rapidly. Four years of crisis have practically changed the face of the world. Extreme poverty and degradation have been the fate of workers in the capitalist world. In the Soviet Union, the other world advances in giant strides. Thus far these two world systems have been able to coexist without open warfare. But the imperialist powers always drive for a way out through a war against the Soviet Union. Neither the antagonisms within capitalist society nor between the capitalist powers can be solved peacefully. The workers in all capitalist countries face the alternative: either intensified suffering and war-slaughter under capitalism and fascism, or the revolutionary way out, the way heralded by the Soviet Union.

CHAPTER XXXIV

Recent Tendencies, 1933-1936

THE following main tendencies characterize this period:

(a) Inability of the ruling class to overcome the crisis.

(b) Contradictions in the ruling class over the uneven distribution of profits under the New Deal.

(c) Disillusionment of large sections of workers, farmers and petty bourgeoisie with the Democratic and Republican parties, giving rise to the development of a Farmer-Labor Party movement.

(d) The struggle for industrial unionism in the trade union movement.

(e) Growing menace of fascism.

(f) Inner crisis of the Socialist Party—widening gulf between the left-wing Militants and the "old guard" reactionaries.

(g) The growth of the influence of the Communist Party and the development of a movement for a united front.

The glowing promises of President Roosevelt to usher in prosperity through his New Deal did not materialize. The country still finds itself in the depression. The National Recovery Act has been ruled out by the decision of the United States Supreme Court which declared the N.R.A. unconstitutional for the simple reason that it was no longer needed by the uppermost strata of the ruling class. The N.R.A. had accomplished its mission. Prices had soared sky-high, the standard of living of the masses had been lowered, the profits of the big bankers, great corporations and trusts had been restored and greatly increased, the illusion of the workers that the N.R.A. guaranteed the right to organize and strike had begun to be dangerous. The Supreme Court had to act according to the wishes of the Bankers' Association and Manufacturers' Association.

The lower strata of the bourgeoisie did not share the profits of the New Deal. Hence the growing dissatisfaction in the ruling class itself with the present situation and the rise of such movements as Father Coughlin's "for social justice"; Townsend's "two hundred dollars a month old age pension," Sinclair's "Epic" in California, and "share-the-wealth" in Louisiana.

It is true that with the birth of the Works Progress Administration (W.P.A.) and the provision of four billion dollars for public works projects, employment increased toward the end of 1935 by about two and half million people. However, as officially admitted, about twelve million workers are still unemployed and there is no prospect of their being absorbed into the regular processes of production. All agree that even with the complete return of "prosperity," over ten million men and women will remain a permanent army of unemployed.

The increase of production—which at the end of 1935 has reached about 90 per cent of the 1923-1925 average, but remains about 30 per cent below the level of 1929—has been achieved through further rationalization: speed-up and new machinery. Furthermore, this increase has no firm basis; it is shaky and impermanent. It primarily affects the production of machinery and other so-called capital goods to replace the obsolete, worn-out ones. Secondly, it has not been accompanied by a proportional increase in the purchasing power of the masses. On the contrary, with the continual lowering of the standard of living, the purchasing power has been further reduced. In his speech at Atlanta, Ga., November 29, 1935, President Roosevelt admitted: "National surveys prove that the average of our citizenship lives to-day on what would be called by the medical fraternity a third-class diet, for the very simple reason that the masses of the American people have not got the purchasing power to eat more and better food."

The American workers did not accept the attack upon their standard of living without resistance. The year 1934, for instance, has gone down in history as a year of very militant strike struggles. That these were mainly local strikes does not make them less significant. Particularly the newly organized workers fought with a militancy which in many respects was unequalled before. The struggles of the workers of San Francisco and of the entire Pacific Coast, of Milwaukee, Toledo, Minneapolis, and of dozens of the textile centers in the South and in other parts of the country, show clearly once more that the American workers are able to fight and will fight.

The San Francisco General Strike, organized in sympathy with marine strikers on the Pacific Coast, lasting from July 17 to July 20, 1934, and involving over 125,000 workers, was an historic event in every respect and struck the greatest fear in the hearts of the big employers. It smashed the conspiracy of the shipping interests to wipe out the marine workers' organizations.

There was but one national strike during this period—the textile strike of 1934, conducted by the United Textile Workers of America. It started on September 1 and lasted about three weeks when it was suddenly called off by the union leaders under the Winant Report which conceded none of the strikers' basic demands. The workers demanded a 30-hour week, minimum wages, increase in wages, union recognition and the abolition of the stretch-out system. The strike was lost and about 80,000 workers in the South were locked out. All promises of the government to give them a fair deal were forgotten as soon as they were driven back into the factories.

The year of 1935 witnessed comparatively few strikes. The strike of the anthracite miners in the Wilkes-Barre, Pa., district, the general strike in Terre Haute, Ind., and the threatened general strike in Barberton, Ohio, were outstanding. Most of the strikes of 1935 affected the workers of the federal and state projects and were partially successful in forcing some concession from the government in the form of higher pay and shorter hours.

The brutality of the ruling class in all these strikes can be compared with its brutality in the general railroad strike of 1877. Local and state governments freely gave armed aid to the employers everywhere. The Labor Research Association estimated that over forty thousand National Guardsmen in nineteen states were called out to suppress the workers in twenty-two strikes. President Roosevelt threatened to send thousands of soldiers of the regular army to crush the textile workers. According to the figures collected by the International Labor Defense, forty-nine workers were murdered by thugs or militiamen in 1935 alone during strike and other struggles.

Fascism gained tremendously in the United States during this period. It is true that as yet it is not a coördinated single movement based upon a single program or around a single individual (it assumes all sorts of forms and manifestations), but its growth cannot be disputed. Its aim is clear: to destroy the labor movement and to set up a bloody fascist dictatorship of the Hitler type. For instance, in 1934 the Congress investigation disclosed that the Wall Street bankers went so far as to begin an actual mobilization of an army of five hundred thousand men to march on Washington and set up a dictatorship. General Butler was asked to lead this fascist army, but he refused.

The reactionary forces working for fascism are found in such organizations as the Manufacturers' Association, the United States Chamber of Commerce, the American Liberty League, Hearst's press, Bankers Association, National Civic Federation, the leadership of the American Legion, etc. Then we have such fascist or semi-fascist movements as the Ku Klux Klan, the Order of '76, Silver Shirts, etc.* Some of these organizations are very small as yet, but they are growing and their influence has been on the increase. If they are not checked in time they will merge into a consolidated movement and will openly proclaim war upon the working class. Roosevelt's government does not stand in the way of the development of fascism in America. There is but one power to stop and crush this monster: the united power of the working class.

Since the advance of fascism in Germany in 1933 and in Austria in

* For a detailed description of these organizations see *Labor Fact Book,* Vol. III, International Publishers, 1936.

1934, the unity of action on the part of the working class against this common enemy has become the most urgent problem all over the world, including the United States. In 1933 the Communist International issued its appeal to the workers of the world to form a united front against fascism and recommended that all Communist Parties immediately appeal to the Social-Democratic Parties, as well as all the trade unions, with concrete proposals for the realization of joint action. On March 30, 1933, the Communist Party of the United States appealed to the Socialist Party and the A. F. of L. for a united front to fight the fascist menace in this country. The N.E.C. of the S. P., at its meeting, April 1933, by a vote of 6 to 5, rejected this proposal. However, the appeal made a deep impression upon socialists and trade unionists, and in some parts of the country local united action was achieved.

In 1934 the Communist Party again proposed united action to the National Convention of the S. P., which turned over the question to the incoming N.E.C. At its December meeting the N.E.C. decided to postpone action on the united front with the Communist Party nationally until the national convention of the S. P., to be held in 1936. In practice, however, there has been a steadily-growing coöperation between the C. P. and S. P. even nationally. The S. P. has been supporting the struggle for the release of the young Negro communist, Angelo Herndon, and at the Atlantic City Convention of the A. F. of L. militant socialists and communists fought side by side for progressive policies.

Despite the failure of the efforts of the C. P. to win the S. P. for a common struggle against war and fascism nationally, in this period we have been witnessing the steady growth of a powerful anti-war and anti-fascist movement in which the communists are playing an important part. The First United States Congress Against War and Fascism took place September 30 to October 2, 1933, representing over a million organized workers, farmers, professionals and middle class elements, and organized the American League Against War and Fascism. The Second Congress was held on September 28-30, in Chicago, in 1934, representing 1,807,201 people, while the Third Congress took place on January 3-5, 1936, in Cleveland, and represented about two million people.

The Socialist Party has been keeping itself aloof from this mass movement. At the January, 1936, Congress, the S. P. had official observers who declared the readiness of the Party to participate in an inclusive anti-fascist and anti-war mass movement. The weakness of the whole movement has been that it has failed to attract large international unions of the American Federation of Labor.

A strong progressive trend has been making itself felt in the American Federation of Labor and challenging the power and policies of the reactionary section of the leadership. It demands new forms of organization and new methods of work to fight the employers' offensive and to face the menace of fascism. Such was the historic meaning of the Atlantic City Convention (55th) of the Federation held on October 7-20, 1935.

It is true that the progressive forces lacked cohesion and clarity, but, for the first time in the last two or three decades, they penetrated even the top leadership of the Federation. The struggle at the Atlantic City Convention had added significance in the fact that it was not over positions in the leadership, but over vital, pressing problems of the working class. Although only about forty communists and their sympathizers were among the delegates, the influence of the Communist Party was felt in all the struggles of the progressives at the convention.

The largest and most solid progressive force was rallied on the question of industrial unionism or the organization of the unorganized. It was led by John L. Lewis of the United Mine Workers of America and ably supported by Gorman of the Textile Workers, Hillman of the Clothing Workers, Howard of the Printers, and Dubinsky of the Women's Garment Workers. The Old Guard—Green, Woll, and Frey—fought back the onslaught just as stubbornly. The progressives lost by 10,933 votes against 18,024. But the fight will go on. Those progressive forces which appeared at the convention held a conference immediately afterward and set up a Committee for Industrial Organization representing eight powerful Internationals whose purpose will be to carry on the struggle started at Atlantic City.

Another vital issue at the Atlantic City Convention was that of a Labor Party. The progressives were hopelessly divided. Lewis, Hillman, and others refused to fight for it. Of the top leaders only Francis Gorman remained progressive, introduced the best resolution for a Labor Party and fought for it on the floor. He was supported by the block of the Federal locals, but they had only a few votes at the convention. The resolution was defeated without a record vote. The Labor Party caucus, however, was attended by delegates representing 5,000 votes out of 29,000 votes at the Convention.

The Atlantic City Convention performed a historic task when it repudiated the National Civic Federation, a red-baiting and open-shop outfit of the employers and Old Guard of the Federation. It decided that "no officer of the A. F. of L. shall act as an officer of the N.C.F., or be a member thereof." It forced Woll and Ryan to withdraw from this outfit.

The Convention condemned Italian fascism for its war against Ethiopia, and the fascist activities of Father Coughlin. It favored an amendment to the United States Constitution to take away the power from the Supreme Court to annul social legislation enacted by Congress. For the first time no resolution was introduced against the Soviet Union. In all probability the Atlantic City Convention will go down in history as a turning point for the A. F. of L.

The years 1934 and 1935 were important for the unity of the trade union movement. In view of changed conditions, the Communist Party, early in 1934, started a struggle for the unification of the trade union movement—for the merger of the revolutionary unions with the old unions under the banner of the A. F. of L. The Trade Union Unity League, as a national center for the revolutionary unions and opposition groups in the old unions, was liquidated. To-day all energies of the workers are concentrated on the work in the A. F. of L. unions, to build them into powerful instruments of the class struggle.

An inspiring historic movement in America is taking place among the youth in the form of the American Youth Congress, which represents over two million youth of various political and religious affiliations. It is led by the young communists, socialists, and anti-war and anti-fascist forces in general. The students' movement against war and fascism has been developing very rapidly. Anti-war strikes have swept high schools, colleges and universities in 1934 and 1935. The merging of the National Students League which was led by communists and the socialist-led Students League for Industrial Democracy, into the American Student Union at the end of 1935, has been a great achievement for the youth movement.

An important event in the labor movement during this period is the inner crisis of the Socialist Party. As it was in the period of 1917-1921, so it is to-day; the question is: reformism or revolution. To-day once more a majority in the Socialist Party want to take the road of revolutionary socialism, and once more the Old Guard (Oneal, Waldman, Lee, Solomon, Cahan) stand in the way.

The party is divided: the majority led by Norman Thomas, the Old Guard led by Oneal and Waldman. Both factions have their papers: *Socialist Call* and *The New Leader* respectively. The fight is very bitter. The New York state organization is definitely split. The National Executive Committee at its meeting January 4, 1936, lifted the state charter and put the entire organization under its direct control until the elecion of new officials. The old state leadership of Waldman, Oneal and Lee refused to surrender and continue to function as the Socialist Party in New York. The fight will be carried to the National Convention to be held in May, 1936, for the control of the party nationally.

Factional rumblings in the Socialist Party were heard as early as 1932, at the Milwauke convention. Norman Thomas was accused of conspiring to replace Morris Hillquit as chairman of the party. The Old Guard would not have it. Two years later, in 1934, at the Detroit convention, there appeared two definite factions—those clinging to the old decrepit reformism and those wanting new ways. The struggle at the convention centered around the "Declaration of Principles" on the question of the attitude toward war and the question of the road of the working class to victory.

In the name of the Old Guard Mr. Waldman declared that if this "Declaration" is adopted, it will be "the end of the Socialist Party," that the document is "provocative," "anarchistic," "illegal," "communistic," "wild," "irresponsible," etc. (*The New Leader,* June 9, 1934). However, the convention adopted the "Declaration" by a vote of 10,822 to 6,512. Later, the membership, through a referendum vote, accepted it by a vote of 5,993 to 4,872.

The gulf between the two factions was getting wider and wider in 1935. The "Declaration of Principles" was almost forgotten, and the disagreements in every-day tactics and policies became the center of contention. In the trade unions, the "militants" are against the reactionary policies of Green-Woll, but the Old Guard supports these policies. On the question of the Soviet Union, the "militants" recognize the Soviet Government as a working class government that is building socialism, but the Old Guard would support any counter-revolution aiming to overthrow the Soviets. On the question of the United Front, the "militants" favor at least partial joint action with the communists, while the Old Guard says that the socialists should keep away from the communists as from "lepers."

The growth of Communism in the United States in this period, as an organized movement and as an ideology, has been considerable. The membership of the Communist Party has increased to over thirty thousand. Its influence in the trade unions, in the anti-war and anti-fascist movement, among the Negroes, the unemployed, the working class youth, the students, the professionals, and the middle class groups, has been greatly extended.

In view of the change in objective and subjective conditions in the world and the United States, the party has changed its tactical line on two important questions, the trade unions and the Labor Party. We have already dealt with the struggle of the party for the unity of the trade union movement. A word on the Labor Party movement will be in place.

From 1929 to 1934 the Communist Party definitely rejected the Labor Party slogan as a practical instrument for the mobilization of the working class on the political field against capitalism at that time. There were no signs then of large groups of workers and farmers breaking away from the influence of the Republican and Democratic parties. Any Labor Party established at that time would have been only a caricature of a real mass Labor Party, or "an appendage to the existing bourgeois parties," as Earl Browder, General Secretary of the Communist Party, declared in November, 1934. "Developments in 1934, however, begin to place this question in a new setting, in a new relation of forces." Therefore, the

Communist Party, he pointed out, "must energetically intervene in this process." And on January 6, 1935, at the National Congress for Social and Unemployment Insurance, Browder declared that the "communists are prepared to join hands, with all our force, all our energy, all our fighting capacity, with all who are ready to fight against Wall Street, against monopoly capital, in the formation of a broad mass party to carry on this fight, into a fighting Labor Party based upon the trade unions, the Unemployed Councils, the farmers' organizations, all the mass organizations of toilers, with a program of demands and mass actions to improve the conditions of the masses at the expense of the rich. . . ."

Finally, the Central Committee of the Party, at its enlarged meeting, January 15-18, 1935, definitely decided to work for the establishment of a mass Labor Party. And after the Seventh World Congress of the Communist International—which was held in July-August, 1936, and which put forth the united struggle against war and fascism as the main task before the Communist movement and the working class as a whole in the present period—the Communist Party of the U. S. A. raised the slogan of a Farmer-Labor Party as the form of a people's front against reaction, against the offensive of monopoly capital, and for the defense of civil liberties and democratic rights.

The Farmer-Labor Party idea has been rapidly gaining ground among the workers and farmers. In the Fall elections of 1935 local Labor Party tickets or labor tickets met with some success. In Detroit, for instance, the workers' candidate for city councilman, Maurice Sugar, received 55,000 votes and was defeated by only 14,000 votes. The greatly increased vote for the candidates of the Communist Party in the same elections, the victory of the Socialist Party in Reading and Bridgeport, the large number of votes cast for the candidates of the supporters of the Townsend Plan in the Middle West and of the "Epic" in California, the support of the Farmer-Labor Party idea by several state Labor Federations as well as by hundreds of locals of the A. F. of L. unions, clearly express the mass discontent with the policies of the old bourgeois parties and the growth of the Farmer-Labor Party movement.

The complete usurpation of the powers of Congress by the U. S. Supreme Court with its decision of January 6, 1936, declaring the Agricultural Adjustment Act unconstitutional, can only give further impetus to this movement. The fight to amend the Federal Constitution so as to deprive the Supreme Court of its power to annul social legislation has become one of the major issues before the toiling masses of America. Neither the Republican nor Democratic party will support such an amendment. Only a powerful mass Farmer-Labor Party could be an effective instrument in this struggle. The presidential elections of 1936 may yet see the birth of a Farmer-Labor Party on a national scale.

ERRATA

p. 11, second line from bottom: "transplanted" instead of "transported."
p. 12, last line: this as well as all following references are to the 4th (1921) edition.
p. 17, first quotation: the author of *Domestic Service* is Salmon.
p. 18, second quotation: reference should be to p. 348.
p. 21, 5th line of quotation at bottom of page: "gathered" instead of "fathered."
p. 23, reference in third quotation should be to Vol. II. The quote ends at "Rhode Island," the rest of the passage being a free translation.
p. 24, line 18: reference should be to p. 47.
p. 27, reference to *Documentary History*, etc., Vol. II, should be pp. 86-87.
p. 33, reference to McMaster, *The Acquisition*, etc., should be pp. 35-36.
p. 34, 5th line of last quotation should read: were there who did not deal in Negro slaves and few also were there who did not have a bonded laborer. . . .
p. 47, the reference should be to Vol. II of Hart.
p. 50, first quotation: the reference should be to W. J. Ghent, *The Forum*, August, 1901.
p. 51, last line: reference should be to Oneal, p. 127.
p. 67, first quotation, first line, should read: women and children are rendered more useful, and the latter more easily. . . .
p. 88, reference to Mary Beard should be p. 173.
p. 98, second line, last quotation: "1828" instead of "1829."
p. 105, first quotation, line 5 should read: "they sustained the bloodstained banner of capital and fraud in their crusade." The page reference should be 110. Last line should read: From the last day of October. . . .
p. 120, last quotation, first line should read: On September 2 Lincoln wrote to Fremont that the confiscation of property and liberation of slaves. . . .
p. 124, first reference to Helper should be pp. 71-73; second reference p. 24.
p. 131, 6th and 7th lines should read: "Never before," says Professor Ely, "were there such sharp contrasts in this country between riches and poverty."
p. 143, reference to Hillquit should be p. 192.
p. 144, line 25 should read: By the close of 1873 there were 32 national. . . .
p. 184, line 23 should read: "the national executive committee declined the invitation. . . ."
p. 206, line 8 should read: kind shall have no place in the convention of the. . . .
p. 234, the reference to Budish and Soule should be pp. 169-170.
p. 242, line 18: the date should be January 11, 1912.
p. 250, line 12 should read: and Theodore Roosevelt (*Ibid.*, p. 362).
p. 275, first reference to Foster should be p. 173, second reference p. 175.
p. 277, the quotation from Foster is from his book, *The Great Steel Strike*.
p. 278, first quotation: the reference is to the 1919-1920 *American Labor Year Book*.
p. 319, line 28: the date should be August 21-31, 1925.

INDEX

A

Advance, The, 336.
Agricultural Workers Industrial Union, 367–368.
Alarm, The, 185.
Amalgamated Ass'n of Iron and Steel Workers, 154, 169, 194, 196, 210, 213, 214, 268, 270.
Amalgamated Clothing Workers of America, 233, 234, 248, 252, 277, 307, 308, 324, 328, 336–337.
Amalgamated Textile Workers of America, 298.
American Alliance for Labor and Democracy, 251.
American Federation of Labor, 101, 134, 167, 171, 180, 181, 191-198, 200, 201, 204–207, 210–213, 226–230, 233, 239, 244, 266–69, 295, 306, 308, 309, 310, 311, 313, 323, 328, 329, 334 ff., 347, 357, 358, 366; *see also,* Class Collaboration, Eight-hour movement, Knights of Labor, Samuel Gompers.
American Federation of Textile Operatives, 343.
American Federationist, The, 244.
American Railway Union, 216–219; *see also,* Pullman strike.
American Revolution, 39–53, 54, 56, 61.
American society, 11.
American Workers Party, 331.
Amter, Israel, 360.
Anarchists, 183–188; *see also,* Haymarket affair.
Arbeiter Zeitung, 186.
Association of Fall River Mechanics, 105.
Auto Workers Industrial Union, 346, 349, 362.

B

Bacon, Nathan, 37.
Bakunin, Michael, 183, 184.
Baltimore & Ohio Plan, 336; *see also,* Class Collaboration.
Barry, T. B., 177.
Berkeley, governor of Virginia, 37, 38.
Bill of Labor Grievances, 228–229.
Billings, Warren, 254.
Bonus March, 364, 365.
Boston Tea Party, 40; *see also,* American Revolution.
Bovay, Alvin E., 103.
Bricklayers' and Masons' International Union, 144, 152, 166.
Bridgeman Convention, 340.
Brisbane, Albert, 103, 108, 113.
Brotherhood of Maintenance-of Way Employees, 306.
Brotherhood of Railway Carmen of America, 304.
Browder, Earl, 330, 336.
Brown, John, 126–127.
Buchman, J. R., 178.

C

Cameron, A. C., 149.
Cannon, James P., 331.

Carpenters' and Joiners' International Union, 144, 166, 180, 213
Chicago Federation of Labor, 325–326.
Child-labor, 67, 68, 84, 92.
Chinese, anti-Chinese movement in California, 159–160.
Church and Labor, 70, 96, 105, 274.
Cigar Makers' Union, International, 144, 145, 152, 166, 167, 168, 176, 180, 194, 197, 198; *see also,* American Federation of Labor.
Cigar Makers' Union, Progressive, 184, 185, 194.
Cigar Makers' Union, United, 103.
Civil War, 21, 107, 115–153.
Class collaboration, 229, 333–335.
Clay, Henry, 23, 29.
Coach Makers' International Union, 144.
Collins, John, 152.
Colonial life, 12–38.
Columbus, Christopher, 9, 17
Commerford, John, 85.
Committees of Correspondence, *see* American Revolution.
Communes, 113–114; *see also,* Utopian Socialism.
Communist International, 332, 333; Second World Congress of, 339, 343.
Communist Labor Party, 285, 287.
Communist Party of U. S. A., 285, 286, 287, 288, 290, 329, 330, 331, 332, 347, 359, 370; of the Soviet Union, 350; *see also,* Workers' (Communist) Party of America.
Company Unions, 347.
Compensated emancipation, 120.
Conference for Progressive Political Action, 324, 325, 327, 331.
Continental Congress, 43, 54.
Constitution of the United States, 54–60.
Constitutional Convention, 57.
Cooper, Peter, 162.
Cordwainers' National Union, 103.
Crawford, William, 41, 49.
Credit crisis, 354.
Crises, 1819, 65; 1837, 65; 100, 102; 1857, 106, 107, 224; 1921, 225; crisis, 1929–1933, Ch. XXXIII.
Culpepper, John, 38.

D

Daily Worker, The, 321, 331, 347.
Danbury Hatters' case, 244; *see also,* American Federation of Labor.
Daughters of St. Crispin, 144.
Dearborn Massacre, 361–362.
Debs, Eugene V., 156, 216, 217, 218, 219, 230, 237, 241, 315.
Debts, imprisonment for, 50–51.
Declaration of Independence, 48, 54; *see also,* American Revolution.
Delaware, colonization of, 14.
De Leon, Daniel, 200, 202, 203, 230; *see also,* Socialist Labor Party.
Democratic Party, 115, 117, 163.
Dickinson, John, 58.
Douglas, Charles, 84.
Douglas, Stephen Arnold, 119.

INDEX

Dual unionism, 203, 204, 230, 236, 343; *see also*, I. W. W.; Trade Union Educational League.
Dutch West India Company, 12.

E

Eight-hour day movement, 142, 146, 180, 181, 210, 211, 212.
Engel, George, 177, 188: *see also*, Haymarket affair.
Engels, Friedrich, 10, 64, 65, 74, 75, 108, 111, 131, 143, 148, 183.
English workers and Civil War, 131–135.
Evans, Oliver, 103.
"Exceptionalism," 332.
Exports, reduction of, 354.

F

Factionalism, struggle against, 331.
Farmer-Labor Party, 324–326, 339; of Minnesota, 327, 329; shortcomings of, 331.
Farmers' Holiday Association, 367.
Farmers' Union, 367.
Farms, foreclosures of, 353.
Farrington, Frank, 338.
Federal Society of Journeymen Cordwainers, 73, 76.
Federated Farmer Labor Party, 326–327.
Federation of Organized Trades and Labor Unions of the United States of America and Canada, *see* American Federation of Labor.
Federation of Textile Workers, 298.
Fehrenbatch, John, 152.
Feral, John, 97, 98.
Fielden, Samuel, 187.
Fischer, Adolph, 187, 188.
Fitzpatrick, John, 271, 326.
Five-Year Plan, of Soviet Union, 356.
Food and Packinghouse Industrial Union, 346.
Foran, Martin A., 152.
Ford, James W., 370.
Foreign-born workers, 224; *see also*, Immigration.
Foster, William Z., 203, 234, 269, 273, 275, 346, 360, 362, 370.
Fourier, Charles, 109, 110, 113.
Franklin, Benjamin, 49.
Frederickson, C. R., 334.
Free Negroes, 28; *see also*, Civil War.
Fremont, John Charles, 120, 127.

G

Garrison, William Lloyd, 28.
Gastonia Strike, 345–346.
Gazette, Philadelphia, 97.
General Trades' Union, of New York, 83, 85, 98; of Philadelphia, 82.
Gompers, Samuel, 134, 167, 169, 171, 197, 200, 202, 203, 205, 206, 207, 213, 229, 239, 248–250, 266, 271, 273, 295, 334; *see also*, American Federation of Labor.
Grable, E. F., 306.
Grand Division of the Order of Railway Conductors, 144.
Greeley, Horace, 104, 108, 113, 120.
Green, William, 315, 334–335.
Greenback Labor Party, 163.
Greenback Party, 163.
Grotkau, Paul, 184, 185.

H

Hamilton, Alexander, 41, 58, 59.
Hancock, John, 40.

Harbinger, The, 114.
Harper's Ferry, 127, 128.
Hat Finishers' Ass'n, 103.
Haymarket affair, 187, 188; *see also*, Anarchists.
Haywood, William D., 230, 241.
Henning, Edward, 335.
Herron, George D., 237.
Hillman, Sidney, 336, 337–338.
Hillquit, Morris, 11, 112, 129, 149, 157, 165, 183, 200, 215, 329.
Homestead Strike, 213, 214.
Hunger March, 363.

I

Immigration, 31, 66, 101, 139, 140, 224.
Independent Unions, 348–349.
Industrial Brotherhood, 152–154.
Industrial Codes, 347.
Industrial congresses, 102–104.
Industrial unionism, 227; *see also*, Industrial Workers of the World; Trade Union Educational League.
Industrial Workers of the World (I. W. W.), 230, 231, 237, 241, 243, 248, 252, 253, 254, 307, 343.
Industries, development of, 62, 63, 137, 138, 221, 222.
Inflation, 372.
Injunction, 209, 210.
Insurance schemes, of trade unions, 337.
Int'l Alliance of Amalgamated Sheet Metal Workers, 303.
Int'l Association of Machinists, 304, 336.
Int'l Brotherhood of Blacksmiths, 303.
Int'l Brotherhood of Boilermakers, Iron Ship Builders and Helpers of America, 304.
Int'l Brotherhood of Electrical Workers, 304.
Int'l Brotherhood of Foundry Employees, 244.
Int'l Coopers' Union of North America, 144, 152.
Int'l Fur Workers' Union, 342.
Int'l Labor Union, 171–172.
Int'l Ladies' Garment Workers' Union, 245, 307, 324, 341–342; *see also*, Left wing in the trade unions.
Int'l Seamen's Union, 295.
International, Socialist, 212, 257, 258, 280.
Int'l Typographical Union, 103, 152, 154, 166, 297.
International Working Men's Association (First International), 132, 143, 145, 148, 149, 163, 164, 183.

J

Jarett, John, 169.
John, Vincent St., 231, 232, 243.
Journal of the Knights of Labor, 200.

K

Kearney, Denis, 159.
Knights of Labor, 147, 166, 169, 170, 172, 173, 174, 176, 177, 178, 179, 180, 181, 182, 183, 189, 192–198, 200, 202, 210, 214; *see also*, American Federation of Labor.
Knights of St. Crispin, 144, 145, 148, 152.
Knox, Henry, 52, 57.
Ku Klux Klan, 141.

L

Labor banks, 336–337.
Labor, conditions of, 68; hours of, 69, 75,

INDEX

Labor (Continued)
  84, 91; and courts, 77, 78, 79, 80, 93; 105; see also, Ten-hour day movement; Eight-hour day movement.
Labor Herald, The, 298.
Labor party movement, 323-329, 330-331; see also, Political action.
La Follette, Robert M., 328, 329.
Land, expropriation of, 64.
Lawrence strike, 1912, 242-243; see also, I. W. W.
Leisler, Jacob, 38.
Leisler's Rebellion, 38.
Lester, Joseph, 360.
Lewis, John L., 276, 301.
Liberator, The, 28.
Lincoln, Abraham, 115, 117, 118, 129, 134, 139; see also, Civil War.
Ling, Louis, 187, 188.
Lithographers' National Union, 103.
Little, Frank, 254.
Locomotive Engineers, Grand Division of, 144.
Locomotive Firemen, Brotherhood of, 144, 216.
London Company, 12.
Lovestone group, expulsion of from C. P., 332.
Lovestone, Jay, 332.

M

MacLure, William, 113.
Madison, James, 57, 59, 78.
Maintenance-of-Way Men, Brotherhood of, 295.
Manifesto, Communist, 10, 56.
Marine Workers Industrial Union, 346.
Marx, Karl, 10, 65, 75, 117, 131-133, 143, 148, 183, 207.
Maryland colonization of, 14.
Masquerier, Lewis I., 103.
McDonnell, J. P., 171.
McMahon, Thomas F., 310.
McNeill, Geo. E., 171, 172.
Mechanics' Association of New England, 105.
Mechanics' Free Press, The, 86.
Mechanics' Trades Union of the United States, 103.
Militia, 92; see also, Railroad Strike of 1877.
Miners' National Association, 144.
Minnesota Banker, 335.
Minor, Robert, 360.
Mitchell, John, 239, 240, 241, 338.
Molly Maguires, 155, 156.
Money crisis, 354.
Mooney, Thomas, 254, 255.
Moore, Ely, 85.
Morgan, J. Pierpont, 130.
Morning Herald, The, 88.
Most, Johann, 184.
Moulders' International Union, 143, 152.
Moyer, Charles H., 241.
Muste, A. J., 331.

N

National Civic Federation, 229, 334
National Farmers' Conference, 367.
National Gazette, Philadelphia, 90.
National Industrial Recovery Act, 347.
National Labor Board, 372.
National Labor Union, 145-149, 152, 153, 205.
National ͜orer, The, 82.
National ͜ers Union, 345, 348, 3͜8, 359.
National ͜ve Association of t͜ Unite͜ States, 103, 105.

National Reform Association of New York, 103.
National Textile Workers Union, 345, 346, 349.
National Trades' Union, 83, 84, 85.
Neebe, Oscar W., 187, 188.
Needle Trades Workers Industrial Union, 345.
Negro question, 368-369.
Negroes, solidarity and unity of with whites in South, 346.
New Bedford textile strike, 1928, 343.
New Deal, 347.
New England Association of Farmers, Mechanics, and Other Working Men, 84, 95, 103.
New England Workingmen's Association, 103, 105.
New Harmony, 113.
New Lanark, 111, 112.
New Yorker, The, 113.
North American Federation of the International Working Men's Ass'n, see International Working Men's Ass'n.
NRA, 370-373.

O

Ohio Company, 12.
One Big Union, 298.
Open-shop drive, 293, 295, 296.
Opportunism, struggle against in Communist Party, 332.
Opposition work, 348.
Ostrolenk, Bernhard, 353.
Owen, Robert, 104, 108, 109, 111, 112, 113.
Owen Robert Dale, 87.

P

Paris Commune, 161, 164, 172, 179.
Parsons, Albert R., 171, 184, 186, 187, 188.
Paterson Association for Protection of Laboring Classes, 89, 90.
Pennsylvania-Ohio Miners' Relief Committee, 343.
People, The, 200.
Pettibone, George A., 241.
Phalanx, The, 114.
Philadelphia Register, The, 106.
Phillips, Wendell, 42.
Pinkerton Secret Service Agency, 214.
Plasterers' National Union, 144.
"Platform of the Class Struggle," 330.
Plumbers' National Union, 144.
Police brutality, 361.
Political action, 84, 86-89, 159, 165, 174, 199-208; see also, Labor party movement.
Population, U. S., 64, 138, 220, 243.
Powderly, Terence V., 173, 180-183, 196, 198, 200.
Production, decline of during crisis, 351 ff.
Public schools, 89, 90.
Pullman strike, 217-219; see also, American Railway Union.

R

Railroad shopmen strike, 303-305.
Railroad strike of 1877, 161-167.
Railway Employees' Department of the A. F. of L., 304.
Raymond, Harry, 360.
Red International of Labor Unions, 339.
Redemptioner, 14.
Republican Party, 115, 117, 118, 163.
Republican Workingmen's Club of New York, 134.
Revolts, 37, 38, 51, 52, 99, 100.

INDEX

Revolutionary Unions, Ch. XXXII.
Roosevelt, Franklin D., election of, 370.
Rosenberg, W. L., 199.
Russian Revolution, 280.
Ruthenberg, Charles E., 322, 326.

S

Sacco, Nicola, 312-314.
Saffin, William, 152.
St. Paul Convention, 329.
Saint-Simon, 109, 110.
Sanial, Lucien, 200.
"Save the Union" Committees, 343.
Seattle general strike, 1919, 278.
Servants, indentured, 14.
Schilling, George, 171.
Schwab, Michael, 186, 187.
Shay's Rebellion, 56.
Ship Carpenters' and Caulkers' International Union, 144.
Shoe and Leather Workers Industrial Union, 346, 349.
Sigman, Morris, 342.
Sims, Harry, 359.
Siney, John, 154.
Sixth World Congress, of Communist International, 350-351.
Slavery, Negro, 12, 20-28, 59; White, 12-19.
Social Democratic Herald, The, 241.
Social Democratic Workingmen's Party of North America, 163, 164.
Social Insurance, demand for by Communist Party, 330.
Socialist Labor Party, 165, 183, 184, 199, 200.
Socialist Party, 235-237, 256-263, 282, 283, 291, 311, 315, 324, 328, 329; *see also*, World War.
Socialist Trade and Labor Alliance, 202, 203, 230.
Sovereign, James R., 200.
Soviet Union, achievements of, 355-357.
Spanish-American War, 221.
Spies, August, 184-188.
Stalin, Joseph, 350.
Steel and Metal Workers Industrial Union, 346.
Steel strike, 268-274, 276, 283.
Stephens, Uria Smith, 147.
Steward, Ira, 171.
Strasser, Adolph, 167, 171.
Strikes, aims of, 75-76.
Supreme Court, U. S., 58.

T

Tailors' National Union, 144.
Ten-hour day movement, 91-93, 95, 98, 99, 105.
Textile strike, 1912, 242-243; 1919, 279; 1922, 297, 298; 1925, 308, 309.
Trade Union Educational League, 324, 325, 339 ff.
Trade Union Unity League, 344 ff.
Trotskyism, 331-332.
Turner, Nat., 123.
Typographical Society, Philadelphia, 73; New York, 73.

U

Unemployed Councils, 362 ff.
Unemployment, 351, 359 ff.
Unemployment Insurance, 366.
Unions, Revolutionary, Ch. XXXII.
United Farmers League, 367.
United Front, 346-347.
United Garment Workers of America, 233, 234, 246, 276.
United Hebrew Trades, New York, 200.
United Mine Workers of America, 213, 216, 239, 240, 244, 293, 294, 301, 324, 342, 343, 348; strikes, 1894, 216; 1897, 219; 1922, 298-301.
United Shoe and Leather Workers Union, 349.
United Textile Workers of America, 298, 309-311, 343, 345-346.
Unity, Communist policy on, 346-347.
Upholsterers' National Union, 103.
Utopian socialism, 108-114.

V

Vanzetti, Bartolomeo, 312-314.
Virginia, colonization of, 14.
Volkszeitung, New York, 199.

W

Walker's Appeal, 28.
War, preparations for, 372-373.
Washington, George, 12, 41, 43, 49, 57, 59; *see also*, American Revolution.
Weaver, James, 163.
Weavers' Protective Association, 156.
Weisbord, Albert, 310.
West Indies Company, 20, 40.
Western Federation of Miners, 216, 230, 231, 232, 241, 353; *see also*, I. W. W.
Weydemeyer, Otto, 171.
Whalen, Grover, 360.
Wiggins, Ella May, 345.
Wilson, Woodrow, 59, 134, 249, 251, 260, 276.
Woll, Matthew, 334.
Woman-labor, 67, 68, 84, 92, 99; Factory Girls' Association, Lowell, 83; Female Society, Lynn, 83; Female Union Association, New York, 83; Lowell Female Reform Association, 102; United Seamstresses' Society, Baltimore, 83.
Workers' (Communist) Party, 313, 316-328; *see also*, Communist Party.
Workers Ex-Servicemen's League, 364.
Working Men's Advocate, The, 87, 88.
Workingmen's Advocate, The, 152, 199.
Workingmen's Party, of California, 159; of New York, 87, 88; of Philadelphia, 84, 86; of United States, 165.
Working Men's Republican Political Association, 88, 89.
World War, 221, 222, 225, 247, 251, 256, 265, 280; *see also*, American Federation of Labor; Socialist Party.
Wright, Chester M., 340.
Wright, Frances, 87, 113.

Y

Young Workers' (Communist) League, 323.